9/91 - 2

Miners, Norman.

Hong kong under imperial
rule, 1912-1941

·MAY 1 5 1989

DEMCO.

EAST ASIAN HISTORICAL MONOGRAPHS

General Editor: WANG GUNGWU

Hong Kong under Imperial Rule, 1912–1941

EAST ASIAN HISTORICAL MONOGRAPHS

General Editor: WANG GUNGWU

The East Asian Historical Monographs series has, since its inception in the late 1960s, earned a reputation for the publication of works of innovative historical scholarship. It encouraged a generation of scholars of Asian history to go beyond Western activities in Asia seen from Western points of view. Their books included a wider range of Asian viewpoints and also reflected a stronger awareness of economic and socio-cultural factors in Asia which lay behind political events.

During its second decade the series has broadened to reflect the interest among historians in studying and reassessing Chinese history, and now includes important works on China and Hong Kong.

It is the hope of the publishers that, as the series moves into its third decade, it will continue to meet the need and demand for historical writings on the region and that the fruits of the scholarship of new generations of historians will reach a wider reading public.

Other titles in this series are listed at the end of the book.

Hong Kong under Imperial Rule, 1912–1941

NORMAN MINERS

WITHDRAWN

HONG KONG   OXFORD   NEW YORK
OXFORD UNIVERSITY PRESS
1987

Oxford University Press

Oxford New York Toronto
Petaling Jaya Singapore Hong Kong Tokyo
Delhi Bombay Calcutta Madras Karachi
Nairobi Dar es Salaam Cape Town
Melbourne Auckland

and associated companies in
Beirut Berlin Ibadan Nicosia

First published 1987
Published in the United States
by Oxford University Press, Inc.,
New York

Library of Congress Cataloging-in-Publication Data

Miner, Norman.
Hong Kong under imperial rule, 1912–1941.
(East Asian historical monographs)
Bibliography: p.
Includes index.
I. Hong Kong—Politics and government. I. Title.
II. Series.
DS796.H757M56 1987 951'.2504 87–21992
ISBN 0-19-584171-9 (U.S.)

British Library Cataloguing in Publication Data

Miners, Norman
Hong Kong under Imperial rule, 1912–1941.
— (East Asian historical monographs).
1. Hong Kong — History
I. Title II. Series
951'.2504 DS796.H757
ISBN 0-19-584171-9

Printed in Hong Kong by Calay Printing Co. Ltd.
Published by Oxford University Press, Warwick House, Hong Kong

Preface and Acknowledgements

My interest in the administration of Hong Kong before the Second World War arose while I was writing a book on the government of Hong Kong today. The area on which I found it most difficult to acquire detailed information was the extent of the influence exerted on the local administration by the British government, since all communications that pass between ministers, civil servants, and the Hong Kong government are strictly confidential, and the possibility of disagreement between any of the three is never publicly admitted. Because of this secrecy some Chinese are suspicious that many of the Governor's actions are taken under instructions from London without regard to the best interests of the colony, in spite of protestations by officials that this is not the case.[1] So in order to clarify the position I turned to look at the period before the Second World War, for which almost all the correspondence between Hong Kong and London that survives is now available for research.

This study is primarily based on these papers, which are preserved at the Public Record Office in London. None of the Governors from May to Northcote has left any significant deposit of his private papers, although some letters survive in other collections, and Sir William Peel wrote a brief memoir of his colonial service. There are several detailed accounts of the internal arrangements of the Colonial Office written by civil servants who worked there between the two World Wars, but these contain very few specific references to Hong Kong. However, I have been fortunate to be able to interview a few of the Hong Kong officials who still survive from this period, and I am most grateful to Sir Sydney Caine, Mr David MacDougall, and the late Mr Roland Todd for their patient readiness to answer my questions.

A number of books have been written about Hong Kong during the Second World War, but there is as yet no detailed history of the colony from the end of Lugard's governorship in 1912 to 1939. Endacott's *History of Hong Kong* was written before the records of this period were open to investigation. So I have begun with a short general account of the history of the colony during this period to provide a background for the following chapters which deal with particular institutions and policy areas. While writing this book I discovered a surprising number of incidents and crises which closely paralleled events in the post-war period, but I have refrained from drawing attention to these possible comparisons.

To avoid confusion the minister responsible for the Colonial Office is always referred to as the Secretary of State, and the title of Colonial Secretary is used only for the deputy to the Governor of Hong Kong. The Wade-Giles system of romanization has been retained for Chinese terms and names since this was the system used in the original British documents upon which this study is based.

I am grateful to Frank Cass and Co. Ltd. for permission to incorporate material from my article, 'The Hong Kong Government Opium Monopoly 1914–1941', which was published in the *Journal of Imperial and Commonwealth History*, Vol. XI, 1983. Quotations from Crown-copyright material in the Public Record Office appear by kind permission of the Controller of Her Majesty's Stationery Office.

All the photographs in this book are reproduced, with permission, from the collections in the Public Record Office of Hong Kong. The photographs from the *South China Morning Post* are reproduced with permission. The endpaper map is reproduced, with the permission of the government of Hong Kong, from *Hong Kong Administrative Report for 1930*.

N. J. MINERS
Department of Political Science
University of Hong Kong

Contents

Tables

Plates

Introduction

EVER since Hong Kong became part of the British Empire in 1842 the Secretary of State for the Colonies has had almost unlimited power to direct the affairs of Hong Kong and to determine in detail what should and what should not be done. He appointed the Governor and other senior officers of the colonial service who were bound, just like any civil servant in Britain, to obey any instructions issued by a minister or by officials at the Colonial Office acting in his name. In practice, even in the heyday of imperialism, Governors were allowed considerable discretion to devise policies that were appropriate to their particular territories. The distances involved and the time taken for dispatches to travel between the Governor and the Colonial Office, even when supplemented by telegrams, meant that most sudden crises had to be dealt with by the Governor acting on his own authority, and the Secretary of State could often be informed only after the crucial decisions were taken. But on less urgent matters Governors were expected to consult the minister before embarking on any new policy initiative, in order that they might act in conformity with his views. Colonial governments were required to transmit a mass of reports and returns to London about all aspects of their administration. The Colonial Office in turn sent out frequent circular dispatches giving details of government policy, particularly in foreign affairs, information on developments in other colonies, and advice on how to deal with general problems which Governors were recommended to adopt.

How much effect did this stream of instructions, recommendations, and advice actually achieve? Governors never, or only very rarely, made public their dissent from the policies emanating from London, whatever disagreements and objections they might have voiced in their secret correspondence, but this outward show of compliance with ministerial directives does not necessarily mean that these policies were faithfully executed in practice. It is no easy task to ensure that the commands of a superior are carried out a thousand miles away, as every imperial power has discovered. In ancient China the irrelevance of imperial edicts from Peking was epitomized in the traditional saying, 'The heavens are high and the emperor is far away.' In the Spanish Empire in South America the king was the supreme sovereign and lawgiver, but colonial officials were able to combine an attitude of total submission and loyalty to the Crown with frequent actual disregard for royal orders.[1] The conventional formula used was *se acata pero no se cumple,* 'the law is accepted but not complied with'; or more simply 'I obey, but do not enforce'. Were the officers of the British Colonial Administrative Service more apt to give obedience to their imperial sovereign than Chinese mandarins or Spanish viceroys?

This book is an attempt to explore the actual consequences in Hong Kong of instructions issued from London, and the local repercussions of imperial policy over a period of 30 years between the revolution of 1911 which overthrew the Ch'ing dynasty and the temporary extinction of British colonial rule in 1941 by the Japanese occupation. The year 1912 marked a significant turning-point in Hong Kong's colonial history. Before that date China was united under a single government which maintained correct relations with the Western powers and made no attempt to destabilize the colony. But after the republican revolution the central government ceased to be able to exercise effective control over the whole of China and power in the provinces passed into the hands of those who were able to seize and hold it, normally the regional military commanders. Hong Kong was then faced with a succession of regimes in Canton (Guangzhou), which were often unfriendly to the colony and had the power to inflict considerable damage to its prosperity by interference with its trade and by encouraging internal agitation against the colonial government. Hong Kong's precarious position in the face of Chinese nationalism forced successive Governors to seek to reach some accommodation with those in authority in Canton. These approaches brought them into conflict with the Foreign Office, which continued to recognize the generals who controlled Peking (Beijing) as the legitimate government of China and strongly disapproved of Hong Kong's attempts to come to terms with those who held power in Kwangtung (Guangdong) province.

This study is based largely upon the official records of the Hong Kong government and in particular upon the correspondence between the successive Governors and the Colonial Office, which is preserved in the Public Record Office in London. A large number of these records have been discarded as unimportant: before 1914 almost all files were preserved, but by the 1920s only around 15 per cent survived the weeding-out process. This makes it difficult to form any quantitative estimate of the extent to which the Colonial Office interfered in the trivial day-to-day activities of the administration. But most dispatches dealing with significant events seem to have been preserved, and the minutes written on them by Colonial Office officials give considerable insight into the attitudes which informed the government of the Empire during this period. Unfortunately all the local files of the Hong Kong government were destroyed in the Japanese occupation and its aftermath, so no record remains of the reactions of the Governor and his advisers to dispatches from the Colonial Office. We can, however, find some evidence of their views by looking at the minutes of the Executive Council, the debates and decisions of the Legislative Council, and what the government actually did in response to promptings from London.

The first chapter gives an outline chronological narrative of the years from 1911 to 1941. This is followed by an account of the organization of the Colonial Office, the functions it performed, and the ministers and civil servants who formulated policies for the Empire or reacted as best they could to events in all parts of the globe. The next five chapters look at various institutions of the Hong Kong government, the changes that took place over 30 years, and the extent to which the Colonial Office was able to exercise effective supervision over the activities of the Hong Kong government. The remainder of the book examines the development of policy in three areas where the Hong Kong administration was under pressure from London to institute reforms: the *mui tsai* system, the tolerated houses, and the control of opium-smoking. The abolition of licensed prostitution can be fully understood only in the light of the system which existed in the nineteenth century; and the problems faced by the government opium monopoly were intimately connected with the campaign to eradicate opium-smoking in China which began in 1906. So in these case studies it has been necessary to extend the historical investigation back for a number of years before 1912 and to include a good deal of information about the changing situation in China. Finally the concluding chapter attempts to estimate the extent to which the Colonial Office was able to influence and control what was done in Hong Kong and the relative importance of ministers and civil servants in determining policy.

1 The History of Hong Kong, 1911 to 1941

THE revolution against the Ch'ing (Qing) dynasty began on 10 October 1911, when the military garrison in Wuchang in central China mutinied and seized control of the city. The other main cities of Hupeh (Hubei) province quickly came under the control of the revolutionaries and their success emboldened other areas to rebel. Within a month half of the provinces of China had declared their independence. On 9 November the Viceroy of Kwangtung took refuge with the British Consul and the whole province went over to the revolutionary cause. Jubilation at the end of Manchu rule spilled over into the colony and many hoped that foreign domination could also be brought to an end in Hong Kong. There was widespread disorder and violence; shops were looted; police attempting to make arrests were stoned and prevented from taking action by rowdy mobs; bomb-making factories were discovered; Europeans were attacked on the streets and there was a rush to buy firearms for self-defence.[1]

The Governor, Sir Frederick Lugard, took strong measures to deal with this situation. Soldiers with fixed bayonets made daily route marches through the streets of the city; on 30 November emergency powers under the Peace Preservation Ordinance were invoked by proclamation, giving the police wide powers to disperse crowds, enter houses, and make arrests; and on the same day an amending bill was rushed through the Legislative Council in one meeting to give magistrates the power to impose the penalty of up to 24 lashes with a cat-o'-nine-tails for a wide range of offences, in addition to any other penalty prescribed by law. In the three months from December 1911 to February 1912, 51 prisoners were flogged with the cat-o'-nine-tails for such offences as theft, assaults on the police, and resisting arrest. At the same time the garrison was reinforced with two battalions of infantry and a battery of artillery sent from India. These measures had their effect and, before Lugard departed in March 1912, he felt sufficiently confident that the disturbances were under control that, as soon as the Chinese New Year celebrations were over, he rescinded the proclamation invoking emergency powers.[2]

However, conditions had not yet returned to normal when the new Governor, Sir Henry May, arrived in July. While he was proceeding from Blake Pier to the City Hall to be sworn in, a Chinese man pushed his way through the watching crowd, ran up to the sedan-chair in which May was travelling, and fired a revolver at his head, narrowly missing him. The would-be assassin, who was mentally deranged and not part of a wider conspiracy, was quickly arrested and the ceremonial inauguration of the Governor passed without further mishap.[3] But unrest continued. Stones and other missiles were thrown at the Governor's car when he appeared in public, and assaults on the police and attempted rescues of prisoners continued to occur. So many law-breakers were sentenced to prison that the gaols became overcrowded and some prisoners had to be released before completing their terms, in order to make room for others. There was also trouble in the rural areas where armed bands of criminals from China made raids across the border. Troops from two Indian battalions of the garrison were deployed along the border and went out on patrol through the New Territories. There was an upsurge in piracy in the waters around the colony and in the Pearl River Delta (Zhujiang Chang). In one particularly daring raid in August 1912 a gang of 40 pirates landed by night on Cheung Chau and raided the police station, killing three Indian constables, and making off with the weapons held there, together with the government tax revenues which were stored in the station safe.[4]

A fresh irritant to nationalist sentiment was an ordinance passed in April 1912 forbidding the importation and circulation of Chinese copper coins. As a result of the past activities of the Hong Kong government and of the Chinese mints in Kwangtung, the quantity of copper coins in circulation exceeded monetary requirements, and so all copper coins were traded at a discount of 7 per cent to their face value. In order to rehabilitate the currency the government proposed to withdraw lower-denomination coins from circulation as they were paid into the Treasury and to forbid the use of coins struck in Canton, thus increasing the demand for Hong Kong coins. This measure to outlaw Chinese coins was regarded as insulting to the new republican government in Canton, and when in November 1912 the Governor persuaded the management of the tramway companies and the Star Ferry Company to refuse to accept Chinese coins a boycott of the tramway running from Shaukiwan to Kennedy Town was organized. Passengers were intimidated from boarding the trams by gangs of roughs and posters were put up threatening injury to any Chinese who used the trams. The main instigators of the boycott were the money-changers, the guilds of engineers and artisans, and various patriotic organizations and secret societies. At first the government tried to enlist the support of prominent members of the Chinese community, such as the District Watchmen Committee and leading merchants. But their speeches and example were ineffectual in inducing the mass of the population to resist intimidation and break the boycott. After three weeks May introduced a new Boycotting Prevention Bill which was passed through all of its stages at a single meeting of the Legislative Council. This imposed stringent penalties for threatening violence, picketing, and inciting to boycott and authorized the government to levy a penal rate on the inhabitants of any area where a boycott occurred and pay the proceeds to the company which was suffering loss of trade. At the beginning of January 1913 the government published notification of its intention to impose this penalty on all the districts through which the tramway ran, but deferred implementation on receiving a petition from the property-owners and occupiers who promised that they would attempt to influence their servants and employees to use the trams again. Spurred by the fear of financial losses these efforts were successful: the numbers using the trams gradually increased and by the end of the month fare receipts were back to normal. Accordingly no penal rate was levied and the tramway company was compensated by a payment from government revenue.[5]

The defeat of the boycott movement gave a considerable boost to the government's authority. As a result, in May 1913, further ordinances were enacted to ban the circulation of foreign silver and nickel coins, and foreign banknotes. Popular enthusiasm for revolutionary change suffered a further setback in July when the republican government of Kwangtung province proclaimed its independence of Peking in the so-called 'Second Revolution'. The provincial forces under General Chen Chiung-ming were quickly defeated by troops loyal to the central government under General Lung Chai-kwong, and Sun Yat-sen and other leading members of his party fled to Hong Kong. However, although the regime of General Lung lasted for three years it was unable to restore stable conditions throughout Kwangtung. Numerous bands of robbers, often composed of disbanded revolutionary soldiers, continued to infest the province and crossed the border to ransack villages in the northern parts of the New Territories. Trains on the Kowloon–Canton Railway were held up and the passengers were robbed. Piracy on the high seas was frequent. Sometimes the pirates embarked on ships under the guise of passengers and then attempted to take over the vessel. In one incident where the officers put up stout resistance the pirates set the ship on fire and 300 lives were lost. In 1916 Canton again announced its independence of the central government when Yüan Shih-k'ai proclaimed himself emperor, and over the next seven years battles took place between armies loyal to various factions and a succession of rulers briefly took control of Canton.[6] Throughout these convulsions Hong Kong remained relatively orderly and peaceful. Refugees from the successive bouts of fighting sought shelter in the colony and many prominent Cantonese moved their families there for safety. Because of the prevailing uncertainty Hong Kong's entrepôt trade with southern China suffered, since merchants kept their stocks as low as possible and were unwilling to commit themselves for the future.

The outbreak of the First World War in Europe in August 1914 was completely unexpected in Asia, and Hong Kong, as part of the British Empire, suddenly found itself at war with Germany and Austria. German firms had long been active and German merchants formed the largest foreign community in Hong Kong.[7] Although the German population was only one-tenth of the size of the British civil population, the aggressive business methods of the German firms and their willingness to extend long-term credit on easy terms to Chinese customers aroused the envy and hostility of the British merchant houses. After the declaration of war all German women and children were obliged to leave and all men of military age were interned. German businesses were taken over by the government and by 1916 they were all liquidated and their assets sold off, much to the joy of their British competitors. German businesses continued to operate freely in China, notably in Canton where there were twice as many German business men as British, until China declared war on Germany in 1917.[8]

Hong Kong was not involved in any hostilities during the First World War and the colony suffered few hardships apart from the commercial dislocation caused by embargoes on dealings with enemy firms and controls placed on the export of certain strategic goods and materials to neutral countries, which threatened the port's entrepôt trade. The patriotic enthusiasm of the British community was shown by the large number of men who volunteered for military service overseas (579 out of a total male population of 2,157) and the gifts and loans raised to support the war effort. In addition to the normal military contribution and the cost of local defence forces, over HK$10,000,000 was voted by the Legislative Council as a gift to Britain (equivalent to the total government revenue for 1914).[9] Individual Chinese also made contributions and Chinese property-owners agreed to a special additional assessment of 7 per cent on the rates which raised over HK$2,000,000 in the last two years of the war.[10]

Because of the war May's governorship was extended beyond the normal term of six years. In September 1918 he left the colony for a short leave, but while away he suffered a stroke and decided to send in his resignation. His last months as Governor were marked by two disasters. In February 1918 during the annual race meeting at Happy Valley a matshed stand collapsed and caught fire and more than 600 Chinese died in the resulting conflagration. At about the same period there was a severe outbreak of cerebro-spinal meningitis which caused about a thousand deaths. A report by Dr Olitsky from the Rockefeller Institute in New York put the blame for the epidemic on the gross overcrowding in the tenements on the northern shores of Hong Kong island where the large numbers of refugees who had crowded in since 1912 were accommodated in dank fetid cubicles which were made by partitioning off the floors of rickety ancient buildings that were infested with rats. The only remedy for these appalling conditions was wholesale demolition of the insanitary structures and rebuilding but such a programme of urban redevelopment was beyond the resources of the government; and, in the absence of effective means of controlling the influx of refugees or forcing the surplus population to leave, new buildings would soon have become as overcrowded as the old.[11]

The new Governor was Sir Edward Stubbs, but he did not take up his appointment until September 1919. During the unusually long interim period of a year the Colonial Secretary, Claud Severn, was Officer Administering the Government (OAG). He presided over the celebrations at the end of the First World War, and he also had to deal with the problems caused by the world-wide shortage of cereals and the consequent rise in prices which occurred in 1919. The rice crop in Siam (now Thailand) had been a partial failure and India and Indo-China had placed controls on the export of rice. The Colonial Office warned Ceylon (now Sri Lanka), the Straits Settlements (now part of Malaysia), and Hong Kong of the dangers of the situation early in 1919 and in May proposed concerted arrangements to obtain supplies, suggesting that an embargo should be placed on the import of rice from Siam on private account in order to prevent private traders from bidding up the price. The Hong

Kong government declined to follow this advice for fear that any such action would permanently damage the colony's large entrepôt trade in rice, and the Colonial Office left the matter to Hong Kong's discretion. In July 1919 the Hong Kong government finally decided to enter the market to make bulk purchases of rice wherever supplies were available for resale to the Chinese population. This rice reached the colony just in time at the end of July, after rioting and the looting of rice shops had already started in Kowloon. The government also used emergency powers to forbid the export of rice from the New Territories, to seize stocks, and to fix the market price. The provision of unlimited government supplies at a fixed price stabilized the situation and prevented further unrest. The shortage ended suddenly in September with the unexpected arrival of fresh supplies from China and the government was then forced to dispose as best it could of its large stocks of poor quality rice which had been bought at the top of the market. Fortunately for the government the unofficial members of the Executive and Legislative Councils had approved the policy of buying rice to stave off unrest at a joint meeting held in July and so were inhibited from any criticism of the massive loss of HK$2,700,000 which was incurred in disposing of the government's stocks on a falling market. In September 1919 an ordinance was passed by the Legislative Council without dissent, retrospectively validating all that the government had done.[12]

The rise in the price of rice affected a population which was already suffering from a severe inflation. This was partly caused by the shortages of the war years, and also by the influx of refugees, which had brought about a huge increase in rents. Wages had not gone up to meet these rises in the cost of living, which employers regarded as a temporary consequence of the war, even though a Salaries Commission appointed in 1919 had recommended wage increases of up to 30 per cent for the public service. Few of the workers were organized in any kind of trade union, but a leading role was taken by the Chinese Engineers Guild which was composed of engineers and fitters from most of the leading European firms. In April 1920 they presented their employers with a demand for a 40 per cent wage increase, and when it was refused they went out on strike. The strike began in the Taikoo dockyard and the Royal Naval Dockyard and quickly spread to the Hong Kong Electric Company, the tramways, and other large firms. This happened at the time of the Ching Ming festival. The men went off to Canton to attend to their ancestors' graves and then stayed there, forcing the employers to negotiate with the strikers' committee by telegraph. The government had to call in the help of the army and navy to keep the electric light and refrigerating plants working. The strike lasted less than two weeks. The employers were obliged to increase their offer to 32.5 per cent. This settlement was accepted and the strikers returned and took up their duties again. This speedy victory encouraged other skilled and semi-skilled workers to follow the engineers' example. Within a year the number of trade unions had increased from 31 to 70 and in 1921 strikes were called by shipwrights, carpenters, furniture-makers, masons, quarrymen, and eating-house employees, resulting in wage increases of around 30 per cent.[13]

A census held in 1921 found that the civil population had increased by 37 per cent over that of 1911, to 625,166. Almost all the growth had taken place in the urban areas of Hong Kong island and Kowloon. The census probably considerably underestimated the numbers actually living in Hong Kong since it was taken during the Ching Ming festival when many had left to visit Kwangtung. The figures were also affected by a widely disseminated rumour that the government intended to build a huge bridge across the harbour to Kowloon resting on 99 piers and that a certain number of young children of both sexes were required to be buried alive under the foundations of each pier to ensure its stability. Many mothers became convinced that the purpose of the census was to enable the government to make a suitable choice of victims and so a large number of children were concealed from the census-takers. This bizarre episode vividly illustrates the distrust that then existed between the mass of the Chinese population and their British rulers.[14]

During the ten years from 1911 to 1920, fewer than 2,000 new houses were built in the urban areas to accommodate the increase of more than 150,000 in the Chinese population. Landlords naturally took advantage of this shortage to crowd in more tenants and increase rents. The profits to be made attracted speculative investment from rich men in Kwangtung, who were seeking a safe haven for their wealth under the British flag, and away from the continuing chaos in Kwangtung. As houses changed hands the new owners were quick to eject old tenants and subdivide floors into yet smaller cubicles, and relet at higher rentals. A draft bill to forbid rent increases was discussed in 1919 when Severn was administering the government, but no conclusion was reached. Stubbs was strongly opposed to any action, believing that any such interference with the free market would deter investment in new buildings, which was the only long-term solution to the housing problem. Instead he pressed ahead with reclamation and road-building to open up new areas for development and accelerated the procedures for the approval of new building plans and the reconstruction of old tenements. But public outcry at the escalation of rents, and the labour unrest fuelled by these rises, finally forced him to take action. In June 1921 a bill was introduced to freeze rents at the levels of December 1920. This measure aroused heated controversy, and a number of petitions were presented to the Legislative Council from supporters and opponents of the bill. One of these organized by the guilds representing 80,000 workers profusely thanked the Governor for introducing the bill and for treating them as though they were 'your little red babies'.[15] The ordinance was meant to be a temporary measure to forbid increases for one year only. But the housing situation was no better in 1922 and the legislation was successively extended one year at a time until it was allowed to lapse in June 1926, when the exodus of population resulting from the strike and boycott (discussed below) brought a swift end to the housing shortage.

This restriction on rent increases did not dampen investors' enthusiasm for buying leaseholds of Crown land. The revenue realized at government land auctions rose from HK$264,000 in 1919 to HK$1,634,000 in 1921, to HK$2,722,000 in 1922, and to HK$3,489,000 in 1923 at the height of the land boom. The government did all it could to increase the supply of land and in 1921 began negotiations to take over the army barracks which occupied prime sites in the centre of Victoria and Kowloon and to rehouse the military in more remote areas. The War Office insisted that Hong Kong must pay the full market value of the land and bear the cost of reprovisioning the army units involved. This ruling infuriated Stubbs and the unofficial members of the Legislative Council but the War Office and the Treasury in London refused to make any concession. An eminent surveyor, Sir John Oakley, was sent out from England in 1923 to assess the value of the land, and his award of just under HK$17,000,000 was grudgingly accepted by the government and the Legislative Council in March 1924. By this time the land boom was already past its peak. In June 1925 Stubbs asked for the valuation to be reconsidered in view of the general decline in land prices, and the whole scheme was indefinitely deferred in 1926 during the general strike and boycott, because of lack of funds. As a result the barracks in the centre of Victoria remained in army hands until after the Second World War.[16]

Meanwhile the affairs of China continued in a chaotic state. Sun Yat-sen briefly returned to power in Kwangtung in1917, but he was ousted a year later by local war-lords. In October 1920 they were in turn defeated by an army under General Chen Chiung-ming, who brought back Sun Yat-sen. In May 1921 he was formally elected President of China in Canton by the surviving members of the Chinese parliament of 1912. The British government continued to recognize the northern war-lords who occupied Peking as the legitimate government of the whole of China. So the Hong Kong authorities, who had no liking for Sun Yat-sen, banned all gatherings to celebrate Sun's inauguration and a proclamation was issued by the Secretariat for Chinese Affairs to warn the population against contributing to the loans being raised by the new regime. The announcement described the promoters of these loans as 'unscrupulous and senseless persons' and predicted the imminent bankruptcy of Sun Yat-sen's government.[17] These insulting remarks caused much anger in Canton and relations between the two cities, never very cordial, reached a new low point. Canton had always resented Hong Kong's commercial success and from time to time plans were made to deepen the Pearl River and to develop the port of Whampoa in order to compete for the trade of South China.[18] For 20 years the Kwangtung authorities, wishing to deprive Hong Kong of the trade from the Yangtze (Chang Jiang) valley, refused to link the railway from Canton to Hankow (Han Kou) with the Kowloon–Canton railway. Sun Yat-sen had become more socialist in his thinking since 1919 and after his return to power in 1920 his government encouraged the growth of trade unions and attempted to build a base of support among the working class. The existing workers' organizations in Canton already had links with their counterparts in Hong Kong, and this co-operation soon provided the means to deal a damaging blow to Hong Kong's prosperity.

The Chinese Seamen's Union was established in Hong Kong in 1921 with help from Canton and in November it put in a claim for wage increases of 30 to 40 per cent and also demanded that in future all seamen should be recruited through the union acting as an intermediary and not through compradors. The shipping companies temporized and refused to make any offer, so the seamen went on strike on 13 January 1922. The strikers, following the example set by the engineers in 1920, immediately travelled by rail to Canton where arrangements had already been made to house, feed, and pay them. They were entertained by the mayor, Sun Fo, the son of Sun Yat-sen, and by decree all temples and public places in the city were made available to them. As more ships arrived in the harbour the crews deserted and joined the strike. The shipowners quickly offered a wage increase, conceding rather less than half of the seamen's demands. This was rejected by the union who put forward their own terms for a settlement which included the establishment of an Arbitration Board at Canton and the demand that in future all crews should be engaged through the Seamen's Union. These terms were in turn rejected on 27 January in a message sent to Canton by Stubbs. On 31 January the stevedores, cargo carriers, coal coolies, and talleymen working in the port all went on a sympathetic strike and also travelled to Canton. The union sent parties of armed men to various points on the coast to interrupt the normal shipment of fresh food to Hong Kong, and trains on the Canton–Kowloon railway were systematically searched and all foodstuffs were removed. In reply to this intensification of the strike the Hong Kong government declared the Seamen's Union to be an unlawful society, closed down its premises, and arrested some of its officials. Three other unions were similarly banned a week later. Various attempts to reach a settlement by negotiation took place during February while food ran short in Hong Kong and prices rose steeply. The union was able to finance the strike and pay a dole to the strikers by forcing the railways in Kwangtung province to collect a 30 per cent surcharge on all tickets for its benefit, and a similar levy was imposed on the river steamers sailing from Canton.[19] The strike committee's actions had the tacit consent of the Kwangtung authorities.

On 28 February the union instructed all workers in the colony to join the strike and proceed to Canton. This call, enforced by widespread intimidation, was obeyed by most of the work-force. Bakers, cooks, clerks, drivers, coolies, and domestic servants all stopped work. Even at Government House the entire Chinese staff joined the stoppage. Soldiers and naval ratings had to be drafted in to keep essential services going. The government rushed a new Emergency Regulations Bill through the Legislative Council in a single day and took powers to censor letters, to commandeer vehicles and foodstuffs, and to impress workers to carry out essential duties. To prevent a further mass exodus to Canton, all Chinese wishing to leave the colony were required to obtain passes from the police, and the train service to Canton was suspended. The strikers then set out to cross the border on foot. One large body of domestic servants attempting to pass through Sha Tin on their way to the frontier was intercepted by the police; when they refused to disperse the police superintendent in charge ordered his men to open fire, killing three among the crowd outright and wounding eight others, one of whom subsequently died.[20]

The shooting at Sha Tin took place on 4 March, when negotiations to end the strike had finally started in Hong Kong. The British Consul-General in Canton, J.W. Jamieson, acted as a mediator between the shipping companies, the seamen, and the Canton government at the talks. The terms of the settlement gave the seamen considerably more than the owners had offered in January, but less than their original demands, and the strikers were to receive half pay for the period of the strike and until they were re-engaged on a new ship. The cost of these payments was to be borne by a fund subscribed by the shipping companies and guaranteed by Sir Robert Ho Tung. The seamen's delegation then went on to meet represent-atives of the Hong Kong government, from whom they received assurances that the banning order on the Seamen's Union would be lifted, that union members who had been arrested would be released, and that compensation would be paid to the victims of the Sha Tin shooting. The prisoners were released and the order declaring the union an illegal society was rescinded on 6 March, and the strikers began to return from Canton on the same day. The union had won a famous victory, the shipping companies had lost millions of dollars while their vessels lay idle for eight weeks, and the Hong Kong government had been forced into an ignominious retreat.[21]

As soon as the strike was over the government began preparing against a repetition. The War Office was asked to increase the garrison by an extra battalion. Methods of gathering intelligence were improved. A register was compiled of Europeans able to undertake essential services. Depots were constructed to hold stocks of coal and other supplies and more lorries were acquired.[22] During the rest of the year further strikes were called in some 20 trades and industries. Most won substantial pay increases, but in a few cases such as the restaurant workers' strike the employers resisted excessive demands and were able to engage new staff to carry on their business in spite of intimidation. The Secretary for Chinese Affairs attempted to persuade the employers to set up a federation and so form a united front against further labour agitation. He also encouraged the formation of a rival seamen's union which somewhat reduced the membership of the Canton-dominated organization.[23]

Chen Chiung-ming, the Civil Governor of Canton, had been helpful in the setting up of the negotiations which brought the strike to an end, and the Hong Kong government regarded him as a conservative and stabilizing element within Sun Yat-sen's regime. So the government was delighted when Sun's attempt to advance northwards against the war-lords failed and General Chen staged a *coup d'état* in June 1922 expelling the Kuomintang (Guomingdang) leaders. In August the Hong Kong government proposed to make a loan of HK$3,000,000 to help the new administration in Canton to establish itself in power, but the Foreign Office vetoed the proposal, insisting that the British government must remain neutral.[24] General Chen's regime lasted barely six months before it was overthrown in January 1923 by forces loyal to Sun Yat-sen. Stubbs regarded Sun's return with foreboding, expecting renewed enmity between Canton and Hong Kong and a resurgence of labour agitation, but he was very pleasantly surprised to find that Sun had apparently changed character and was now anxious for good relations with the colony. He expressed willingness to allow the building of a railway loop to join the Hankow–Canton line to the Kowloon–Canton line and asked for the loan of British experts to help reorganize the Kwangtung administration.[25] There was no sign of overt support from Canton for strikes called by the Hong Kong unions and by the end of the year Stubbs had become an enthusiastic supporter of the pretensions of Sun Yat-sen's southern government, much to the annoyance of the British ambassador in Peking and the Foreign Office. Friendly relations with Canton continued throughout 1924, although the Hong Kong business community and the government became increasingly concerned at the presence of Russian advisers and the close links between the newly reorganized Kuomintang party and the Communists. In December Sun Yat-sen went to Peking at the invitation of one of the northern war-lords and remained there until he died in March 1925. His death led to a struggle for power between the right-wing and left-wing factions of the Kuomintang. This conflict was not resolved until Chiang Kaishek, the commandant of the Whampoa Military Academy, was able to attain supremacy in May 1926.

On 30 May 1925 the police in the International Settlement at Shanghai opened fire on a demonstration, killing nine Chinese and wounding many more. This incident provoked protests and demonstrations in many parts of China. In Canton the labour leaders called for a general strike in Hong Kong and South China against British imperialism. The seamen were the first to come out, on 19 June, and men in other trades soon followed. Some workers were unenthusiastic for a strike which had no immediate economic motive and the Engineers Guild voted overwhelmingly to stay at work. But on 23 June a mass demonstration held in Canton was fired upon from the British and French concession on Shameen (Shamian) Island, leaving 52 Chinese dead. The news of the 'Shameen massacre' generated increased support for the strike and by the middle of July almost all businesses in the colony had been affected, and most of the junior staff of government had joined the stoppage. As in 1922 the strikers were instructed to leave for Canton where the strike committee had arranged food and accommodation for them. It was estimated that by the end of July, 250,000 strikers and their families had left for Canton, and once they had arrived they were forcibly prevented from returning.[26]

The Hong Kong government had been preparing to deal with such a situation for three years. On 21 June the Volunteer Defence Corps was called out for duty, and the next day emergency regulations were brought into force. Military guards were posted at vital points and troops made route marches through the city. Naval ratings were detailed to run the cross-harbour ferries and keep the electricity supply working; and volunteers from the European community were mobilized to keep essential services running and were enrolled as special constables. Controllers of food, transport, and labour were appointed, and unskilled workers were engaged at relatively high rates to take the place of workers who had gone on strike. To encourage workers to remain at their jobs and resist intimidation the government promised to pay compensation of HK$2,000 to the family of anyone who lost his life as a result of continuing at work, and a Labour Protection Bureau was set up under a retired Chinese general, consisting of about one hundred ex-soldiers and others whose role was to threaten labour agitators and deter intimidation. These energetic measures were relatively successful and by September the worst of the strike was over; a number of workers had made their way back to the colony or replacements had been engaged from elsewhere along the China coast; and most businesses had resumed operations, though on a reduced scale.[27]

The most serious threat to the colony was now the boycott organized by the strike committee in Canton, with the active support of the Kwangtung government. An embargo was imposed on all trade between Hong Kong and any part of Kwangtung; all British and Hong Kong Chinese shipping was banned from entering any port, as was any foreign vessel which had called at Hong Kong or was carrying British or Hong Kong goods. All ships entering Canton and other southern ports were inspected by pickets posted on the wharves by the strike committee, who imposed fines or confiscated merchandise for any breach of these regulations.[28] This boycott was effectively enforced for 15 months until October 1926, causing immense damage to the commerce of Hong Kong. Trade with South China could only be carried on if the goods were transhipped to Shanghai or some other northern port and then sent on to Canton by a foreign shipping line with all identifying marks removed. The number of ships entering Hong Kong harbour dropped by 60 per cent.[29] Many firms went bankrupt and others were only able to survive by receiving advances from a trade loan of £3,000,000 arranged by the Colonial Office from the Straits Settlements and the West African Currency Board.

In September, three months after the strike began, the strike committee and the Canton government issued a list of conditions on which they were prepared to call off the strike and boycott. Apart from the reinstatment of all employees and the payment of wages in full for the period of the strike, they demanded a large number of political changes in the colony including the election of Chinese to the Legislative Council, the abolition of all discrimination against Chinese, an eight-hour working day, and a 25 per cent reduction in all rents.[30] These conditions were immediately rejected by Stubbs and no further attempt at negotiations took place until December. Stubbs adopted a very bellicose attitude, proposing that the Canton regime should be coerced into submission by means of a blockade of the Pearl River, bombing the Boca Tigris forts at its mouth, or by military action against Canton, to be carried out by the British in co-operation with those forces in southern China who were loyal to the Peking government. The Foreign Office considered and rejected all of those courses of action, fearing that any use of force would lead to a fresh outburst of anti-British feeling in China which would permanently embitter relations, expose British communities in other ports to acts of retaliation, and lead to an even greater loss of trade than Britain was experiencing at that time. Military action could only be contemplated in conjunction with the other treaty powers and they had no wish to intervene in a quarrel which concerned Britain alone.[31] Instead the British government favoured a policy of patient inaction, waiting in the hope that more moderate leaders might come to power in the Kuomintang and exert effective control over the strike committee. The committee was acting like an independent government in Canton, with its own police force of armed pickets and its own courts and prisons to punish those who offended against the boycott regulations or attempted to return to Hong Kong.

In October 1925 Stubbs left after six years as Governor and was succeeded by Sir Cecil Clementi, who adopted a much more conciliatory attitude towards Canton and attempted to open informal talks with the authorities there. As a result conversations were held between officials of the Hong Kong and Canton governments in December and a delegation of Chinese merchants visited Canton in January 1926. These talks proved fruitless, and during February the strike committee attempted to organize a second general strike in Hong Kong, but without success. In March the Canton government proposed negotiations, but these did not get beyond preliminary conversations, when Hong Kong made it clear that there was no question of paying the huge sum of money demanded as compensation for the strikers. Clementi regarded any such payment as a surrender to blackmail, which would expose the colony to a renewal of the strike and further demands for money at any time in the future. A new round of negotiations took place in July. The Hong Kong delegation continued to refuse payment of compensation, but offered to make a loan to the Canton government for the construction of public works, which could provide employment for the strikers who could not be reinstated. No agreement could be reached, even although it appeared that the Canton government was ready to end the boycott provided that it could lay its hands on a substantial sum of money which was needed to finance the forthcoming military expedition of Chiang Kai-shek against the northern war-lords.[32]

In a surprise move in September British naval forces sailed up the Pearl River to Canton and landed marines who cleared the strike pickets from the wharves. A gunboat was left lying alongside to prevent their return. This demonstration of force and the threat of further naval action at a time when Chiang Kai-shek's northern expedition had reached the Yangtze, but had been repulsed at Wuchang, seems to have frightened the Canton government. An announcement was made that the boycott would be terminated in

October, provided that Britain raised no objection to the imposition of a tax of 2.5 per cent on all imports and 5 per cent on luxury goods. The right of China to fix its own tariffs had not yet been conceded by the treaty powers, but Britain acquiesced in this proposal as a means of ending the long-running dispute. The boycott was finally ended on 10 October when the strike committee organized a massive demonstration in Canton to celebrate their achievements and vowed to continue the struggle against imperialism by other means. Trade with Canton then gradually returned to normal, although intermittent attempts to picket British ships and merchandise continued for some time, and the shipping companies which had engaged new crews during the strike were compelled to discharge them and re-engage their former employees through the Seamen's Union.[33] However, in spite of these difficulties the outcome of the 15-month strike and boycott was a clear victory for the Hong Kong government; the colony had survived the attempt to bring about its commercial ruin, none of the political concessions demanded by the strikers had been granted, and no payments had been made either to the strikers or to the Canton government. But trading companies had lost immense sums — up to HK$500,000,000 according to one estimate[34] — and the shock to business confidence in the colony's future affected its prosperity for years afterwards.[35]

Trade recovered very slowly from the effects of the boycott. In Canton the strike committee remained in existence until the end of 1927 and from time to time there were threats that the boycott might be renewed. Steamers on the Hong Kong–Canton service were harassed by a series of strikes called by the Seamen's Union on trivial matters.[36] At the end of 1926 the national leadership of the Kuomintang had moved from Canton to Nanking (Nanjing), leaving General Li Chai-sum as head of the provincial government of Kwangtung. His political leanings were to the right-wing faction of the party, and during 1927 he had difficulty in imposing his authority on the more radical socialist elements and the trade union leaders who were dominant in Canton. But in December 1927 the Communists staged an uprising in the city and seized control of the central district for three days until they were overwhelmed by troops sent in from outside. Some 6,000 Communists and their supporters were killed in the fighting and in the massacre that followed. After this bloody episode General Li was able to restore order to the province and re-established amicable relations with Hong Kong. Li and Clementi exchanged official visits in March 1928 and it seemed that a new era of friendly co-operation between the two cities was beginning. Co-ordinated operations were undertaken against the notorious haunt of pirates at Bias Bay (Daya Bay) to the north of Hong Kong and a permanent Chinese garrison was established there.[37] Clementi was helpful in extraditing criminals who had fled to the colony and he put no obstacles in the way of Li's attempts to raise a loan from the Hong Kong business community.[38] General Li did not remain in power very long: in March 1929 he was arrested on the orders of Chiang Kai-shek on suspicion of disloyalty. But General Chan Ming-shu who succeeded him continued to maintain friendly relations with Hong Kong.

Throughout 1927 the Hong Kong government was constantly on the alert for any sign of Communist penetration of the labour unions, and took severe measures to anticipate the danger of politically motivated strikes and agitation. New emergency regulations were promulgated to exercise more stringent control over meetings, demonstrations, and processions. The General Labour Union was proscribed in April, the Hong Kong branch of the Seamen's Union in May, and the Knitting Workers' Union in December. In July a new Illegal Strikes and Lockouts Ordinance was passed, forbidding politically motivated strikes which were not called in furtherance of a trade dispute, and making it unlawful for any union to be affiliated to an organization outside the colony. All of these restrictions and prohibitions remained in force for the next 15 years, until after the Second World War.[39] But in fact there were no further serious labour disputes during this period. The strike and boycott of 1925–6 had left the unions impoverished and unpopular, and the trade depression of the 1930s was not conducive to labour militancy. The union movement did not revive until 1937–8, when it was stimulated to renewed activity by patriotic motives in support of the war against Japan.[40]

In 1928 the major cause of public anxiety was not the political situation but the weather. Rainfall in the 12 months from June 1928 was the lowest ever recorded. The reservoirs on Hong Kong island and in Kowloon almost ran dry, strict water rationing was introduced, and large brick-built tanks were erected on the waterfront and were kept filled by ships which brought water from as far away as Foochow (Fuzhou), Shanghai, and Japan. The situation was so desperate that aeroplanes were sent up from Kai Tak airport to sprinkle powdered kaolin on the passing clouds, but without any appreciable results.[41] The drought finally ended in July 1929. By then decisions had been taken to lay a pipeline under the harbour to carry water from Kowloon, and to start work on the first large reservoir in the New Territories at Shing Mun. There was another severe water shortage in 1932, which accelerated plans to start work on the second stage of Shing Mun, later renamed the Jubilee Reservoir. Throughout the whole of the period from 1914, estimates of the future demand for water and the need for fresh sources were invariably outstripped by the growth of population.[42] The census held in 1931 found that the population had risen to 849,751, a 36 per cent increase over 1921.

The 1931 census also discovered that 24 per cent of the working population (111,156 out of 470,794) were employed in manufacturing industry.[43] This figure caused some surprise since it had always been assumed that the vast majority of the work-force were employed in shipping and the trades and services directly connected with the harbour such as the dockyards, and in warehouses, banking, and insurance. Sugar-refining and cement-manufacture had long been important industries but in the 1920s and 1930s a large number of small factories were set up for the manufacture of knitwear, hosiery, cigarettes, perfumery, glassware, rubber shoes, and electric torches and batteries.[44] This increase prompted the need for factory legislation. In 1922 the first such bill was passed, to forbid the industrial employment of children, and this was followed in 1927 by a Factory Accidents Ordinance which empowered the Governor in Council to make regulations for the safe operation of machinery and provided for the appointment of factory inspectors. In 1929 a bill was passed to allow the government to regulate the conditions of employment of women and young persons.

The further growth of manufacturing industry was threatened by the treaty powers' concession of tariff autonomy to China in 1929. China immediately increased its import duties. These were collected by the staff of the Chinese Maritime Customs for the benefit of the new central government of China at Nanking, but they also served as a barrier to protect Chinese products from foreign competition, and so affected Hong Kong's trade with the mainland. One immediate result was to make the smuggling of merchandise from Hong Kong to China much more lucrative. Since roughly a quarter of China's total imports went through Hong Kong a serious loss of potential revenue occurred. Therefore negotiations to conclude a commercial treaty took place between China and Hong Kong during 1929 and 1930. The Chinese Maritime Customs wanted to set up an office in Hong Kong to collect the new Chinese duties before merchandise was transhipped into coasting vessels for carriage to China. The colonial government had always opposed an official presence of the Chinese Maritime Customs in Hong Kong and before granting this concession it tried to secure certain compensating advantages for local business interests, such as the right of British-registered ships to trade on China's inland waterways and the admission of Hong Kong manufactures into China without payment of duty. The Nationalist government refused to entertain these proposals and threats were made that if no agreement was reached Hong Kong shipping might be harassed by the launches of the Maritime Customs and a virtual blockade might be mounted outside the colony's waters. A draft agreement was eventually negotiated in October 1930 between the Governor and the Inspector-General of the Maritime Customs which would have allowed a Customs Commissioner to operate in Hong Kong, but this agreement was then rejected by the Central Executive Committee of the Kuomintang on the ground that the granting to Hong Kong of the customs facilities enjoyed at a treaty port would be detrimental to the interests of Canton. Certain officials of the Kwangtung government had a very profitable interest in the smuggling operations and had lobbied at Nanking against the ratification of the treaty.[45] Although the Chinese authorities had been responsible for the failure to conclude an agreement there were frequent complaints from China about the activities of Hong Kong smugglers in the years that followed.

In 1930, during the course of these negotiations, Clementi had been unexpectedly transferred from Hong Kong to become the Governor of the Straits Settlements. His successor was Sir William Peel, who proved to be more phlegmatic and relaxed in his temperament than Clementi. His five years as Governor were relatively uneventful. The only serious incident was a nasty riot which erupted in September 1931 after the Japanese invasion of Manchuria. Japanese residents were assaulted, shops selling Japanese goods were looted, and all Japanese property that the rioters could lay their hands on was destroyed. A family of six Japanese living in an isolated villa were murdered. The arson and looting continued over five days both on Hong Kong island and in Kowloon, and on the fourth day the army had to be called in to prevent the police from being overwhelmed. On several occasions, the police opened fire to disperse mobs and at least five Chinese were killed in the shooting.[46] This was the worst outbreak of street violence since the 1912 disturbances: the strikes of the 1920s had been comparatively peaceful since the striking workers had all departed to Canton.

The main anxiety during the 1930s was the deteriorating state of the economy. Hong Kong was not much affected in the early years of the world depression which began in 1929. The sharp drop in the world price of silver from 1929 to 1931, which caused the value of the Hong Kong dollar to depreciate by more than half against the pound sterling, gave an inflationary stimulus to the economy. This produced a temporary boom in the sales of Crown land, which peaked in 1931.[47] The value of imports and exports, measured in Hong Kong dollars, was as high in 1930 as in 1924.[48] But over the next four years there was a steady decline. In 1935 imports and exports were down to exactly half their 1931 values. Apart from the general depression in world trade Hong Kong suffered in particular from the reduction in its trade with China, which was the source of 35 per cent of its imports and the destination of 50 per cent of its exports at this time. This reduction was partly the result of the continued unsettled conditions in South China, where the provincial government of Kwangtung was generally in dispute with the national government in Nanking and occasionally in open rebellion against it. Another cause was China's increased protectionism, which was expressed in the sharp increases in her tariff wall from 1931 onwards. The gradual rise in the exchange value of the Hong Kong dollar from 1931 to 1935 also had some effect.[49]

Hong Kong's domestic exports of manufactured goods received some help during the 1930s from the system of Imperial Preferences instituted as a result of the Imperial Economic Conference held in Ottawa in 1932. As a free port, Hong Kong could do little to encourage the sale of Empire produce in its local market, but it did provide preferential rates of duty on Empire-produced tobacco and alcoholic drinks, and imposed a first-registration tax on foreign motor vehicles to assist British and Canadian car manufacturers. Certain countries of the Empire refused to extend reciprocal preferences to Hong Kong products, but in some lines of trade Hong Kong producers were able to take advantage of preferential rates of duty in ways that had not been foreseen. Manufacturers of rubber shoes and boots were able to capture markets in the West Indian colonies and in Britain. This led to protests from established suppliers and Britain even threatened to impose quotas on imports from Hong Kong, although it did not in fact do so.[50]

The trade depression was at its worst in 1935. In November Hong

Kong went off the silver standard, following similar action by the monetary authorities in China. The government then intervened in the currency markets to stabilize the value of the currency, using the assets of the newly created Exchange Fund. This mechanism was used to bring about a substantial devaluation of the Hong Kong dollar, which dropped from HK$10 to the pound in September to HK$16 to the pound in December. This depreciation, together with a strong recovery in the Chinese economy, produced an increase of 26 per cent in Hong Kong's total trade during 1936 and a further growth of 35 per cent in 1937.[51] However, the immediate effect of the devaluation was a large increase in projected government expenditure, since much of it was payable in pounds sterling. In order to balance the budget the government therefore felt obliged to impose a levy of up to 20 per cent on the salaries of all but the lowest-paid civil servants. This expedient aroused intense resentment in the service, but the government did not feel sufficiently confident of the financial outlook to restore the payment of full salaries until July 1937.[52]

As a consequence of the move to a managed currency the government withdrew all silver coins from circulation, replacing them with a cupro-nickel token coinage. The government also took over the silver bullion which the banks held as backing for their note issue, exchanging the silver for certificates of indebtedness issued by the Exchange Fund. Most of this silver was then sold by the Fund and the sums realized were invested in British government securities. The interest received on these investments provided the government with a new source of revenue, which amounted to approximately HK$4,000,000 a year. In 1938, the Governor, Sir Geoffry Northcote, proposed to set aside part of this windfall to finance a scheme for the redevelopment of the older urban area of Victoria and the provision of housing for the poor.[53] Unfortunately the outbreak of the Second World War in 1939 frustrated the implementation of these plans.

In July 1936 Chiang Kai-shek crushed the revolt of the South-western Political Committee of the Kuomintang, led by the rulers of Kwangsi (Guanxi) and Kwangtung provinces. In September he visited Canton and invited the Governor of Hong Kong, Sir Andrew Caldecott, to come and see him there. Chiang's main interest at the meeting was to discuss British co-operation in defensive measures against a possible Japanese attack on South China, but Caldecott pointed out that as Governor he was responsible only for the internal affairs of Hong Kong and could not enter into any commitment on wider issues. However, Chiang emphasized his hopes for the widest possible co-operation with Britain in road and rail development and promised that he would arrange for the construction of a loop line to connect the Kowloon–Canton and Canton–Hankow railways, provided that this could be done without publicity. Caldecott raised the question of reviving the 1930 negotiations for a commercial treaty between Hong Kong and China, but Chiang showed no interest.[54] It was apparent that the Kwangtung authorities continued to be unenthusiastic for any changes which might enhance Hong Kong's prosperity at Canton's expense. The mayor of Canton paid an official visit to Hong Kong in November and was eager to discuss the participation of British capital in schemes for the development of southern China. But at the same time other officials in Kwangtung were actively encouraging residents in the Walled City of Kowloon to resist plans to resettle them elsewhere, on the ground that the Walled City was Chinese territory. China's right to sovereignty over the Walled City was based on the terms of the 1898 Lease but this issue had remained dormant since 1900 until China reasserted its claim in 1934.

In July 1937 Japanese troops clashed with Chinese forces near the Marco Polo bridge in Peking and this incident rapidly escalated into an undeclared war between China and Japan. Peking and Tientsin (Tianjin) were quickly occupied. In August Japan attacked Shanghai and then advanced towards Nanking, which fell in December. Chiang Kai-shek moved his capital to Chungking (Chongqing) and fighting continued throughout 1938 in northern and southern China. In October Japanese troops landed at Bias Bay and within nine days captured Canton. The colony was not directly involved in the fighting, but Hong Kong fishing junks were sunk by Japanese warships, Chinese vessels were attacked while taking refuge in the colony's territorial waters, and areas in the northern part of the New Territories were accidentally bombed. Refugees from the fighting in northern China began to move into the colony by sea soon after the war began, and when the Japanese invaded Kwangtung many more flooded in across the land border. Some 1,300 defeated Chinese troops also entered the colony and had to be interned. These arrivals put a huge strain on the colony's resources. All vacant accommodation was soon occupied, rents rapidly increased, many slept on the streets, and the government was forced to set up temporary camps. It was impossible to close the land border, but an attempt was made to stem the influx by sea by insisting that any refugee who wished to land must possess at least HK$20. This amount was raised to HK$100 in June 1939, but with little effect. By September 1939 it was estimated that the population had doubled and was over two million.[55]

Despite all these problems the war provided a considerable boost to the economy. When Shanghai was attacked merchandise that would normally have been sent to the Yangtze ports was diverted to Hong Kong and most of the war supplies needed by the Chinese army were shipped to Hong Kong and then sent on by rail to central China. The long-promised rail link to the Canton–Hankow railway was put in hand as soon as hostilities commenced and was completed by December 1937. At the same time a road link between the colony and Canton was opened up for the first time by the construction of a temporary bridge across the Shum Chun (Sham Chun) river. By early 1938 half of China's foreign trade was passing through Hong Kong and this continued until the fall of Canton in October.[56] Many refugees were by no means destitute, and government revenue from taxes on opium, tobacco, and liquor showed sharp increases. New factories were set up as industries were transferred from China and the total number of factories increased from 541 in 1936 to 948 in 1939. These included two factories making gas masks for the Chinese army and others making military equipment.[57] Several foreign firms expressed interest in assembling aircraft in Hong Kong but these proposals were not pursued when the government made it clear that it could not allow the export of military aeroplanes to China while the conflict continued.[58]

British policy towards the Japanese invasion of China was at best equivocal. There was considerable sympathy for China's plight, but the British government was faced with the danger of war against Germany in Europe and had no forces that could be spared for action in the East; so it was unwilling to countenance any overt action which might provoke Japanese hostility. Quantities of military supplies were allowed to pass through Hong Kong in transit to the Chinese army and the Governor, Sir Geoffry Northcote, was permitted to pay an official visit to Canton in June 1938 as a gesture of solidarity with China.[59] But in spite of pressure from the Chinese members of the Legislative Council the Hong Kong government declined to offer any financial aid to China for the relief of war victims; the Hong Kong Red Cross Society was not allowed to send a detachment to the war zone; and the Hong Kong authorities, on instructions from

London, suppressed the report of a commission of enquiry which produced evidence that the Japanese had attacked and sunk unarmed Hong Kong fishing vessels. After the capture of Canton, Hong Kong quickly established communication with the Japanese occupation forces to arrange for the resumption of rail and river traffic.

The outbreak of war in Europe in September 1939 made no immediate difference to the situation in the East. Registration of the European population for compulsory service had been instituted earlier in the year, but none was allowed to volunteer for service in Europe as had been permitted in the First World War; all able-bodied men were needed for local defence.[60] Shelters were dug, precautions against air raids were taken, gas masks were issued to the defence forces and government employees, and the colony was put in a state of readiness to meet the imminent possibility of a Japanese invasion. The long-awaited attack finally came on the morning of 8 December 1941. Resistance lasted barely two weeks and the Governor was forced to surrender to the Japanese on 25 December.

2 The Colonial Office

In 1912 the Secretary of State for the Colonies was responsible for the government of some 40 crown colonies and protectorates where the administration was carried on by governors and officials appointed by him and answerable to him. The number of these dependent territories rose to 50 after the First World War.[1] He was also responsible for relationships with the five self-governing dominions (Canada, Australia, New Zealand, South Africa, and Newfoundland). A separate Dominions Office was not established until 1925 but the same minister held both portfolios until a separate Secretary of State for the Dominions was first appointed in 1930. The governments of the colonies and other dependencies had been established over the past three hundred years by various acts of the Crown (Orders in Council, Charters, and Letters Patent), which, except in the case of some of the oldest West Indian colonies, reserved ample power to the Crown to control all aspects of government. The Secretary of State, acting formally in the name of the Crown, was entitled to issue directives to the Governor on any matter connected with the administration of a colony and the Governor was bound to carry out all such instructions or risk the possibility of dismissal, since he held his office during the pleasure of the Crown. The Secretary of State was also empowered to disallow any ordinance passed by a colonial legislature, or to prevent its enactment by instructing the Governor to refuse his assent. Detailed instructions for the administration of the colonies were laid down in the *Colonial Regulations,* which were 'Directions to Governors for general guidance given by the Crown through the Secretary of State for the Colonies'. These listed a large number of matters on which the Governor could not take action without first obtaining the permission of the Secretary of State.

The only colonial issues which fell outside the jurisdiction of the Secretary of State were matters of defence and foreign policy. The troops stationed in a colony came under the control of the Secretary of State for War and the arrangements for their pay and accommodation were the subject of negotiations between the Colonial Office and the War Office. In all actions which affected relations with foreign governments and international organizations governors were expected to conform with the policy of the Foreign Office, and if a governor failed to do so the Colonial Office, acting on the request of the Foreign Secretary, was obliged to send him appropriate instructions. The Secretary of State, as a member of the Cabinet and subject to its collective will, was also required to carry out any Cabinet decision affecting a colony, although in practice Cabinet discussion of the internal affairs of any colony was extremely rare.[2] Subject to these limitations the Secretary of State for the Colonies possessed complete authority to prescribe what should be done in any colony and to supervise and control all the actions of the local administration.

Parliament had no direct responsibility for the government of the colonies. It was entitled to pass laws applicable to any or all of the colonies and if it did so such Acts of Parliament would supersede or repeal any ordinance passed by a colonial legislature. But in practice Parliament did not legislate except when uniformity was desirable throughout the United Kingdom and the Empire as a whole, on such matters as defence, shipping, air navigation, treaties, and nationality issues. If the Secretary of State wished to change the law in any colony he instructed the Governor to introduce the necessary bill in the colony's Legislative Council. Colonial budgets required the approval of the Secretary of State, not Parliament. The estimates for the Colonial Office itself had to be approved by Parliament and the annual debate on this vote provided an opportunity for the minister to give a general survey of developments in the colonial empire and for members to make speeches drawing attention to the problems of particular colonies. But the only money voted by Parliament for the benefit of any colony was the very small sums allocated for colonial development, certain research organizations, and grants-in-aid for particular colonies which were temporarily unable to balance their budgets. (The only money which Hong Kong received from Imperial funds was an annual grant of £300 to finance certain scholarships at the University of Hong Kong.)[3] Members of Parliament directed questions to the minister and made speeches on colonial issues or abuses which might concern them. If this pressure was sustained, and particularly if it came from members of his own political party it might on occasion persuade the Secretary of State to send new instructions to the Governor concerned. There are a few instances where a campaign in Parliament on a particular Hong Kong issue seems to have been a major influence in changing the minister's mind. But Parliament could never force a change of policy on the

Colonial Office and the Secretary of State was normally able to satisfy the House of Commons that the course of action he was pursuing was the right one. There was never an occasion when the Secretary of State was the subject of a motion of censure or where an attempt was made to force him to resign.[4] Interest in colonial affairs was weak and intermittent, and was normally confined to a few Members of Parliament. Although the Secretary of State was, constitutionally speaking, responsible to Parliament, sentiment in the House of Commons seems to have impinged only very rarely upon the determination of colonial policy.

Few Secretaries of State held the portfolio for very long. As Table 1 shows, between 1910 and 1941 there were 17 changes of minister, with an average length of tenure of 23 months. (However, since Malcolm MacDonald held the post twice and J.H. Thomas three times, the average was in fact 28 months for each minister.) The majority knew very little of colonial issues before becoming Secretary of State and their short tenure did not allow them sufficient time to acquire the necessary expertise before they lost office or moved on to a more exalted ministerial position. Of those who had some previous acquaintance with colonial matters, three had previously served in the Colonial Office as Parliamentary Under-Secretary of State (Churchill, Amery, and Ormsby-Gore), and Lord Passfield had worked for 10 years as a civil service clerk in the Office 40 years before he became its head. Three other Secretaries of State had had experience of Dominion affairs: Viscount Milner had been High Commissioner in South Africa from 1897 to 1905; the Duke of Devonshire had been High Commissioner in Canada from 1916 to 1922; and MacDonald had served in the Dominions Office from 1931 to 1938 as Parliamentary Under-Secretary and then as Secretary of State. But even those ministers who entered office with an intimate knowledge of some parts of the Empire were ill equipped to deal with the multifarious problems posed by some 50 colonies in all quarters of the globe and to give directions to their administrations. It is commonly said that all ministers are heavily dependent on their civil servants for their first six months or more after taking up a new ministry and in the case of the Colonial Office the learning period must have been far longer. Some ministers were preoccupied by particular problems which left them little time to think about less troublesome areas: Milner was away at the Versailles Peace Conference immediately after his appointment to the Colonial Office and then went off for five months to settle the problems of Egypt;

Table 1   Office-holders at the Colonial Office, 1910–1941

Date	Office-holder

Secretaries of State

November 1910	Lewis Harcourt (later Viscount Harcourt)
May 1915	A. Bonar Law
December 1916	Walter Long (later Viscount Long)
January 1919	Viscount Milner
February 1921	Winston Churchill
October 1922	Duke of Devonshire
January 1924	J.H. Thomas
November 1924	L.S. Amery
June 1929	Lord Passfield (formerly Sidney Webb)
August 1931	J.H. Thomas
November 1931	Sir P. Cunliffe-Lister (later Viscount Swinton)
June 1935	Malcolm MacDonald
November 1935	W. Ormsby-Gore (later Lord Harlech)
May 1938	Malcolm MacDonald
May 1940	Lord Lloyd
February 1941	Lord Moyne

Parliamentary Under-Secretaries of State

March 1911	Lord Lucas
October 1911	Lord Emmott
August 1914	Lord Islington
December 1916	A. Steel-Maitland
September 1917	W. Hewins
January 1919	L.S. Amery
April 1921	E.F.L. Wood (later Earl of Halifax)
October 1922	W. Ormsby-Gore
January 1924	Lord Arnold
November 1924	W. Ormsby-Gore
June 1929	W. Lunn
December 1929	Dr Drummond Shiels
September 1931	Sir R. Hamilton
September 1932	Earl of Plymouth
July 1936	Earl De La Warr
May 1937	Marquess of Dufferin and Ava
May 1940	G.H. Hall

Date	Office-holder
Permanent Under-Secretaries of State	
1911	Sir John Anderson
1916	Sir George Fiddes
1921	Sir J. Masterton-Smith
1925	Sir Samuel Wilson
1933	Sir John Maffey
1937	Sir Cosmo Parkinson
February–	
May 1940	Sir George Gater
1940	Sir Cosmo Parkinson

MacDonald reckoned that half of his time as Secretary of State was taken up with the situation in Palestine.[5] Most ministers must have found themselves in the position of Lord Passfield who described his work in 1930: 'I have to authorize daily by initialling innumerable decisions one after another, on endless matters on which I can form only the roughest kind of judgement, on the advice of others.'[6] A few ministers seem to have had a clear idea of certain policies they wished to have implemented and the time and energy to push them through. This was true of Amery, who was an enthusiastic advocate of the economic development of the Empire and the federation of the East African colonies. Cunliffe-Lister was eager to promote trade within the Empire by the system of imperial preferences. MacDonald was similarly determined to push forward social and economic progress and secured the enactment of the Colonial Development and Welfare Act of 1940. But other Secretaries of State appear to have had little permanent impact on the direction in which the colonial empire was moving, although the decisions which they took on particular issues that came before them, and the governors they selected or whose selection they approved, were of crucial importance for particular colonies during their period in office.

Parliamentary Under-Secretaries of State changed as frequently as their chiefs: between 1910 and 1914 they numbered 16. Only three went on to higher ministerial office: Amery, Ormsby-Gore, and E.F.L. Wood (the future Earl of Halifax). The Under-Secretary's functions were rather limited. When the Secretary of State was a member of the House of Lords his junior was always a member of the House of Commons, responsible for answering questions and replying to debates on behalf of the Colonial Office. He might also be made chairman of some office committees, he wrote comments on certain files before they were seen by the Secretary of State, and he might approve action proposed on less important issues which his chief had no time to look at. When the Secretary of State was away on foreign tours he acted as head of the department. Amery (under Milner) and Ormsby-Gore (under Amery) both had quite lengthy periods of independent command: the latter was acting Secretary of State for seven months while Amery was engaged in a world tour of the Empire. Apart from these brief intervals very few Parliamentary Under-Secretaries were able to make an impact upon policy-making. Milner sent Amery to settle a crisis in Malta where he drew up a new constitution for the island. Dr Drummond Shiels, Passfield's junior for most of the Labour government of 1929–31, was the prime mover in drafting a number of circular dispatches which urged colonial governors in unusually emphatic terms to improve the treatment of young offenders, set up workmen's compensation schemes, and apply the conventions of the International Labour Organization in their territories. He was also forthright in the minutes he wrote on files passed up to Passfield and seems to have persuaded his chief to override the officials' advice on a number of occasions.[7] But such Parliamentary Under-Secretaries were very much the exception.

Permanent Under-Secretaries, the senior civil servant in the department, stayed in office much longer than their political masters: there were six in the years 1911 to 1942, with an average tenure of five years.[8] Three of them came from within the department: Sir John Anderson, Sir George Fiddes, and Sir Cosmo Parkinson. One was a civil servant who was transferred from the Department of Labour, Sir James Masterton-Smith, and two were former colonial governors: Sir Samuel Wilson who had governed Trinidad and Jamaica and Sir John Maffey who came from the Anglo-Egyptian Sudan.[9] Of the others Anderson had been Governor of the Straits Settlements immediately before he returned to become Permanent Under-Secretary, and Fiddes had served on Milner's staff in South Africa. So all but two of the civil service heads had first-hand experience of administration in the field. This did not necessarily make them more sympathetic to the difficulties of other governors. Anderson was severely critical of May's handling of the tramway boycott in 1913, drawing upon his own experience in handling a similar situation in Singapore.[10]

The staff of the Colonial Office was divided into the first division, the administrative officers who in practice took most of the decisions, and the second division, the clerical staff, typists, librarians, and messengers. Entry to the first division was by the civil service examinations, which were normally taken by university graduates. Candidates were allowed to state which departments they preferred, and positions in the Treasury or the Colonial Office were usually favoured by those who passed at the top of the list.[11] New entrants were appointed as Second Class Clerks (renamed Assistant Principals in 1920). They moved up after a few years to become First Class Clerks (Principals), then Principal Clerks at the head of a department (Assistant Secretaries), and might be promoted to Assistant Under-Secretary in charge of a group of departments. Some newly appointed officers were perhaps over-conscious of their intellectual achievements and when set to write minutes on dispatches they sometimes displayed a rather arrogant or patronizing attitude as they dissected the logical flaws in the case put up by a colonial administration.[12] Their more senior colleagues also indulged occasionally in witticisms at a governor's expense, but they were more ready to accept the views of the man on the spot. Colonial governments would have had their requests refused much more often if the official reply had followed the sense of the first minute on the file.

Until the 1920s very few civil servants had any personal experience of conditions in the colonies. Stubbs had been sent out to Malaya and Hong Kong to investigate staff salaries in 1910 when he was a First Class Clerk in the Eastern Department, but this was exceptional. The information on which officials took their decisions came primarily from written communications and the dispatches, returns, and annual reports received from colonial governments, supplemented by visits to the Colonial Office by governors and other senior officials when on leave and occasional delegations of business men or from missionary or philanthropic organizations who went to put their case on a current issue to the minister or senior officials. Amery inaugurated a deliberate policy of arranging for members of staff to go out to the colonies on special missions or as secretaries to commissions of enquiry.[13] It was easier to spare staff for visits to the West Indies or to Africa than to the Far East when a sea voyage to Hong Kong and back took three months, but in the 1930s J.A. Calder and E. Gent of the Eastern Department were able to comment on Hong Kong dispatches on the basis of first-hand acquaintance. The Warren Fisher Committee of 1930 recommended that measures should be taken to promote interchange between the Colonial Office and staff overseas. As a result a number of Assistant Principals were sent out to a colony for a period of duty and picked officers of the Colonial Administrative Service were seconded for two or three years to work in the Colonial Office.[14] Such officers, who were commonly known as 'beachcombers', did not serve in the department concerned with their own territory, since it would have been unseemly for a junior officer to write a minute on his own Governor's dispatches. But they were available in the Office to elucidate a difficulty and they might be consulted informally on a troublesome issue; for example, McElderry, a Hong Kong cadet, was asked his views on the opium issue and wrote a memorandum which differed significantly from the stand taken by the Governor.[15]

The internal organization of the Colonial Office was based on a number of geographical departments and one general department. The number of geographical departments varied slightly at different times: there were six in 1912 and eight in the 1920s following the acquisition of the former German colonies, officially known as mandated territories, after the First World War. In 1930 there were seven departments: West Indies, Far Eastern, Middle East, West Africa, East Africa, Ceylon and the Mediterranean, and Tanganyika and Somaliland. These departments were responsible for almost all matters relating to the territories in their particular area. The General Department looked after only such matters as defence, ceremonials, postal services, patents, copyright, Colonial Regulations, and circular dispatches.[16] Officials tended to stay in one department for a long period and became experts in the problems of their particular area. After the recommendations of the Warren Fisher Committee were accepted, new departments dealing with Recruitment and Personnel were set up, followed by an Economic Department in 1936 and a Social Services Department in 1939. But for most of the period covered by this book the geographical departments were predominant, with the emphasis being laid on the need to adapt policy to the local conditions and circumstances of each colony rather than the imposition of some blueprint for social and economic advance on the colonial empire as a whole. No such general policy existed. Circular dispatches were sent out from time to time to all colonies and dependencies drawing governors' attention to innovations that had been found effective in one colony, suggesting desirable reforms, or asking if the colonies wished to adhere to some new international convention. But these dispatches were seldom phrased as imperative directives and governors could and did decide that such proposals were inappropriate or unnecessary in their particular territory. For example, the Hong Kong government declined to pass an ordinance providing for compulsory workmen's compensation, in spite of circular dispatches sent out in 1930 and 1937 strongly urging the adoption of such legislation.[17]

If the staff of one of the geographical departments were in need of expert advice to help with a problem raised by one of their territories they might get in touch with one of the other ministries in Whitehall which dealt with similar matters in Britain. Alternatively they could seek help from one of the advisory committees or special advisers attached to the Colonial Office. A Legal Adviser who drafted constitutional instruments and checked all ordinances passed by colonial Legislative Councils had always been a part of the Colonial Office establishment at the level of Assistant Under-Secretary. A Chief Medical Adviser was appointed in 1926, an Economic and Financial Adviser in 1928, Advisers on Fisheries, Agriculture, and Animal Health in 1928, 1929, and 1930, and a Labour Adviser in 1938. An Advisory Committee on Education in Tropical Africa had been set up in 1921, consisting of part-time members with a full-time secretary. In 1926 the Committee's scope was extended to the whole of the colonial empire with a second secretary responsible for the non-African colonies. Other advisory committees were set up in the 1930s such as the Medical and Sanitary Committee, the Committee on Nutrition in the Colonies, and the Labour Advisory Committee.[18] These advisers and advisory committees saw and commented on the relevant portions of the annual administrative reports sent in by all colonies and were consulted on any proposals which governors might put forward in their budgets or at other times. Occasionally their views were decisive. For example in 1936 the Hong Kong government submitted a draft bill to amend the Dangerous Drugs Ordinance which would have made trafficking in heroin punishable by flogging. A number of officials and the Secretary of State, Ormsby-Gore, expressed reservations about the bill and it was referred to the newly established Penal Advisory Committee which recommended that instead of flogging the penalties for this offence should be doubled.[19] So the Governor was instructed to introduce a bill on these lines. Normally the views expressed by such advisers were incorporated in the replies sent to a governor as suggestions for future policy, or they might form the basis for a circular dispatch.

All correspondence received at the Colonial Office was registered, placed in a file, and passed to the appropriate geographical department. The first minute on it was written by an Assistant Principal who referred to the appropriate precedents and previous correspondence on the subject. The file then made its way up the hierarchy to the Principal, Assistant Secretary, Assistant Under-Secretary, and Permanent Under-Secretary, gathering further minutes on the way until it was put before the minister, or was stopped by an official who decided that he could properly dispose of it. A reply was then drafted by a lower official on the basis of the minutes, and this was then approved and sent off. Before the First World War a surprisingly large number of files went up to be seen by the Secretary of State, many on quite unimportant matters. Files dealing with issues that were the subject of questions in Parliament or on matters which might possibly be raised there always went to ministers, sometimes on quite trivial issues,[20] as did all cases where officials proposed to overrule a governor's views, except in minor matters of pay and allowances. Petitions addressed to the Secretary of State were normally seen and the proposed course of action approved by the Parliamentary Under-Secretary in the 1930s, although this had not been customary in earlier years.[21] Other than this, officials decided which items it was necessary or desirable for ministers to see, in the light of their expressed interests and the time at their disposal. There are a few instances where it seems that politically sensitive issues were deliberately kept from ministers' eyes. Proposals to create a European reservation on the Peak in 1904 and another European reservation on Cheung Chau in 1919 were approved by officials without reference to the Secretary of State.[22] This may have been done to spare the minister embarrassment, or out of apprehension that he might make a wrong decision. A file was never put before the Secretary of State without a definite recommendation on what action should be taken. If the officials who had minuted earlier were in disagreement, the Permanent Under-Secretary always indicated which policy alternative was preferable, and on most occasions the Secretary of State acquiesced in his view by initialling the file. On very rare occasions a minister might spontaneously make an unforeseen decision on a file which came before him. One such instance occurred in October 1939 when Malcolm MacDonald unexpectedly minuted on a telegram from Hong Kong offering to donate a large amount to Britain for the war effort: 'I am inclined to discourage these gifts. They do not really help us much; the money could be well spent in the colonies concerned, and if one colony starts others will feel that they have got to follow suit.' A meeting of Assistant Under-Secretaries quickly decided that a general embargo on gifts might be politically dangerous; any action to rebuff such patriotic offers would be misunderstood in the colonies and would be inconsistent with the fact that a number of such gifts had already been accepted; so it was suggested that each case ought to be considered on its merits. This view was put to MacDonald, and he agreed to the officials' advice.[23]

The Colonial Office did not attempt to govern the colonies. It was not in a position to take direct executive action itself and it did not attempt to prescribe in detail what should be done. There were 50 colonial governments and each was responsible for the administration of its own territory. Individuals and groups in a colony were deliberately discouraged from appealing to the Colonial Office rather than to the Governor when discontented with a government decision.[24] The function of the Colonial Office, as the officials concerned described it, was to supervise the activities of the colonial governments and to supply direction, advice, and help.[25] In carrying out their supervisory role officials sought to ensure that the code of good administration laid down in *Colonial Regulations* was fully complied with, that colonial budgets were balanced and expenditure properly controlled, and that colonial service officers were fairly treated and received their due entitlements in pay and allowances. Such supervision could only be effective if the Colonial Office received adequate information about what governors were doing or were proposing to do. The colonial governments were, with few exceptions, financially self-sufficient and were quite capable, in normal circumstances, of managing their own affairs without any reference to London. So Governors were required to seek permission from the Colonial Office before they were allowed to spend all but the smallest sums of money or alter the conditions of service of any public official. They were also obliged to send home annually a set of administrative reports on the work of all departments of government, a detailed 'Blue Book' of statistics, and a large number of periodical returns, reports, and publications. Those listed in the 1928 edition of *Colonial Regulations* totalled 74. All ordinances passed by the Legislative Council had to be forwarded to the Secretary to State together with full explanations so that he could decide whether or not the law should be disallowed. All this information should have been sufficient to enable the Colonial Office to exercise effective control and prevent any abuses. But it was still possible for policy to be changed as a result of an executive instruction issued by a governor, and the Colonial Office might never hear of this except by accident. There were no roving inspectors sent out from London to report on what was actually taking place in a colony, as was the practice in the French colonial empire. So there were occasions when the Colonial Office discovered what was really happening only as a result of an item in a newspaper, a petition from a colonial officer, or a chance reference in a letter of complaint.

Supervision was largely a negative activity, an elaborate system to check that colonial administrations were keeping to the rules of conduct that had been laid down. The Colonial Office also sought to supply direction and to offer positive guidance as to what governors ought to be doing. Guidance implies that ministers and officials had some idea of the objectives that they were aiming to achieve, but it is difficult to find any single authoritative pronouncement which defined the central purposes of colonial policy during the period between the First and Second World Wars. The nearest approximation might be the set of obligations which Britain assumed in 1919 when it took over responsibility for the government of various German colonies as mandates from the League of Nations. Britain then undertook 'to promote to the utmost the material and moral well-being and social progress of the inhabitants'. This formulation of the duty of trusteeship had in effect been written into the Covenant of the League of Nations by British statesmen and it embodied what one governor called 'the ordinary and recognised principles of colonial administration'.[26] Another way of identifying the objectives of colonial government is to look at the actual content of the decisions taken and the circular dispatches sent out in the period up to 1939. This exercise would suggest that the following purposes were implicit in British colonial policy: to ensure security, public order, and justice; to promote the welfare of the inhabitants and to safeguard them from oppression; to suppress uncivilized customs and practices; to develop the economies of the colonial territories; and to assist British trade and commerce. Preparation of the colonies for eventual self-government and independence was not an accepted goal until the end of the 1930s and it was not proclaimed without qualification as the central purpose of British colonial policy until after the Second World War.[27] In practice these goals could conflict with one another, and at different times one policy aim might be predominant: for example in the 1930s the emphasis was placed on the encouragement of trade within the Empire for the mutual benefit of Britain and the colonies themselves. However, although the Colonial Office and the Governors might be in general accord over the principles on which colonial policy should be based, they did not necessarily agree on their applicability to specific issues. The views expressed by enlightened opinion in Britain as to what constituted undesirable practices which ought to be stamped out (for example opium-smoking or child slavery) might be very different from the outlook of colonial administrators who could see the difficulties and dangers of interfering with a long-established and valued social custom. In such circumstances governors might prefer to leave well alone rather than run the risk of stirring up trouble by ill-considered efforts at reform.

When such a conflict arose between the authorities at home and a colonial administration the received wisdom in the Colonial Office was that it was best to trust the judgement of 'the man on the spot' who had first-hand knowledge of the complications of the local situation and who would have to deal with any disturbances that might arise from the attempt to implement a directive from London. But it was easier for officials in the Colonial Office to counsel the need for restraint than for the minister to accept this advice when he was under pressure to put an end to some local practice from Members of Parliament who had no conception of the complexities of the local situation and the difficulties of enforcement. Another reason for not always deferring to the views of 'the man on the spot' was the need for consistency. Governors remained in charge of a colony only for six years, or sometimes less, and a new governor might take a completely different view of the feasibility of some reform than his predecessor.[28] There was also the possibility that Governors in neighbouring colonies might follow divergent policies when dealing with the same problem. So the Secretary of State could appear to be guilty of inconsistency, if not of weakness. Several circular dispatches on labour questions in the 1930s referred to the fact that the governors of adjacent colonies had, for no apparent reason, taken quite opposite views on the practicability of adopting certain conventions of the International Labour Organization in their territories.[29]

When the Colonial Office found itself faced by an intransigent Governor on some major issue the Secretary of State did not normally use his powers to override the Governor's protests. This was done in a few instances, but more usually the Colonial Office would suggest the appointment of a special committee or commission of enquiry with members from Britain or a visit by an expert to investigate the problem at first hand. This was often done not so much in the hope that the committee would discover a solution that had not occurred to the Office as with the object of marshalling authoritative outside support for some line of action which the staff wanted to take.[30] When the committee reported and produced a unanimous verdict (which was not always the case) the Governor would be invited to implement its recommendation. This technique enabled the minister to satisfy his critics in Parliament and at the same time afforded the governor an opportunity to deploy his arguments and have them independently assessed. Governors were aware of this tactic and so tended to resist any suggestion from London that a commission should be appointed; for example, Stubbs in 1921 strenuously protested against a proposal to sent out a commission to investigate the *mui tsai* issue, and in 1930 Peel similarly objected to a commission to examine whether licensed brothels should be closed down.

Apart from supervision and direction, the other function of the Colonial Office was to provide help and assistance to the colonial territories. The Office recruited the staff needed by colonial administrations or arranged for their transfer from other colonies. When a colony needed assistance from another department of the British government or sought a modification of policy in some area which affected its interests (for example where the import regulations made by the Board of Trade affected a colony's exports) the Colonial Office forwarded the representations made by the colonial administration and almost invariably supported them with all the arguments it could muster, even on occasions when officials doubted the wisdom of the Governor's views.[31] Sometimes the Secretary of State would approach his ministerial colleagues directly. Such efforts often failed, since the Colonial Office did not carry much weight among the other departments in Whitehall where ministers and officials were likely to pay greater attention to wider British interests or to the particular concerns of British public opinion. The Colonial Office supported the applications put forward by Hong Kong for some of the funds available under the Colonial Development Act of 1929 without success; but when the British government agreed in 1929 to give the Boxer Indemnity Fund back to China, the Secretary of State was able to persuade the Cabinet to allocate

£250,000 of this money to the University of Hong Kong.[32] The Office argued repeatedly with the War Office about the amount of money which Hong Kong should be required to pay towards the maintenance of the British garrison, but was unable to secure any real reduction. There was frequent correspondence with the Foreign Office over problems arising between Hong Kong and China on such matters as trade, the representation of the Chinese government in the colony, and the relationship between Hong Kong and Canton. The colony's revenue from its opium monopoly was liable to be affected by Britain's general policy on the international traffic in narcotic drugs, a matter which lay within the responsibility of the Home Office. On all of these matters the Colonial Office supported the representations made by the Governor with all the arguments it could master, and tried to ensure that the interests and needs of Hong Kong were given due weight in the determination of British policy.

3 The Governor and the Executive Council

'IN a Crown Colony the Governor is next to the Almighty.'[1] So said Sir Alexander Grantham, Governor of Hong Kong in the years 1947–57. The Colonial Regulations described his position more precisely: 'The Governor is the single and supreme authority responsible to, and representative of, His Majesty. He is, by virtue of his Commission and the Letters Patent constituting his office, entitled to the obedience, aid, and assistance of all military, air force, and civil officers.'[2] Within the colony the Governor was, and is, the head of the administration and all officials were bound to obey his instructions. He was obliged to consult with his Executive Council on all major policy decisions, but for most of the period covered by this book six out of the nine members of the Council were officials and he was fully entitled to disregard the Council's advice, if he thought fit. The Legislative Council made laws for the colony, but more than half the members consisted of officials who were bound to vote as he directed. All bills were introduced into the Council by order of the Governor and the official majority could be used to defeat any amendment put forward by the unofficial side. The Governor thus had virtually complete control of the executive and legislative branches of government.

The Governor of Hong Kong received £4,800 a year. This sum was paid out of the colony's budget but it was fixed by the Colonial Office and remained unaltered from 1904 to 1955. Hong Kong was one of 10 first-class colonies in the Empire and the Governor's salary was the seventh highest, being just below that of the Captain-General of Jamaica.[3] He was paid almost as much as the Secretary of State, who received £5,000, and considerably more than the Permanent Under-Secretary at the Colonial Office, who was paid £3,000. The Governor also received an entertainment allowance of £1,200, which was increased to £2,200 in 1930 in accordance with the recommendations of a salaries commission.[4] As head of the social life of the colony and its representative to the outside world, the Governor was subject to heavy ceremonial demands. In addition to holding numerous receptions, lunches, and dinners for the leading members of the European and Chinese communities, he was obliged to extend a welcome to the many important foreign guests who touched at the colony in the course of a world tour. Stubbs claimed that in his governorship he had had to entertain the heirs to four thrones, a dozen other royal princes, and innumerable admirals, generals, ambassadors, and statesmen. The memoirs of other Governors are filled with similar lists of celebrities.[5]

There were seven Governors of Hong Kong between 1912 and 1941 (see Table 2). All came from similar social and educational backgrounds. Their fathers comprised a bishop, three clergymen, two judges, and an Indian civil servant. All attended English public schools and went on to Oxford or Cambridge, except for May, who was educated at Harrow and Trinity College, Dublin. All were career members of the Colonial Administrative Service except for Stubbs, who had entered the Colonial Office as a junior clerk in 1900 and had then transferred to Ceylon as Colonial Secretary in 1913. Of the rest, all except Northcote, who spent his first 30 years in Africa, were Eastern cadets: May and Clementi had begun their service in Hong Kong, Peel and Caldecott in Malaya, and Young in Ceylon.

The selection of a new Governor was made as a result of discussions between the Secretary of State and his Permanent Under-Secretary, normally on the basis of a list of possible candidates drawn up by the Personnel division. Peel is the only Governor who has left an account of how he was chosen. When on leave in 1927 he was asked by the head of the Eastern Department if he would like to be considered for one of the smaller governorships and he replied that he would prefer to remain at his existing post as Chief Secretary of the Federated Malay States. Three years later during his next leave he was invited to meet the Secretary of State, Lord Passfield, and afterwards he was asked if he would let his name be put forward for the governorship of Hong Kong. Since this was a first-class post he agreed to accept it. He then attended an audience with the King and was given a full briefing on the Hong Kong situation by the Colonial Office, and another concerning relations with China by the Foreign Office.[6] Other future Governors were offered promotion while serving abroad, without first being looked over by the Secretary of State.

It was almost unknown for an officer to be promoted to the position of governor in the territory where he was already serving. Three of the seven had been Governors elsewhere before being transferred to Hong Kong: May in Fiji (1911–12), Northcote in British Guiana (1934–5), and Young in Tanganyika (1938–41). The other four were all Colonial Secretaries when promoted: Stubbs and Clementi in Ceylon, Peel in the Federated Malay States, and

Table 2   Governors and Colonial Secretaries of Hong Kong, 1912–1941

Date	Incumbent
Governors	
July 1907–March 1912	Sir Frederick Lugard
July 1912–September 1918	Sir Henry May
September 1919–October 1925	Sir Edward Stubbs
November 1925–February 1930	Sir Cecil Clementi
May 1930–May 1935	Sir William Peel
December 1935–April 1937	Sir Andrew Caldecott
November 1937–September 1941	Sir Geoffry Northcote
September 1941–December 1941	Sir Mark Young
Colonial Secretaries	
June 1911	Warren Barnes
February 1912	Claud Severn
May 1926	Thomas Southorn
November 1936	Norman Smith
December 1941	Franklin Gimson

Note: When the Governor was absent from the colony the Colonial Secretary took over the position of Officer Administering the Government (OAG), except from August 1940 to March 1941 when Lieutenant-General C.F. Norton was OAG.

Caldecott in the Straits Settlements. May's appointment was unusual in that, apart from one year in Fiji, he had spent his whole career in Hong Kong where he had served as Captain Superintendent of Police and as Colonial Secretary. In 1912 Hong Kong was in a very unsettled state after the revolution in China, and when Sir Frederick Lugard was unexpectedly moved to Nigeria the Legislative Council petitioned that May should return to be his successor. The Secretary of State agreed to his suggestion in the belief that Hong Kong needed a governor who had an intimate knowledge of the territory and a reputation as a strong disciplinarian to deal with the current wave of unrest.[7]

Hong Kong was a long-established colony and the routine business of administration normally ran very smoothly under the direction of the Colonial Secretary. Sir William Des Voeux had commented 25 years earlier, 'A Governor might pass the whole of his tenure of office, without falling into official disfavour, by doing little more than sign his name to the productions of others, and the place would be a paradise to a man inclined to be idle.'[8] Times were not so easy in the twentieth century when Governors had to cope with the problems posed by the First World War, labour unrest, strikes and boycotts, the financial crises of the 1930s, and the effects of the Sino-Japanese war. But the duties of a Governor normally allowed time for visits to be paid to Canton, Macau, French Indo-China, and the Philippines, and there was leisure enough for all the sport that he wished to enjoy.[9] Peel played a round of golf every week and rode with the Fanling hunt across country in the New Territories, jumping down the paddy-field terraces and occasionally ending up bogged down in the mud.[10]

The arrival of a new Governor gave the opportunity for a reappraisal of existing policies and a consideration of new initiatives to tackle long-standing problems. But in fact it is difficult to point to any notable innovations that can be associated with a particular Governor. Most new policies seem to have been introduced in reaction to unforeseen events rather than as the outcome of a far-sighted vision of the colony's future needs. Thus May has been praised for his Education Bill of 1913, which required all schools to be registered with the Director of Education and conform to regulations laid down by the Governor in Council. But his dispatch to the Colonial Office makes it clear that his motive was not to improve the standard of education in vernacular schools but to prevent them from being used as centres for anti-British propaganda in the aftermath of the Chinese revolution.[11] Stubbs pushed forward a large programme of public works and the building of new roads to open up fresh areas for development. He was able to do this because the colony was enjoying large budget surpluses from buoyant land sales. His predecessor and successors would have been happy to do the same, but they were straitened by lack of funds.

The most active of the Governors during this period was Clementi. He was fertile in devising new schemes which would reduce the colony's liability to pay the costs of the British garrison.[12] He reiterated in numerous dispatches his criticisms of British policy towards China, insisting that the Foreign Office ought to recognize that the government in Peking had lost control of most of the country and that Britain should therefore deal separately with the 18 provincial governments.[13] He pressed tirelessly for a British initiative to take over the New Territories, or alternatively for permission to grant land leases expiring beyond 1997 so as to demonstrate Britain's determination never to give up the Leased

Area.[14] Although the Colonial Office and the Secretary of State gave support to Clementi's views his efforts came to nothing. The War Office and the Treasury rejected all his financial proposals and the Foreign Office was not prepared to allow the whole of British policy in the Far East to be determined by the needs of Hong Kong. In domestic matters Clementi was able to achieve a few permanent changes: the first appointment of a Chinese member to the Executive Council; the enlargement of the Legislative Council; and the initiation of moves for the improvement of public health which led, under his successor, Peel, to the transformation of the Sanitary Board into the Urban Council.

A Governor was not bound to continue with the policies laid down by his predecessor. Instances can be found where specific plans that had been agreed were changed or abandoned but this was normally for financial reasons and not solely the result of an arbitrary decision by a new Governor. For example Stubbs scrapped plans to put a tax on salt which had been devised by May, partly because additional revenue was no longer needed, but also because he felt that such a tax would press too heavily on the poor.[15] Clementi reversed Stubbs's decision to set up a separate new Port Development Department.[16] Peel originated a scheme to build a new Government House at Magazine Gap and redevelop the existing site for the construction of offices and a new city hall. This was approved by the Colonial Office in 1932 but Caldecott halted all action on the project three years later, partly because he doubted whether the sale of part of the existing site would raise enough money to finance the building costs, and also because he disliked the new site which Peel had chosen for Government House. Then in 1938, when the colony's financial position and the property market had improved, Northcote reactivated Peel's scheme but he proposed major changes in the plans.[17] As a result of these vacillations little was done before the outbreak of the Second World War and it was left to the Japanese to demolish the crumbling structure of Government House and rebuild it on its existing site. On more important matters, however, there is an impressive continuity of policy through a succession of governors, with only minor inconsistencies between one incumbent and the next.

The Governor was the sole channel of communication between the colonial administration and the Secretary of State. All dispatches to London were signed by him, although this did not necessarily mean that he did more than add his name to a draft which had been composed in the Colonial Secretariat. A governor's dispatches might sometimes be published by the Colonial Office in a Command Paper or shown to Members of Parliament, so an important dispatch was sometimes accompanied by another, marked 'Secret' or 'Confidential', containing information which it might be impolitic or embarrassing to reveal.[18] Governors also wrote personally to the Permanent Under-Secretary or to officials in the Eastern Department giving the background behind particular policy decisions or asking for favourable consideration for a particular project. Some governors used this method of communication more than others. Stubbs in particular wrote frequently to his former colleagues, especially to Sir Gilbert Grindle, an Assistant Under-Secretary who had formerly been head of the Eastern Department when Stubbs had been a junior clerk 10 years earlier. As a result of this, and his intimate knowledge of the procedures and prejudices of the Office, his submissions seem to have been treated more leniently than those of his predecessors, and he was permitted to vary the terms of land leases and to sell certain land lots by private treaty and not by public auction, without needing to refer each case separately to London for approval.[19] But when he asked for further extension of the area in which he might act at his own discretion, officials demurred and insisted that the detailed reports required under Colonial Regulations must still be forwarded.[20]

All governors chafed at the niggling supervision over their routine activities exercised by the Colonial Office and its occasional rejections of new projects and policy changes which they considered essential. Various strategies were used to circumvent actual or anticipated Colonial Office opposition. Some governors were more punctilious than others in their adherence to Colonial Regulations and the procedures laid down: of the seven who governed Hong Kong, Northcote and Peel seem to have been the most compliant to Colonial Office control while Stubbs and Clementi were the least; but all governors made use of these tactics to some degree and many examples will be found in the chapters which follow.

The simplest ploy was to ignore letters sent from London. This accidental oversight tended to occur particularly when officials were enquiring about some customary practices or administrative procedures, to reveal the details of which might prove embarrassing for the local administration. This tactic was rarely successful. The Colonial Office itself was not always efficient in answering dispatches within a reasonable time, but it had a good filing system and reminders were sent to colonies which failed to reply to its letters. Once the Office believed it had discovered that something was being done amiss it was generally able to insist on being supplied with the information it wanted.

Another method was for the Governor to issue executive instructions to the public service to take action and say nothing to London. So long as this course of action required no changes in the law and no special financial provision which would appear in the annual estimates there was a very good chance that the Colonial Office would never hear of it, and might even be quite happy to be kept in ignorance. The only ways in which London might accidentally learn what was taking place was from a speech by an unofficial member of the Legislative Council reported in *Hansard,* from a newspaper report, or from a letter written to a Member of Parliament by a chance visitor to the colony. The most extraordinary example of the success of this tactic was the system of licensed prostitution in Hong Kong which was instituted by executive action and lasted for 30 years in total disregard of the policies laid down by the Secretary of State and approved by Parliament.

Another method of procedure was for the Governor to take action and then report what he had done to London, asking for covering authority.[21] This was quite frequently done in financial matters where Colonial Office approval was required for many trifling expenditures and changes in establishments. In practice the Governor sometimes spent the money first and asked for permission afterwards, when it was too late for officials in London to withhold their assent. All that the Colonial Office could do was to point out that the regulations had been contravened, as the Governor was well aware, and require him to pay greater attention to them in future. Sometimes no attempt at all was made to seek covering authority from London and this omission was only noticed when the colony's accounts were checked by the Colonial Audit Department. Another way round the regulations was to include new expenditures in the annual budget and ask for permission at the same time as the Estimates were submitted to London. It was in practice impossible for the Colonial Office to ask for the deletion of any particular item from the Estimates, since the Appropriation Bill had to become law by the end of the financial year and it had usually passed through all its stages in the Legislative Council before the Colonial Office had commenced, let alone completed, its own examination of the Estimates.

When the Secretary of State asked a Governor to take action or to pass legislation which the latter considered unwise or inappropriate to conditions in the colony the Governor might accede to the request in his reply to London, but in fact fail to take the necessary action. This was a rare response, since it amounted to deliberate deception, but it did occur. For example, in response to circular dispatches, the Hong Kong Legislative Council passed a Minimum Wage Ordinance in 1932 and a Trade Boards Ordinance in 1940.[22] In both cases the intention of the Colonial Office was that the colonial administration should fix minimum wage levels in industry and punish employers who failed to pay their employees at the statutory rate. But, although the necessary legislation was passed, not a single order was made under either ordinance to fix the rate of wages in any industry or occupation.

The usual response by a Governor when he received a directive from London instructing him to do something which he disapproved of, or refusing him permission to take the action he considered appropriate, was to reply requesting that the Secretary of State's decision might be reconsidered. All sorts of arguments might be brought forward to cast doubt on the reasons adduced by the Colonial Office. A Governor would often emphasize that his proposals had the unanimous agreement of the Executive Council and were supported by the unofficial members of the Legislative Council, and copies of the proceedings of the Council might be forwarded to London with the Governor's dispatch. The views of the District Watch Committee could also be mentioned as evidence of Chinese opinion, and occasionally the Governor might refer to the possibility of civil unrest if his views were disregarded. Stubbs in particular was fond of making ominous reference to the troubles that might arise, presumably because he knew that such hints would be taken seriously in Whitehall. If such expostulations had no effect a Governor might return to the charge a second time with fresh arguments, or he might put forward a modified proposal which made some concession to the Colonial Office viewpoint. It is surprising how often a determined Governor was able to get his own way if he was sufficiently persistent. Officials in London were very reluctant to overrule 'the man on the spot' when they had few or no alternative sources of information about local conditions. The Secretary of State was rarely self-confident in his own judgement; in almost all important issues where a Governor failed to get his own way the minister was faced with pressures from the House of Commons or from important pressure groups in Britain which he was unwilling to oppose.

Governors held their position, like all other officers in the public service, during the pleasure of the Crown and were liable at any time to be transferred or removed from office by the Secretary of State. This possibility was actually contemplated in the case of Stubbs in 1923 at the request of the Foreign Office, as it was considered that Stubbs's apparent support and encouragement of the regime of Sun Yat-sen in Canton was a serious embarrassment to British policy in China. This situation had arisen out of the chaotic conditions in the province of Kwangtung during the 1920s, which had persisted since the 1911 revolution. In April 1921 Sun Yat-sen had been elected President of China by an assembly in Canton, but a year later he was driven out by General Chen Chiung-ming and fled to Shanghai. In January 1923 Sun's supporters were able in their turn to drive out General Chen, and Sun returned to Canton in February. On his way back by ship he called at Hong Kong and stayed there for three days. During this period he was entertained by the Governor and addressed the staff and students of the University of Hong Kong where he had been educated. In his speech he praised the efficiency of the British administration. Sun was at this time hoping to secure the support of the British for his political ambitions.[23] Stubbs had no great respect for Sun Yat-sen and had been ready in January, if the Foreign Office had not intervened to oppose this move, to lend HK$3,000,000 from Hong Kong's reserves to General Chen to help prevent his defeat.[24] But now that Sun was once more in power in Kwangtung he was eager to establish friendly relations with him, remembering how the authorities in Canton had damaged Hong Kong's interests by their support for the 1922 general strike when Sun was last in power. In March 1923 Stubbs proposed to make a loan to Sun for the purposes of railway construction, but permission to do this was refused by the Colonial Office because of objections raised by the British minister in Peking, Sir R. Macleay, who cited the opposition of the government in power in Peking to any aid for what was, in its view, a rebellious province. Macleay also opposed granting a request made by Sun in May for the loan of British experts to help reorganize the provincial administration.[25]

Meanwhile Sun Yat-sen's government was very short of money. He attempted to obtain loans and gifts from Chinese business men in Hong Kong and also laid hands on the revenue collected by the Salt Administration which should have been paid to the central government. In July a launch belonging to the Salt Administration took refuge in Hong Kong harbour and when Eugene Chen, Sun's secretary, demanded the surrender of the vessel to the Canton authorities Stubbs was ready to comply until he was ordered by the Foreign Office to intern it.[26] In December 1923, Sun's government tried to seize control of the revenues of the Chinese Maritime Customs in Kwangtung, claiming that the military faction then in control of Peking had no right to be considered the legitimate government of China. Eugene Chen chose to present Sun's claims to the Customs' revenue not through the foreign consuls at Canton but by a direct approach to Stubbs, coupling his demands with the threat that if the surplus of the Customs' revenue was not paid over he would retaliate against Hong Kong and British trade in South China. Stubbs was well aware of the power of the Canton authorities to stir up labour trouble inside Hong Kong so he forwarded Eugene Chen's message to Macleay in Peking, strongly urging that the treaty powers should accede to Sun's demands. This action infuriated Macleay in Peking and the Foreign Office in London.[27] The treaty powers were planning a united demonstration by naval forces to overawe Canton in order to preserve the integrity of the Maritime Customs, which was the main security for the payment of China's foreign debts. Stubbs's apparent willingness to act as an intermediary for Sun Yat-sen was seen as an encouragement of Sun's defiance of the central government. So the Foreign Secretary, Lord Curzon, wrote to the Secretary of State suggesting that Stubbs's actions were highly improper and that the serious situation in South China 'would be materially assisted by the speedy removal of Sir R.E. Stubbs from Hong Kong'.[28]

A telegram was immediately sent to Stubbs in the name of the Secretary of State warning him that, although he was entitled to make representations to London and to the British legation in Peking about the effects of British policy on Hong Kong, he was wrong in taking any positive action contrary to the British government's policy on China, and that unless he mended his ways he would be transferred forthwith. The Colonial Office did not propose to dismiss Stubbs, but consideration was given to transferring him to govern the Straits Settlements in place of Sir Lawrence Guillemard, whose management of the colony's finances had incurred Colonial Office censure.[29] Such a move would not have been a demotion since both Hong Kong and the Straits Settlements were first-class governorships. This plan, however, was not put into effect. Stubbs wrote a personal letter to the Secretary of State expressing regret for his actions, but at the same time emphasizing that his motive had been to safeguard British trade in South China which would be put at risk if the authorities in Kwangtung and the neighbouring provinces were hostile.[30] By the time this self-justificatory apology had reached London a general election had taken place (in December 1923), in which the Conservatives had lost office and a Labour government had taken over. Nothing further was said about Stubbs's transfer. But he did not become noticeably more circumspect as a result of his reprimand. At the end of December he let fly a new protest when another Salt Administration launch which had been captured at Swatow (Shantou) from the Cantonese authorities was sent to Hong Kong. He described this action as 'a deliberate attempt to embroil us with Canton' and an attempt to 'drag this government into the disputes of Chinese factions'. The Foreign Office was not amused at his reference to the Chinese Maritime Customs as a Chinese faction, and instructions were again sent to him that the vessel should be interned.[31]

Stubbs did not suffer for his outspokenness. Though deploring his caustic tongue and occasional lack of judgement the Colonial Office had a high regard for his financial acumen. He served out his full six years in Hong Kong and then went on to govern successively Jamaica, Cyprus, and Ceylon. When he finally retired in 1937 he had been a Governor for 18 years, a record among twentieth-century British Governors. When he departed from Hong Kong in 1925 the Foreign Office was concerned as to who his successor might be and asked to be consulted. The Colonial Office, jealous of its prerogatives, demurred at this, but did let it be known that Clementi, the Colonial Secretary of Ceylon, was under consideration. The Foreign Office raised no objection, noting: 'We have heard nothing but good of him.'[32] The Foreign Office was much deceived, since Clementi proved to be even more bellicose towards China in defence of Hong Kong's interests than Stubbs ever was. In 1930 Clementi was moved to the more prestigious post of Governor of the Straits Settlements. His successor was Sir William Peel, an older man who was on the verge of retirement when offered the governorship. He proved much more amenable and was able to maintain cordial relations with the British legation in Peking throughout his governorship.[33]

The Executive Council

The Governor was required to consult with his Executive Council on all questions except where he judged that the matter was urgent, trivial, or highly confidential.[34] The Executive Council consisted of the General Officer Commanding (GOC) British Forces and five officials, together with two unofficial members until 1920, and three thereafter. No Chinese was a member of the Council until 1926 when Clementi recommended the appointment of Sir Shou-son Chow. Before then the views of the Chinese had been represented in the Council by the Secretary for Chinese Affairs who presided over meetings of the District Watchmen Committee. The official purpose of this committee was to superintend the operations of the District Watch Force, a body of constables paid for by the Chinese merchants, but in practice the 14 Chinese members of this committee comprised the élite of the Chinese community, who channelled their views to the government through this forum.[35] Before 1912 Lugard had occasionally held joint meetings of the Executive Council with the unofficial members of the Legislative Council so as to tap a broader spectrum of views, but May discontinued this practice. Stubbs held one such joint meeting during the 1922 general strike, and Clementi held several during the 1925–6 strike and boycott.[36]

The Executive Council normally met once a week. A great deal of its business concerned routine administrative matters. It approved all draft bills before they were submitted to the Legislative Council, and after their enactment it approved all regulations made under them. The Council confirmed a wide range of administrative decisions such as banishment orders on prisoners who had served their sentences and on other undesirable persons, the connection of water supply to private houses, the erection of water closets,[37] the grant of prospecting licences, and the registration and deregistration of societies. It also acted in a semi-judicial capacity to consider appeals against decisions by the Director of Public Works not to authorize building plans, and it enquired into all cases where public servants had transgressed against government regulations, recommending dismissal or some lesser penalty. From 1918 the Executive Council decided all applications to live on the Peak. This was a requirement introduced by the *Peak District Residents Ordinance* of 1918, and it was used as a device to exclude Chinese and other Asians without writing this discrimination into the law. Only one Chinese was granted permission to live on the Peak between 1918 and 1941:

Mme Chiang Kai-shek.[38] A similar system was set up to create a European reservation in part of Cheung Chau in 1919, but a few Chinese were permitted by the Executive Council to live there in the 1930s.

The requirement that all significant government decisions should come before the Executive Council was the main check upon the autocracy of the Governor. Although most of the members of the Council were officials discussion was evidently quite free; officials disagreed with each other, votes were taken, and proposals were sometimes toned down or substantially modified. Very occasionally the Governor found himself in a minority. Once, in December 1915, May found the whole of the Council arrayed against him. The question at issue was the disposal of the German and Austrian civilians who had been interned at the outbreak of the First World War. The Secretary of State had suggested that they should be shipped to Australia, but May strongly opposed this on the grounds that the colony would be bound to pay for their transhipment and for the cost of their maintenance, which would be twice as expensive in Australia as in Hong Kong. The other members of the Council, led by the GOC British Forces, argued that the presence of these prisoners constituted a grave danger to the colony; the Indian troops in the colony might mutiny, as had happened in Singapore, and if they did so they would release and arm the Germans. Other members pointed out that the use of the Volunteer Corps on guard duties put a considerable burden on many firms which were short of staff. Faced with this united opposition from both the official and unofficial members May gave way and agreed that enquiries should be made as to the cost of shipping the internees to Australia.[39]

The Governor was specifically permitted by the *Royal Instructions* to act against the advice of the Council, provided that he immediately reported the facts to London. May did this twice, but on both occasions the question concerned the penalty to be imposed on a public officer who had been found guilty of a breach of government regulations.[40] In these matters the final decision on whether or not the officer should be dismissed was taken by the Colonial Office and not by the Executive Council, so the fact that the Governor on both occasions recommended dismissal against the views of the majority of the Council did not settle the officer's fate. None of the Governors who followed May went against the Council's advice in disciplinary matters and no Governor ever acted unilaterally in defiance of the views of the majority.[41] However, there were a few occasions where it seems that the Governor temporarily acquiesced in the Council's advice but raised the subject again at a later meeting and obtained the decision he wanted. For example, in August 1917 all the members of the Council who spoke opposed May's suggestion that the sale of alcoholic drinks in bars and clubs on credit should be prohibited by law; but a month later when a draft bill to ban the signing of chits for such purposes was put before the Council the majority agreed that it should go forward for consideration by the Legislative Council.[42]

All death sentences imposed by the Hong Kong courts were considered in the Executive Council with the aid of a report submitted by the judge who had presided at the trial. But although members of the Council expressed their views on each case and a vote was taken, the *Royal Instructions* made it clear that the exercise of the royal prerogative of mercy was delegated to the Governor alone: 'In all such cases he is to decide either to extend or withhold a pardon or reprieve according to his own deliberate judgement, whether the members of the Executive Council concur therein or otherwise, entering, nevertheless, on the Minutes of the Executive Council a Minute of his reasons at length in case he should decide any such question in opposition to the judgement of the majority of the members thereof.'[43] On only two occasions were the views of the Executive Council set aside by the Governor. In January 1933 and October 1934 Peel decided to exercise the prerogative of mercy when the Council advised by a majority of five to four that the death sentence should be carried out. The reasons he put down in the minutes were the narrowness of the majority in the Council, the provocation suffered by the prisoner at the hands of the murdered man, and the public support shown for the plea of commutation.[44]

It was the settled policy of the Colonial Office never to interfere with the exercise of the Governor's discretion, whichever course he had taken. Legally speaking, it was open to the Secretary of State to advise the King to override the Governor and commute the death sentence when the Governor had decided not to exercise the prerogative of mercy; or he could communicate directly with the Governor asking him to re-examine the case, if there was a possibility that a miscarriage of justice had occurred. But neither of these courses of action was ever followed. The rationale for this policy was that the relevant facts of the case were available only in the colony, and if the Secretary of State were to intervene he would have to obtain a full account of the evidence and in effect try the case again in London, which would lead to unacceptable delays for the condemned man.[45] The existence of this rule also served to protect the Secretary of State from pressures exerted in the House of Commons for a reprieve. Occasionally attempts were made to induce the Secretary of State to intervene, but all such approaches were firmly rebuffed by the Colonial Office. For example, in 1934 the Bishop of Hong Kong wrote to the Secretary of State asking him to intervene in a case where the Governor, acting on the advice of a six to two majority of the Executive Council, had refused to commute a death sentence, in spite of the fact that the jury had made a recommendation for mercy. A junior official minuted on the Bishop's letter suggesting that a telegram might be sent asking the Governor to postpone the execution and submit a report, but the more senior staff all firmly quashed this proposal. Instead the Governor was instructed to inform the Bishop that the prerogative of mercy had been delegated to the Governor, to whom any representations should be made, and that the Secretary of State was unable to intervene.[46]

In an unusual case in 1914 the Foreign Secretary, Sir Edward Grey, attempted to influence the Governor's decision. A sepoy of the Baluchistan Infantry Regiment stationed in Canton to protect the European reservation of Shameen had shot and killed his subahdar (Indian company commander) after he had been reprimanded for gambling. Normally at this time crimes committed by British subjects in China would have been tried in the court of the British Consul, but, as a capital sentence was involved, the case was transferred to Hong Kong. The prisoner was found guilty by a jury in December 1912 and sentenced to death, but the case was appealed to the Privy Council in London. This was not because there was any doubt that the sepoy was guilty of murder, but on the issue of jurisdiction: he came from Afghanistan and the question was whether the British or the Chinese authorities should have tried the case. It took 18 months before the appeal was heard and dismissed by the Privy Council. If the case had been heard by His Majesty's Supreme Court in China, the power to exercise the prerogative of mercy would have rested with the Foreign Secretary, but since it was tried in Hong Kong this responsibility lay with the Governor. Sir Edward Grey took a personal interest in the case and asked that the Governor should be informed of his view that, because of the long delay which had elapsed since the sentence of death was passed, the penalty should be commuted to life imprisonment, and that he would have taken this course if the decision had rested with him. A telegram was immediately dispatched to May and a copy of the letter giving the Foreign Secretary's views was sent on to him. This letter made it clear that the Foreign Secretary recognized that the decision was the Governor's alone. The matter was brought before the Executive Council and a majority recommended that the law should take its course. This advice was in accord with May's own views. He considered that in spite of the delay the death sentence was fully justified in the interests of military discipline, and he fortified his judgement by privately consulting the colonels of the four Indian regiments then stationed in Hong Kong. The execution was carried out in July 1914.[47]

A very similar case occurred 24 years later, but with a different outcome. In January 1937 a Chinese cabin-boy on a cruiser of the Chinese Maritime Customs shot the European captain while the ship was in Hong Kong's territorial waters, and then attempted to commit suicide. He was arrested and the Kwangtung authorities asked for his extradition to China, but the Hong Kong courts decided that he should stand trial in the colony. He was convicted of murder and sentenced to death in August 1937. Leave to appeal to the Privy Council was granted but judgement was not delivered until December 1938, when the jurisdiction of the Hong Kong courts to try the case was upheld. The British Attorney General who had conducted the case for the Crown before the Privy Council suggested to the Colonial Office that, since the prisoner had already spent 15 months in the condemned cell while an important point of maritime law was decided, the Governor should consider granting a reprieve. This view was conveyed to Northcote without any mention of the source of the suggestion, and he decided with the unanimous agreement of the Executive Council to commute the sentence to life imprisonment. This is the only case that can be found where the Secretary of State intervened effectively to influence the Governor's exercise of the prerogative of mercy.[48]

4 The Legislative Council and the Control of Legislation

THERE were no significant changes in the composition of the Legislative Council before the Second World War. From 1896 to 1929 the Council consisted of the Governor, seven officials, and six unofficial members; in 1929 four new members were added to it, two officials and two unofficials, leaving the balance between the two sides unaltered. Four of the officials sat on the Council ex officio (because they held a particular government office): the senior officer commanding the military garrison, the Colonial Secretary, the Attorney General, and the Treasurer. The other three official seats were invariably filled by the Secretary for Chinese Affairs, the Director of Public Works, and the Captain Superintendent of Police. When the Council was enlarged in 1929 the Secretary for Chinese Affairs became an ex-officio member and the two additional official seats were taken by the Director of Medical and Sanitary Services and the Harbour-master.[1]

The Governor presided over the Council and also had the right to vote, though he normally refrained from doing so in any division since the official side already had an overall majority of one, provided all the official members were present.[2] Governors did not stand aloof from the debates as impartial chairmen: they frequently made statements on particular bills and interjected comments in the course of the discussion. Until 1926 the Governor always introduced the Budget Estimates with a long exposition of the government's finances, and also gave a detailed reply at the end of the Budget debate. Clementi began the practice of making only a short statement at the beginning of the Budget debate, leaving the Colonial Secretary to explain the Estimates in detail. From 1938 Northcote transformed these introductory remarks into a broad general survey of the government's policies for the coming year.

There were four European unofficials throughout the period. Two were nominated by the Governor, one was chosen by the votes of the unofficial Justices of the Peace, and one was chosen by the Hong Kong General Chamber of Commerce. The longest-serving member was Sir Henry Polluck, who sat continuously on the Council from 1903 to 1941. Most of that time he served as the nominee of the

Justices of the Peace, but on several occasions he moved to the official side when asked to act as Attorney General while that post was temporarily vacant. The members representing the Chamber of Commerce were changed more frequently; the longest serving was Mr P.H. Holyoak who remained on the Council for 11 years (1915–26), but thereafter most of the Chamber's representatives stayed for only two or three years. There was a similar turnover among the business men and lawyers nominated by the Governor. Few remained in the colony long enough to serve a second four-year term and most sat for three years or less. The firm of Jardine, Matheson and Co. was represented on the Council for almost the whole period, apart from the years 1921–6, usually by the Governor's nomination, but occasionally elected by the Chamber of Commerce.[3] There was much greater stability among the Chinese members, who were two in number up to 1929 and three thereafter. Mr R.H. Kotewall served for 12 years (1923–35) and most stayed for the full period of two terms, as did the Portuguese member, Jose Braga (1929–37).

Service on the Council did not impose an onerous burden on its members. It met on average 18 times a year and few sessions were prolonged. Most bills passed through all their stages in two meetings, without any comment at all by the unofficials, after a brief speech by the official member introducing the measure. Clementi ascribed the 'businesslike brevity' of the Council's proceedings to the fact that disagreements were normally thrashed out beforehand in informal discussion in the Executive Council or in specially appointed committees; as a result the formal enactment of legislation could take place without the need for long debates and obstructive tactics.[4] Very occasionally the feelings of the unofficials were so aroused that members chose to make a full public statement of their position, as over the *mui tsai* legislation of 1923 or the controversies over civil service pay in the 1930s. But such public displays of disagreement were rare and when Peel came to Hong Kong from Malaya he noted the absence of the 'friendly ferocity' which characterized the meetings of the Legislative Council of the Federated Malay States.[5]

The longest sessions of the year took place at the time of the Budget in October when the debates on the annual Estimates usually filled a quarter of the pages in the year's *Hansard*. Unofficials felt free to comment critically and at length on any aspect of the government's policies and officials then replied defending their actions or inactivity as best they could. Stubbs once described this annual event as 'the unofficials' half holiday'.[6] During the rest of the year criticism was largely confined to putting down questions for official replies. The average number of questions was about 25 a year but the total reached as high as 68 in 1918 and 61 in 1929 after the Council was enlarged. These figures compare very favourably with the passivity of the Legislative Council in the 20 years after 1946. Unofficials also occasionally moved resolutions critical of the government.

In the earlier half of the period, during the governorships of May and Stubbs, opposition to the policies of the administration was almost invariably spearheaded by the European members, particularly Polluck and Holyoak. The Chinese members voted with their European colleagues as a gesture of solidarity but did not take the lead in raising controversy over matters which primarily affected the Chinese population. Wei Yuk served on the Council for 21 years (1896–1917) but he hardly ever spoke more than a few sentences. When he was the senior unofficial member he always asked a European unofficial to make the first speech in the Budget debate on his behalf. Ho Fook (the half-brother of Sir Robert Ho Tung), who succeeded to Wei Yuk's seat (1917–21), explained in his valedictory speech to the Council that the Chinese members had learned that the best way to serve the interests of the Chinese community was for their two representatives to approach unofficials quietly and tactfully instead of by asking questions and proposing resolutions in the Council.[7] However, in 1919 he and his colleague Lau Chu-pak (1913–22) did make a dignified public protest against the bill to create a European reservation on Cheung Chau. This bill was passed with only the two Chinese members voting against; the official side and the European unofficials were all in favour, hypocritically claiming that this was no more than a measure to protect the missionaries (who had developed the area) from economic competition, and was not a case of racial discrimination.[8] This was an exceptional occasion. Normally the Chinese members took little part in the proceedings of the Council and confined their remarks in the Budget debate to pressing a few issues of interest to the Chinese such as the need for larger government grants to vernacular schools and the conditions of employment for Chinese in the civil service.

One important reason for the passivity of the Chinese was the existence of the District Watch Committee as the main channel by which the government was made aware of the views of the Chinese community.[9] This Committee was formally in charge of a force of

120 Chinese policemen and detectives who were maintained by subscriptions levied on the Chinese merchants. In fact the 14 members of the Committee comprised the leading Chinese in the colony and met frequently under the chairmanship of the Secretary for Chinese Affairs. The advice of the Committee was sought on every question of interest or importance to the Chinese, and the government was always most anxious to obtain the Committee's support when any changes were proposed which might affect Chinese interests or cause offence to their sentiments. The Committee was consulted, for example, over the measures proposed to deal with the tramway boycott of 1912, on future trade policy in 1917, on the industrial employment of children in 1922, the proscription of the General Labour Union in 1927, the suppression of tolerated brothels in 1930, and the regulation of Chinese banks in 1935.[10] On these and all other occasions when the views of the District Watch Committee coincided with his own the Governor customarily reported their opinions to London as a strong if not decisive argument in favour of the policy he was pursuing. Clementi inaugurated the custom of inviting the Committee to meet every three months at Government House, thereby giving increased prestige to its members. The District Watch Committee provided the government with its principal means of exercising control and influence over the Chinese population by co-opting its natural leaders.[11] The Chinese no doubt saw it as a means whereby they might exert influence over the colonial government. So, for example, in 1921 legislation was introduced at the instance of the Committee to abolish the penalty of the 'stocks', by which a convicted Chinese was compelled to wear a wooden board around his neck. However, the Committee was not always a very active body: sometimes, for example when criticizing the arrogant insensitivity of British merchants or rebutting European objections to the custom of employing *mui tsai,* the Committee could generate a lively discussion; but more generally, as the Secretary for Chinese Affairs reported to the Governor in 1921, 'The District Watch Committee sits dumb and I usually have to elicit opinions with a sort of verbal bootjack.'[12]

Towards the end of the 1920s and in the 1930s the Chinese members in the Legislative Council began to play a more active role. On three occasions the three Chinese members pressed their opposition to a government policy to a division when objecting to proposed new charges for water supply, and once in 1936 they voted together against increased penalties for offences under the *mui tsai* legislation. The European members did not support them in these votes. When Lo Man-kam joined the Council in 1935 he quickly established a reputation as the leading critic of the government, a role played by Polluck 20 years earlier. In the four years 1936–9 he asked more questions than the rest of the Council put together, many of which drew attention to cases of discrimination against the Chinese. His maiden speech in the Council was on a motion which he had put forward himself criticizing the size and expense of the public service and demanding retrenchments. Later in the same year he introduced a motion asking for the end of censorship of the Chinese press, which had been imposed under emergency regulations for the past 11 years, since 1925, but which did not affect English-language newspapers. This was defeated by 14 votes to 2, with only Braga supporting him.[13]

In any division the official side was sure of a majority and a decision by the unofficials to press their opposition to a vote achieved nothing except to place on record their emphatic disagreement with the government's policies, in the hope that this would be noted by the authorities in London.[14] The ultimate step open to the unofficials was to stage a mass resignation from the Council and so precipitate a constitutional crisis. This has never occurred in Hong Kong, though such action took place in the Straits Settlements in 1895. There were two occasions when similar action was con-templated in Hong Kong: in 1908 one of the unofficials hinted at the possibility during the debate on the closure of the opium divans, in protest against a policy which was being imposed on Hong Kong by the Secretary of State without any consultation with the local authorities; and in 1928 the unofficials privately threatened a mass resignation if immediate action were not taken by the government to improve the water supply by the construction of a pipeline to bring water across the harbour from Kowloon to the island. On both occasions the unofficials secured substantial concessions.[15]

The attitudes of different Governors to the use of the official majority were not uniform. May was not a man to compromise when he was convinced of the correctness of his own judgement. During his seven years as Governor, the official majority was mobilized to defeat a united unofficial opposition on 14 occasions. Six of these were votes against imperial policy on matters such as the size of the Defence Contribution, or in protest against the slowness of the government in effecting the complete extirpation of German commercial interests during the First World War and its unwillingness to accept the demand of the General Chamber of Commerce that all Germans should be forbidden to return and restart their businesses for at least 10 years after the war was over. In these instances the Governor was acting on instructions from London to use the official majority to defeat the unofficials' motion. But on the other eight occasions the unofficials were objecting to policies decided on by the local administration without reference to London, on matters such as taxation policy, the administration of the medical department, or the grounds for granting exemption from compulsory military service to European British subjects. On all of these matters May was convinced that he was right and refused to make any concession to conciliate his opponents and secure an agreed outcome. These votes were reported to London when the ordinances were routinely sent to the Colonial Office after they had passed through the Legislative Council, and the Colonial Office then made no criticism of May's actions. There were, however, two occasions when May saw fit to consult the Secretary of State beforehand as to whether he should use the official majority to overcome the unanimous opposition of the unofficials: once in May 1914 on a proposal to purchase a gunboat for anti-piracy patrols in Hong Kong waters, and once in 1917 when he wished to extend compulsory military service for European residents into the post-war period. On both occasions the Colonial Office instructed him to desist. On the gunboat issue this was because of naval objections; on conscription, officials felt that it was premature to antagonize the unofficials on a matter which could be left until the war was over. An official minuted, 'The governor is an Irishman whose judgement cannot invariably be trusted', and the Secretary of State initialled his agreement.[16]

Stubbs was as confident of his own opinions as May, but he followed a much more conciliatory approach, seeking to convince the unofficial side of the reasonableness of the government's policy and achieve a consensus rather than overriding all opposition by the brute force of the official majority. One means by which he sought to achieve this was by remodelling the committees of the Legislative Council on the lines of the system used in Ceylon, where he had previously served as Colonial Secretary.[17] Until 1920 the Finance Committee, which met to approve all proposals for new expenditures that were not included in the annual appropriation bill, consisted of all the members of the Council except for the Governor. This meant that the official side had an overall majority of one (seven to six) and could ignore any objections raised by the unofficials. On four occasions during May's governorship the official majority had been used in the Finance Committee to overcome the unanimous opposition of the unofficials. Stubbs changed the composition of the committee so that it included only three officials, the Colonial Secretary, the Treasurer, and the Director of Public Works, together with all six unofficial members, who thus were in a majority. This gave the unofficials real powers of decision over public finance, and though it was still possible for the Governor to refer any item to the full council if defeated in the committee, this never in fact proved to be necessary. Over the next 20 years there was only one occasion when the government was defeated on a division in the Finance Committee, but there were a number of instances when the government side was persuaded by criticism in the committee to withdraw a proposal completely or resubmit it after amendment. The Finance Committee met in public and showed a keen eye for economies, however paltry; at one meeting an item of HK$8 for shoeing a pony was criticized when one member objected that he could get such a job done for HK$3.[18] On at least one occasion the committee's view was effective in frustrating a directive from London. In 1920 the Colonial Office sent a circular dispatch to all colonies inviting increased contributions for the support of the Imperial Institute in London and suggesting that Hong Kong should give £1,000. The unofficials unanimously opposed so large a grant and Stubbs wrote to the Secretary of State: 'I feel confident that your Lordship would not wish me to make use of the official majority in this matter as I am aware that some at least of the official members share the opinions of their unofficial colleagues and I recommend that the proposal to give £500 should be accepted.' The Colonial Office acquiesced in this compromise.[19]

There were two other committees of the Legislative Council. One was the Public Works Committee which until 1920 consisted of the Director of Public Works and four other members. Stubbs enlarged this to include all the unofficials. This concession had little practical effect since the committee had no decision-making power; it met intermittently to hear details of the government's public works proposals and comment on them before they were incorporated in the annual finance bill.[20] The other committee was the Law Committee, consisting of the Attorney General, the Secretary for Chinese Affairs, and three unofficials, usually lawyers. It met very occasionally when it was necessary to thrash out an acceptable form of words in order to amend a bill so as to meet objections which had been voiced by unofficials in the second reading debate. Stubbs made no changes here.

The other innovation instituted by Stubbs concerned the vexed question of subsidiary legislation. On a number of occasions during May's governorship various unofficials, notably Mr C.G. Alabaster, a barrister, had objected to bills which delegated the power to make regulations to the Executive Council, on the ground that all legislation ought to be made by the Legislative Council. To settle this dispute Stubbs proposed that in future whenever a bill gave the Executive Council power to make regulations they should be laid before the Legislative Council which would have the power to vote to annul them by passing a resolution to that effect at its next meeting, if it so wished. This satisfied all the unofficial members except Alabaster, and the matter was then dropped. The procedure was never in fact made use of in the next 20 years, but it has remained on the statute book and was resorted to for the first time in 1974.[21]

While Stubbs was Governor there were only two occasions when the unanimous views of the unofficials were overridden. One was on an amendment to the *mui tsai* bill, where the Governor was acting under direct instructions from London that there could be no compromise over the prohibition of the engagement of new *mui tsai*. The other occasion concerned a minor local issue. In 1923 the unofficials put forward a motion proposing the repeal of an ordinance passed five years earlier at May's insistence to forbid the sale of drinks at hotel bars except for ready cash. May at the time had been much concerned about drunkenness in the colony and believed that the practice of signing chits at the bar in payment for drinks encouraged overindulgence. Stubbs allowed the official members to vote according to their own judgement on the motion, since he regarded it as a matter to be settled according to the general view of the community, and the officials all voted against making any changes in the law.[22] Stubbs also allowed a free vote to the officials when a bill imposing rent controls was being debated in committee, but on this occasion the unofficials themselves were not united. The officials voted solidly against one amendment, following Stubbs's lead, but split their votes on the second after Polluck had protested that the Governor had effectively influenced the officials' vote by expressing his own opinion; so on the next amendment he ostentatiously refrained from making any comment and the unofficials were able to pass their amendment with the aid of three official votes.[23]

Not all disagreements between the unofficial members and the government were pressed to a vote. In 1920 Stubbs decided not to attempt to force through the Council by the use of the official majority a bill to compel Europeans to serve in the Volunteer Corps. He reported to London that he personally regretted this, but he had felt obliged to give way to the strength of public opinion against any such proposal now that the war was over.[24] Similarly in 1922 after the general strike the Executive Council approved the introduction of a bill into the Legislative Council to require all Europeans to register for service in any future emergency. But after the bill had had its first reading the European unofficials privately made known their opposition to the measure. No public speeches were made, but the government decided not to proceed further with the bill.[25]

Stubbs's successor, Clementi, was even more successful in charming the unofficials into agreement with his views. There was not a single disagreement pressed to a division in the first three years of his governorship, and although there were two divisions in 1929 in both of them the government's view was supported by at least one of the unofficials. Only one serious dissension arose between the government and the unofficials during Clementi's governorship, on the question of measures to deal with the colony's perennial water shortage. The unofficials were in favour of building a new reservoir at Shing Mun in the New Territories and bringing the water to Hong Kong island by means of a pipeline to be laid under the harbour. Clementi was concerned about the dangers if the colony had to rely upon a water supply from the leased territory which might revert to China in sixty years' time, and preferred to enlarge an existing reservoir in the Aberdeen valley on Hong Kong island. While he was away on leave in Britain in 1928 the unofficials became convinced that the Aberdeen scheme would provide insufficient water for the colony's future needs and informed the acting Governor that they were unanimously opposed to voting any money for it. The acting Governor telegraphed this news to London, adding that he did not favour using the official majority to force the project through, since the unofficials had been very helpful to the government in recent years. Officials at the Colonial Office also deprecated the use of the official majority in such a matter. Clementi was consulted and he asked for the vote to be postponed until his return. He was then able to persuade the unofficials to accept a package of measures which included the immediate completion of a cross-harbour pipeline and a small reservoir in Kowloon, detailed investigations for a new reservoir in the Shing Mun valley, and the authorization for construction work on the Aberdeen scheme to begin.[26] Clementi thus proved his consummate ability to win the support of the unofficials when he set his mind to it. But this did not stop him from exaggerating the importance of unofficial opposition when that happened to suit his purposes. When pressed by the Home Office to consider abandoning the government opium monopoly he insisted that it would be impossible to get such a policy accepted by the Legislative Council, since it would involve the colony in maintaining a preventive service to track down smuggled opium without any countervailing revenue to pay for it.[27]

Clementi departed from Hong Kong in 1930, leaving his successor, Sir William Peel, to deal with the contentious issue of public service pay. In 1928 Clementi had appointed a commission consisting of the Chief Justice, Sir Henry Gollan, and two unofficial members, Sir Shou-son Chow and Mr P. Lauder, to review the salaries of the public service. Their report was delivered in September 1929 and recommended substantial increases, which were justified on the basis of the rise in the cost of living since the last general revision of salaries in 1920. On the previous occasion the new salaries had been accepted by the unofficial members without opposition at a time of economic prosperity and rising government revenue. The situation in 1930 was very different, and the recommended increases were strongly opposed by the Hong Kong General Chamber of Commerce as being overgenerous to the public service, out of line with the salaries paid by commercial firms, and too expensive for the taxpayer at a time when trade was depressed. An additional reason for opposition was that the commission had recommended that expatriate officers whose salaries were denominated in sterling should be paid in Hong Kong dollars at the current rate of exchange instead of using the sliding scale which had hitherto been in force. In 1930 the value of the Hong Kong dollar was depreciating rapidly against sterling, and the effect of the commission's recommendation was to give an unexpectedly large increase to expatriate officers when their salaries were converted into Hong Kong dollars at the current rate of exchange. This vastly increased the cost of the new scheme. The General Chamber of Commerce argued fiercely against the revised salaries in Hong Kong, and the China Association also lobbied in London, asking that the

Secretary of State should refuse to endorse the commission's report.[28] When these actions failed, the unofficial members of the Legislative Council made it clear that they would vote against the salary revision and ask for the whole question to be reconsidered by a new committee.

The outright opposition of the unofficials was very upsetting for the Hong Kong government. It had previously been assumed in Hong Kong that officials should not vote on their own salaries and Peel consulted the Colonial Office as to whether it was constitutionally correct to use the official majority on such an issue. The Colonial Office replied that this was in order; the Colonial Office's Legal Adviser minuted that if it were not, the officials would be at the mercy of the unofficials.[29] So a resolution to approve the recommendations of the Salaries Commission, with certain minor modifications, was put before the Legislative Council in June 1930 and passed by the votes of all the officials after a long and bitter debate. All the unofficials voted against the resolution except for the two members of the Salaries Commission, who abstained. The debate ended with the Governor accepting a further motion moved by the unofficials to set up a Retrenchment Committee to propose economies in the staffing and management of the public service.

This was not the end of the matter. The exchange value of the Hong Kong dollar against sterling continued to fall, further increasing the cost of the salary revision. At the time of the Budget debate in October 1930, Mr P. Lauder, an unofficial who had been a member of the Salaries Commission, suggested that expatriate civil servants should have half of their salary converted into dollars at the current rate of exchange, and the other half at a fixed rate of HK$13.30 to the pound. The Governor readily accepted this proposal, but, because the scheme had been passed only three months previously, he had great difficulty in persuading the Colonial Office to accept this change in the scheme. It was only the further decline in the value of the Hong Kong currency to more than HK$20 to the pound which forced the Colonial Office to agree. European public servants were outraged by this decision. They sent a petition to London and persuaded various Members of Parliament to take up their grievance by questions and speeches in the House of Commons. This lobbying was so successful that the Secretary of State instructed Peel to restore the full convertibility of sterling salaries at the current rate of exchange from January 1932.[30] This decision was revealed when the Estimates were presented to the Legislative Council in

October 1931. It caused an immediate outcry among the unofficials, all of whom voted in favour of a resolution to reduce the Estimates by the amount needed to pay the increased salaries. The Appropriation Bill was only carried by the united votes of the official side. The unofficials were well aware that the government was acting under instructions from London and their vote was a protest against the policy of the Colonial Office rather than against that of the local administration. This was the last occasion before the Second World War on which the official majority was mobilized to defeat the unanimous view of the unofficials. There were a number of divisions later in the 1930s, but in all of them the government was able to persuade at least one, and usually more, of the unofficials to accept its point of view.

Colonial Office Scrutiny of Legislation

Once a bill had been passed by the Legislative Council and had received the Governor's assent it became law and was enforced by the Hong Kong courts. A copy of the ordinance was then dispatched to the Colonial Office, together with an explanatory memorandum by the Attorney General and a copy of the debate on the bill, if any, in the Legislative Council. The ordinance could then be disallowed by His Majesty's Government, which had the effect of repealing it from the date when notice of disallowance was promulgated in the colony. The Letters Patent set no time limit upon the notification of disallowance so in theory an ordinance could be disallowed at any time; but in practice, to avoid uncertainty, the Governor was normally informed within a few months that the Crown's power of disallowance would not be exercised, and this information was published in the Government Gazette.

Some bills were examined in draft at the Colonial Office before enactment by the Legislative Council. The Governor was, and is, forbidden by Article XXXVI of the *Royal Instructions* to assent to 10 classes of legislation unless he has previously obtained the consent of the Secretary of State. The most important of these are bills affecting banking, the issue of currency, and the control of the armed services, bills contrary to any treaty, bills prejudicing the rights, property, trade, or shipping of British subjects, and bills which discriminate against the non-European population. Drafts of all such bills were invariably sent to the Colonial Office so that any criticisms could be taken into account and changes could be incorporated in the bill before it was introduced into the Legislative Council. Bills on other sensitive subjects were also sent to London in draft beforehand to anticipate objections and to avoid the possible need to introduce amending legislation after the bill had been passed by the Legislative Council.

The great majority of the bills and ordinances scrutinized in the Colonial Office were found to be free of any fault and non-disallowance was immediately notified to Hong Kong. On average about 30 new ordinances were passed each year, but most of them were minor amendments to existing legislation to take account of changing circumstances and the latest decisions of the courts. Others were bills which were initiated as a result of the circular dispatches that were sent to all colonial territories enclosing copies of legislation which had recently been passed either in Britain or in one of the colonies, and which the Colonial Office considered could be usefully adopted elsewhere. For example, Hong Kong was the first colony to legislate for the control and censorship of public cinematograph displays in 1910, and a copy of the Hong Kong ordinance was included in a circular dispatch recommending legislation on the subject; and in 1937 a Hong Kong ordinance giving power to impose a black-out of all lights in the event of an air raid was similarly circulated.[31] Such legislation normally followed the model Act of Parliament or ordinance very closely and so required little attention in London. Other bills entirely prepared in Hong Kong were carefully examined to see if they were properly drafted to achieve their objective and to ensure that they were not objectionable on policy grounds. Bills were routinely sent to other departments of state for advice on technical matters and to ensure that their interests were not adversely affected. For example ordinances relating to banking or finance were sent to the Treasury and the Bank of England, those on company law, trade marks, patents, insurance, and shipping went to the Board of Trade, those on prisons and asylums to the Home Office and bills on issues affecting China, such as the extradition of criminals and deportation, were seen by the Foreign Office. The Legal Adviser to the Colonial Office, who looked at every colonial ordinance, was particularly vigilant to censure legislation which curtailed the liberty of individuals or gave excessive powers to the government; for example where the onus of proof was shifted on to the accused, where immunity from civil action was granted to officials or statutory bodies, or where the power to make arrests was conferred on junior officials. These were all matters which should have been noticed and objected to by the unofficial members, but the passage of legislation through the Legislative Council was usually so rapid and the examination of it there so cursory that the task of protecting civil liberties from the encroachment of the executive was carried out by the Colonial Office instead of by the unofficial members of the legislature.[32]

Certain ordinances were sent for comment to professional organizations in Britain: for example an ordinance on the sale of drugs to the Pharmaceutical Society and one on the registration of nurses to the General Nursing Council. Pressure groups and commercial firms were never invited to give their views. Such organizations did sometimes approach the Colonial Office directly when an ordinance was under consideration, seeking to secure changes which had not been raised during the bill's passage through the Legislative Council, or which had already been refused by the Hong Kong authorities. The Colonial Office also rarely received petitions from individuals or groups or organizations in Hong Kong asking that an ordinance should be disallowed: one such case occurred in 1911 when the staff of the new University of Hong Kong petitioned against a bill which made the Director of Education an ex-officio member of the University Senate.[33] Very occasionally such interventions were successful: in 1932 the firm of Butterfield and Swire asked for an amendment to the Companies Ordinance to remove the obligation that the company should file a copy of its balance sheet for public inspection, on the ground that it was a private company and such a requirement did not exist in British legislation; so the Colonial Office wrote suggesting that British practice should be followed and Hong Kong complied.[34] But normally the Colonial Office took the attitude that the colonial government was the best judge of what suited local circumstances and should not be overruled by the Secretary of State. The objections voiced by the pressure group might be conveyed to Hong Kong, but if the government declined to agree, the government's view was normally decisive. So, for example, in 1929 an attempt by the British American Tobacco Company to secure changes in the method of calculating the excise duty on tobacco was rebuffed after the Governor had explained to London the reasons for the government's decision.[35]

There was one exceptional instance where the Colonial Office insisted, in deference to pressures from the China Association, that Hong Kong should make changes in spite of its reiterated objections.

In 1932 the Hong Kong government published a draft bill giving itself general powers to reclaim land and to build piers, breakwaters, warehouses, and other public works on the foreshores and seabed of the colony, and to extinguish all private rights of access, and to remove any piers, wharves, or landing places, subject to compensation to be determined by a judge. The bill was sent to London before introduction into the Legislative Council, since it could be said to affect the property and shipping of British subjects outside the colony. Strong objections were raised by a number of firms, including Butterfield and Swire and Jardine Matheson, who protested against the possible loss of their sea frontages and access to their wharves and godowns by government reclamations, apparently fearing that government might use its wide powers to set up new piers, warehouses, and ferry services to compete with existing private operators. They were also dissatisfied with the arrangements for assessing compensation, asking that the judge should be assisted by commercial assessors and that there should be a right of appeal against the judge's award to all courts right up to the Privy Council. The campaign against the bill was orchestrated locally by the Hong Kong General Chamber of Commerce and in London by the China Association. The Foreign Office was persuaded to approach the Colonial Office on their behalf, arguing that the general powers to extinguish private property rights contained in the bill would be seized upon by the Chinese government as a useful precedent for confiscatory action against the foreshore and riparian rights of British firms in the treaty ports. All of these objections were put to the Hong Kong government by the Colonial Office. In his reply the Governor agreed to redraft the bill to allow for an improved procedure to appeal against proposed reclamations, and to allow commerical assessors to assist the judge in determining the amount of compensation. But he declined to forego the general powers to reclaim land in the harbour and to construct public works, claiming that these were necessary to validate existing reclamations, and that it would be cumbersome to obtain separate legislative approval for every future project. Such procedures would, in his view, cause unreasonable delays to the improvement of the harbour; the objections voiced were no more than a cover to protect the vested interests of the existing shipping firms; China would act as it pleased in any case, and would not be affected by what was being done in Hong Kong. These concessions failed to satisfy the protesters and the campaign against the bill continued, aided by questions in the House of Commons and personal approaches to the Secretary of State, Sir Philip Cunliffe-Lister, by the China Association. Colonial Office officials were inclined to support the Governor, being habitually sceptical of the self-interested pleas made by business men, but Cunliffe-Lister overruled his advisers and directed that the general bill should be withdrawn and that legislation should be enacted periodically when needed to validate specific public works. The first such ordinance was passed in 1936. The China Association was successful on this occasion since the issue of private property rights was a sensitive one for a Conservative minister and because it had been able to gain the support of the Foreign Office to assist its campaign.[36]

Disallowance of an ordinance after it had been passed by the Legislative Council and assented to by the Governor was extremely rare. In the whole history of the colony this power has only been exercised 15 times. Eight of these were in the first three years of the Legislative Council's existence from 1844 to 1847 and the other instances were in 1856, 1867, 1884, 1889, 1906, 1907, and 1913. This last case was over an issue of little significance. In 1902 Britain had become a party to an international agreement, the Brussels Sugar Convention, which obliged its members not to subsidize the production or export of sugar and to prohibit or levy differential duties on the import of subsidized sugar from other sources. Hong Kong along with other colonies had acceded to the Convention in accordance with the advice of a circular dispatch sent to all colonies, and in 1904 a short ordinance was passed empowering the Governor in Council to make regulations to prohibit the import of bounty-fed sugar into the colony. Hong Kong itself produced no sugar but it did refine and export sugar imported from the Dutch East Indies (now Indonesia). In 1912 Britain announced its formal withdrawal from the Convention, to take effect in 1913, but at the same time informed the other signatories that she still intended to abide by the general principles of the Convention. The colonies were informed of this by a circular dispatch and the Hong Kong government promptly introduced a one-clause bill repealing the ordinance of 1904. When this ordinance was received in London it was routinely passed to the Board of Trade and the Foreign Office for comment. When Britain had announced its withdrawal, no undertaking had been given on behalf of the colonies, and the Foreign Office suddenly realized that the West Indian colonies might be open to reprisals if it was thought that the colonial empire had also withdrawn from the Convention; so the Colonial Office was informed that it would have been better if Hong Kong had done nothing, to avoid drawing attention to the position of the colonies, and that it should now, if possible, revert to the previous position. The simplest way to achieve this was to disallow the 1913 ordinance, which would automatically reinstate the ordinance of 1904. The Governor was asked if he had any objection to this being done. He had none, and accordingly notice of disallowance was promulgated.[37]

Although this was the last time that disallowance was actually used against a Hong Kong ordinance the possibility was mentioned in the Colonial Office on three other occasions. In 1913 disallowance of the Boycott Prevention Ordinance was suggested, when the Permanent Under-Secretary and the Secretary of State both took strong exception to the wide powers conferred upon the government to punish those inciting a boycott and to levy a penal rate on the district affected. Sir John Anderson, the Permanent Under-Secretary, commented: 'The special rate provisions are most objectionable. The most omniscient and judicial-minded of governors should not be trusted with such powers', and May was ordered to repeal the ordinance; alternatively it could be disallowed in London, if this would cause him less embarrassment. In the event May was able to argue that the ordinance was useful as a deterrent, even if it was never put into force, and he was allowed to retain it temporarily on the statute book and to defer its repeal to a suitable occasion in the future. A few years later, when there was a new minister and a new Permanent Under-Secretary, May secured the reversal of this instruction and the ordinance remained unrepealed until 1939.[38]

In 1919 the Colonial Office noticed that an ordinance which transferred the property of certain German missionary societies to the Custodian of Enemy Property with the power to sell or otherwise dispose of it was contrary to article 438 of the Treaty of Versailles. The Legal Adviser proposed disallowance but the Permanent Under-Secretary, Sir George Fiddes, decided that it was only necessary to send a telegram to the Governor forbidding him to take any action under these newly acquired powers.[39] Similar action was taken over an ordinance passed in 1927. In the previous year nine ships had been hijacked in the waters around the colony by pirates operating from Bias Bay in Chinese territory. A court of enquiry had been set up to investigate one of these incidents, the piracy of the SS *Sunning* in November 1926, and an interdepartmental conference was called by the Foreign Office in London to consider appropriate counter-measures. Before any decision was reached the Hong Kong government enacted a bill to repeal the existing Piracy Prevention Ordinance and bring in new regulations designed to make ships more secure against seizure by pirates who had got on board in disguise among the passengers. This hasty action before the Foreign Office committee had reported annoyed the Colonial Office and one official suggested disallowance. But instead a telegram was sent directing the Governor to suspend the introduction of the new regulations. Three months later, when the Foreign Office conference had decided what instructions should be sent to the naval and military authorities in China, Hong Kong was notified that the ordinance would not be disallowed and that the new regulations might be brought into force.[40]

On all of these occasions disallowance was contemplated in order to deal with legislation which had been passed precipitately by the Hong Kong government without thought of possible repercussions or objections that might be raised in Britain. There were also two other instances when disallowance was mentioned in the Legislative Council even though the Colonial Office had given no indication that action along these lines might be taken. In both cases the government wished to justify its refusal to accept an amendment put forward by one of the unofficial members. In 1924 C.G. Alabaster, speaking on behalf of shipping interests, suggested the deletion of a section in the Opium Ordinance under which the owners of a ship where concealed opium had been discovered were deemed to be guilty of allowing it to be used for smuggling, unless they could prove that they had taken every reasonable precaution to prevent this. Alabaster claimed that it was unfair to lay the burden of proof on the shipowners. In reply the Governor, Stubbs, refused to accept any change, on the ground that the British government would certainly disallow any bill which made it easier for those involved in smuggling opium to escape punishment.[41] In 1932 the government put forward a bill to allow divorce on the lines of recent changes in British law. An unofficial suggested that the grounds for dissolution of matrimony should be further liberalized, but the Attorney General warned that the ordinance would certainly be disallowed if it went beyond the British Act on which it was modelled.[42] It is possible that in both 1924 and 1932 the Colonial Office might have exercised the power of disallowance if the bills had been amended as the unofficials wanted, but such drastic action seems rather unlikely.

The normal procedure when the Colonial Office took grave exception to a colonial ordinance was to write to the Governor asking him to introduce amending legislation, unless he wished to raise any objection; pending his reply no decision would be taken as to whether or not the ordinance should be disallowed. This implied threat of disallowance served to encourage the government to take action. For example in 1920 the War Office was consulted over an ordinance to reconstitute the Hong Kong Volunteer Regiment after the war and found fault with the ordinance because it made provision for the nomination of NCOs and officers by their companies. The War Office considered the election of officers, in whatever form, extremely objectionable, so the Colonial Office wrote to Hong Kong insisting that this provision must be removed before the ordinance could be sanctioned.[43] In 1931 the Colonial Office asked that a new Deportation (Amendment) Ordinance should be repealed and re-enacted, after it received a letter from the Chief Justice of Hong Kong complaining that the judges had not been consulted over the bill which, in his view, made a judge part of the machinery of executive action for deportation without any power to influence the result. The Legal Adviser to the Colonial Office suggested a compromise procedure for the conduct of enquiries before deportation, which the government then accepted.[44] In 1936 an ordinance to regulate gunnery practice by the British forces in Hong Kong was found to be defective because it made it an offence for a ship to be in a proclaimed firing area. Hong Kong was ordered to remove this clause since it purported to legislate with extra-territorial effect over the high seas, and this was beyond the competence of a colonial legislature.[45]

But such peremptory directives were very rare; no more than 10 examples can be found in the period from 1912 to 1940.[46] More usually, when the Colonial Office was unhappy about an ordinance, a dispatch would be sent to Hong Kong detailing the points of criticism which had been noted in the Colonial Office, or by another department which had been consulted, and requesting the Governor to furnish an explanation. The Governor would then reply, either setting out the peculiar circumstances of Hong Kong which rendered it necessary to depart from British precedents; or else pointing out that a similar clause already existed in another Hong Kong ordinance to which the Colonial Office had previously raised no objection. This usually satisfied the officials, and non-disallowance was then signified. This did not mean that the Colonial Office was entirely satisfied with the ordinance. The dispatch notifying non-disallowance sometimes also included further comments and suggestions for the improvement of the legislation, which the Governor was invited to consider incorporating on a suitable occasion in the future. These might be minor points of drafting, to clear up an ambiguity or clarify a definition, or might be matters of substance. For example, in 1927 the Colonial Office suggested that an ordinance to provide safeguards against factory accidents, which had closely followed an Act of Parliament passed in 1901, might be usefully updated to include the higher standards imposed by British legislation of 1926; and on the Asylums Ordinance of 1934 the Colonial Office noted that it was considered undesirable that prisoners should be kept in an asylum before trial.[47] Such suggestions were normally complied with, but they were not mandatory, and occasionally, whether by accident or design, no action was taken. For example, in 1927 an Illegal Strikes and Lockouts Ordinance was passed which, among other provisions, made it in effect a criminal offence for a public servant to go on strike. The Colonial Office noted that this provision was more sweeping than that in the British act on which the legislation was modelled, but did not ask for an amendment since it was considered important that there should be no appearance of disagreement between Hong Kong and London on this issue. It was noted in the dispatch signifying non-disallowance that this clause should be amended on a suitable occasion, but in fact it remained unaltered for 20 years, until 1948.[48]

Correspondence concerning legislation was hardly ever brought to the attention of ministers, since it was mainly concerned with matters of detail. Occasionally a file might be passed up to a minister when there was a possibility that the matter might be raised in Parliament. An instance of this occurred in 1932 over an ordinance which made it easier for the police to prosecute prostitutes for soliciting in public. This was shown to the junior minister, the Earl of Plymouth, and, as was expected, he accepted the advice of officials that the local authorities should be allowed to decide what measures were necessary to keep their streets clean.[49] The Secretary of State never looked at legislation except when it was a matter of immediate public controversy in Britain, as over the issue of *mui tsai*.

5 The Public Service

Size and Composition

In 1914 the establishment of the public service was 4,447 posts. By 1939 this total had grown to 10,004 posts, an increase of 125 per cent.[1] This growth was roughly parallel to the increase in population over the period, from 462,466 in the 1911 Census to an estimated permanent population of 1,050,000 in 1939 (excluding refugees).[2] The most obvious difference from the present public service was the large proportion of Europeans employed. These numbered 515 in 1914 (11.6 per cent of the service) and by 1930 the number had increased to 956, still representing 11 per cent. There was then a slight decrease during the following decade to 889 in 1939 (9 per cent). Europeans were employed in many lowly posts, as ordinary constables in the police force, warders in the prisons, inspectors in the Sanitary Department, overseers of labour in the Public Works Department, and as clerks in all branches of the government. The cost of their salaries, which were calculated in sterling, placed a severe burden on the finances of the colony. A European police constable in 1914 was paid £100 a year, at the time equivalent to HK$1,142. This was more than seven times as much as a local Chinese or Indian constable, who received HK$150 a year; and this does not take into account the additional cost of accommodation and leave passages. In 1939 the lowest-ranking European in the police force, a lance-sergeant, received £190 a year, then equivalent to HK$3,040, while his Chinese counterpart received HK$396 a year. Every Governor on his appointment called attention to the large number of Europeans in the public service compared to the number in other colonies, but until 1930 there was no pressure from the unofficial members of the Legislative Council for the replacement of Europeans by local staff. Quite the reverse.[3] In 1914 the European unofficials pressed for an increase in the number of European nurses at the government civil hospital in spite of the expostulations of the Governor that it already had far more European staff than comparable hospitals in the Straits Settlements, Fiji, or Ceylon. In 1920 there were demands for an increase in the European contingent of the police force, even though its establishment had just been increased from 160 to 183. The Colonial Secretary pointed out that Singapore had fewer than 40 European police and that in the whole of Ceylon there were only 23 for a population at least six times as great as that of Hong Kong.[4]

Various reasons were given for the large number of expatriates employed. Heads of departments claimed, on very dubious evidence, that European subordinates were more trustworthy and less corrupt than Chinese and were more efficient at their work. There was also the question of loyalty to the British Crown: the great majority of the population and of the locally recruited public servants were not British subjects and so could not be considered completely reliable in an emergency.[5] For this reason the Chinese contingent in the police force was outnumbered by the European police and those recruited from India. In 1913 the police comprised 175 Europeans (14.3 per cent), 472 Indians (38.6 per cent), and 576 Chinese (47.1 per cent). During the seamen's strike of 1922 which developed into a general strike the government was very dissatisfied with the performance of the Chinese police, particularly their failure to prevent the intimidation of labourers who wished to continue at work. As a result 23 sergeants and constables were dismissed or retired from the force and as many were reduced in rank or otherwise disciplined.[6] After the strike the size of the European and Indian contingents was increased and a new source of recruitment was opened up in Weihaiwei, a British colony in North China. In 1922–3, 200 police were recruited there and the Weihaiwei Chinese continued as a separate element in the force until 1941. In 1939 the police force comprised 306 Europeans (13.8 per cent), 774 Indians (34.9 per cent), 844 Cantonese Chinese (38 per cent), and 296 Chinese from Weihaiwei (13.3 per cent).

Political reliability was not the only reason for the number of Europeans employed. A number of clerical posts were filled by the sons of subordinate European staff who wished to make a career in Hong Kong. They entered the Senior Clerical and Accounting Staff (which was in practice reserved for Europeans until the 1930s) as probationary clerks at a salary of HK$900 a year (compared to HK$450 for a new Chinese entrant) and then were rapidly promoted to senior posts, the salaries for which were calculated in sterling.[7] Police and prison warders were commonly recruited from the ranks of the British army. Soldiers serving in the colony who were due to retire when their regiment returned to Britain were glad to take their discharge in Hong Kong in order to take up a post with the colonial government rather than face unemployment in Britain. This method of recruitment saved the government the expense of paying the passages to Hong Kong of staff engaged in Britain, and also provided a better class of recruit. The minimum pay for a constable in the Metropolitan Police in Britain in 1920 was £188 a year, compared to £120 offered by the Hong Kong police force. So when the Hong Kong government in 1920 asked the Crown Agents in London to recruit 48 constables for service in the colony they had great difficulty in finding men of suitable physique and character, and a number of those who were sent out on this occasion proved unsatisfactory and had to be sent back home.[8]

The life of a low-paid European in Hong Kong cannot have been very pleasant. Many found solace in drink. According to the Governor, Sir Henry May, speaking in 1918, less than half of the European subordinate staff who came to Hong Kong survived to earn their pensions; the rest died, were dismissed, or were invalided out of the service, and most of these casualties were caused by excessive drinking. Over the years 1908 to 1917, 17 per cent of the strength of the European contingent of the police were dismissed or died from overindulgence in alcohol, and drink was a contributory factor in the dismissal, invaliding out, or death of a further 29 per cent of the force.[9]

Marriage between European officers and Chinese or Eurasian women was not expressly forbidden by government regulations, but it was discouraged in a number of ways. Police officers who married Chinese were not allowed to re-enlist after the expiration of their original five-year contract. Overseers in the Public Works Department and sanitary inspectors who married Chinese or Eurasians without the permission of the Governor were forbidden by regulation to occupy government quarters. Similar restrictions were imposed on prison warders.[10] The rationale for this discrimination was that Chinese or Eurasian women willing to marry Europeans generally came from the lowest social class and it was undesirable that officials whose job it was to enforce the law on the Chinese population should be open to influence by the relatives of their wives. There were also objections from European staff and their wives who did not wish to live in the same block of quarters as Chinese women. By the 1930s these administrative measures to discourage intermarriage were relaxed a little and subordinate staff who married Chinese were paid a rent allowance instead of being allocated government quarters, provided they had given at least four years' satisfactory service.[11]

In the higher ranks of the public service there were a few cases of officers marrying Chinese, but the practice was frowned upon, since it normally meant that such officers could not be promoted to a position in another colony. For example, in 1918 Dr Woodman applied to be transferred elsewhere. A Colonial Office official noted on his file that he was of average ability according to his confidential reports 'and his social position is not as good as it might be, largely bacause his wife is not of European origin. Reply discouragingly.'[12]

Localization of the Public Service

Chinese and European staff had their pay calculated on a different basis. In the nineteenth century all members of the public service had had their salaries fixed in dollars. But in the latter part of the century the Hong Kong dollar which, like the currency of China, was based on silver, depreciated against sterling, which was based on gold. This decline continued until 1916 when the value of silver suddenly began to increase. The lower value of the Hong Kong dollar particularly affected European staff, who received fewer pounds for their dollars when on leave and when remitting money to their families in Britain, and who had to pay more for goods imported from Europe. So they were at first compensated by being paid a special allowance in dollars in addition to their salaries. In 1904 the system was changed and all new European staff had their salaries denominated in pounds sterling. When on leave in Britain they drew their pay in pounds, but in Hong Kong their salaries were converted into dollars at a variable rate. In 1913 four-fifths was converted into dollars at a fixed rate of HK$11.40 to the pound and one-fifth at the current market rate. This system was changed by the 1919 Salaries Commission which recommended the conversion of the entire salary at a fixed rate of HK$10 to the pound. This scheme was further modified during the 1920s by the introduction of a sliding scale of conversion, the aim of which was to give European officers a relatively stable number of dollars independent of the fluctuations in the exchange rate, but with some benefit when the rate of exchange declined.

All Chinese and Portuguese from Macau had their salaries fixed in dollars, with the exception of three inspectors of vernacular schools in the Education Department. (The salary for these posts had originally been fixed in sterling and remained so when Chinese staff took over the positions. This anomaly was noticed and adversely commented on by the Retrenchment Committee of 1930, but it remained unaltered.)[13] Europeans, whether recruited locally or in Britain, were invariably given sterling salaries until the end of the 1920s. Thereafter a few were engaged in Hong Kong on local terms (in 1936 these totalled 52) and might be transferred to a sterling salary after a number of years.[14] The distinction between sterling-paid and dollar-paid officers did not disappear until 1948, when all salaries were put on a dollar basis.

No serious attempt was made to increase the number of posts held by local Chinese until the 1930s. Before then there was a surprising absence of any pressure for sinization from the unofficial members of the Legislative Council, including the Chinese members. The Colonial Office favoured more local appointments, primarily as a means of economizing on salaries, but little attempt was made to press the Hong Kong government to take any specific action. In 1923 Stubbs requested permission to engage graduates of the University of Hong Kong for posts in the Medical Department and the Public Works Department which carried an initial salary of less than HK$5,000 a year without the need to refer each individual case to London for approval.[15] The Colonial Office agreed to this request, but few such appointments were made. By 1930 there were 10 Chinese medical officers, all but one of whom had qualified locally. Their initial salary was HK$4,500 a year whereas a European doctor started at £700 (equivalent in 1930 to HK$10,266). The Education Department employed 30 Chinese graduate teachers, but the Public Works Department showed no desire to recruit local graduates; there were seven Chinese in the department earning over HK$4,000 a year in 1930, but all had reached their positions after long service in the lower ranks.

The desirability of replacing European staff by Chinese first became a public issue in 1930 after the publication of the Report of the Salaries Commission. This led to a great outcry from the public, and the unofficial members of the Legislative Council opposed the increased salaries proposed for public servants and the new taxes needed to finance them. In order to mollify the critics the Governor cut back some of the increases proposed by the commission and agreed to the appointment of a retrenchment committee, composed entirely of unofficials, to advise where economies could be made in the personnel and administration of the government. This committee carried out a thorough investigation of all departments and made detailed recommendations for reductions in staffing and for the replacement of Europeans by Chinese wherever possible. When forwarding these proposals to London the Governor, Sir William Peel, reported that he had already given instructions to heads of departments to take action along these lines. In 1932 three Chinese clerks were appointed to the Senior Clerical and Accounting Service for the first time, and arrangements were made to recruit six Chinese as probationary sanitary inspectors, a grade which had previously been open only to Europeans. In 1934 three Chinese with a secondary school education were engaged for training as sub-inspectors of police. Those on the first course proved unsatisfactory and their training was discontinued, but the experiment was renewed in 1936 with an intake of 10, and by 1939 the police force contained 36 Cantonese sub-inspectors. The number of Chinese graduates of the University of Hong Kong employed by the government increased from 40 in 1930 to 86 in 1936; 57 of these were in the Education Department, 25 were doctors, three were in the Public Works Department, and one was a railway engineer.[16]

Progress in replacing Europeans by local staff was slow, in spite of the pressures exerted by the Chinese and Portuguese members of the Legislative Council, who were increasingly vocal on this subject in the 1930s, and the support for sinization expressed by Governors from Sir William Peel onwards. European staff could not be dismissed to make way for Chinese before they reached retirement age, so vacancies arose only from natural wastage and from increases in the establishment of the public service as a whole. Over the period from 1930 to 1939 there was a small expansion in the total size of the public service, from 8,663 in 1930 to 10,004 in 1939, but the number of Europeans on sterling salaries decreased only slightly, from 956 to 889. Some heads of departments were reluctant to employ local staff: one strenuously resisted the Governor's demand in 1936 that newly trained Chinese staff should be used to replace his European inspectors and not, as he wished, to supplement them; and in 1939 a new Governor, Sir Geoffry Northcote, much to the surprise of the Colonial Office, supported a request from the Prisons Department that four additional European warders should be added to the establishment.[17]

The low salaries offered to local appointees in comparison with those paid to Europeans of the same grade may also have been a disincentive to local applicants. The disparity between European and Chinese rates of pay actually increased during the 1930s as a result of the depreciation of the Hong Kong dollar, but there was no suggestion from government or the unofficials during this time of financial stringency that the salaries of local officers should be raised towards European levels. One unofficial, Lo Man-kam, went so far as to deny that Chinese expected to receive salaries equal to those drawn by European officers, contradicting the Colonial Secretary who had made this assertion as an excuse for the slow pace of localization.[18] However, in 1938 the government did find it necessary to make an upward adjustment in the pay of certain Chinese medical officers in order to prevent them from resigning to go into private practice. Their maximum salary was increased to HK$10,800, but this was still below the starting salary for a European doctor of £700, which was then equivalent to HK$11,200.

The Cadet Service

There was never any question of accepting Chinese into the Hong Kong Cadet Service (since 1960 known as the Administrative Officer grade). From 1904 all candidates for Eastern cadetships in the Straits Settlements, the Malay States, and Hong Kong were required to be of pure European descent on both sides of the family in order to be eligible to take the civil service examination. The government of Ceylon permitted Ceylonese with British university degrees to sit the examination in London, and from 1920 one-third of all appointments to the Administrative Service in that colony were reserved for Ceylonese. Entry to the Malayan Civil Service was reserved for Europeans, as in Hong Kong, but a junior grade, the Malay Administrative Service, was instituted in 1910 for indigenous officers and some of these Malays were later promoted to the Malayan Civil Service. But no such opportunities were made available to Chinese in Hong Kong.[20]

Candidates for the Home Civil Service, the Indian Civil Service, and Eastern cadetships all took the same examinations in London. Those with the best results normally chose the Home Civil Service or India and the remaining examinees usually opted for Ceylon, Hong Kong, or Malaya, in that order of preference. In 1932, following the report of the Warren Fisher Committee of 1929, the examinations for Eastern cadetships were abolished and a unified Colonial Administrative Service was set up. Entry to this was on the basis of an interview and an extensive investigation of an applicant's background and character, a system which had been used to select administrative officers for the African colonies for many years. Most of the Hong Kong cadets had been educated at English public schools and had then gone on to Oxford or Cambridge.[21] Immediately after their arrival in Hong Kong they were sent to Canton for intensive language study for two years, taking examinations every six months. When they were fluent in spoken and written Cantonese, they took up their duties in the Hong Kong administration. After 1932 cadets also spent one year on a colonial service course in Britain before arriving in Hong Kong, so they did not commence work until three years after their appointment. On average two cadets were recruited each year between 1919 and 1939.

The cadets formed a small élite group. They numbered 26 in 1913, 38 in 1930, and 35 in 1939, but this figure includes the probationers doing language study in Canton and those on leave, normally one-fifth of the total at any one time. Cadets occupied most of the top positions in the government, filling all the senior posts in the Colonial Secretariat, the three police magistracies, and most headships of departments except for those that required specialist technical competence such as Public Works, the Railway, the Royal Observatory, Prisons, Audit, the Botanical and Forestry Department, the Medical Department, and the post of Harbour-master. Cadets served as Secretary for Chinese Affairs, Superintendent of Imports and Exports, Postmaster-General, head of the Sanitary Department, and as Attorney General (until 1930), Colonial Treasurer (until 1931), Superintendent of Police (until 1935), and Director of Education (until 1938). Some cadets read for the Bar while on leave and after their call a few went on, after serving as a magistrate or as Deputy Registrar of the Supreme Court, to appointment as a puisne judge.

In theory all senior posts in Hong Kong were open to officers throughout the colonial empire. When one of these positions held by a cadet fell vacant the Governor was required to report the vacancy to London, so that the Colonial Office could decide whether it should be filled by promoting an officer from another colony. But the Governor almost always recommended the promotion of a Hong Kong cadet, emphasizing the importance of filling the position with an officer who was fluent in Cantonese and had a knowledge of Chinese culture and traditions and the local political situation. Reference was also made to the grave effect on the morale of the cadet service and its attractiveness to future candidates if senior posts to which cadets had aspired in the past were given to outsiders.[22] (The adverse effect on the feelings of professional officers if the top post in their department was held by a cadet was not mentioned.)

Colonial Office officials were sceptical of such special pleading, but in fact only one administrative officer from another colony was transferred to Hong Kong in the period from 1913 to 1940. This occurred in 1926, soon after the arrival of a new Governor, Sir Cecil Clementi, who was himself a former cadet. Both the Colonial Secretary and the Assistant Colonial Secretary had been transferred out of Hong Kong and Clementi recommended the promotion to Hong Kong of W.T. Southorn, the Assistant Colonial Secretary of Ceylon, where Clementi had previously been stationed. The normal policy of the Colonial Office was to discourage Governors from nominating to high positions individuals who had previously served under them in another colony, but on this occasion the Promotions Committee in London decided to accept the Governor's recommendation after considering and rejecting other possible candidates.[23]

During the 1930s a number of posts which had customarily been occupied by cadets were taken over by professionally trained officers. After the institution of the unified Colonial Legal Service in 1933 cadets were no longer eligible for appointment as judges since they lacked the requirement which was then laid down of four years' practice at the Bar. In 1931 the post of Colonial Treasurer was filled by the transfer and promotion of E. Taylor, the Deputy Treasurer of Sierra Leone, on the retirement of C.M. Messer. This transfer was insisted on by the Colonial Office over the Governor's protests, after a long period of dissatisfaction with the management of the colony's finances.[24] When E.D.C. Wolfe retired as Inspector-General of Police in 1935 the Governor, Peel, recommended that the post should go to his deputy, T.H. King. King had served in the Hong Kong police force for 30 years since he joined it as a police probationer in 1904. The Colonial Office welcomed the Governor's proposal and quickly approved his appointment after only a cursory survey of senior police officers of comparable seniority in other colonies.[25] There was more difficulty over the appointment of a professional educationist to be Director of Education. The Advisory Committee on Education at the Colonial Office had commented adversely on the Hong Kong annual Education Reports for some years and in 1927 the Governor was advised of the desirability of filling the post of Director with an experienced educationist when it next fell vacant. However, when the post became vacant in 1932 the Governor put forward a cadet officer, N.L. Smith, stressing the need for the Director to be fluent in Cantonese and thoroughly

conversant with the local political situation, in view of the efforts
being made by the Kuomintang party to gain influence in the
vernacular schools. He added that the senior professional officers
in the department were unsuited for the post since they were either
close to retirement or lacked administrative experience. The Colonial
Office reluctantly agreed to Smith's promotion provided that he took
a course of study on educational methods in England during his next
period of leave. Fifteen months later Smith was moved to become
Secretary for Chinese Affairs and the Governor again recommended
a cadet, G.R. Sayer, to succeed him, giving the same reasons as
before. Officials were very unhappy about this, but were unwilling
to override the Governor or dispute his views about the competence
of the senior staff of the Education Department. So Sayer's
promotion was accepted, but the Governor was pressed to agree to
a visit by an expert from Britain to advise on the whole Hong Kong
education system. The Governor made no objection and an Inspector
of Schools, Mr E. Burney, visited Hong Kong and produced a
report which was published in 1935. In it he was particularly critical
of conditions in the vernacular schools and the short tenure of
recent Directors of Education, and recommended that a first-rate
educationist should be appointed to the vacant post of Senior
Inspector of Schools who would succeed to the Directorship on
Sayer's retirement. The Executive Council approved this proposal,
and C.G. Sollis was recruited from Malaya. He became Director of
Education in 1938.[26]

Comparatively few Hong Kong cadets were promoted out of the
colony. Three moved to Colonial Secretaryships elsewhere: Clementi
in 1913 to British Guiana, Fletcher in 1926 to Ceylon, and Grantham
in 1935 to Bermuda. Three others were transferred to other colonies,
presumably at their own request. Otherwise the Hong Kong cadet
service stayed a small close-knit group. Those holding senior positions
remained unchanged for long periods: Irvine was Director of
Education for 23 years, from 1901 to 1924; Hallifax was Secretary
for Chinese Affairs for 21 years, from 1912 to 1933; Wolfe was
Superintendent of Police for 17 years, from 1918 to 1935; Kemp was
Attorney General for 15 years, from 1915 to 1930; and Messer was
Colonial Treasurer for 13 years, from 1918 to 1931. After working
together in the same offices for decades on end, and living in close
proximity on the Peak, without any possibility of moving away to
administer remote provinces as was possible in Ceylon or Malaya,
it is very likely that their outlook would become rather narrow and

that they would be resistant to new ideas. Critics of the administration referred to its parochial outlook and profound conservatism. One official in London described Hong Kong in 1934 as 'the most self-satisfied of all the colonies, except Malaya'. Another criticism of the cadets was that they had little sympathy with the leaders of republican China and for the changes that had taken place there since 1911.[27] This probably applied particularly to those senior cadets whose outlook had been shaped by their studies in China before the revolution. The derogatory attitude displayed by the Hong Kong authorities towards the Kuomintang government of Sun Yat-sen and his successors in Canton embittered relationships in the 1920s and made the settlement of disputes between the two cities more difficult.

Salaries and Allowances

Until the 1930s, when a deliberate effort was made to standardize terms and conditions of employment, there was no unified colonial service throughout the Empire. Each colony had its own public service and paid its officials and provided allowances and pensions according to its own salary scales and local regulations. The conditions offered might be mean or generous depending on the relative wealth of the colony and the difficulty or ease it had experienced in attracting suitable staff. Thus the West African colonies, with their unhealthy climate and lack of amenities, were obliged to offer higher rates of pay and more frequent periods of leave than Hong Kong or Malaya in order to recruit the qualified staff that they needed.[28] The Colonial Office exercised some control, in that the Governor was forbidden by *Colonial Regulation* No. 283 to increase the number of public servants employed or to make any alteration in their rates of salary or other emoluments unless such changes had previously been sanctioned by the Secretary of State. This meant in practice that any alteration in the General Orders of the Hong Kong government with regard to such issues as rent allowances, leave entitlements, passages, or pensions had to be submitted to London for approval before it could be promulgated in the colony and the funds needed to pay for the change in service conditions could be included in the annual Estimates.

Normally the initiative for making any changes came from the colonial government. Sometimes the need for an increase in the establishment and changes in salaries or emoluments arose from a reorganization of the work of a department which was instituted by the Governor. He also received frequent representations from individuals or groups of officers complaining about their pay or allowances on the ground that the nature of their work had changed, or that more favourable terms of service were offered in other dependencies such as Malaya. From time to time petitions were drawn up and signed by discontented officials for submission to the Secretary of State. These were all forwarded to London along with the Governor's comments, sometimes explaining why no concessions were possible or desirable, or occasionally admitting the justice of the petitioners' case and proposing to make changes which went some way to meet their demands. Officials at the Colonial Office almost always accepted the Governor's views when drafting a reply to such petitions: they never suggested a more liberal response than the Governor proposed, even though they might on rare occasions express some sympathy with the petitioners' grievance, but they sometimes cut back the Governor's recommendations for an improvement in allowances on the ground that he was being too generous in the light of the colony's financial situation or the conditions offered in other colonies. For example, in response to a petition in 1926, Clementi proposed to allow officers of over 45 years of age to go on leave with full-passage allowances after three years of service instead of four. The Colonial Office demurred and insisted that, although such officers might be allowed to go on leave after three years, they should be required to pay one-eighth of the cost of their passages themselves if they did so.[29]

On the rare occasions when the Governor was overruled by the Colonial Office this was not the end of the matter. He could, and sometimes did, return to the charge with fresh arguments and if he persisted in maintaining his position officials in London would often give way. For example, in 1915 Sir Henry May sent a dispatch proposing to institute a system of rent allowances for senior officers who were not housed in government quarters. The Colonial Office rejected this on the ground that a scheme of rent allowances would only encourage private landlords to increase rents by an equivalent amount and so would give no relief to the officers whom it was intended to benefit. This had recently been the effect of a similar scheme instituted in Ceylon. So May was advised that it would be preferable to build more government quarters. May wrote back claiming that there was an absence of accessible building sites on the Peak, the only convenient area suitable for expatriates. He enclosed a memorandum written by the Director of Public Works which explained that any new developments would require the construction of expensive roads or tramways and that certain sites which might be developed were unsuitable since they were 'badly exposed to the afternoon sun'. The Colonial Office was unimpressed and suggested that a start should be made on a phased programme of building. In his next reply the Governor put forward proposals for the construction of 20 flats and asked that pending their completion he might be allowed to institute a system of rent allowances for the 100 senior officers concerned, who were suffering considerable hardship from the rising cost of living. At this point the Colonial Office gave way and agreed to the grant of allowances on a temporary basis until a general revision of salaries could be instituted when the First World War was over.[30]

The only occasion when the Colonial Office took the initiative in proposing a revision of salaries and allowances was in connection with the scheme for the setting up of a unified colonial service. Unification was recommended by the Warren Fisher Committee and was approved in principle by a conference of colonial governors held in London in 1930. The main features of the scheme were that in future all new entrants selected by the Colonial Office were appointed to the colonial service as a whole instead of to the public service of a particular colony; they were eligible to be considered for promotion to senior posts in the unified service in other colonies; and they accepted a liability to be transferred to another colony at the discretion of the Secretary of State, although an officer could refuse to be transferred if the pay and conditions of the new post were substantially worse than those attached to his present position. Apart from the provisions for compulsory transfer these changes were largely nominal and did no more than formalize existing practice. The Colonial Office was anxious to increase the scope for moving officers from one dependency to another but the main obstacle to this desirable interchange of staff was the many different rates of pay and allowances, the result of which was that the smallest and economically weakest colonies tended to offer the worst terms of service, and so were unable to attract the aspiring officers with the ability to tackle their problems. In order to meet this difficulty, a number of committees were set up in the Colonial Office to examine conditions of service and to make detailed proposals for the unification of the various branches of the colonial service such as the administrative, legal, medical, police, and other services. One committee under the Earl of Plymouth, the Parliamentary Under-

Secretary of State, examined the multiplicity of leave and passage regulations to be found in the 50 colonies and dependencies and drew up a set of principles which would be applicable throughout the colonial empire. These were then sent out to all Governors in 1935, inviting their observations and strongly suggesting the desirability of adopting the proposed framework with such local adaptations as might be necessary. The Hong Kong government decided that because of the prevailing financial stringency it could afford to do no more than make some trifling changes to its leave regulations, but it did take the opportunity to reduce the passage entitlements of certain officers in line with the committee's suggestions.[31] In 1936 the salary scales recommended for the unified Colonial Administrative Service were similarly notified to Hong Kong. The Governor, Sir Andrew Caldecott, declined to standardize local salaries on this basis as the colony was still suffering from an acute financial crisis. The new salary scales were adopted in the following year for the benefit of newly appointed cadets only.[32]

There were only two general revisions of salaries for the Hong Kong public service between the First and Second World Wars. There had been a marked rise in the cost of living during the First World War, estimated at around 30 per cent, and in 1918 the Colonial Office agreed to the Governor's proposal that a temporary 10 per cent bonus should be added to all salaries to give some immediate relief. As soon as hostilities were over, a local commission was appointed with the approval of the Colonial Office to enquire into the pay and emoluments of the public service. The commission consisted of the Chief Justice as chairman, two European unofficial members of the Legislative Council, another European business man, and a cadet. When it reported in March 1919 it recommended salary rises ranging from 12 to 30 per cent and radical changes in the system of official allowances.[33] While the commission was sitting, Sir Henry May resigned from the governorship and his successor, Sir Edward Stubbs, did not take up his appointment in Hong Kong until October. Stubbs recommended substantial changes in the report, modifying most of its proposals either up or down so that he practically rewrote the entire document. The Colonial Office deliberated at length and finally accepted almost all of Stubbs's revisions, although it returned to the commission's view on a few points.[34] The new salaries were incorporated in the Budget Estimates for 1921 and were passed without dissent. The colony was still enjoying a post-war boom, the opium revenues were high, and the unofficial members did not quibble over the rises of 20 to 30 per cent in public service salaries for which the officers had waited so long. These rises were not overgenerous, considering the estimate of the commission that the cost of living had risen by 50 per cent since the last salary revision in 1908.

By 1925 pressures were again growing within the service for a further rise. Colonial Office officials privately expressed some sympathy with these grumblings, being aware of the difficulty experienced in recruiting staff for Hong Kong at the existing salaries, but the fall in government revenues brought about by the strike and boycott of 1925–6 made any such revision impossible at that time. By 1928 the colony's finances had returned to surplus after three years of Budget deficits and the Governor, Sir Cecil Clementi, proposed the setting up of another salaries commission consisting of local business men under the chairmanship of the Chief Justice, along the lines of that of 1919. Colonial Office officials demurred, preferring the appointment of a full-time commissioner from Britain who could take a broader view than a local commission on the question of comparability with other colonies and the salaries needed to attract recruits. But Clementi, who was on leave in London, overbore the doubts of the officials by emphasizing the need for a speedy decision.[35] So the commission was set up locally in October 1928 and reported a year later. Unlike the 1919 commission it included one Chinese member, Sir Shou-son Chow, the senior Chinese unofficial on the Legislative Council.

The commission recommended an increase of approximately 20 per cent in the pay and allowances of Chinese employees and an increase of 15 per cent in the sterling salaries of European staff; the value of this increase locally was dependent on the rate of exchange between the Hong Kong dollar and the pound sterling. The Governor listened to various representations from the public service and outside bodies, proposed a number of minor modifications to the commission's report, and then sent it to the Colonial Office for approval. Officials there were not very happy with the report: they doubted the commission's estimate that the local cost of living had risen by 15 per cent since 1920 and feared that the cost of implementation would prove too heavy a burden for the Hong Kong finances. Several business firms and the China Association in London wrote directly to the Colonial Office complaining that the rises were unduly generous and that the additional taxation needed to pay for them would be insupportable at a time when trade was depressed. Never-

theless officials stifled their doubts and recommended acceptance
of the commission's proposals as modified by the Governor, deferring to the judgement of the local authorities. The Secretary of
State, Lord Passfield, agreed and a telegram was sent to Hong Kong
signifying approval.[36] In June 1930 the new salary scales were
endorsed by the Legislative Council by the use of the official
majority; none of the unofficial members voted in favour.

The main reason for the unofficial opposition, which had grown
rapidly after the publication of the commission's report, was the
depreciation in the value of the Hong Kong dollar against sterling.
One of the report's recommendations was that public servants on
sterling-denominated salaries should have their salary converted into
dollars at the current rate of exchange, or at a fixed rate of HK$10
to the pound if the dollar appreciated above this level. In fact the
dollar steadily declined in value from HK$10 to the pound at the
time when the commission reported to HK$13.30 to the pound by
January 1930 and had reached HK$16 to the pound when the report
was put to the vote in June. The government refused to believe that
this unprecedentedly low value would be maintained and gave an
estimate of the cost of the new salaries based on a rate of HK$13.30
to the pound. These hopes were too sanguine. When the Budget
Estimates were presented to the Legislative Council four months later
the rate of exchange was HK$15 to the pound, and to pacify the
unofficials the Governor accepted a suggestion from one of them
that sterling-paid officers should have only one-half of their salary
converted into dollars at the current rate and the other half at a fixed
rate of HK$13.30 to the pound.[37] The effect of this proposal would
be to reduce the number of dollars paid to European officers by 8
per cent. The Governor then asked the Colonial Office to approve
this change, pointing out that Europeans would still be receiving more
dollars then they had received before the salary revision. Officials
at the Colonial Office were divided: some were prepared to accept
the Governor's proposal in order to balance the budget; others,
including the head of the newly formed Personnel Branch, regarded
this as equivalent to a breach of faith on the government's part, since
no indication had been given in June that the sterling conversion
arrangements, which were an integral part of the commission's
report, were subject to revision at the government's discretion. The
Legal Adviser to the Colonial Office commented that colonial
officers, as servants of the Crown, had no legal right to complain
about any alteration in their pay or terms of service, but it would

be dishonourable for the government to breach the terms of a pay settlement only four months after it had been enacted. The issue went up for decision to the Secretary of State, Lord Passfield, who decided that the Governor must be overruled.[38]

Passfield's decision lasted only 10 days. The Governor, Sir William Peel, immediately telegraphed asking for the matter to be reconsidered, since the value of the dollar had now plunged to the unprecedentedly low level of more than HK$20 to the pound. This fall would impose an additional cost on the budget of HK$2,250,000 in respect of sterling salaries alone, unless some limit were placed on the rate of conversion.[39] This serious financial prospect over-bore the Colonial Office's concern to protect the conditions of employment of its servants. Passfield agreed to rescind his decision and the Governor was allowed to do as he wanted.

This decision satisfied the unofficial members of the Legislative Council, but it outraged the European public servants who suffered a cut in the pay they had enjoyed since the Salaries Commission report had been adopted. A petition signed by 552 officers was sent to the Secretary of State which stressed the unfairness of singling out the European public servants alone for a reduction in salary and emphasized the many possibilities available for raising taxation. Officials at the Colonial Office expressed considerable sympathy with the petitioners but advised the Secretary of State that the Governor should not be overridden, and the petitioners were so informed. This rebuff stimulated a further petition signed by 573 expatriate officers which reiterated the arguments that they had already put forward. At the same time a number of Members of Parliament were approached to take up the issue by questions to ministers and speeches in the House of Commons. This combined assault persuaded Lord Passfield to telegraph to the Governor in August 1931 that he considered that salary conversion at the market rate of exchange must be restored, unless this made it impossible to balance the budget. Peel replied giving details of the taxation increases that would be necessary and suggested that it would be sufficient to convert three-quarters of the salary at the current rate and one-quarter at a fixed rate of HK$13.30 to the pound. By this time the Labour government had fallen, but the incoming minister of the new National government, Sir Robert Hamilton, accepted the advice of his civil servants that Hong Kong could and should afford the cost. So in September 1931 Hong Kong was instructed that full convertibility must be restored from January 1932. The Governor did not attempt to argue further against the Colonial Office's decision.[40] As it happened the dollar began to strengthen against the pound from September, following the decision of the National government to go off the gold standard. By December the pound was worth HK$14.10. So ironically when full convertibility was restored in January 1932 as the public servants had wanted they in fact received fewer dollars in their pay, as a result of the depreciation of the pound, than they were receiving at the time of their protest.

For the next four years sterling salaries were converted at the current rate of exchange, subject to an upper limit of HK$10 to the pound and a lower limit of HK$20 to the pound. The Hong Kong dollar remained at a low value during 1932 and 1933 and then gradually appreciated until it reached HK$10 to the pound in the early months of 1935. Then in October 1935 Hong Kong followed China in going off the silver standard and the value of the dollar against sterling rapidly depreciated, dropping to HK$16 to the pound by December. This sudden drop in the exchange rate, which substantially increased the dollar cost of all payments fixed in sterling, made a large budget deficit inevitable. In September 1935 the acting Governor had already taken the precaution of securing permission from London to impose a levy on salaries if that should become necessary and the Colonial Office had reluctantly agreed. In January 1936 the new Governor, Sir Andrew Caldecott, submitted detailed proposals for a salary levy on all except the lowest-paid officers, together with a scheme for all sterling salaries to be converted at four different rates during each quarter of 1936. These rates gave sterling-paid officers more dollars to the pound than they had received in the first 10 months of 1935 but fewer than they were entitled to at the current exchange rate from November onwards. The quarterly adjustments were intended to take account of the expected rise in the cost of living as the cheaper dollar worked its effect on local prices. These changes in the conversion rate had not been foreshadowed when the acting Governor wrote in September, but on this occasion the Colonial Office raised no objection; instead officials concentrated on the details of the incidence of the salary levy, but their questions and criticisms did not persuade Caldecott to modify his proposals.[41] The rates at which the salary levy was imposed were reduced in July 1936 and January 1937, and the levy was finally abolished in June 1937. The Colonial Office pressed the Governor to make larger reductions in the salary levy and to abolish it earlier, but Caldecott declined to be deflected from the path of financial caution either by suggestions from London or the complaints of public servants in Hong Kong. By October 1936 the conversion rate for sterling salaries and the current rate of exchange had coincided, so the conversion rate was then fixed at HK$16 to the pound and remained at this level thereafter.

On this as on all other occasions the initiative for instituting a review of salary scales came from the Governor and his views determined the final outcome. Changes in the conversion rate for European salaries, which could have much the same effect as a salary rise or a salary levy, were also invariably proposed by the Governor. The most important curb on the Governor's freedom of action was not the Colonial Office, which generally accepted his views after a period of anxious cogitation, but the political need to pay attention to the views of the business community and the taxpayers. In 1919 and 1928 the Governor attempted to pre-empt their opposition by giving local business men membership of the Salaries Commission, thereby ensuring that they had a major voice in determining the details of salary increases that were generally agreed to be necessary. These tactics worked in 1920, but not in 1930. Faced with the extraordinary currency fluctuations of the 1930s, successive Governors chose to cut public service salaries by manipulating the exchange rate at which sterling salaries were paid or by a straight salary levy rather than offend the business community through a steep rise in taxation. The Colonial Office always acquiesced in the Governor's proposals, except in 1931 when officials felt that the Hong Kong government had been guilty of a breach of faith with its employees and forced the abandonment of an artificial exchange rate rather sooner than the Governor wished.

Appointments, Promotions, and Dismissals

The most important control exercised by the Colonial Office was that over appointments, promotions, and dismissals in all the colonial territories. Colonial Regulations laid down that appointments to vacancies in the public service could be made by the Governor only when the applicant was resident in the colony and the initial salary of the post was less than £400 a year. When the initial salary was less than £200, the Governor's decision was final.[42] In the case of offices with an initial salary between £200 and £400 the appointment had to be reported to London in a quarterly return for approval, but in practice the Governor's decision was never questioned. If the post was to be filled by recruitment in Britain the selection of candidates was made by the Colonial Office, except for technical staff, who were chosen by the Crown Agents, and teachers who were chosen by the Board of Education. The Governor of Hong Kong was permitted as a special concession to offer graduates of the University of Hong Kong who were resident in the colony employment in posts carrying an initial salary over £400 a year without reference to the Colonial Office, but he could not recruit European residents to such posts.[43] At most he could engage them temporarily on a provisional basis and then report the matter to London, where officials would check their qualifications and send for testimonials before the appointment was sanctioned or, as very rarely happened, was refused.[44]

When a vacancy occurred in a senior post carrying a salary of over £400 a year the Governor was required to report the vacancy immediately to London. Such posts were almost invariably filled by promotion from within the colonial service. The Governor might appoint an officer to act temporarily in the post, but the decision on whether to confirm the acting appointment or to offer the position to an officer from another colony was entirely a matter for the Secretary of State. In practice, in all but the most senior posts, the decision was taken by a Promotions Committee composed of senior Colonial Office officials who considered the merits of qualified officers of appropriate seniority throughout the dependent territories on the basis of the annual confidential reports sent to London by the Governors. Such vacant positions were not advertised. It was open to officers to write in to the Colonial Office offering their services if they came to hear of a vacancy in another colony, but such applications had no discernible effect on the process of selection. When reporting a vacancy the Governor usually recommended the promotion of an officer in the department concerned; occasionally he specifically asked that an officer from outside should be selected if he was satisfied that there was no one suitable in the department. For example, in 1928, and again in 1937, when the post of Director of Medical and Sanitary Services was about to become vacant by retirement, the Governor asked the Colonial Office to find a replacement from elsewhere. But, whatever the Governor said, the Colonial Office always drew up a list of potential candidates from other colonies and the decision as to who should be offered the post was taken by the Promotions Committee. Although officers were appointed to the public service of a particular colony the possibility of promotion to senior posts elsewhere was one of the attractions of the colonial service, and this was specifically mentioned in all offers of appointment made after the unification of the colonial service was agreed in 1930. Offers of promotion could be, and sometimes were, refused. Often this was because the salary and allowances attached to the new post were less in total than those attached to the officer's existing position. In some cases there might be several refusals, so that the Promotions Committee would eventually find itself obliged to offer the position to the local officer put forward by the Governor. Thus in 1930 a local barrister, C.G. Alabaster, recommended by the Governor, was appointed to the post of Attorney General only after three other lawyers in Nigeria, Kenya, and Ceylon had all turned down the offer.[45] When such an appointment occurred, the Governor's judgement on the relative merits of the local candidates was never overridden, even on the occasions when he recommended the supersession of a senior officer by his junior, or the promotion of a cadet to the headship of a department over the head of the senior professional officer.

The Colonial Office also exercised strict control over the termination of officers' appointments. The Governor was empowered to dismiss on his own authority only those officers who were earning less than £200 a year, and even in these cases the officer might appeal to the Colonial Office for the decision to be reviewed. In the case of an officer earning more than £200, Colonial Regulations required that the matter should be fully investigated by a committee of the Executive Council. If dismissal was recommended, the conclusion had to be considered by the full Executive Council and the officer might then be suspended from duty while the report of the committee was transmitted to London. The Colonial Office could then confirm, vary, or annul the penalty proposed. The Governor was also empowered to recommend to the Colonial Office that an officer should be removed on the grounds of general inefficiency.[46] In such a case the Executive Council was not consulted. All cases were carefully scrutinized by Colonial Office officials, but the decision taken by the Hong Kong government was almost invariably confirmed. In two instances the Governor's view was upheld even though it had not received the support of the Executive Council. In 1912 a band of pirates made a night attack on the police station on Cheung Chau, killed three Indian police constables, and stole HK$1,000 in tax revenues held in the station safe together with a quantity of firearms. The Superintendent of Police, F.J. Badeley, was held to be responsible for the outrage since he had allowed the European sergeant in charge and other police to sleep away from the station, but the Executive Council disagreed as to the penalty to be imposed. Only the Governor and the Colonial Secretary were in favour of compulsory retirement, but the Governor rejected the majority view of the Council and recommended to the Colonial Office that Badeley should be required to retire, if he could not be transferred to another colony. Officials and the Secretary of State supported the Governor's view and Badeley was told to resign. Similarly in 1916 the Colonial Office confirmed the Governor's proposal that the Secretary to the Sanitary Board should be dismissed from the service for drunkenness and absence from duty, despite the fact that a majority of the Executive Council had voted against this penalty being imposed.[47]

However, there were at least three occasions when the Governor's view was not accepted. In 1916 Sir Henry May asked the Colonial Office to retire the headmaster of Queen's College on the grounds of general inefficiency. The Colonial Office scrutinized the evidence submitted in the dispatch and decided that the reports on his conduct by the Director of Education were insufficient to justify compulsory retirement. May was unwilling to accept this decision and requested that the headmaster, who was then on leave, should be subjected to 'a severe medical examination as to his physical fitness to perform the duties of a headmaster, a post which requires much energy'. This was done, but the physician to the Colonial Office declined to co-operate with May's evident desire to be rid of Mr Dealy and pronounced him fit to return and carry out his duties.[48] The two other instances were very minor. In 1932 the Colonial Office confirmed the dismissal of a Eurasian clerk, but modified the financial penalty of a reduction in his gratuity which had also been imposed. In 1935 the Colonial Office allowed a Chinese foreman who was being retired for inefficiency to retain his full pension.[49]

6 Finance

THE Hong Kong government has always had difficulty in finding sufficient sources of revenue to finance its activities. The colony has no natural resources such as minerals or agricultural products which could be taxed by levies on exports. In other colonies tariffs on imports and exports provided a major source of revenue, but this expedient was impossible in Hong Kong because the very reason for Hong Kong's existence was the entrepôt trade through its harbour, which depended on its status as a free port.[1] An incomes tax was considered to be impossible, because of the united opposition of the Chinese and European business men and the practical difficulties of elucidating the accounts of Chinese businesses in order to make a fair assessment of the incomes of individuals and companies. The possibility of imposing an incomes tax was briefly considered and rejected in 1916, and thereafter the question was not again made the subject of a serious investigation until a committee was appointed in December 1938.[2] By this time Hong Kong, the Gold Coast, and the Straits Settlements were the only important British colonies where a tax on incomes did not exist in some form.

In 1912 the largest and most dependable source of revenue was the rates levied on urban property, then known as the 'assessed taxes'. In that year they yielded HK$1,495,290 or 18.3 per cent of a total government revenue of HK$8,180,694.[3] All buildings were reassessed annually and the percentage of the rate was based on the services provided in particular areas. The maximum percentage, which was levied in the central district of Hong Kong island, was 13 per cent, comprising 8.75 per cent for the presence of police patrols, 1.5 per cent for street lighting, 2 per cent for a filtered water supply, and 0.75 per cent for the services of the fire brigade. This system remained in force until 1931 when the various percentages (apart from a 2 per cent deduction where piped water was not provided) were consolidated into a single charge, on the ground that the differential provision of services was already reflected in the rents charged, and hence in the rateable value, of property in particular areas.[4] However, the old formula is still recalled when the Chinese refer colloquially to the rates as *'chai heung'* (literally 'police food money'). Revenue from the rates increased steadily over the next 30 years as more houses were built, rents were raised, and outlying areas such as Tsuen Wan were brought under assessment. There was only one general increase in the rates during the period 1912 to 1939; that was in 1930 when the standard percentage was raised from 13 to 17 per cent. In 1939 the government received HK$5,987,126 from the rates, amounting to 16.3 per cent of its total revenue.

The next largest item of revenue in 1912 was the rent paid by the farmer who held the government opium contract, which amounted to HK$1,183,000 and provided 14.5 per cent of government revenue. Apart from opium the only other vice or luxury that was taxed was alcohol. Duties on imported liquor and an excise tax on Chinese wines and spirits distilled in the colony were first imposed in 1909 to compensate for an anticipated decline in the rent paid by the opium farmer after the opium divans were closed down on instructions from London. In fact liquor duties yielded HK$705,574 in 1912, nearly three times the reduction in the opium contract. Taxes on alcohol, together with the revenue of HK$238,000 from the licence fees for public houses and restaurants, provided 11.5 per cent of government revenue. In 1912 there were no duties on tobacco. These were first introduced in 1916 and the rates of duty were successively raised in 1921, 1930, and 1931. In 1931 revenue from tobacco surpassed that from opium for the first time and continued to increase throughout the 1930s, at a time when the income from opium practically disappeared. In 1939 government revenue from the rates, opium, liquor, and tobacco provided 40 per cent of the government's funds, compared to 44 per cent from rates, liquor, and opium in 1912.

Revenue from the sale of land leases made only a very small contribution to government revenue in 1912: HK$163,784, or 2 per cent of revenue. Land sales were very volatile: during the boom years of the early 1920s sales soared to a peak of HK$3,488,300 in 1923 (14 per cent of revenue), a record figure which was not reached again until after the Second World War. After 1923 they dropped back to a low point of HK$143,683 in 1927, less than 1 per cent of revenue. A more dependable source were the rents from the leases of Crown land and other government property. These provided HK$873,732 in 1912, 10.7 per cent of revenue. Unfortunately this was not a very buoyant source, since rents were generally low and were fixed in most cases for a period of 75 years. By 1938 the revenue had little more than doubled to HK$1,899,215, which then amounted to only 5.1 per cent of revenue.

A further 10 per cent of revenue in 1912 came from the various

Table 3   The Main Sources of Revenue, 1912–1939

	1912 (%)	1921 (%)	1930 (%)	1939 (%)
Rates on property	18.3	13.2	15.1	16.3
Opium monopoly	14.5	22.2	10.2	2.5
Liquor duties and licences	11.5	7.4	7.5	5.6
Tobacco duties	—	6.0	9.4	15.3
Sales of land leases	2.0	9.2	10.3	5.2

Sources: Blue Books and *Estimates of Revenue and Expenditure* (annual).

commercial and semi-commercial undertakings of government, the post office, the Kowloon–Canton Railway and the waterworks. The remaining 33 per cent came from a long list of miscellaneous licences, fees, charges, and dues which seemed to cover practically every imaginable trade and activity, from auctioneers' licences to undertakers' licences, from Sunday cargo-working permits to fees for the medical examination of emigrants. The largest single item was stamp duties (HK$1,151,312, or 14 per cent of revenue) which also included the yield from estate duties. The rates of estate duty were fairly low: in 1912 the maximum charge was 8 per cent on estates valued at over HK2.5 million. The top rate was raised to 12 per cent in 1931 and to 20 per cent in 1936. Nevertheless the occasional death of a multimillionaire could have a very noticeable effect on government finances: in 1933 the portion of the estate of the shipping magnate, Lord Inchcape, which was invested in Hong Kong yielded HK$1,812,140 (5.6 per cent of that year's revenue). One other minor but unusual source of income was the conservancy contract for the sale of the colony's night-soil to China, where it was used as agricultural fertilizer. This brought in HK$76,800 in 1912, 1 per cent of revenue.

The main sources of revenue during the period 1912 to 1939 are shown in percentage terms in Table 3.

On the expenditure side of the government accounts the largest item was the military contribution paid to the British government towards the cost of the British army garrison. This contribution had been fixed in 1900 at 20 per cent of the gross revenue of the colony after the deduction of certain specified items such as the premiums on the sale of land leases, contributions paid by government officers to the widows and orphans pensions fund, and the expenditure of certain productive undertakings such as the Kowloon–Canton Railway and (after 1914) the government opium monopoly. These enterprises were assessed at 20 per cent of net receipts, but no deductions were allowed for the post office and the waterworks, since these enterprises had been in operation before 1900. In most years the military contribution covered less than half of the actual cost of the garrison; the only years when the contribution actually exceeded the cost were 1917–18 and 1918–19 when the garrison was unusually small because of the demands of the First World War in Europe; at the same time the rate of exchange between the Hong Kong dollar and sterling was exceptionally high.

The size of this contribution to the imperial treasury was a frequent subject of complaint by the unofficial members of the Legislative Council as being an onerous and unjustifiable burden on the colony's finances. It was pointed out that the Hong Kong garrison was maintained not solely for the colony's defence but also as a reserve force for imperial purposes in China, such as the defence of the International Settlement in Shanghai, and it was claimed that Hong Kong was forced to pay out a greater portion of its revenue for defence than practically any other colony. In 1911 and 1913 the unofficial members proposed motions in the Legislative Council objecting to the payment which were defeated only by the use of the official majority.[5] In public successive Governors defended the reasonableness of the contribution, but in confidential dispatches to the Colonial Office they emphatically supported the unofficials' complaints and inveighed against the extravagance of the military establishments in the colony. Stubbs in particular castigated 'the apparent desire of the War Office to make two colonels grow where one grew before' and grumbled that 'acres of some of the best building land in the heart of the city are merely dotted here and there with insignificant buildings and a large area in the best part of Kowloon is sparsely inhabited by mules'.[6] The Colonial Office privately sympathized with such views: one minute refers to 'the inequity of the extortion to which the Eastern Colonies are subjected'. But the formula for the assessment of the military contribution had been fixed by an agreement between the War Office, the Colonial Office, and the Treasury in 1900, and the Colonial Office could do nothing to help Hong Kong without the concurrence of the other departments.

From time to time Governors of Hong Kong put forward

suggestions for marginal modifications of the formula, or for a completely new method of assessment. In 1926 Clementi proposed that the contribution should be fixed at 12.5 per cent of the entire rateable value of the colony. Calculations were made which showed that this method would have significantly reduced the sum paid to Britain in a number of the preceding years, so the War Office naturally rejected the proposal. They also suspected that the Hong Kong government might succumb to the temptation to underassess property values, if most of the revenue from the rates was destined to go to the British government. Clementi then tried to have certain items of revenue excluded from the assessment on the ground that they should properly be regarded as municipal revenue, pointing out that in the Straits Settlements the revenue of the municipality of Singapore was excluded from the military assessment. But the War Office promptly replied that this had already been taken into account when the colony's contribution had been fixed in 1900; if such items were to be excluded from the assessment then the percentage would have to be adjusted upwards to compensate. The Treasury and the War Office were at most prepared to accept minor adjustments in the system, for example by allowing the expenditure on new productive undertakings such as the wireless telegraphy service and the revenue raised to pay the servicing charges on new loans to be deducted from the government's total revenue before the 20 per cent contribution was assessed. Such arguments over the detailed application of the formula laid down in 1900 led to protracted and sometimes acrimonious correspondence between the Colonial Office and the War Office, which usually produced only trifling concessions.[7]

The Hong Kong government tried by every legitimate means to reduce the revenue assessable for the military contribution and these efforts had a distorting effect over the whole field of government accounting. A particular example of this was the system (which still exists) whereby Crown leases were sold for a high cash premium and a nugatory annual Crown rent was charged. This had the desirable effect, from the colony's point of view, of maximizing the capital revenue from premiums, which was not assessable for the military contribution, and minimizing the rental income, which was so assessed.[8] Another objection to the military contribution system was that it provided a convenient argument against any expansion of the sphere of government activity. If ever consideration was given to raising additional taxation in order to provide for a new or expanded government service, for example to increase grants for education or to implement a rise in public service salaries, it was necessary to raise an extra 25 per cent over and above the estimated cost of the new service in order to provide for the extra defence contribution that was thereby incurred. This additional burden on the taxpayer, which brought no benefit at all to the colony, could be used by the unofficial members as an argument against any new government spending proposals.[9]

In spite of these and similar objections, the system continued to operate until 1938 when the new Financial Secretary, Sydney Caine, proposed that in future Hong Kong should pay a fixed sum for the military contribution, which would be subject to reassessment every five years. Caine had been an official at the Colonial Office for 10 years and was well aware of the objections which had caused the rejection of Clementi's proposal of 1926. He therefore suggested that the annual sum should be fixed for the first five years at HK$6,000,000, an amount greater than that paid in any year prior to 1938. The War Office and the Treasury were quick to accept this apparently generous offer from Hong Kong, and the long-standing argument over the contribution was finally settled. In fact Hong Kong's proposal was very finely calculated: the colony's revenue was rising rapidly at the time as a result of the Sino-Japanese War and in consequence the payment to His Majesty's Government in 1939 and 1940 was considerably less than it would have been if the contribution had been worked out under the old formula.[10]

Apart from the military contribution most of the rest of the Budget in 1912 was spent on the running of the government machine: general administration took 10 per cent; law and order (the courts, the Legal Department, the police, the fire brigade, and the prisons) took 14 per cent; servicing the public debt and the payment of pensions to retired public servants accounted for 13 per cent; while government commercial undertakings (the post office and the Kowloon–Canton Railway) took 7 per cent. The Public Works Department spent a quarter of the budget: 10 per cent covered staff costs and the maintenance of existing buildings, roads, and reservoirs, and 15 per cent went on new construction, which was known as Public Works, extraordinary. This item in the Estimates showed the greatest variation over the years. When revenue was buoyant the government embarked on large new projects; when revenue fell this was the area where it was easiest to economize. Expenditure on social services, by the most generous interpretation, absorbed 11 per cent of the

Table 4   The Distribution of Government Expenditure by Function, 1912–1939

	1912 (%)	1921 (%)	1930 (%)	1939 (%)
Defence	19.7	14.7	14.1	20.0
General administration	10.5	14.2	19.7	14.2
Law and order	13.8	13.3	14.0	14.4
Public debt and pensions	12.6	8.1	9.5	10.6
Commercial undertakings (post office, the railway, and so on)	7.0	8.9	4.7	5.4
Public works, recurrent expenditure	10.6	10.1	12.8	11.3
Public works, extraordinary	14.6	19.4	10.1	4.8
Education	3.4	5.0	7.3	6.6
Medical and health	3.0	2.4	4.2	6.5
Sanitary services	4.5	3.4	3.1	3.1
Grants to charities and voluntary agencies	0.3	0.5	0.5	3.1

Note: Grants to the University of Hong Kong are included under 'Education'.

Sources: Blue Books and Estimates of Revenue and Expenditure (annual).

Budget: education took 3.4 per cent, which was largely spent on 13 government schools; the Medical Department took 3 per cent, which was mainly spent on four government hospitals; and 4.5 per cent was spent on street cleaning and public health by the Sanitary Department. Grants to voluntary agencies and charities came to a mere 0.3 per cent. As can be seen from Table 4, these percentages varied very little over the next 20 years, apart from the large fluctuations in the allocation to the Public Works Department. By 1939 social services expenditure had increased to 19.3 per cent of the Budget, and in this total grants to voluntary agencies had gone up to 3.1 per cent.

The control exercised by the Colonial Office over a colony's expenditure was, formally speaking, absolute, and could be extended down to the minutest detail. The Colonial Regulations laid down that the authority for incurring any expenditure consisted of a formal vote or enactment by the colony's Legislative Council and the sanction of the Secretary of State. The Governor was forbidden to make any addition to the fixed establishment of the colony, or to alter the rates of salary or emoluments of any officer without the previous sanction of the Secretary of State; nor was he permitted to propose the execution of any important public work to the

Legislative Council unless such sanction had already been obtained. The annual Estimates of Revenue and Expenditure were required to be submitted to London after their passage through the Legislative Council in sufficient time to allow them to be considered in detail by the Colonial Office and receive the Secretary of State's assent before the beginning of the new financial year. If any additional sums were needed during the financial year the Governor was obliged to obtain the agreement of the Legislative Council and the Secretary of State before such expenditure was incurred.[11] This requirement was only waived when the payment was of a casual or non-recurrent nature and cost no more than HK$1,200 (at the time equivalent to approximately £150). This limit was fixed in 1916 and being so low it was in practice often ignored: sometimes requests for the retrospective approval of sums of HK$50,000 or more were submitted to the Colonial Office in the 'Quarterly Returns of Unforeseen Expenditure' months after the money had been spent. Such cavalier disregard of the *Colonial Regulations* was intermittently the subject of criticism in the annual audit report. In 1930 the limit was raised to HK$10,000 (equivalent to £625), when the Governor pointed out that the limit set for Hong Kong was far lower than that in other colonies with similar budgets. But at the same time the Governor was warned that in view of this concession he would be expected to observe the limit more carefully in future. In 1935 the Governor asked for the limit to be raised further but the Colonial Office refused, pointing out that it should normally be possible to obtain the necessary authority beforehand if the details were sent to London by airmail, and that in a real emergency the Governor might authorize the expenditure and then obtain covering sanction immediately afterwards.[12]

As a consequence of these regulations the Colonial Office received numerous requests to approve individual items of expenditure. In some cases they were for payments to be made in the current financial year to meet needs which had not been foreseen when the Estimates were drawn up; in other cases they related to the next financial year and were put to the Colonial Office for approval before being inserted in the annual Estimates. This procedure was normally followed in the case of some new or unusual item of expenditure in order to anticipate questions that might be raised when the Estimates were being examined and so avoid delays in their approval. Assent to any to these requests was never automatic. Colonial Office officials could and did raise queries, ask for additional information, and even occasionally refused permission to spend. Such refusals would have been a little less rare if the junior clerks at the Colonial Office, who wrote the first minute on the file, had had their way. More senior officials generally accepted the Governor's proposals, citing precedents where such payments had been allowed in other colonies, for example when sanctioning a small grant to be made to a sports club for junior staff.[13] But Governors were not invariably successful: for instance in 1913 the Colonial Office refused permission for the District Officer, New Territories, to live rent free in his bungalow at Tai Po; and in 1938 a proposal from the Director of Education to create a new post of music master at a government school was rejected, on the ground that Hong Kong could not afford any unnecessary expenditure at that time. Other proposals were sometimes arbitrarily reduced: in 1912 May asked if the Hong Kong government could be allowed to spend HK$14,000 a year to establish a medical professorship at the new University of Hong Kong, but the Colonial Office decided this was far too extravagant and cut the figure down to HK$10,000; and in 1939 the Colonial Office objected to a grant of HK$50,000 to the newly formed Hong Kong Tourist Association and consented to the expenditure for such a grant only when the amount was reduced to HK$10,000.[14]

New expenditure proposals might also be inserted in the annual Appropriation Bill without previous sanction from London, although such proposals usually entailed fairly minor changes only. The Draft Estimates for the next financial year were normally submitted to the Legislative Council in September and at the same time a copy was sent to London. By the time the Colonial Office began its examination of the Budget the bill had normally been passed and it was then too late for London to ask for individual items of expenditure to be deleted. In theory the Secretary of State was entitled to exercise the power of disallowance to repeal the Appropriation Ordinance in its entirety, but it would then be impossible to pass a new Budget through the Legislative Council before the end of the financial year on 31 December. So the Budget had to be accepted as it was, in order to avoid financial chaos. There was only one occasion when the Colonial Office objected to a particular item of expenditure and instructed the Governor not to spend the sum which had been approved by the legislature. This was in the Budget for 1930 when the unofficials had unanimously opposed the provision of HK$25,000 to set up a division of the Royal Naval Volunteer Reserve in Hong Kong. The Governor, Clementi, persuaded the unofficials to leave the provision in the Budget on condition that he reported their views to London. In these circumstances the Colonial Office decided that the new unit should not be established.[15] The Hong Kong government seems sometimes to have taken advantage of the Colonial Office's unwillingness to object to individual items in the Estimates when it wished to embark on some new item of expenditure which was not certain to receive Colonial Office approval. For example in 1921 Stubbs did not ask for special permission to make loans from the colony's surplus balances to officers to enable them to build or buy their own quarters, but instead included the item in the Budget proposals, where it passed unnoticed. This failure to obtain permission was only remarked in 1933 when Peel wished to make similar loans and punctiliously asked for the requisite approval beforehand.[16]

The examination of the annual Estimates in the Colonial Office was the most rigorous check on the financial policies of the Hong Kong government. Officials commented on them in exhaustive detail, although in practice they rarely discovered any point which had not already been mentioned during the Budget Debate in the Legislative Council. After 1930 they were also examined by the newly appointed Financial and Economic Adviser to the Colonial Office, Sir John Campbell. Ministers were hardly ever involved with this exercise. The resulting official view on the Budget and the future financial policy that should be followed was sent to the Governor in January when he was formally notified that the Appropriation Ordinance would not be disallowed. The *Colonial Regulations* laid down that the annual revenue and expenditure should be conservatively estimated and that in ordinary circumstances total estimated expenditure should not exceed the estimated revenue. The Colonial Office went further than this to advise the desirability of running a surplus in order to build up the colony's reserve funds. In 1928 it was suggested that ideally the reserves should be equal to a year's expenditure. In fact this figure was never achieved. Reserves reached a high point of nearly HK$16 million in 1923 at the height of the land boom (approximately 65 per cent of revenue in that year), but with the effects of the strike and boycott of 1925–6 they quickly plunged to HK$3.5 million at the end of 1926. They were then gradually rebuilt. In the 1930s the Colonial Office accepted the more modest aim of a minimum reserve of HK$10 million, equivalent to four months' revenue.

Another lever to exercise control over the colony's finances was the power to refuse permission to raise a loan. Loans were authorized by an ordinance passed by the Legislative Council and the Colonial Office had to agree the amount of the loan, the terms on which it should be raised, and the schedule of public works to be constructed with the funds obtained. In practice the terms of any loan were decided in the light of market conditions in London or Hong Kong as advised by the Crown Agents in London and the Hongkong and Shanghai Banking Corporation locally. Two loans were floated in the years between the First and Second World Wars, both on the Hong Kong market: HK$5,000,000 at 6 per cent in 1927 and 1928 and HK$14,000,000 at 3.5 per cent in 1934. It was Colonial Office policy that in established colonies loans should only be raised to pay for productive undertakings which might be remunerative in future, such as the construction of Kai Tak airport or new waterworks. Accordingly the Colonial Office initially refused permission for Hong Kong to build a new gaol at Stanley out of loan funds. But the Governor persisted in putting this item forward, pointing out that the estimated cost of HK$4,500,000 was too great to finance out of current revenue. The Colonial Office finally agreed that a sum for this construction could be included in the schedule of the 1934 loan, though insisting that the item should be subject to reconsideration if sufficient surplus revenue was available at some future date.[17] In fact the matter was never raised again.

The stress laid by Colonial Office officials on the need to balance the Budget and build up the reserves was intended to safeguard the colonies from the danger that they might be forced to apply to the Treasury for a Grant in Aid in order to meet their commitments. This was a very disagreeable situation to be in, since it meant that the colony's Estimates had to be submitted to the Treasury in London before presentation to the Legislative Council, so that they could be drastically pruned in order to reduce or eliminate the cost to the British taxpayer. During the slump of the 1930s many colonies were forced to go to the Treasury for assistance in this way. Hong Kong was fortunate to avoid this fate in the 1930s, though it came very close to it in 1936. The only time this century when Hong Kong finances were placed under Treasury control was in the years 1945–7, immediately after the end of the Japanese occupation.

Governors were less worried about the dangers of running deficits than the Colonial Office, and the colony's reserves were frequently drawn down to finance expenditure in anticipation of being able to replenish them in future by the floating of a loan. As a result the amount of money actually available in the surplus balances to cover a deficit on current expenditure was normally far below the nominal assets of the colony. For example, in October 1937, over HK$10,000,000 had been advanced out of the surplus balances, which nominally stood at about HK$12,000,000, leaving actual liquid reserves of only HK$2,000,000. This situation worried Colonial Office officials, who suggested the need for immediately raising a new loan. But the Governor, Northcote, demurred, pointing out that revenue was in fact coming in very satisfactorily in excess of the Budget Estimates as a result of the Sino-Japanese war.[18] There was never any shortage of arguments to justify a deficit Budget; these included the surplus achieved in the previous financial year, the healthy state of the reserves, the backlog of essential public works, or the difficulty in raising taxation in a year when trade was depressed. Of the 27 Budgets submitted for the years 1913 to 1939, 24 estimated a deficit and only three expected a surplus. These last were the Budgets for the years 1918 to 1920. (The out-turns for the financial years were in fact much better than this: 18 years ended with a surplus and only nine with deficits.) The revenue and expenditure of the Hong Kong government for the years 1912 to 1939 are given in Table 5.

The most enterprising Governor in this respect was Stubbs. In his first four Budgets, submitted for the years 1921 to 1924, he budgeted for deficits of HK$2 million, HK$3 million, HK$4 million, and HK$3.5 million respectively, although in fact he achieved substantial surpluses in the first three years. Stubbs had been an official at the Colonial Office for 13 years before he left to become Colonial Secretary in Ceylon in 1913 and the Colonial Office was prepared to trust his judgement. But when in September 1924 he put in a Budget with an estimated deficit of HK$8.6 million for 1925 even his former colleagues became worried and suggested that the public works vote might be cut by perhaps HK$2 million. Stubbs immediately sent back a dispatch defending his programme in detail: Hong Kong was developing rapidly and as soon as affairs in China had settled down the colony would enter upon an era of unparalleled prosperity; the public works were either essential for good administration or public health, or were proposals for roads or reclamation work which would soon pay for themselves by the consequent sale of land for new buildings. Stubbs followed up this dispatch with a personal letter to the Deputy Permanent Under-Secretary, Sir Gilbert Grindle: 'If you can't share my view on this

Table 5   The Revenue and Expenditure of the Hong Kong Government, 1912-1939 (HK$)

	Revenue	Expenditure	Surplus/Deficit
1912	8,180,694	7,202,543	+ 978,151
1913	8,512,308	8,658,012	− 145,704
1914	11,007,283	10,756,224	+ 251,059
1915	11,786,107	15,149,268	− 3,363,161
1916	13,833,386	11,079,914	+ 2,753,472
1917	15,068,105	14,091,000	+ 977,105
1918	18,665,248	16,252,171	+ 2,413,077
1919	16,524,974	17,915,925	− 1,390,951
1920	14,689,671	14,489,593	+ 200,078
1921	17,728,131	15,739,652	+ 1,988,479
1922	22,291,064	18,563,002	+ 3,728,062
1923	24,783,762	21,571,904	+ 3,211,858
1924	24,209,639	26,726,428	− 2,516,789
1925	23,244,365	28,238,432	− 4,994,067
1926	21,131,581	23,521,715	− 2,390,134
1927	21,344,535	20,845,064	+ 499,471
1928	23,005,040*	21,230,242	+ 1,774,798
1929	23,554,475	21,983,256	+ 1,571,219
1930	27,818,473	28,119,646	− 301,173
1931	33,146,716	31,160,774	+ 1,985,942
1932	33,549,716	32,050,283	+ 1,499,433
1933	32,099,278	31,122,715	+ 976,563
1934	29,574,286	31,149,157	− 1,574,871
1935	28,430,550	28,291,636	+ 138,914
1936	30,042,984	29,513,523	+ 529,461
1937	33,196,367	32,111,222	+ 1,085,145
1938	36,735,855	37,175,898	− 440,043
1939	41,478,052	37,949,116	+ 3,528,936

* Excludes HK$1,963,358 received from a public works loan.

Notes: This table gives the final outcome of the year's finances. This was often very different from the original Estimates, as a result of changes in the exchange rate of the Hong Kong dollar and other unforeseen events.

matter of the Estimates, for Heaven's sake acquiesce in it. You have known me for 25 years and you know that I am not an enthusiast or a visionary and I tell you without hesitation that the potentialities of this place are amazing. I have not dared show your telegram to my Executive Council as they would go up in the air.'[19] He went on to emphasize the colony's financial strength, prophesying the imminent deaths of a baronet who was steadily drinking himself to death, and of Sir Paul Chater, whose estates, Stubbs confidently predicted, would soon enrich the colony's exchequer with at least HK$1,000,000 and HK$3,000,000 respectively in death duties.[20] So the Colonial Office was reluctantly persuaded to sanction Stubbs's enormous deficit. This was a pity since neither they, nor Stubbs, could have foreseen that in August 1925 Hong Kong would be hit by the great strike and boycott, which lasted for 16 months and completely crippled the colony's trade.

This was an extreme example of the Colonial Office's culpable compliance, but it did not differ in essence from the officials' accustomed attitude of being prepared to trust the judgement of the man on the spot. Normally when doubtful over the prudence of a Governor's fiscal judgement officials would approve the Estimates but suggest the general desirability of increased taxation or request that a careful watch should be kept on how the revenue was coming in, and if there was a shortfall the Governor should be prepared to think again about initiating some of his public works projects.[21] If the officials were very worried, they might require the Governor to submit monthly returns of revenue and expenditure, as happened in 1936. The object of such returns seems to have been to stimulate the Governor to take early corrective action, rather than for the enlightenment of the officials in London. Occasionally suggestions were made as to possible new sources of taxation; for example, when the 1920 Budget was approved the taxation of motor vehicles was pointed to as a possible way of helping to pay for the roads programme. But the Hong Kong government saw no reason to comply with this advice for another 10 years. The initiative for imposing new taxes or raising old ones was always left to the Governor since he was in the best position to judge what level of taxation the colony would find tolerable.

In general the Hong Kong government was very loath to raise rates of taxation or to seek new sources of revenue. Hong Kong was then, and still is, very lightly taxed, as Governors occasionally pointed out to the Legislative Council, but the unofficial members were never reluctant to assert that the colony's trade and prosperity would be ruined if any new exactions were imposed on the taxpayer. So the government rarely attempted to carry through more than marginal adjustments. In times of prosperity when revenue was buoyant new taxes were unnecessary; but when trade was poor the government was unwilling to impose new taxes for fear that this might deepen the depression. However, there were times of crisis when the Budget could not be balanced and the reserves were too low to draw on. In such circumstances there was no alternative to additional taxation since the Colonial Office would never allow a colony to raise a loan to cover a deficit in current expenditure.

The first such crisis in the period 1912–40 arose in 1915. Several factors were responsible. The outbreak of the First World War in 1914 imposed additional costs for the defence of the colony and for the internment of the German and Austrian residents. In 1914 the colony had been on the point of raising a loan to finance the final stages of the construction of the Kowloon–Canton Railway, but it was unable to go to the market for such a loan in wartime and so the costs of completing the project had to be financed out of current revenue and by drawing down the colony's reserves. Expenditure was also swollen by the cost of demonetizing large quantities of subsidiary coins. For many years Hong Kong had been putting large quantities of small coins into circulation, which were widely used throughout Kwangtung province. At first this had been a very lucrative venture for the colony since the face value of the coins was less than their metal content. But after mints in China began to produce large quantities of these small-denomination coins, the supply had become so excessive that by 1912 they were changing hands at a discount of 10 per cent to the silver dollar. So the Hong Kong government had banned the circulation of foreign coins in the colony, and instituted a policy of not reissuing small coins received in revenue, largely by the opium monopoly and the railway; instead the coins were shipped to England and sold for their metal content. It was hoped that by reducing the number of small coins in circulation the actual exchange value of the coins could be brought back to their nominal value.[22] This exercise involved the government in a loss of approximately 20 per cent of the face value of the coins, which cost the revenue HK$825,000 in 1914 and HK$1,400,000 in 1915. It also meant that there was a delay of several months between the receipt of the coins by the Treasury in Hong Kong and the sale of the metal by the Crown Agents in London; it was only after the sale that the proceeds were credited to the government accounts. As a result of these three factors — the war expenditure, the completion of the railway, and the cost of the demonetization programme — in

December 1915 the reserves of the colony were entirely exhausted and it was running an overdraft at the Hongkong and Shanghai Banking Corporation of nearly HK$2 million. The apparent seriousness of the financial position was realized at the Colonial Office only when the Budget Estimates for 1916 were being examined in December 1915; urgent instructions were then sent to the Governor ordering him to suspend the demonetization programme, impose additional taxation, and investigate the possibility of raising a local loan of HK$2 million to pay off the overdraft. The Hongkong and Shanghai Banking Corporation was viewed with considerable suspicion in London during the First World War because of its close links with Germany and it was considered of vital importance to rescue the Hong Kong government from its clutches.[23]

The Governor, Sir Henry May, did not take such a dismal view of the situation as the Colonial Office did. He pointed out that suspension of the demonetization programme would save very little money, since the government was not engaged in buying coins in the open market, but only in disposing of the money unavoidably received in revenue; if these coins were to be put back into circulation through the banks the government would still lose money to the amount of the prevailing discount. The overdraft which so worried the Colonial Office was caused by an unusual delay in selling off the surplus coinage for its metal content, and by the end of March 1916 the overdraft could be reduced to no more than HK$100,000. As regards new taxation May pointed out that he had already submitted a proposal to the Colonial Office for the institution of a tax on salt, as part of a proposed commercial treaty with China, on which he was still awaiting a decision. It was estimated that this would bring in HK$600,000 a year. In addition he was considering increased taxation on alcohol and a new tax on tobacco. The Colonial Office was suitably chastened by this exposition of the true situation and signified their approval of the Governor's proposals.[24] In the event the salt tax was not imposed since the commercial agreement with China was never concluded. But in spite of this the accounts for the year 1916 showed a surplus of HK$2,753,472 instead of the expected deficit of HK$413,769. The new taxes on alcohol and tobacco only contributed HK$390,000 to this result, and were in fact completely unnecessary.

This huge surplus in 1916 was largely due to the vast profits being made by the government opium monopoly. May had pushed up the price of government opium to take advantage of the disappearance of competing smuggled supplies from China, where the authorities were energetically engaged in the suppression of the drug. The government's net revenue from opium rose from HK$1,183,200 in 1913 to over HK$8,000,000 in 1918. The budget surpluses generated as a result enabled the government to pay off the HK$3,000,000 debt on the cost of building the Kowloon–Canton Railway over and above the amount raised by the original loan in 1905, and to make generous gifts to Britain for the war effort of over HK$5,000,000 in the years 1917–18. It also enabled the government to write off a huge loss of HK$2,700,000 sustained in 1919 on transactions in rice, when the government bought up large quantities during a world-wide shortage and resold it locally to stabilize prices and prevent rioting. Another beneficiary from the surplus revenue was the University of Hong Kong: in 1920 the government gave it a grant of HK$1,700,000, of which HK$570,000 was to pay off the university's bank overdraft and accumulated debts and the rest was to supplement its inadequate endowments and provide an income for the future.[25]

The revenue of the opium monopoly declined sharply after the First World War from HK$8.6 million in 1918 to HK$4.3 million in 1920. The estimated deficit in the Estimates for 1921 was over HK$2 million and additional taxation appeared to be unavoidable. In April 1921 stamp duties and taxes on tobacco and alcohol were raised sharply. In fact these measures were not needed, since sales of monopoly opium revived in 1921 as the result of an energetic campaign against opium smuggling, and the government revenues also benefited substantially from the land boom of 1920–4. These factors made it possible to rescind a very unpopular move to increase the assessed taxes (rates) from 13 to 20 per cent, which had been passed by the Legislative Council in April 1921. This decision was reversed in June after widespread protests that landlords were using the increase in rates as an excuse for excessive rent rises. Buoyant revenues for the next few years enabled the government to initiate many new public works projects, which proved very expensive to complete when income contracted in 1925 during the great general strike and boycott. All possible economies in spending had to be made, but no new taxes were imposed, in order to avoid deepening the depression induced by the strike.[26]

The finances of the colony recovered slowly from the effects of the strike. At the end of 1927 the credit of the colony was sufficiently restored for a small loan to be floated locally to finance new public works, and in 1928 Clementi proposed the setting up of a commission to review salaries in the public service, which had last been revised in 1920. The Salaries Commission reported a year later, recommending increases averaging 15 per cent at a cost estimated at HK$1,300,000. The Governor made some slight modifications to the commission's views and sent them to London, where the Colonial Office reluctantly approved the amended proposals, commenting that they appeared to be overgenerous. The cost of the proposals depended crucially on the sterling value of the Hong Kong dollar, and by the time the revised salaries were due to be put before the Legislative Council for approval in June 1930 the exchange rate had depreciated from HK$11 to the pound in 1929, when the commission reported, to HK$16 to the pound. In consequence the cost of the revised salaries had increased to HK$2.5 million. The unofficial members were not prepared to approve this amount, and the inevitable increases in taxation to pay for it, at a time when businesses were suffering severely from the fall in the dollar's value. The new Governor, Peel, pruned back the increases further to HK$1.7 million, but the unofficials were not mollified and voted against the financial resolution, which then had to be carried by the use of the official majority. Subsequently postal rates were raised, duties on tobacco were increased, a new tax on petrol was imposed, and the assessed taxes (rates) went up by 4 per cent.

Unfortunately for Hong Kong the value of its dollar continued to fall against sterling, dropping below the rate of HK$20 to the pound in January 1931. The government calculated that if this rate continued for the rest of the year the projected Budget deficit would be more than doubled to HK$5.6 million and that further measures of taxation were therefore needed. These were made slightly more tolerable for the unofficial members of the Legislative Council by a cut in the rate at which sterling salaries were to be converted into dollars. Light dues on shipping entering the harbour were doubled from two to four cents a ton, a new tax was imposed on entertainments, and estate duties were raised in January 1931. In February tobacco and liquor taxes were raised and the price of monopoly opium was increased. In August the value of the dollar was still low (HK$21 to the pound) and so at the time of the Budget in October tobacco duties were raised yet again, petrol duty was increased, and a new tax was imposed on perfumes and toilet preparations. These duties were followed by new taxes on gambling and sweepstakes in December. The unofficial members complained that new taxes were becoming almost a weekly occurrence and during the Budget Debate they proposed a motion to reduce public service salaries. All the unofficials present voted in favour, and the motion was only defeated by the use of the official majority.[27] Relief for the dollar came unexpectedly when the Labour government in Britain resigned in August 1931 and the new National government soon afterwards went off the gold standard and allowed the pound sterling to float downwards. As a result the Hong Kong dollar appreciated to a value of HK$14 to the pound by December. This late improvement and the increased taxation unexpectedly allowed revenue to exceed expenditure for 1931.

The exchange rate then remained fairly stable at around HK$15 to the pound for the next two years, giving Hong Kong a welcome respite from fresh taxation. The 1932 government accounts showed another surplus and in commenting on the 1933 Budget the Colonial Office advised the Governor that he should not overlook the possibility of some reductions in taxation. The rationale behind this suggestion was that a surplus tended to encourage the unofficial members to press for spending on new public works, which might then lead to a permanent increase in the colony's recurrent expenditure. Such an increase might be difficult to finance when fortune changed.[28] Hong Kong took little notice of this well-meant advice. The only reduction in taxation put forward was a cut in light dues of approximately 20 per cent which would be achieved by the introduction of a new method of calculation. Shipping interests and the General Chamber of Commerce had lobbied vigorously in Hong Kong and London for some reduction and the Governor decided that it was politic to make a small concession.[29] Otherwise the new taxes imposed in 1930 and 1931 were prudently left unchanged. This was fortunate since Hong Kong was soon hit by the effects of the world-wide depression and the revenue steadily declined from HK$33.5 million in 1932 to a low point of HK$27.5 million estimated for 1935. No new taxes were needed to meet this shortfall, although a few minor changes were made in rates of taxation, mainly in order to give effect to the new system of Empire preferences agreed at the Imperial Economic Conference at Ottawa in 1932.

The fall in revenue produced a deficit of HK$1.5 million in the government accounts for 1934. The deficit would have been much greater but for the rise in the exchange value of the dollar during the course of the year. This rise was caused by the decision of the United States government to embark on a policy of purchasing silver, with the deliberate intention of driving up the price. The rise in the price of silver also pushed up the value of the silver-based Hong Kong dollar. The United States continued this policy in 1935 and the Hong Kong dollar rose further, reaching an unprecedentedly high value of HK$8 to the pound in March. Meanwhile China had taken steps to prevent the appreciation of its own silver-based currency by imposing various taxes and controls on the export of silver in October 1934, and finally in November 1935 it broke the link between its dollar and silver and moved to a managed currency. As a result of these measures the disparity between the values of the Hong Kong and Chinese currencies widened, giving Shanghai a marked competitive advantage over Hong Kong in the China trade. A Currency Committee in the Colonial Office which included representatives of the Treasury, the Bank of England, and commercial banks kept a close watch on the situation, receiving weekly reports from the Governor. By March 1935 this committee had reached the conclusion that the Hong Kong government should follow China's example and depreciate its currency by the imposition of an export tax on silver, but opinion in Hong Kong opposed this move, preferring to wait on events.[30] This temporizing view continued to be predominant in Hong Kong until China went off the silver standard completely in November. This move forced Hong Kong to take action. At the time of China's devaluation the export of silver from Hong Kong was prohibited and in December an ordinance was hurriedly passed to call in all silver currency in circulation, release the three note-issuing banks from the obligation to exchange banknotes for silver, and take over all the silver bullion and coin held by the banks. An Exchange Fund was set up under government control to manage the Hong Kong currency in future. As a result the value of the Hong Kong dollar fell rapidly from HK$10 to the pound in September to HK$16 to the pound in December and thereafter stabilized at around this level.

The plunge in the value of the dollar, which had been deliberately engineered by the government in the general interests of the Hong Kong economy, made havoc of the Budget for 1936. Hong Kong was still affected by the trade depression, and revenue for 1936 was estimated at HK$1.6 million less than that of 1935. As always, estimates of expenditure depended on the exchange value of the dollar: at HK$10.60 to the pound the budget would balance; at HK$14 to the pound a deficit of over the HK$5 million was anticipated. The unofficial members were opposed to any increases in taxation; indeed in the Budget Debate the senior Chinese unofficial, R.H. Kotewall, called for reductions in taxation to stimulate the economy.[31] So the government decided that there was no alternative to a levy on the salaries of all public servants earning above a basic minimum. The levy was graduated, ranging from a cut of 12.5 per cent on salaries of over £1,400, down to 2.5 per cent on salaries of £240 or HK$240 a year. The Colonial Office assented to the levy only with great reluctance, objecting in particular to the disparity in the incidence of the levy on sterling-paid and dollar-paid officers.[32] The Governor was unwilling to modify his plan, claiming that the exemption levels which had been set represented the bare minimum of subsistence for each class of officer. He did, however, bow to the insistence of the Colonial Office that the levy should be accompanied by an increase in taxation so that sacrifices to balance the budget were not imposed on public servants alone. In the course of 1936, therefore, taxes on tobacco, alcohol, and petrol were raised and the top rate of estate duty was increased from 12 to 20 per cent. The salary levy naturally aroused bitter resentment throughout the public service and lengthy petitions were sent to the Secretary of State by the European and Chinese staff criticizing the administration's financial policies in detail and objecting to the fact that they were being penalized by a tax on their incomes which was borne by no other section of the community. The Colonial Office refused to intervene on their behalf. Many colonies had been forced to impose salary levies in the early 1930s during the depths of the world depression. Hong Kong was exceptional in having to resort to this expedient to balance its Budget at a time when other colonies had been able to do away with such levies.

There was some revival in trade in 1936 with a consequent increase in government revenue and this, together with the effects of the salaries levy and increased taxation, unexpectedly produced a very small surplus in the government accounts for the year. However, the Estimates for 1937 anticipated another large deficit and the salary levy was continued with the agreement of the Colonial Office for a further six months, though at a reduced rate. In the search for fresh ways of increasing revenue, a committee of the Executive Council was set up to investigate the possibility of imposing a tax on salt, an expedient that had not been considered since 1916.[33] Relief for the government finances came from an unexpected quarter: the outbreak of the Sino-Japanese war in July 1937. Much trade was diverted through Hong Kong from Shanghai, refugees began to flood into the colony, and their expenditure swelled the government's receipts from indirect taxation and caused a new boom in land sales. In the ensuing prosperity, revenue increased from HK$30 million in 1936 to HK$41 million in 1939. Expenditure also rose, both on new public works and on civil defence against a possible Japanese attack. In August 1938 a programme of protective measures against air raids and precautions against gas warfare was initiated which entailed costs of over HK$5 million. These expenditures were all financed without the need for any fresh taxation until the outbreak of the Second World War in Europe in September 1939.

The financial problems which faced Hong Kong in the 1930s were paralleled in many other colonies which were forced by low prices for their commodity exports during the world depression to cut budgets drastically, impose salary levies and, as a last resort, apply for direct financial assistance from the British Treasury. The Colonial Office became increasingly concerned that Governors did not pay sufficient attention to the fiscal implications of their policies because they did not have access to expert financial advice when new administrative measures were being devised. The structure of colonial administrations until the 1930s made no provision for such a senior financial and economic adviser. Instead there was a Colonial Treasurer who was the chief accounting officer responsible for the general management and supervision of the receipts and expenditure of public monies and the proper observance of all financial procedures. But in most colonies he was not consulted as a matter of course on the formulation of all government policies and long-term financial planning. It was the Colonial Secretary, not the Treasurer, who was responsible for drawing up the annual Estimates and presenting them to the Legislative Council. In June 1932 the Secretary of State sent out a circular dispatch to all colonies drawing attention to the need to elevate the status of the Treasurer, suggesting that he should not be considered merely as one of a number of heads of departments but should have access to all secretariat files and be consulted at an early stage before policy decisions were taken. The proposals in this circular were not mandatory and Governors were invited to send in their comments. In practice few changes were made as a result of this initiative. So in 1937 a further circular dispatch was sent out, instructing all except the smallest colonies to institute the office of Financial Secretary.[34] He should rank next after the Colonial Secretary in the structure of the government and should be a member of both the Executive and Legislative Councils. He was to be responsible for the preparation and presentation of the annual Estimates, he should comment on the financial implication of all new policy initiatives, and his advice on all questions of an economic or financial character should not be overridden without reference to the Governor, to whom he should have direct access. He was not to be personally concerned with the detailed control and supervision of accounting procedures; these duties of the Colonial Treasurer should be devolved to a new official with some such title as Chief Accountant or Accountant General.

In the case of Hong Kong the post of Colonial Treasurer had long been reserved for a member of the cadet service, who was unlikely to have had any special financial training. From 1918 to 1930 the post was held by Mr C.M. Messer, who had previously been Captain Superintendent of Police. Colonial Office officials did not have a high opinion of his financial acumen and he had been criticized for lax supervision by a committee of enquiry after a Treasury clerk had misappropriated government funds amounting to HK$15,329 in 1928. The following year he was due to retire at the age of 55 and the Colonial Office took advantage of this opportunity to reject his application for an extension, which was supported by the Governor, and to insist that his successor must be an officer with proper financial qualifications from outside the colony.[35] When the Hong Kong government made objections the Colonial Office pointed out that the Treasurer's post had not been permanently removed from the cadet service and that cadets who had suitably qualified themselves by attendance at courses of instruction in Britain might be considered for such promotion in future. The appointment was offered to Mr E. Taylor, the Deputy Treasurer of Sierra Leone, who was appointed to the treasurership in 1931 after serving for a year under Messer. The Colonial Office expressed satisfaction at the marked improvement in Hong Kong's financial documentation as a result of this change. Taylor joined the Executive and Legislative Councils as an ex-officio member, but the preparation and presentation of the Estimates continued to be in the hands of the Colonial Secretary. In accordance with a long-established local procedure the draft Budget was scrutinized item by item by a committee consisting of the Governor, the Colonial Secretary, and the Treasurer, with each head of department appearing before them in turn.[36]

Taylor reached retirement age in 1937. The Governor, Caldecott, asked the Colonial Office to find a replacement from outside the colony and the position was offered to Sydney Caine, who had been an official at the Colonial Office since 1926.[37] During this period he had served in the Eastern and Economic Departments and had frequently commented on dispatches from Hong Kong, so he was very well qualified to deal with its problems, although much younger than his two predecessors. On arrival in July 1937 he took up the newly created post of Financial Secretary. Caine remained in Hong Kong for only a little over two years, until he was recalled to the Colonial Office at the outbreak of the Second World War. But during this short period he was instrumental in bringing about a number of innovations: the replacement of the 20 per cent military contribution by a fixed annual sum, the alteration of the Hong Kong financial year from the calendar year to the year from April to March, and the moves towards the introduction of a tax on income. As a result of his urging a Taxation Committee was set up in 1938 which reported in favour of an income tax, after considering and rejecting the many objections urged against it.[38] So when the Second World War broke out in September 1939 the groundwork had been laid which made it possible for the Governor, Northcote, to propose the introduction of an income tax to the Legislative Council, not because the colony was itself in need of further revenue, but in order to make a fitting contribution to Britain for the war effort. The detailed proposals were considered by a further committee after Caine's return to Britain and substantially modified: instead of a tax levied on the whole of a person's income, separate taxes were imposed on salary income, income from property, and business profits. In order to disarm opponents the bill included a clause providing for its automatic repeal immediately after the war was over. Because of this concession, which was approved by the Colonial Office, the bill was passed through the Legislative Council without a division in 1940.[39] The taxation of salaries, property income, and business profits thus came to an end in 1946, but taxation was reinstituted on a permanent basis by a fresh vote of the Legislative Council in 1947.

In no other area of administration was the Governor so tightly constrained by a detailed straitjacket of rules and regulations as in matters concerned with finance. All but the most minor decisions were required to be referred to London for official sanction. In practice, however, Governors enjoyed a surprisingly wide latitude. The detailed requirements of the *Colonial Regulations* were not infrequently ignored, depending on the meticulousness of different

Governors and the efficiency of their financial staff. The broad guidelines on policy laid down in the *Colonial Regulations* and in the advice conveyed by official dispatches from the Secretary of State could almost always be set aside if a Governor was sufficiently determined and persistent in pressing his point of view on the colony's needs. The Colonial Office very occasionally exerted its authority by refusing minor financial requests which were not sufficiently important for the Governor to raise a protest at the refusal; on major matters, even where officials had grave doubts as to the correctness of local financial policy, the Governor was invariably allowed to have his own way, since the Colonial Office was well aware of the fallibility of its own prognostications of future financial trends and lacked the detailed knowledge of local conditions on which the Governor based his case.

7 The Structure of Government

THERE were no significant changes in the constitutional arrangements for the government of Hong Kong between 1912 and 1941. At the end of this period, as at the beginning, the Legislative Council had a clear official majority, all the unofficials were nominated by the Governor, and on the Executive Council officials considerably outnumbered the few nominated unofficials. There were a few minor changes: the number of seats on the Executive and Legislative Councils was marginally enlarged; a Chinese member appeared for the first time on the Executive Council and the number of Chinese on the Legislative Council increased from two to three; but little else was changed apart from the transformation of the Sanitary Board into the Urban Council in 1936.

Such stability in constitutional structure was not unusual in the colonial empire at that time. The main exception was Ceylon which advanced from a stage of development rather behind that of Hong Kong in 1912 to reach a position of virtually complete internal self-government by 1931, with local ministers dependent on a Legislative Council elected by universal adult suffrage. However, Ceylon's progress paralleled, and was stimulated by, the constitutional changes in its mighty neighbour, India. Hong Kong's constitutional inertia was no different from that of its nearest colonial neighbour, the Straits Settlements. This lack of progress in Hong Kong was not caused by an absence of local pressures for change. In the early years there were several agitations by European residents for political changes in their own interests, and there was a brief spark of interest from the Chinese at the time of the 1925–6 general strike and boycott. But thereafter an almost complete apathy descended on the colony.

In 1912 Hong Kong possessed a constitutional feature unique among the Eastern colonies: the presence of two unofficial members in the Executive Council. This resulted from the 1894 petition of the British residents who had sought to achieve an unofficial elected European majority in the Legislative Council with complete control over local expenditure. This demand had been rejected by two Secretaries of State, Lord Ripon in 1894 and Joseph Chamberlain in 1896, principally on the ground that it would be wrong to hand over the administration of the colony to a small oligarchy of 800 transient British business men and merchants who would rule over a Chinese population of a quarter of a million, whose taxes contributed 90 per cent of the colony's revenue. However, since there was no municipal council in Hong Kong, such as existed in most of the larger colonies, and since it appeared to be impracticable to set one up in view of the difficulty of drawing a line between colonial and municipal affairs, Chamberlain decided that two unofficial members, normally drawn from those sitting on the Legislative Council, should in future join the officials on the Executive Council.[1] No stipulation was laid down as to the race of these members. The first appointees were Paul Chater, a British subject of Armenian ancestry, who remained on the Council without interruption for 30 years from 1896 to 1926, and the head of Jardine, Matheson and Co., whose successors continued to occupy that seat for the next 10 years.

The other result of the 1894 petition was quite unintended and unforeseen by the European signatories, the increase in Chinese representation on the Legislative Council from one to two members. The Secretary of State was impressed by the disproportion between the contribution of the Chinese community, in the payment of taxes and generally to the prosperity of the colony, and their meagre representation on the Legislative Council (consisting of a single Chinese among four Europeans); so he decided that the number of unofficials should be increased by one. The revised *Royal Instructions* did not lay down that the new member must always be Chinese, but the Colonial Office dispatch made it clear that this was the intention. The increase on the unofficial side was balanced by the addition of another official member, the General Officer Commanding (GOC) British Forces in the colony. As a result the Legislative Council consisted of the Governor, seven official members, and six unofficials.

Governors did not find it easy to find suitable Chinese to fill the seats customarily reserved for them. It was desirable that any Chinese member should be fluent in English so as to be able to take a full part in the business of the Council, be recognized as a man of standing and influence within the Chinese community, be a British subject (normally by birth within the colony), and be loyal to the British Crown. Chinese possessing all these qualifications were rare, since most of the Hong Kong Chinese had come to the colony from Kwangtung and intended to return there. Eurasians of mixed Chinese and British blood were generally unsuitable for appointment since they were looked down upon by pure-bred Chinese who habitually referred to them as 'the Bastards' (according to Stubbs in 1920).[2] However such was the difficulty in finding acceptable Chinese that one of their seats was filled by a Eurasian, Ho Fook, the half-brother of Sir Robert Ho Tung, from 1917 to 1921, and later from 1923 to 1935 by Robert (later Sir Robert) Kotewall, a gentleman of Parsee ancestry with a Chinese mother, but who was a fine Chinese scholar and was accepted by the Chinese as being one of themselves.[3] Kotewall's place was taken in 1935 by Lo Man-kam, a Eurasian who had been educated in Britain and had qualified there as a lawyer.

The question of loyalty to Britain arose most acutely in 1913. The Chinese unofficials then were Sir Kai Ho Kai, a member since 1890, and Wei Yuk, a member since 1896. Sir Kai had been knighted in 1912 on the recommendation of Lugard in recognition of the support given by the leaders of the Chinese community to the strong measures introduced by Lugard to deal with the disorders in the colony at the time of the 1911 revolution in China. But though Sir Kai favoured the suppression of turmoil in the streets of Hong Kong he had continuing and close connections with the revolutionary regime in Canton. He drafted an elaborate constitution for the new Kwangtung government, supported various financial expedients to which that regime resorted in order to raise money from the Hong Kong Chinese, and secured appointments for his relatives in the new government. He was also alleged to be connected with an anti-British newspaper published in Canton and to be a patron and adviser to the Sze Yap Association, which played a leading role in the 1913 boycott of Hongkong Tramways Limited. In consequence of these and other supposed acts of disloyalty, the Governor, Sir Henry May, wrote to the Colonial Office in 1913 proposing that Sir Kai's membership of the Legislative Council should not be renewed when his fourth six-year term expired in 1914. May supported his case by referring to the way in which Sir Kai had used his position on the Council to exact gifts from various guilds and organizations (for example, HK$600 a year from the opium-farmer and a similar amount from the pawnbrokers' guild); moreover he was no longer a ready or reliable source of information to the government on Chinese or local politics. But, although May averred that Sir Kai had lost the confidence equally of the Chinese community and the British authorities, he was unwilling to offend him openly by not recommending him for a further term on the Council. So he asked the Colonial Office if it would be possible for the British minister in Peking to recommend Sir Kai to the President of China, Yüan Shih-k'ai, for employment on some foreign mission.[4] The Colonial Office naturally declined to be involved in an attempt to foist Hong Kong's unwanted councillors on to the Chinese government. Instead the Colonial Office saved May the embarrassment of openly snubbing Sir Kai by laying down a new general rule that members of colonial legislatures should not, save in exceptional circumstances, be reappointed for more than one term, and instructed May to inform Sir Kai that in view of his distinguished record of 24 years' service he would now be permitted to retire. Accordingly in February 1914 Sir Kai made his last appearance in the Legislative Council and departed in a blaze of glory to a chorus of hypocritical adulation in which the Governor played the leading role. Five months later Sir Kai died, leaving so little money in his estate that the Hong Kong government undertook the cost of educating his five sons as an act of charity.[5]

Sir Kai's colleague, Wei Yuk, had been associated with one of his schemes for the issue of banknotes by a Chinese bank in Hong Kong which would be used to pay off a bond issue that had been raised by the Canton government. May regarded Wei Yuk's activities as proof of his financial incompetence rather than disloyalty and told the Colonial Office, 'Wei Yuk still retains as much of my confidence as it is safe to repose in any Chinese.' Officials in London were not so sanguine, but hoped that Sir Kai's downfall would serve as a salutary warning to his colleague. They were accordingly surprised when only a month after Sir Kai's valedictory eulogy they received a dispatch from May recommending that Wei Yuk should be reappointed to the Legislative Council for a further period when his second term expired later in the year. May admitted that this would be somewhat embarrassing after the general rule against reappointment had just been invoked to get rid of Sir Kai, but he professed himself unable to find any suitable replacement except a Eurasian. The Colonial Office at first demurred at this proposal, but then allowed May to have his way.[6]

This was not by any means the last time that the connections of the Chinese members with the Chinese government or factions within China caused awkwardness for the Hong Kong authorities. In 1921 the senior Chinese unofficial member, Lau Chu-pak, raised a fund among the Hong Kong merchants to support General Chen Chiung-ming, in the hope of persuading him to sever his connection with

Sun Yat-sen and come to terms with the government in Peking. And in 1938 the first Chinese member of the Executive Council, Sir Shou-son Chow, upset the Governor, Sir Geoffry Northcote, by serving on a committee to promote the sale of Chinese government bonds.[7]

The rule limiting service on the Legislative Council to two terms was never rigidly enforced. The Colonial Office decided that it need not apply to the two seats which the Governor customarily filled in accordance with elections held by the Justices of the Peace and the Hong Kong General Chamber of Commerce.[8] This was a tradition which had been followed by Governors since 1849 and 1883 respectively, although it was nowhere mentioned in the *Royal Instructions* or in any other legal document. As a result of this custom Henry Polluck was able to serve on the Council uninterruptedly for 38 years from 1903 to 1941, a record which is unlikely ever to be surpassed. When commenting on his nomination for yet another term in 1939 an official at the Colonial Office referred to him as the 'senile' rather than the 'senior' member of the Council — he was then aged 76 — but the Governor, Northcote, felt constrained to continue to put forward his name so long as the Justices of the Peace persisted in re-electing him without opposition.[9] The nominees of the General Chamber of Commerce were changed more frequently. The two-term rule provided a convenient excuse for removing other unwanted members of the Council when their terms expired. But if the Governor wished the rule to be waived, usually in the case of a Chinese member, no objection was raised from London.[10]

When in 1896 the Secretary of State had directed that two unofficial members should be added to the Executive Council, he had observed that it was obviously desirable that they should as a rule be chosen from among the unofficial members of the Legislative Council, although the choice should be inspired by personal merit without regard to race. This policy was followed until 1906 when Sir Paul Chater was permitted to give up his seat on the Legislative Council after 18 years service there, while retaining his seat on the Executive Council. His colleague, Mr Hewett, remained a member of both Councils until his sudden death in 1915. The choice of a successor put the Governor in a quandary. The man pre-eminently qualified to succeed him was Mr Henry Polluck, KC. He had been a member of the Legislative Council since 1903 and was the senior unofficial there. He had also acted as Attorney General for three years between 1896 and 1901 and had consequently been an official member of the Executive Council during this period. But unfor-

tunately for Polluck, the Governor, Sir Henry May, felt considerable
personal antipathy towards him, an attitude which was demonstrated
publicly in a number of acrimonious exchanges in the Legislative
Council, notably on one occasion when May abruptly brought the
proceedings of the Council to an end by walking out of the chamber
while Polluck was still speaking. Polluck did not help his cause by
putting down a series of six questions in the Council which pointedly
drew the Governor's attention to his qualifications for the vacant
Executive Council seat.[11] May sent a dispatch to London which
disparaged Polluck's abilities and his judgement and recommended
another leading member of the bar, Mr Ernest Sharp, KC, who
was, in May's judgement, 'the ablest man outside government
service in the colony'. Alternatively he put forward the name of Mr
Stabb, the general manager of the Hongkong and Shanghai Banking
Corporation, who might be willing to accept appointment to the
Executive Council, but whose company would not allow him to sit
on the Legislative Council. The Colonial Office was not at all happy
with May's proposal, which would mean that neither of the unofficial
members on the Executive Council would be sitting on the Legislative
Council. But they had no reason to challenge May's estimate of the
individuals concerned from a distance, and so Sharp's nomination
was accepted.[12]

Polluck had to await the arrival of the next Governor, Sir Edward
Stubbs, before he was appointed to a permanent seat on the Executive
Council in 1921. Stubbs did not dissent from May's opinion as to
Polluck's capabilities, writing: 'He is rather exceptionally stupid, but
he is an honest, straightforward gentleman whom I have always
found eminently reasonable when matters have been fully explained
to him', but he considered it desirable that one of the unofficials
on the Executive Council should concurrently serve on the Legislative
Council. In order to achieve this without disturbing the two existing
unofficials, Sir Paul Chater and E.H. Sharp, whom Stubbs wished
to retain, he proposed that the number of unofficials on the Executive
Council should be increased to three. The Colonial Office readily
agreed to this, since the unofficial members would still be
outnumbered by the officials three to seven (the Governor, the GOC
British Forces, the Colonial Secretary, the Attorney General, the
Treasurer, the Director of Public Works, and the Secretary for
Chinese Affairs).[13] Polluck was appointed for an initial term of
five years, and the *Royal Instructions* were subsequently amended
to fix this period for all future appointments. Previously Chater

and Sharp had been appointed without a terminal date and retained their seats on the Council until their deaths in 1926 and 1922 respectively. Polluck was subsequently reappointed three times, and retained his membership of both the Executive and Legislative Councils until 1941.

However in 1916 Polluck could not foresee his future eminence, and his response to this snub by May was to join Mr Holyoak, the nominee of the General Chamber of Commerce, in organizing a petition for constitutional reform in the colony. This was sent to London in March 1916, having been signed by 556 persons. All but 12 of the signatories were British subjects of European race and they included most of the leading British business men in the colony. The Chinese were not invited to sign and the two Chinese unofficial members refused to have anything to do with the petition. The petitioners asked that two more unofficial members should be added to the Executive Council and that all four unofficials there should in future be elected, two by the Justices of the Peace, and two by the General Chamber of Commerce. It was further requested that the number of unofficials on the Legislative Council should be increased from six to 10 by the addition of four Europeans, and that in future the eight European seats should be filled by election, four to be selected by the Justices of the Peace, and four by the General Chamber of Commerce. This would given an unofficial majority of two (10 unofficials against the Governor plus seven officials), but not an elected unofficial majority, since the two Chinese members would continue to be nominated by the Governor. The only reason adduced by the petitioners was the fact that the official majority in the Legislative Council was 'constantly' employed to vote down the unofficial members, although the only instance given of the overriding of public opinion was a recent argument between the Governor and Polluck over the government's alleged failure to recruit sufficient European nurses for the government hospital.[14]

The petition received very short shrift from the Colonial Office officials. It was pointed out that the proposal to elect members of the Executive Council was unprecedented in any colony: the Executive Council was the Governor's cabinet and he was entitled to choose as his advisers those on whose judgement he could rely. The petitioners' suggestion of an electoral college was also scornfully rejected. Using figures supplied by the Governor, officials at the Colonial Office noted that the General Chamber of Commerce consisted of 150 members (of whom 25 were not even British subjects) and the Justices of the Peace numbered no more than 120; it was out of the question that this body of 270 Europeans or less, since some were members of both bodies, should have the final say over the business of a colony consisting of some 450,000 Chinese (who contributed the bulk of the colony's revenue), and 12,000 non-Chinese, without any regard to the policy of the British government. The Permanent Under-Secretary, Sir George Fiddes, described the petition as a 'feeble production' and advised its outright rejection, and the Secretary of State, Bonar Law, initialled his agreement. A brief dispatch to this effect was accordingly sent to Hong Kong in August 1916.[15] No detailed arguments for the rejection of the petition were given, but the signatories were referred to the reasons adduced by Lord Ripon and Joseph Chamberlain in their successive replies to the petition of 1894, where it was stated that Hong Kong, being on the borders of a foreign land and the nucleus of wide-reaching British interests in the Far East, must remain under imperial protection and under imperial control, and that no hope could be held out that Hong Kong would ever cease to be a Crown Colony or that it would ever enjoy representative government on any form of franchise whatever.

In May 1916, while the petition was still being considered in London, Holyoak and Polluck had been active in forming a Constitutional Reform Association. Membership was open to all British subjects but only one Chinese was enrolled as a member.[16] Little was heard from this body for the next two years, but once the First World War was over a meeting was called to renew pressure for constitutional change. A large gathering of European residents met at the Theatre Royal on 9 January 1919 and after a lengthy debate passed a resolution asking that unofficial representation on the Legislative Council should be increased from six to nine — thereby giving an unofficial majority of one, and that there should be seven elected members, all British subjects, to be returned as follows: one elected by the General Chamber of Commerce; one by the Justices of the Peace; one by the Chinese General Chamber of Commerce or some other body representative of the Chinese; and four (one of Portuguese race and three of British race) by British subjects on the Jurors List, and those liable for jury service but exempted. The proposal to increase Chinese representation from two to three was a late addition to the resolution. Originally the Constitutional Reform Association had made no mention of such an increase and the Chinese had feared that their weight on the

Council would be diminished if the proposed plan were to be accepted. So a meeting of leading Chinese was hurriedly summoned by the senior Chinese unofficial, Lau Chu-pak, which put forward the suggestion that, in addition to the two already nominated by the Governor, one Chinese member should be elected by the Chinese General Chamber of Commerce. Thereupon the Constitutional Reform Association had incorporated this item in their resolution before their meeting was convened.

The resolution was more moderate than that put forward in the 1916 petition and was drafted with an eye to avoiding the criticisms that had been levelled against the earlier proposals. No changes in the Executive Council were asked for. The use of the list of qualified jurors was a shrewd move. The Jurors List was already used for elections to the Sanitary Board. The list was revised annually and consisted of 'good and sufficient persons resident within the colony between the ages of 21 and 60, of sound mind and not deaf, blind or similarly infirm who have good enough English to understand the proceedings in Court'. In 1920 the list contained the names of 1,500 jurors, of whom only 61 had Chinese names. The requirement that all jurors should have a working knowledge of English ensured that the proposed electorate would be over-whelmingly European, without the need to impose any specifically racial test for the franchise.[17]

At the time of the meeting Sir Henry May had already gone on leave, and the resolution was forwarded to London by the Officer Administering the Government (OAG), Claud Severn. His covering dispatch pointed out the danger that any such constitutional innovations might lead to a loss of business confidence and might discourage investment, and he also emphasized the obvious difficulties of conceding an unofficial majority on the Legislative Council under the Crown Colony system of government:

What would happen were the government to be defeated by the proposed unofficial majority on some crucial question, for example the annual supply bill or some matter of policy common to the whole empire? The only possible course would be for the government to resign, but that it cannot do, as there are no persons available to take up the offices that would be vacant.

Colonial Office officials fully agreed with Severn's arguments, but the Secretary of State, Viscount Milner, directed that a delaying reply should be sent to the authors of the resolution pending consideration of the question by the newly appointed governor, Sir Edward Stubbs.[18]

Stubbs took some time to formulate his views and did not write on this subject until July 1920, some 10 months after his arrival in the colony. He began his dispatch by noting that the general indifference of the community to all matters of public life was almost unbelievable, and described the Constitutional Reform Association as a farcical body of a few dozen persons which had owed its origin to the personal pique of certain persons against the previous Governor and was now practically moribund. Stubbs was against an unofficial majority for the same reasons as Severn had given, but he was prepared to accept an increase in the number of unofficials from six to nine, provided that the official side was similarly augmented. He took a surprisingly liberal attitude to the request for elections and supported the principle that the non-Chinese members of the Legislative Council, apart from the member selected by the General Chamber of Commerce, should be elected, and recommended that no better electorate could be found than the British subjects on the list of jurors, as the resolution asked. However, he deprecated the suggestion that one Chinese member should be selected by the Chinese General Chamber of Commerce since this would mean increasing the influence of the Eurasians that controlled that body; he preferred that all the Chinese members should continue to be nominated by the Governor. If the number of European members were to be increased, the Chinese element on the Council must be increased in proportion, otherwise the politically quiescent Chinese community might be stirred up by agitators to demand redress of this grievance.[19]

Before coming to any decision the Colonial Office consulted Sir Paul Chater, who had been an unofficial member of the Executive Council since 1896 and who happened to be then in London. He was strongly opposed to any change in the colony's constitution and in particular he argued against elections on the ground that it was already difficult to persuade the best Europeans to serve on the Council, and that there was the possibility that junior European clerks might be elected to the Council in preference to the heads of their firms.[20] Officials were more impressed by Chater's fears as to the dangers of elections than by the Governor's willingness to adopt them. Fortified by Stubbs's assurance that there was no widespread agitation for reform, officials decided that it was unnecessary to make any changes in the colony, beyond the appointment of Polluck to the Executive Council. The Secretary of State, Viscount Milner, agreed and Hong Kong was informed of the decision in February 1921. Polluck asked that the correspondence between the Governor and the Colonial Office should be published, as had been done in 1916, but Stubbs refused this request on the ground of confidentiality. However, the views of the Governor favouring the election of the non-Chinese members of the Legislative Council, but not an unofficial majority, were later made public in a reply to a question in the House of Commons in June 1921.[21]

This information stimulated the Constitutional Reform Association to fresh activity. Polluck had ceased to be connected with the Association after he had attained his goal of a seat on the Executive Council in 1921, but under a new secretary, Mr Whyte, yet another petition was drawn up and on this occasion achieved the surprisingly large total of 1,500 signatures from among the British community before it was sent to the House of Commons in January 1922. The petition asked for an unofficial majority in the Legislative Council, and requested that the non-Chinese unofficial members should no longer be nominated by the Governor but should be elected by the British residents of the colony. The petition was accompanied by a pamphlet which referred to various precedents for the granting of an unofficial majority in the Legislative Council, such as Cyprus, Malta, and some of the West Indian colonies, and particularly emphasized the case of Ceylon, which obtained an unofficial majority in 1920; the pamphlet also cited the proposals put forward in 1921 by a committee of the Legislative Council of the Straits Settlements for an unofficial majority in that colony.[22] Similar precedents had been cited in support of the petitions of 1894, 1916, and 1919. The crucial difference between these colonies and Hong Kong, as Colonial Office officials had noted, was that the unofficial majorities elsewhere were composed entirely or predominantly of representatives of the indigenous population, whereas the Hong Kong petitioners were arguing in favour of a majority composed largely of representatives of the transient British community.

The Colonial Office as usual asked the Governor for his comments, and Stubbs again took his time to reply. When he finally wrote some 12 months later in March 1923 he began his dispatch by disparaging the petitioners: although 1,500 persons had signed the document, he wrote, it was not difficult to collect such signatures, and if anyone wished to take the trouble he could just as easily obtain a similar list of signatures to a petition against any change. He further pointed out that only 25 of the names on the petition were those of 'persons of some standing whose opinion might be regarded as entitled to carry some weight. The principal business men of the colony have not added their names.' An official at the Colonial Office commented caustically at this point: 'It is a little difficult to see what evidence of popular demand could be produced which would satisfy Stubbs. Even if a mob came and broke the windows of Government House he would say with some plausibility that few of the leading merchants had been seen taking part in the demonstration.'[23]

Stubbs then went on to deal with the substance of the petition. As in 1920 he was prepared to support in principle the proposal for an increase in the number of European unofficials from four to six, and of the Chinese unofficials from two to three. He would also accept the election of five of the six European members by those on the list of qualified jurors, while the sixth continued to be nominated by the General Chamber of Commerce. But if these changes were to be put into effect the number of official members must be raised from eight to 10, since he strongly opposed the granting of an unofficial majority on the Council. His arguments against this were twofold: firstly that an unofficial majority was unnecessary since he, like previous Governors, had invariably given the fullest consideration to the views of the unofficials and refrained from pressing on with proposals to which they were opposed, except when acting upon orders from London, or when it was necessary to safeguard the colony's finances. His second argument was more weighty: the granting of an unofficial majority composed largely of elected Europeans would cause trouble among the Chinese community, who would probably be incited to demand a similar process of election for the Chinese members and then for an elected Chinese majority on the Legislative Council. Once the democratic principle of popular election had been granted to the Europeans it would be difficult to deny a similar concession to the Chinese without apparent inconsistency. Such a change would mean the end of Hong Kong as a British colony and must therefore be rejected. Such a rejection, however, might lead to serious trouble in view of the disturbed conditions in the neighbouring provinces of China. The revolutionary and Bolshevist ideas prevalent in Canton had a very serious influence on the Hong Kong population, as was shown by the great strike of 1922. Accordingly Stubbs advised the Colonial Office that until times again became normal it would be a grievous mistake to do anything other than reject the petition.

The officials in London were unanimous in advising the Secretary of State to accept Stubbs's recommendation, and so the petition was put aside unanswered. No public announcement was made in the House of Commons, or in Hong Kong, but, as Stubbs had correctly prophesied, the dismissal of the petition did not lead to any agitation. By October 1923 the Constitutional Reform Association had for all practical purposes ceased to exist, and was never revived.[24] The 1922 petition was the last attempt by the European minority in the colony to grasp at power for themselves. Stubbs's fears that this example might incite the Chinese to raise demands for representation were not fulfilled. The only occasion when the question of constitutional reform was raised by the Chinese was during the 1925–6 general strike and boycott. One of the 19 demands of the strike committee in Canton was that the Chinese members of the Legislative Council should be elected and that labourers should be given the vote.[25] But this demand was not pressed with any vigour in the intermittent negotiations which took place over a period of some 15 months. The Governor, Sir Cecil Clementi, assured the Colonial Office, quoting Stubbs's words, that the vast majority of the Chinese took no interest in such matters. In any case such a demand could not be discussed, much less conceded, at the dictation of an alien body.

However, in May 1926 while the boycott was still in effect Clementi created considerable surprise at the Colonial Office by proposing the nomination of a Chinese, Sir Shou-son Chow, to fill a vacancy on the Executive Council caused by the death of Sir Paul Chater. Sir Shou-son had been a member of the Legislative Council since 1921 and had just been knighted in the New Year Honours List. He was only the third pure-bred Chinese to become a knight, and, like his predecessor Sir Kai Ho Kai in 1912, this honour was in part a reward for his consistent support of the colonial authorities in troubled times. Clementi wished to make the gesture of elevating a Chinese to the Executive Council spontaneously before any agitation for such a concession arose, in order to achieve the maximum political effect.[26]

Officials in London were doubtful of the wisdom of such a move, even though they recognized its political value. Could a Chinese be trusted to observe the confidentiality of Executive Council business?

Would not the presence of a Chinese inhibit the discussion of certain items? Would there be a suitable Chinese successor available when Sir Shou-son retired, since the Chinese would expect his seat to be permanently allocated to them and would suffer great loss of face if he were to be replaced by a European in future? There was also the danger that such an appointment in Hong Kong might give rise to agitation for similar changes in the Straits Settlements, where conditions were different. These points were all put to Clementi but they did not cause him to withdraw his proposal. He replied that the possibility that unofficial members might disclose information obtained at meetings of the Executive Council or use it for their personal advantage had always existed and present European members were not above suspicion on this count. He did not anticipate any difficulty in finding a worthy successor when that became necessary, nor did he think that the appointment could be seen as a victory for the Canton strike committee since they had never raised such a demand: and it might have the effect of staving off a demand for elected Chinese representation on the Legislative Council, which, Clementi averred, could not possibly be granted.[27] The officials in London were not completely convinced, and the Governor of the Straits Settlements, Sir Lawrence Guillemard, who had been consulted, also objected to the proposal; but Clementi's assessment of the situation was the decisive factor, and the Permanent Under-Secretary advised the minister that it should be accepted. So Sir Shou-son Chow was appointed to the Executive Council. The Foreign Office was informed after the decision was taken. Later in the year, on the insistence of the Foreign Office, the Governor was instructed that secret telegrams should no longer be communicated to members of the Council, as had been the practice in the past.[28] Sir Shou-son Chow remained on the Council for 10 years until 1936 when he was succeeded by Sir Robert Kotewall.

The care shown by the Colonial Office to take account of possible repercussions in the Straits Settlements of any constitutional change in Hong Kong was part of the general concern of officials to achieve consistency of policy throughout the Empire, except where local conditions militated against this. Four years earlier, in 1922, the danger of stimulating renewed agitation in Hong Kong had been used to dissuade the Governor of the Straits Settlements from pressing for changes in that colony. The attitudes of the Governors of Hong Kong and the Straits Settlements to the issue of constitutional reform provide an interesting contrast. Stubbs, who had previously been an official at the Colonial Office for 15 years, was cautiously prepared to contemplate token changes in response to agitation while insisting on the need to retain an overall official majority in the Legislative Council; Sir Lawrence Guillemard, who had come into the colonial service late in life after 30 years at the Treasury and in the Department of Inland Revenue, had a much more liberal attitude. In the Straits Settlements in 1920 the subject of changes in the Executive and Legislative Councils had been raised informally by the unofficials. Without waiting to ask permission from the Colonial Office, Guillemard arranged for the appointment of a select committee, composed predominantly of unofficial members of the Legislative Council, to make proposals. This recommended that the number of unofficials on the Legislative Council should be increased from 8 to 14 and the number of officials from 10 to 12, giving an unofficial majority of two, whereas previously there was an official majority of two. The committee also proposed that the two unofficials should be elected to the Executive Council by the Legislative Council unofficials. Guillemard welcomed these proposals and commended them to the Colonial Office as being eminently reasonable and in keeping with the spirit of the times; but officials demurred and delayed a decision until Guillemard returned to England on leave, when he was with difficulty persuaded to agree that the official majority in the Legislative Council should be retained, although the number of both officials and unofficials should be increased, to 13 officials and 12 unofficials, and two unofficials should be appointed to the Executive Council. Officials argued that the admitted apathy of the population of the Straits Settlements made further changes unnecessary, and that a greater advance might stimulate demands in Hong Kong.[29]

The same officials who turned down plans for constitutional advance in Hong Kong and the Straits Settlements were at that very time bestowing an elected unofficial majority on the colony of Ceylon. But in that case officials believed that they were faced with a 'genuine local demand' to which concessions had to be made, which was not the case in either Hong Kong or the Straits Settlements.[30] In all cases the first moves for constitutional change had to come from within a colony, and then officials recommended such pragmatic adjustments to the machinery of government as seemed appropriate to local conditions, making an assessment of popular feeling and the possible repercussions elsewhere. There is no sign that Colonial Office officials or any minister had any long-term strategy to expand democratic participation generally in the colonial empire.

The only change in the composition of the Hong Kong Legislative Council in the 40 years between 1896 and 1946 took place in 1929, and this occurred without any prior public agitation whatsoever. Sir Henry Polluck, who had been quiescent for eight years after his elevation to the Executive Council, put down a question for the Governor in the Legislative Council in March 1928, asking whether a representative of Kowloon could be added to the Council. The number of those living on the Kowloon peninsula had grown from 80,000 in 1918 to 250,000 in 1928 and they now formed a quarter of the colony's total population. Clementi professed his sympathy with Polluck's point of view and undertook to discuss the matter at the Colonial Office when on leave in the summer. He then went beyond Polluck's suggestion to propose that the Legislative Council should be enlarged by the addition of two officials and two unofficials; the unofficials should be appointed by the Governor but could be nominated by the Kowloon Residents Association, on the lines of the existing nomination of two members by the Justices of the Peace and the General Chamber of Commerce, and one of them should be a Chinese.[31] The Colonial Office raised no objections to this proposal and the minister initialled the papers without comment. During his discussions on this subject in the Colonial Office Clementi apparently alluded to the political climate in Hong Kong, and an official subsequently minuted, 'The European desire for constitutional reform has been more or less killed by the realisation that any changes would have to be in a Sinophile direction.'[32] This proved to be a very prescient assessment: there was not a single further mention of constitutional reform in the Legislative Council over the next 13 years by either European or Chinese unofficials. Only one isolated reference to the question can be found in all the surviving official records: the Taxation Committee Report of 1939 mentioned, among other objections to the institution of an income tax, the possible danger that 'so radical a departure in fiscal policy would give rise to a demand, now dormant, for popular representation'.[33]

The new members of the Legislative Council took their seats for the first time in January 1929 after the *Royal Instructions* had been amended. The race of the new unofficials was not specified, nor was the method by which they were to be chosen, these matters being left to the discretion of the Governor. One was Dr Tso Seen-wan, giving the Chinese three out of the eight unofficial seats. The other was Jose Pedro Braga, who was of Portuguese origin. This was the first time that those who had moved from Macau to Hong Kong had been given representation in the Legislative Council. Both Tso and Braga were residents of Kowloon and Braga in particular was vociferous in raising the complaints of this area in Council meetings, claiming to speak in the name of the Kowloon Residents Association. But the Governor did not commit himself in any way to give this body a prescriptive right to nominate future members. Tso and Braga both served two four-year terms on the Council, retiring in 1937. Braga was succeeded by L. D'Almada E. Castro who was a member of the committee of the Kowloon Residents Association and was similarly active on the residents' behalf. Dr Tso was replaced by Dr Li Shu-fan, who does not appear to have had any particular connection with Kowloon.[34]

At the same time as Braga and Tso joined the Legislative Council in 1929, the Harbour-master and the Director of Medical and Sanitary Services were added to the official side. The amendment to the *Royal Instructions* also provided for the Secretary for Chinese Affairs to be an ex-officio member of both the Executive and Legislative Councils. Hallifax, who had been Secretary for Chinese Affairs since 1911, had long been a nominated official member of the Councils, but Clementi pressed for this change since he wished to emphasize the importance which the government attached to this office.[35]

A number of other changes to the *Letters Patent* and *Royal Instructions* were made over the period, but they were all of minor significance, directed towards clarifying ambiguities, simplifying procedures, settling questions of the precedence of officials, and bringing the Hong Kong documents into line with changes made in revisions of the *Colonial Regulations*. The whole set of documents, originally issued in 1888, was revised and reissued in 1917, and all subsequent amendments were consolidated in a single document in 1938, when the post of Colonial Treasurer was abolished and the new post of Financial Secretary created. The 1938 revision also finally removed the reference to the post of Lieutenant-Governor in Clause 17 of the *Letters Patent*. In the early days of the colony this position had normally been filled by the General Officer Commanding (GOC) British Forces in the colony, to ensure that he acted as Officer Administering the Government (OAG) when the Governor was away on leave, but no Lieutenant-Governor had in fact been appointed since the retirement of Major-General Whitfield in 1874.[36]

The question of who should act as OAG when the Governor was absent from Hong Kong gave rise to problems on two occasions, in 1920 and in 1940. According to Clause 17 of the 1917 *Letters Patent* (which reproduced the wording of the 1888 *Letters Patent)*, when the Governor was absent he should be succeeded in the first place by the Lieutenant-Governor, if any; if there was none, by 'such person or persons as may be appointed under the Royal Sign Manual and Signet'; finally, in default of any such instructions, the succession passed to 'the person lawfully discharging the function of Colonial Secretary'. In practice from 1885 the second alternative had been used and the succession had been regulated by a dormant commission held by the Governor which came into operation when he left the colony. Under this dormant commission the line of succession was laid down as: firstly, the Colonial Secretary, secondly, the senior military officer in command of the regular forces in the colony, and thirdly, 'the person discharging the functions of the Colonial Secretary'. During the period from 1895 to 1903 which was a time of tension in the Far East following the Sino-Japanese War, the dormant commission was amended to give the senior military officer precedence over the Colonial Secretary, but the former order of succession was reinstated in 1903.[37]

These arrangements caused no problems until April 1920 when it so happened that the Colonial Secretary went on leave and shortly afterwards the GOC British Forces, Major-General Ventris, was unexpectedly sent to Singapore to conduct a military enquiry. This left the military forces under the command of a Colonel Young of the Royal Engineers, who under the terms of the dormant commission would automatically take over as Governor if any accident befell Sir Edward Stubbs. Stubbs did not have a high opinion of Major-General Ventris ('a period of administration by him, though not likely to be satisfactory, would not be obviously unreasonable') but his opinion of Colonel Young was far worse ('his views appear to be somewhat peculiar and his personality is more than somewhat uncouth. That the government of the colony should be administered by Colonel Young is inconceivable'). At the time the colony was facing a series of strikes which had begun in the dockyards, had then spread to the electricity company and the tramways, and threatened to spread further, while there was political instability in Canton, and there were fears that undisciplined and unpaid Chinese troops might stage raids across the frontier in search of loot. Stubbs was affronted that the War Office had not consulted him before posting Major-General Ventris to Singapore at a time when Hong Kong was facing such a crisis, and he penned a furious dispatch to the Colonial Office demanding that the dormant commission should be cancelled forthwith, so that in future when the Governor was absent or indisposed the colony would be administered either by the Colonial Secretary or the acting Colonial Secretary. The dispatch was accompanied by a private letter to the Permanent Under-Secretary (Fiddes) which elaborated on the perils of the situation if the colony should ever be run by Colonel Young ('a man notoriously eccentric to the verge of madness').[38]

Colonial Office officials deprecated the violence of Stubbs's language, but accepted the reasonableness of his case. To deal with the immediate situation the dormant commission was withdrawn and replaced by one which referred specifically to Major-General Ventris, but made no provision for him to be replaced by another army officer. On Ventris's retirement the dormant commission was withdrawn completely, leaving the succession to be regulated by Clause 17 of the *Letters Patent;* that is to say, in the Governor's absence the administration passed first to the Colonial Secretary and then to the acting Colonial Secretary. The War Office was informed of the new arrangements only after they had been finalized and its protests at the exclusion of the GOC British forces from the succession, which had been expected, were ignored.

Twenty years later the competence of an acting Governor was again called into question, but on this occasion it was the military authorities who cast doubt on the ability of a public servant to run the government. In May 1940, the Governor, Sir Geoffry Northcote, went on leave to Britain on the advice of his doctors, and the Colonial Secretary, Mr N.L. Smith, took over as OAG. Smith had spent the whole of his career in Hong Kong. He had been Colonial Secretary since 1936 and had already acted as Governor twice before, in 1935 (when he was acting Colonial Secretary) and in 1937. However in 1940 the colony stood in grave danger of an attack by Japan and it soon became evident to the military and naval authorities that Smith was unfitted to the demands of such an emergency. A month after his assumption of office the Commander-in-Chief of the China station sent the following cable to the Admiralty:

General Officer Commanding and myself are in agreement that there is grave danger to colony of Hong Kong if the present acting governor remains in office. He lacks decision and drive and things are muddling along. If Colonial Office cannot spare a first class man in very near future, we recommend a Military Governor be appointed and that a senior soldier should be sent from India.[39]

This message was immediately passed by the Admiralty to the Secretary of State for the Colonies, Lord Lloyd, who decided that this advice must be accepted. The War Office was asked to suggest an officer and proposed Major-General C.F. Norton, DSO, MC, who, among his other accomplishments, had led an expedition to climb Mount Everest in 1924. This extraordinary appointment was approved by the Prime Minister, Winston Churchill, and a dormant commission, personal to Norton, was issued to enable him to supersede Smith as Governor. Norton was given the temporary rank of Lieutenant-General and flew to Hong Kong from India, arriving at the beginning of August, when Smith reverted to the post of Colonial Secretary. Lieutenant-General Norton served uneventfully for seven months until Northcote returned in March 1941. Northcote had not fully recovered his health and finally retired in September, when he was immediately succeeded by Sir Mark Young, just 12 weeks before the Japanese invasion.

In both 1920 and 1940 Colonial Office officials were quite content to allow the succession to the Governor to take place according to the established rules. They only reacted when alerted to a possibly dangerous situation by the man on the spot, and then they did not attempt to question his assessment of the competence of the potential or actual acting Governor before removing him from the succession.

The Creation of the Urban Council, 1936

There was only one change in the institutions of government in Hong Kong between the First and Second World Wars: the transformation of the Sanitary Board into the Urban Council. However, this was more a change in nomenclature than a change of substance.

The Sanitary Board had been set up in 1883 as a committee of officials, following the publication of the Chadwick Report on the appalling sanitary conditions in the colony. In 1886 four appointed unofficial members were added and in the following year provision was made for two further unofficials, who were to be elected by those ratepayers who were qualified to serve as jurors. For the next 16 years the Sanitary Board as a collective body was responsible for drafting by-laws on all matters of public health (which were subsequently enacted into law by resolution of the Legislative Council) and for the supervision of their enforcement by the staff of the Sanitary Department. This arrangement was not entirely successful: the members of the Board only served on it in a part-time capacity and so were unable to keep a close check on the activities of its officials; and the unofficial members, being themselves usually substantial property-owners, were suspected of being unduly lenient with other landlords over the implementation of the sanitary regulations. In 1901 there was a renewed outcry over sanitary conditions in the colony, expressed in a petition to the government, and another commission of enquiry was sent from Britain to investigate local conditions, consisting of Osbert Chadwick (again) and Professor W.J. Simpson. They recommended the appointment of a Sanitary Commissioner to take full responsibility for the efficient administration of the Sanitary Department. The Commissioner should be a medical man specially trained and skilled in sanitary affairs and he should devote the whole of his time to such duties. Chadwick and Simpson also drafted a new and stricter Public Health and Buildings Ordinance.[40]

These recommendations were carried into effect by legislation passed in 1903, and the Principal Civil Medical Officer (PCMO) was appointed to be both President of the Sanitary Board and head of the Sanitary Department. The unofficial members of the Sanitary Board were not at all happy at being reduced in effect to little more than a consultative committee to the PCMO and three years later they had the opportunity to give public vent to their grievances. Allegations of corruption in the administration of the Sanitary Department led the Governor to appoint a commission of enquiry, consisting of all the unofficial members of the Sanitary Board, to investigate. The commission's report, published in 1907, asserted that bribery and corruption were rampant within the Department. They also claimed that, although the PCMO now had 'despotic powers', the administration of the Department was ineffective since he was too preoccupied with his duties in the government hospitals to spare the time to supervise the work of the subordinate sanitary officials. The solution, in the view of the commission, was to give back to the Sanitary Board full powers to direct the activities of the Department, to decide all promotions and assignments of staff, and to control its expenditure. The Board should elect its own President annually who 'should not under any conditions be a medical man'.[41]

The colonial government agreed that the PCMO was too overburdened by his other duties to direct the work of the Sanitary Department, but did not accept that the solution was to give this responsibility back to the members of the Sanitary Board, who were themselves only part-time members of that body. Instead the post of head of the Sanitary Department and President of the Sanitary Board was given to a cadet officer and the PCMO was removed from the Board and replaced by a medical officer of health.[42] The composition of the Board remained unchanged, consisting of four officials and six unofficials, but the franchise was slightly extended by giving all jurors, and also those qualified for jury service but exempted, the right to vote, whether or not they were also ratepayers. But as there was no change in the essentially advisory nature of the Board this concession made little practical difference. In theory the business of the Board was conducted through 17 select committees, but in fact, in 1929, unofficials were members of only four of these committees, and most of the committees consisted of the head of the Sanitary Department and one other official.[43]

For 16 years after the reorganization in 1908, little was heard of the Sanitary Board and few of the elections were contested. Moves for change first emerged in 1924 when there was an outbreak of typhoid fever which gave rise to much criticism of the Sanitary Department in the local press. In fact, the number of typhoid cases was little different from that in previous years, but a greater number of those affected were Europeans. Dissatisfaction centred on the point that the sanitation services were under the control of a medically unqualified cadet. So a motion was passed at a meeting of the Sanitary Board that it should be reconstituted under a commissioner of public health who should be a medical man possessing a diploma in public health.[44] The unofficials further pressed this point in a debate in the Legislative Council, but the Governor, Stubbs, was adamant in opposing this change, arguing that the Sanitary Department must be headed by a competent administrator who was able to speak Chinese, in order that he should be able to exercise effective control over the largely Chinese staff of the department.[45] After Stubbs departed at the end of 1925 the new Governor, Clementi, asked the PCMO and the head of the Sanitary Department to put forward concrete proposals for the closer co-ordination of their two departments. Agreement was found to be impossible since the PCMO maintained that all sanitary activity was a matter for technical medical control, while the head of the Sanitary Department claimed that matters of simple order and cleanliness, though bearing on public health, did not require such expert supervision and were better left under the charge of those conversant with Chinese language, psychology, and customs.[46]

In 1928 the position of PCMO fell vacant and Clementi asked the Colonial Office to appoint a medical officer from another colony with practical experience in preventive medicine and who was not primarily a clinician, as previous holders of the post had been. The position was eventually offered to Dr Wellington, who was then Chief Health Officer of the Federated Malay States and was well qualified with two diplomas in the field of public health. Before his arrival in the colony the title of the office was changed to Director of Medical and Sanitary Services and the Legislative Council was informed that it was the government's intention that the work of the Medical and Sanitary Departments should be more closely co-ordinated in future, but that no reduction in the duties or the responsibility of the Sanitary Department or the Sanitary Board was contemplated.[47]

When Dr Wellington arrived in Hong Kong in 1929 Clementi proposed to appoint him immediately as head of the Sanitary Department and President of the Sanitary Board. However, this idea was opposed by the Executive Council and as a compromise Clementi agreed that Dr Wellington should at first only be made a member of the Board so that he could observe its workings.[48] He remained on the Board for less than a year and then put forward a voluminous memorandum proposing a radical restructuring of the whole public health organization.[49] Wellington pointed out that although it had been laid down that the Director of Medical and Sanitary Services was responsible for the health of the colony, he had practically no authority to act outside the government hospitals and laboratories. The Sanitary Board was totally independent of him and controlled by far the greater part of the colony's machinery for dealing with public health and was the authority under the only public health ordinance which the colony possessed. He went on to point to specific weaknesses in the by-laws passed by the Sanitary Board and the many gaps in their coverage, and made detailed criticisms of the way the by-laws were, or more often were not, enforced. In his view the only remedy was that the ordinance and regulations should be entirely recast to take account of modern ideas and practices, and that all public health activities should be brought together under medical direction. The Sanitary Department could continue as before under a cadet officer, but its activities would be confined to sanitation in the narrowest sense, that is, town cleaning, scavenging, and conservancy work, together with the granting of certain licences. The Sanitary Board might remain as a purely advisory body and a vent for public opinion.

Such radical proposals aroused a storm of opposition from the cadet service, the Director of Public Works, the unofficial members of the Sanitary Board, and from the public in general.[50] Although the Board had little effective power, it was jealously regarded locally as the one element of self-government allowed in the colony and the Chinese members in particular desired to have some kind of buffer interposed between them and the demands of a professional hygienist who might intrude upon the privacy of their homes and family life, interfere with their freedom to overcrowd tenements for maximum profit, and infringe upon their liberty to live under insanitary conditions and spread diseases to their neighbours. It was five years before a compromise was finally hammered out. Clementi, who had strongly supported Dr Wellington's proposals, left the colony early in 1930 to become Governor of the Straits Settlements and his successor, Sir William Peel, was less inclined to put his weight behind the new plans and override the vested interests involved.[51] Conferences were held without resolving the differences; a committee of the Executive Council was set up to mediate but failed to agree. Finally in 1933 the Governor issued a directive which laid down the general lines upon which reorganization should take place and ordered that drafting of the new ordinances should proceed. When drafting was completed the bills were examined by another committee of the Executive Council, which divided three to two on the proposals. The bills were then considered by a committee of officials, further revised by the Attorney General, and finally submitted to the Executive Council again at the end of 1934. They were approved, amended further during their passage through the Legislative Council, and eventually became law in 1935. The new system was inaugurated in January 1936, by which time Dr Wellington was on the verge of retirement.

Throughout these discussions Dr Wellington had stressed the need to model Hong Kong's public health arrangements on those of a progressive modern municipality, and his original memorandum had given full details of the organization that had been adopted in such cities as Toronto, Shanghai, and the Panama Canal Zone. He also emphasized that sanitation services formed only a small part of the modern science of preventive medicine. Accordingly the most obvious change brought about by the new legislation was the abolition of the Sanitary Board and the creation of a new Urban Council. But in spite of the change of name the functions of the two bodies were almost identical. The Medical Department took over responsibility for the registration of births and deaths and for the prevention of infectious diseases but otherwise the formal powers of the Council to make by-laws and superintend their enforcement over a wide area of public health activities remained unchanged, although its prerogatives were now set out in far more elaborate detail in six ordinances rather than two. It acquired no new responsibilities outside the area of public health. Under the old ordinance of 1903 it had been laid down that: 'The head of the Sanitary Department shall give such directions as may be necessary for carrying out and giving effect to the decisions of the Board.' An identical form of words appeared in the 1935 Urban Council Ordinance, except that 'head of the Sanitary Department' was replaced by 'Chairman of the Urban Council'. If the former Sanitary Board was stigmatized as nothing more than an advisory committee to the Sanitary Department — an accusation which the cadet in charge always emphatically denied — then the Urban Council was in exactly the same position.

The composition of the Council was also little altered. The Chairman of the Urban Council was still to be the head of the Sanitary Department, that is to say, a cadet and not a medically qualified professional. There was now to be a Vice-Chairman, the Director of Medical and Sanitary Services, who was to be the professional adviser to the Council on all matters of public health and sanitation and was to superintend the enforcement of all ordinances, by-laws, and regulations relating to public health. The medical officers of health and the sanitary inspectors were to work under his general direction, but he was required to ensure that any instructions received from the Chairman of the Urban Council were duly carried out. There were three other officials on the new Council: the Director of Public Works, the Secretary for Chinese Affairs, and the Inspector-General of Police, and also eight unofficials, comprising six appointed by the Governor, of whom three must be Chinese, and two elected members. The franchise for the elections was the same as in 1908. Thus the only changes from the old Sanitary Board were the addition of three new members, the Inspector-General of Police and two appointed unofficials, and the substitution of the Director of Medical and Sanitary Services for a medical officer of health.

If we compare the new arrangements with Dr Wellington's original proposals it is clear that he had largely been the loser in the bureaucratic battle. An integrated system of public health under the control of the Director of Medical and Sanitary Services was not created; instead, authority for the making and enforcement of most public health regulations remained in lay hands, in the Urban Council and the cadet officer who was its Chairman.[52] The Building Authority (effectively the Director of Public Works) continued to be the body responsible for approving plans for new buildings and for town planning, waterworks, sewers, and drains, without any reference to the medical authorities. In the New Territories where the Urban Council did not operate, district officers still dealt with matters of hygiene and sanitation. When Wellington retired in 1937 even the statutory requirement that the sanitary inspectors should be grouped under the medical officers of health had not been implemented and they continued to be directly responsible to the head of the Sanitary Department.[53] One reason for this was a lack of sufficient staff, a consequence of the financial stringency caused by the economic depression which necessitated the postponement of a number of other medical improvements which Dr Wellington had planned.

Throughout this whole controversy the Colonial Office was little more than a passive spectator. The need to put greater effort into public health services and preventive medicine rather than building more hospitals and providing curative services was a constant theme of the reports of the Colonial Advisory Medical Committee, which was established in 1922, and of the comments of the Chief Medical Adviser at the Colonial Office, a new position created in 1926.[54] Officials in London were intermittently kept informed of progress in Hong Kong by visits paid by Dr Wellington and successive Governors when on leave, and by occasional dispatches, and from time to time the Colonial Office showed its interest in the discussions by asking for further information, but no attempt was made to put any pressure on the Governor to influence the outcome. The various ordinances of 1935 were routinely submitted to the Colonial Office for the signification of non-disallowance after they had been passed by the Legislative Council, but the only query raised on them was why public servants were denied the right to vote in Urban Council elections. The Governor explained that public servants were not allowed to act as jurors, and so had been excluded from the electoral roll ever since elections had been instituted; the government had no intention of extending the franchise for the new Urban Council from that used for the Sanitary Board. In view of the reluctance of the Governor to make any change officials decided not to press the point further.[55]

The reorganization of the Urban Council was not connected with any wider scheme for municipal government in Hong Kong. In 1894 the Secretary of State for the Colonies, Lord Ripon, had commended the idea of establishing a municipality in Hong Kong, such as existed in other colonies, but his successor, Joseph Chamberlain, had considered this to be impracticable, principally because of the difficulty of drawing a line between colonial and municipal affairs. Thereafter the idea was dropped and the constitutional agitation of 1916 to 1923 was entirely concerned with securing an unofficial majority in the Legislative Council. The absence of a municipal council was referred to by the promoters of the various petitions, but only as an argument for increased representation in the Legislative Council. None of the petitions mentioned the Sanitary Board or advocated changes in its composition or powers so that it could be developed into a Municipal Council. However, once the hope of changes in the Legislative Council was abandoned, the idea of a Municipal Council was once more intermittently put forward by the unofficial members, notably those who were on the Retrenchment Commission of 1930–1, who suggested in their report that the institution of a municipality such as existed in Singapore would produce cheaper and more efficient administration. The members of the commission apparently believed that such a municipality could be run by local business men with greater economy than the existing government departments. This proposal was not worked out in detail and was immediately rejected by the Governor in a dispatch to the Colonial Office as being more likely to lead to wasteful duplication of services.[56] But the idea was not killed by this rebuff, and 15 years later it formed the basis of Sir Mark Young's post-war plans for constitutional reform.[57]

8 The Abolition of the *Mui Tsai* System, 1917 to 1924

WHEN Captain Elliot took possession of Hong Kong in 1841, he issued a proclamation which declared that 'pending Her Majesty's further pleasure, the natives of the island of Hong Kong and all natives of China thereto resorting shall be governed according to the laws and customs of China, every description of torture excepted'. Similarly, when Governor Blake took over the New Territories in 1899 he promised the indigenous inhabitants that 'Your usages and good customs will not in any way be interfered with'. Neither of these proclamations had the force of law, but they have always been regarded by the Chinese as binding the colonial administration not to interfere with the social customs of the Chinese community, and over the past 150 years that of Elliot has been regularly cited by the Chinese whenever they felt the need to protest at some new imposition by the colonial government. In fact neither of these declarations is unqualified: that of Elliot specifically exempted all forms of torture and was subject to the overriding discretion of the Queen, that is to say of the British government; and that of Blake referred to the preservation of 'good' customs only, leaving it open to question who would decide which customs were bad and so liable to be interfered with. However, the two declarations enshrined one of the cardinal principles of British colonial administration, that it was imprudent and dangerous to disturb the native inhabitants of the colonies by any attempt to change their traditional social customs and arrangements.

Such restraint did not extend to the toleration of the practice of slavery. The first ordinance passed by the Legislative Council of Hong Kong when it was constituted in 1844 was one to prohibit the practice of slavery. This ordinance was disallowed by the Crown, not because the British government wished to permit slavery in Hong Kong but on the legal ground that the British Acts of Parliament outlawing the slave trade and subsequently abolishing slavery itself already extended to all dominions of the Crown, including the new colony of Hong Kong, and so any anti-slavery ordinance by the local legislature was unnecessary. This fact was made known to the population by a government proclamation.[1]

However, neither the Chinese nor the colonial administration regarded this announcement as outlawing the traditional Chinese practice of taking small girls to work as domestic servants known among the Cantonese as 'mui tsai' (literally 'little younger sister').[2] This was a custom found all over China under various names by which parents who were too poor to provide adequately for their children presented a daughter to a more well-to-do family. This family undertook to feed, clothe, and shelter the child until she came of age, when a suitable marriage might be arranged for her. Normally the transfer of the child would be effected by the drawing up and signing of a 'deed of gift' or 'sung tip' by which the parents formally gave up their rights to the child, and in exchange received a sum of money, which might amount to HK$10 for each year of the child's age, in compensation for the cost of her upbringing to date.[3] The mui tsai would then be employed on domestic duties in her new home. These might be no more than attendance on one of the daughters of her new master in a wealthy home or might extend to performing all forms of household drudgery in a poorer household. The mui tsai received no wages beyond her food and shelter, although she might receive occasional gifts. Her natural parents might visit her if they lived within a reasonable distance, and might be consulted about her eventual marriage; but in practice the girl's connection with her natural family was often completely severed if she was transferred to a far-distant town, although her parents by custom had the right to redeem her if they refunded the money which had been paid for her transfer. The girl herself had no opportunity to give or refuse her consent to the transaction. Commonly mui tsai were only small children and sometimes were mere babies when the transfer was made. There was normally a plentiful supply of surplus daughters throughout China to be disposed of as mui tsai as a result of the desire of the Chinese to obtain sons who could carry on the family and perform the customary religious rites in commemoration of their ancestors. Daughters could not perform these ceremonies and would in any case leave their father's home on marriage, and so were less esteemed. Since the mass of Chinese both in China itself and in the colony of Hong Kong lived in conditions of grinding poverty and were always liable to be brought to the brink of starvation by floods, drought, pestilence, or banditry, the poor might be driven to part with their daughters in order to secure the means of sustenance for the rest of the family, and in times of famine desperate parents might give away their children rather than see them starve to death. In such circumstances a child who was acquired as a *mui tsai* suffered a better fate than one sold to a brothelkeeper for a life of prostitution. The rich man who took a *mui tsai* into his houshold could then regard himself as performing an act of charity towards the poor.

Critics of the institution, both Chinese and European, did not regard it in this light.[4] They claimed that the *mui tsai* was in fact a slave; she was bought for money, even though the transaction might be formally described as a 'presentation'; she had no right to leave her master; she could be exploited without reserve; she received no pay for her labour; and she could be sold again, sometimes for immoral purposes, if she failed to satisfy her master. It was said that far from being an act of charity the acquisition of a *mui tsai* was a straight commercial transaction whereby the master obtained a child for a small sum of money, enjoyed her free labour for a number of years, and then disposed of her at a profit when she came of age (whether she was sold into prostitution or given in marriage as a first wife or concubine), since her master was entitled to the customary marriage payment when she married. Furthermore, *mui tsai,* being entirely within the power of their masters, were frequently subject to ill-treatment dictated by the whims of their owners and sometimes to gross cruelty. They were also liable to be sexually abused by the male members of the household.

In reply defenders of the system insisted that the Chinese were noted for their kindness to children; most *mui tsai* were well treated; cases of cruelty were rare and would be reported by the neighbours and could be punished by law. *Mui tsai* were not slaves, but were treated as members of the family which had adopted them, although of an inferior status. Upon marriage they and their children were entirely free of any taint of servitude. The work of a *mui tsai* was much the same as any girl would be called upon to do in her own home, and most were better off with their new families than if they had remained with their poverty-stricken natural parents. It was also denied that there was any connection between the adoption of *mui tsai* and the trafficking in girls to be trained as prostitutes; *mui tsai* were acquired for the purpose of domestic service and not to be taught the arts of a courtesan.[5]

The legal position of the *mui tsai* in 1920, when the agitation for reform first became clamant, was that no form of servile status was

[margin note: defenders of Mui Tsai]

recognized by the laws of Hong Kong.[6] In law the *mui tsai* was entirely free to leave her master at any time, and if he should attempt to prevent her he could, in theory, be served with a writ of *habeas corpus* by the girl's parents, or by any other interested party, requiring him to produce the girl before the courts. In practice there had never been recourse to such a procedure. The contract purporting to transfer the girl from her natural parents to her new adoptive family or master was absolutely void in the eyes of the law and unenforceable in the courts, as being contrary to public policy. The status of being a *mui tsai* existed in fact, not in law, and this status was enforced by custom and by the ignorance of the *mui tsai,* most of whom were children who had been taught to believe that they were bound to obey their masters. So the Hong Kong government could not be accused of giving the backing of law to Chinese custom. On the other hand it did nothing to make the *mui tsai* aware of their right to leave their masters and it implicitly gave a degree of recognition to the practice when, in prosecutions for the kidnapping of *mui tsai,* the employer of a *mui tsai* was treated as having the lawful care of her as against the child-stealer. Some slight protection was also given to *mui tsai* by an ordinance of 1910 which made the Secretary for Chinese Affairs the legal guardian of any girl who had been adopted or who had been transferred from her natural parents for a money payment, and empowered him to take such action as should best secure the welfare of any girl who had been mistreated. This provision gave the Secretary for Chinese Affairs wide discretion to take action if a case of cruelty came to his notice, but it was in fact very seldom used.[7]

Whatever the legal status of the *mui tsai,* the custom was widespread in Hong Kong. In 1918 the Governor informed the Colonial Office that practically every household that could afford the expense possessed a *mui tsai.* A few years later the Secretary for Chinese Affairs stated that half the Chinese families in Hong Kong had at least one *mui tsai* and it was likely that the number of *mui tsai* might exceed the number of daughters living with their natural parents.[8] The custom of owning a *mui tsai* extended from the well-to-do right down to the families of clerks and artisans, as was shown by reports of cases in court.[9] A count of the number of *mui tsai* was attempted in the 1921 Census, when 8,653 *mui tsai* were discovered, as compared with 75,000 daughters under the age of 18. But this figure is likely to be inaccurate since some families probably told enumerators that their *mui tsai* were their natural or adopted daughters. In any case the 1921 Census almost certainly gave a very misleading picture of the colony's population since, on instructions from London, it was taken over the Chinese New Year holiday at a time when many people had left Hong Kong to visit their families in China. But whatever the precise figure for *mui tsai* might be, there were clearly a vast number of them in the colony and any attempt to abolish this venerable custom might be expected to arouse considerable controversy and resentment and alienate the substantial economic interests involved. Not surprisingly the Hong Kong government preferred to interfere with the institution as little as possible and was only prepared to consider reforms when pressure was exerted on it from outside.

The question of the legality of the *mui tsai* system had first been raised in 1878. Two long reports on the custom were produced for the use of the Colonial Office by Dr E.J. Eitel, the Inspector of Schools, in 1879 and by Mr J. Russell, the Registrar General, in 1883. After a protracted correspondence the Colonial Office was finally convinced that no action to abolish or modify the custom was necessary or practicable beyond a strengthening of the law against the trafficking in children with a view to prostitution or the training of them for this purpose, and an ordinance on these lines was eventually passed in 1887.[10] For the next 30 years nothing more was heard of the matter until the question was revived in 1917 when a case involving the alleged kidnapping of two *mui tsai* aged 10 and 13 years was heard before the Hong Kong Supreme Court. On this occasion counsel for the defence attempted to rebut the assumption that the *mui tsai* were in the lawful custody of their mistress at the time of their kidnapping, on the ground that the *mui tsai* were really slaves and so, since slavery had been abolished in Hong Kong, their mistress could not be their lawful guardian. The accused was eventually found not guilty on other grounds and the question of the legality of the *mui tsai* system was not decided by the court, but the case attracted considerable local publicity. One person who noticed it was Lieutenant-Colonel John Ward, a British Member of Parliament who happened to be passing through Hong Kong while on active service. Ward caused the case to be brought to the notice of the Secretary of State for the Colonies, demanding to know how it was possible that slavery was apparently tolerated and protected by law in part of the British Empire. Officials at the Colonial Office were completely ignorant of the correspondence of 30 years before and were taken aback by this highly embarrassing revelation. A dispatch was accordingly sent to the Governor pointing out that if it was established that a status equivalent to slavery could exist in the colony it would be necessary to amend the law on the subject; however the Secretary of State did not doubt that this was not the case, and the Governor was asked to send a report on the system and suggest remedies for any abuses that might occur.[11]

This dispatch was sent in December 1917 and the Governor, Sir Henry May, took his time to reply and only did so after a reminder was sent to him four months later. He then sent a brief telegram which was later elaborated in a dispatch sent in August 1918. This gave a full explanation and defence of the *mui tsai* institution, referring the Colonial Office to the reports submitted 30 years earlier. May pointed out that slavery was indeed illegal in Hong Kong, but he insisted that *mui tsai* were not slaves but maidservants who were given board, lodging, and sometimes education in lieu of wages; although the *mui tsai* might in some cases be subject to misuse or ill-treatment the system was often the only alternative to starvation or infanticide. The dispatch contained no proposals for reform.[12]

The Colonial Office was not at all satisfied by this complacent reply. By this time, the officials had found the ancient reports and put before the Governor some tentative suggestions for reform, such as that *mui tsai* should in future be paid wages, and should be given complete freedom to change their employment on giving notice. The aim was to transform the system gradually into one of ordinary paid domestic service. Such a change would make the institution much easier to defend against criticism in Parliament and elsewhere. But officials were well aware of the difficulties of implementing any such reform. One official minuted: 'The Chinese will stand most things, but will stand least of all interference in family affairs. For that reason we interfere in these affairs as little as possible.' The Permanent Under-Secretary similarly warned his minister, 'We can easily cause great mischief if we act too roughly when up against established practice in the East.'[13] The Secretary of State (Walter Long) accepted this advice and a dispatch embodying the suggested reforms was sent to the Hong Kong government. This initiative was quickly rebuffed by Claud Severn, the Officer Administering the Government between the resignation of Sir Henry May and the arrival of the new Governor. He reiterated that *mui tsai* already had full legal freedom to change their employment, but most were too young and inexperienced to take advantage of this, and if they did so there was a great danger that they might fall into the hands of procuresses and end up being sold as prostitutes; *mui tsai* were fed, clothed, housed, and sometimes educated by their masters and this was sufficient recompense for them, considering that many had been saved from near starvation. He claimed that the *mui tsai* system was still universally practised throughout China and concluded, 'There being then no recognition of servile conditions, it would appear that no action is called for which might tend to upset the organization of a vast number of families.'[14]

The Colonial Office was relieved to learn that the system was still prevalent in China itself, which made it easier to defend its continued existence in Hong Kong. Lieutenant-Colonel Ward was now away fighting in Russia and his London correspondent, the Secretary of the General Federation of Trade Unions, had ceased to trouble the Secretary of State on the matter. So officials were quite prepared to accept Severn's arguments for non-interference and advised that the subject could be quietly dropped. The Permanent Under-Secretary agreed to this without seeking to ascertain the views of the new Secretary of State, Viscount Milner.

However, the matter was not allowed to rest there. Lieutenant-Colonel Ward had confined himself to protests expressed in private correspondence, since he wished to avoid handing the enemy a possible propaganda weapon to be used in wartime. But after the First World War was over a number of European residents in Hong Kong began to campaign actively for the abolition of the *mui tsai* system. These included some missionaries, and they were also joined by a few Chinese associated with the Christian churches. Among the campaigners was a Mrs Haslewood, the wife of a Lieutenant-Commander in the Royal Navy, whose intemperate letters to the newspapers attacking the system caused offence to the leaders of the Chinese community. The new Governor, Sir Edward Stubbs, asked the Commodore to persuade the Commander to restrain his wife from her crusade, and when he refused to do so the Admiralty was requested to arrange for his transfer.[15] Haslewood retired to Britain shortly afterwards where he and his wife set about energetically enlisting support for the cause of the oppressed slave girls of Hong Kong by writing to the press, to various philanthropic societies, to Members of Parliament, and to other prominent persons. Every scrap of information appearing in the Hong Kong press relating to *mui tsai*, cruelty to children, child labour, or prostitution was called in evidence to expose the shocking conditions existing in the colony. The Secretary of State found himself frequently answering questions in Parliament on the subject asked by Lieutenant-Colonel Ward and others, or signing replies to personal letters addressed to him by eminent persons whose views could not be lightly brushed aside, such as the Archbishops of Canterbury and York. Representations were received at the Colonial Office from organizations such as the Fabian Society, the League of Nations Union, the International Woman Suffrage Alliance, and the Anti-Slavery and Aborigines Protection Society. Officials were kept busy drafting letter after letter explaining that *mui tsai* were not slaves, that all cases of cruelty to children or *mui tsai* were investigated and punished by the courts, and that the adoption of *mui tsai* as domestic servants was unconnected with the procurement of women for prostitution.

The replies sent out by the Colonial Office followed completely the views expressed by the Hong Kong government. Nevertheless, in confidential dispatches, various suggestions were put before the Governor in 1920 and 1921 which might have the effect of mollifying the critics and deflecting the rising chorus of disapproval in Britain. None of these found favour with Stubbs. In April 1920 the Colonial Office suggested that all children taken into adoption should be registered and then made subject to visitation by inspectors. Stubbs rejected this on the grounds that the Chinese would refuse to co-operate and that the requirement to register could only be enforced under stringent penalties by an army of inspectors with inquisitorial powers of entry into every house in the colony. Such a system would be bitterly resented and would alienate the existing loyalty of the Chinese to the British administration.[16] In September 1920 Viscount Milner suggested that the Chinese should be encouraged to form a society for the protection and improvement of the conditions of girl domestic servants, with branches in different districts to hear complaints and mitigate cases of hardship and cruelty. Stubbs replied that such a committee existed already in the Po Leung Kuk. This society had been in existence since 1878 when it had been formed to assist in the suppression of kidnapping and the traffic in human beings. It already maintained a place of refuge for rescued women and children until proper provision could be made for them. The committee of the Po Leung Kuk consisted of prominent Chinese from all parts of the colony and any attempt to set up a new organization would be taken as a slur upon their existing charitable efforts.[17] In May 1921 the new Secretary of State, Winston Churchill, relayed to Stubbs a suggestion made in Parliament by Viscountess Astor, that members from Britain should be added to a committee set up in Hong Kong to supervise the conditions for the employment of children. In August Churchill proposed the appointment of a committee of enquiry from Britain. Stubbs dismissed both proposals; anyone coming from outside the colony would necessarily be ignorant of Chinese customs and modes of thought. In October 1921 the Colonial Office revived an old suggestion that all further transfers of *mui tsai* without the consent of their natural parents should be forbidden by law. Hong Kong had already rejected this on the ground that such a law could be easily evaded because such transfers would then take place secretly without witnesses.[18]

Meanwhile the campaign for the abolition of the *mui tsai* system continued to gain momentum not only in Britain, but also in Hong Kong itself where an Anti-*Mui Tsai* Society was set up with an organizing committee composed almost entirely of local Chinese. To counter its efforts the two Chinese members of the Legislative Council set up a Society for the Protection of *Mui Tsai*, thereby implementing Milner's suggestion which Stubbs had declared to be out of the question six months earlier. Meanwhile ministers in London continued to explain and defend the institution in Parliament and in private correspondence. Effectively the policy that there should be no attempt to interfere with the *mui tsai* system had been decided by the 'man on the spot', the Governor of Hong Kong, and the Colonial Office was acting as his spokesman, a position which ministers and officials were finding increasingly uncomfortable. Eventually in February 1922 the Secretary of State, Winston Churchill, decided that he would do so no longer. Faced with yet another list of parliamentary questions on the subject he dictated the following minute to his Permanent Under-Secretary:

I am not prepared to go on defending this thing. Ask that all these questions should be put off for a week in order that I may make a comprehensive reply after receiving full reports I am calling for. Put to the Governor my intention to state that no compulsion of any kind will be allowed to prevent these persons from quitting their employment at any time they like.

I do not care a rap what the local consequences are. I am not going on defending it. You had better make it perfectly clear.   W.S.C., 21/2/22.

There is no clear evidence of the reasons for Churchill's abrupt reversal of Colonial Office policy. He may have been influenced by a conference of over 20 societies held in London under the auspices of the Anti-Slavery and Aborigines Protection Society which had just issued an appeal for a public enquiry. He was also under more subtle pressure to take action: his friend Colonel Josiah Wedgwood had written to him, 'This *mui tsai* business is a small thing that you might put right with credit. It must go soon and you should do it.'[19]

Once the minister had decided on a change of policy it became the task of the Colonial Office to translate it into practical administrative measures. A telegram was drafted to be sent to the Governor, and after its terms had been strengthened by Churchill, who added the suggestion about the issue of identity discs, it was sent, the text being as follows:

Mui Tsai. I am not at all satisfied. Unless I am able to state that this institution does not involve the slightest element of compulsory employment (which is the essence of slavery) and that every *mui tsai* of a certain age is in law and practice free if she wishes to leave her adopted parents or employers, I cannot defend its continued existence in a British colony. So far as administrative measures can make it so this freedom must be real. Would it be possible for example to give each child on attaining age of discretion (say twelve years) a numbered identity disc which she could at any time post to Secretary for Chinese Affairs whose duty it would then be to secure her release? A commission (including local advocates of reform) should be appointed to consider:
(a) What legislative and administrative measures are necessary to bring about complete abolition of compulsion in employment of *mui tsai* over age (the possibilities of the plan suggested above or other measures of securing real freedom to leave employment might be enquired into).
(b) To recommend precautions to secure *mui tsai* under age an equivalent measure of protection. In view of the practical difficulty of a child asserting her legal freedom particular attention should be paid to devising some means of affording them some safe and secret means of appeal to the Chinese Secretariat in case of ill-treatment.
(c) To investigate fully the possibility of preventing the transfer of *mui tsai* without the consent of their natural parents or the Chinese Secretariat.
(d) To report what measures should be taken by government to cope with the anticipated result of the measures adopted.

You should obtain the commission's report and send it to me with your recommendations before you leave the colony in June. You should in any case issue a proclamation immediately making it clear to employers and employed that the status of *mui tsai*, as understood in China, will not in future be recognized in Hong Kong and in particular that no compulsion of any kind to prevent girls over age freely leaving at any time their adopted parents or other employers will be allowed. Please telegraph as soon as possible the substance of the proposed proclamation.   CHURCHILL.[20]

This instruction reached Stubbs at a most inconvenient time. The colony was paralysed by a nearly universal general strike called in support of the Seamen's Union; even the personal servants at Government House had joined the walk-out, and Stubbs was fully occupied in devising the necessary emergency measures. This was certainly not the moment for further antagonizing the Chinese by interference with their family arrangements. It was three weeks before he was able to reply to Churchill's directive. He reported that he had set up a committee composed of members of the Society for the Protection of *Mui Tsai* and the Anti-*Mui Tsai* Society to devise measures for ending the system as soon as possible; but he had not issued any proclamation since both societies were agreed that the process must be gradual and that measures to provide for the girls' future must be devised before they were encouraged to leave their employers, for fear that they would fall into the hands of procuresses.[21] Officials advised acceptance of the Governor's proposal, but Churchill was obdurate, and insisted that a proclamation must be issued without delay and that the system must be abolished within one year. On the same day Churchill made a statement to this effect in the House of Commons which was greeted with general applause.

Stubbs made one further attempt to evade issuing the proclamation, but Churchill was not prepared to go back on his pledge to the House of Commons, so a notice was issued in Hong Kong on 14 April. This was drafted by Stubbs and approved by the Colonial Office before publication.[22]

The following proclamation is issued by the Governor under instructions from His Majesty's Government.

Slavery is not allowed to exist in the British Empire, and therefore it must be understood that *mui tsai* are not the property of their employers. Those of them who wish to leave their employers and who have reached years of discretion must be allowed to apply to the Secretary for Chinese Affairs who will consider their cases.

Girls are warned that they must not leave their present employers until they have some employment to go to for fear they should fall into the hands of procuresses.

Masters and mistresses are specially warned against any attempt to prevent *mui tsai* from seeing the Secretary for Chinese Affairs.

This announcement was much more limited than Churchill's original intentions. Instead of the general charter of freedom for all *mui tsai* over the age of 12 years to leave their employers which Churchill had envisaged in his original telegram and in his statement to the House of Commons, this proclamation did no more than restate the existing legal position that slavery was forbidden within the British Empire. It did not permit *mui tsai* to leave their masters but instructed them to remain with them. Only *mui tsai* who had reached 'years of discretion' were permitted to apply to the Secretary for Chinese Affairs to be released, and even then release was not automatic but at the discretion of the Secretary for Chinese Affairs.

Stubbs's foreboding that publication of this proclamation would lead to a rush of *mui tsai* fleeing their employers proved to be groundless. Not a single application for release was received by the Secretariat for Chinese Affairs. This is very surprising in view of the fact that even in a normal year (1919) the Po Leung Kuk gave shelter to 44 'runaway maidservants'.[23] Probably one reason for this was that the Hong Kong government made no attempt to disseminate the announcement very widely. The notice was put up in Chinese on government notice-boards, but most *mui tsai* were not allowed the freedom to roam the streets at will and few of them were literate. The government knew the whereabouts of the 8,653 *mui tsai* enumerated in the Census of 1921, but no attempt was made to contact them individually, in spite of the fact that this was recommended in the report of the joint committee of the Society for the Protection of *Mui Tsai* and the Anti-*Mui Tsai* Society. Stubbs regarded the lack of response as proof of his frequent assertion that the vast majority of the *mui tsai* were happy and contented with their position.

The joint committee presented its report to the Governor on the methods which should be adopted to carry out the abolition of the system at the end of May. The report was by no means a radical document. It began by pointing out that there were around 10,000 *mui tsai* in Hong Kong; that it was beyond the resources of the government to provide maintenance for all of them; and that the economic interests of the owners of *mui tsai* could not be ignored. Accordingly it recommended that no new engagements or transfers of *mui tsai* should be allowed; that all existing *mui tsai* should be registered and should be obliged to continue to serve their present masters until they reached the age of 20 years by Chinese reckoning (approximately 18½ years by English reckoning), when they would be free to leave their employer if they so wished. A *mui tsai* under the age of 20 could only regain her liberty if she was redeemed by her parent, who would be obliged to repay to her employer a part of the original purchase price in proportion to the number of years she had still to serve. Otherwise a *mui tsai* could only be removed if her employer decided she was 'persistently troublesome and disobedient' in which case the Secretary for Chinese Affairs would make other arrangements for her employment, custody, or care as he might think fit. These proposals were far removed from Churchill's determination to effect the abolition of the institution within one year, and they showed the gap which existed between the ideas of feasible changes advocated by reformers in Hong Kong and the views of militant philanthropists in England. As Stubbs pointed out to the Colonial Office, these proposals gave explicit legal recognition for the first time to the status of being a *mui tsai* and provided for the enforcement of compulsory labour up to the age of 20 years. Under the proposed system the employer would be in a far better legal position than he was at present to retain control of the *mui tsai* and obtain full value for the money he had spent, either in unpaid labour or in the amount paid for her redemption.[24]

Realizing that the report of the joint committee would be unacceptable to Churchill, Stubbs proceeded to outline his own more far-reaching proposals: all *mui tsai* over the age of 18 years were to be permitted to leave their employment; those below 18 years of age must be restored to their parents either on their own demand or that of their parents without any payment; all remaining *mui tsai* were to be registered and those aged over 10 years were to be paid a minimum wage; no girl in future was to be taken as a *mui tasi* and no one was to be permitted to employ a female domestic servant aged under 10 years unless she was a former *mui tsai*. Stubbs then went on leave to Britain where he explained his proposals in more detail at the Colonial Office. Churchill accepted this scheme even though it allowed for the institution to continue, albeit in a modified form, for a further 18 years, since existing *mui tsai* under the age of 18 years whose parents could not be traced or who were unwilling to receive them back would still be required to stay with their masters, unless the Secretary for Chinese Affairs could be persuaded that they were being ill-treated. The most surprising concession made by Stubbs was to propose the registration of *mui tsai*, an idea which he had previously rejected as impractical, unenforceable, and obnoxious to the Chinese community.

While Stubbs was on leave in Britain a bill on these lines was drafted, but when it was published in September 1922 it met with strong objections from the representatives of the Chinese community.

Opposition was not directed to any particular features of the bill, but to the whole idea of abolishing the *mui tsai* system which, it was claimed, worked in the best interests of the girls themselves and of their parents, and saved numerous infant girls from the fate of being drowned at birth. This upsurge of protest was reported to the Colonial Office by the Officer Administering the Government and officials turned to Stubbs in England for advice as to what should be done.[25] He took a very gloomy view of the prospects not merely for the reform of the *mui tsai* system, but for the future of Hong Kong itself:

This is the beginning of the end. I told you the other day that I believed we should hold Hong Kong for another fifty years. I put it now at twenty at the most . . . We hold our position in Hong Kong because the Chinese are satisfied to be ruled by us so long as we do not make our yoke heavy and are willing to listen to their views and meet their wishes in matters which affect them nearly. They do not like us, but are passively loyal. If we interfere with their customs to an extent which they believe to be unreasonable, this passive acquiescence will be turned into more or less active opposition.

As to the immediate problem of the *mui tsai*, Stubbs suggested that all the most contentious matters where co-operation from the Chinese was essential, including registration of *mui tsai* and the payment of wages, should be placed in a separate part of the bill which would be brought into operation only at a later date when opposition had died down.[26] This suggested compromise was welcomed by officials and approved by the Parliamentary Under-Secretary, Edward Wood, in the absence of Churchill, who was ill with appendicitis. Action was then further delayed by the dissolution of Parliament and a general election campaign, so that the telegram to Hong Kong authorizing this further weakening of the reform programme was not sent until the end of November when it was issued in the name of the new Secretary of State, the Duke of Devonshire.

The *mui tsai* bill, amended in accordance with Stubbs's latest suggestions, was introduced into the Legislative Council in December 1922 and passed into law in February 1923. At first Stubbs expected that all the unofficial members, both British and Chinese, would be united in opposing the bill and it would be possible to obtain its passage only by the use of the official majority, a highly undesirable procedure when dealing with such a sensitive issue. However, the Hong Kong trade unions tried to exploit the situation for political purposes and petitioned the government in favour of the bill, hoping

1 A panoramic view of Hong Kong, early twentieth century
Source: The Public Records Office of Hong Kong

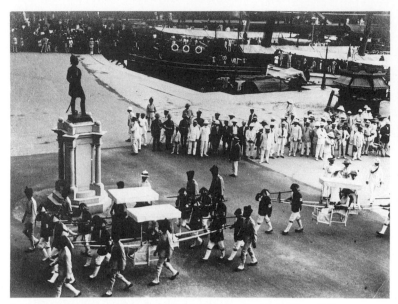

2 The inaugural procession of Sir Henry May leaving Blake Pier, 1912
Source: The Public Records Office of Hong Kong

3 Sir Henry May with his staff
Source: The Public Records Office of Hong Kong

4 Sir Edward Stubbs with the Prince of Wales and party at Government House, 1922
   Source: The Public Records Office of Hong Kong

5 Sir Cecil Clementi reviewing Indian troops, 1925
   Source: The Public Records Office of Hong Kong

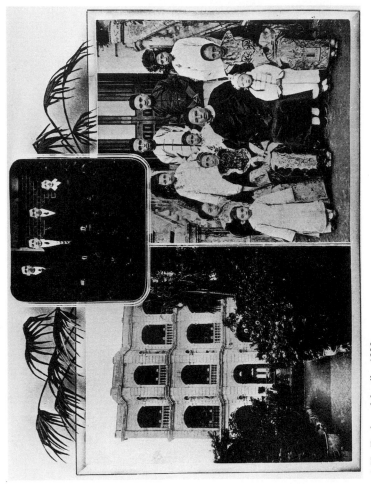

6 Ho Fook and family, 1920s
Source: The Public Records Office of Hong Kong

7 Sir Cecil Clementi with General Li Chai-sum, Governor of Canton (*seated, fifth and sixth from left*) and other officials, 1928
Source: The Public Records Office of Hong Kong

8 Sir Andrew Caldecott inspecting the St John Ambulance Brigade, Hong Kong, 1937
Source: South China Morning Post

9 Sir Robert Ho Tung (*seated, third from right*) and guests at a reception for General
Wu Teh-chen, Governor of Canton (*on Sir Robert's left*), 1937
Source: South China Morning Post

10 Sir Geoffry and Lady Northcote at the New Territories Agricultural Show, 1938
Source: South China Morning Post

11 Sir Robert Kotewall opening a bazaar at St Paul's College, 1939
Source: South China Morning Post

12 Sir Geoffry Northcote reviewing troops at the King's Birthday celebration, 1939
Source: South China Morning Post

that when the bill was put through by the government over the opposition of the unofficials they would be able to claim a victory over the representatives of the 'bourgeoisie'. The unofficials were unwilling to 'give face' to the unions in this way, and so decided not to vote against the bill.[27] Instead the unofficials spoke against it and proposed a number of amendments, most of which were designed to strengthen the law against ill-treatment or cruelty to *mui tsai*. All of these were accepted by the government with the exception of one which attempted to postpone implementation of the clause prohibiting the employment of any new *mui tsai*. This clause was then carried by the official majority with all the unofficials voting against, after Stubbs had pointed out that he was under instructions from London that there could be no compromise on this point. The third reading of the bill was passed unopposed.[28]

As soon as the bill was passed Stubbs wrote to London deprecating any immediate attempt to bring into force by proclamation the provisions of Part III of the bill relating to registration and the compulsory payment of wages. He claimed that the promulgation of regulations on these matters would be most unpopular and it would be impolitic to enforce them at a time when the government of Sun Yat-sen in Canton was doing its best to foment anti-British feeling.[29] Officials at the Colonial Office were quick to recommend acceptance of this proposal. Winston Churchill had been replaced as Secretary of State for the Colonies by the Duke of Devonshire, who had no personal commitment to the abolition of the *mui tsai* system, and so Stubbs was authorized to do as he wished and take no further action.

Since Part III was not implemented, the Female Domestic Service Ordinance 1923 (to give its official title) accomplished very little. Most of its clauses did no more than reiterate the existing legal position: that slavery was illegal; that the payment of money for the transfer of a female child conferred no legally enforceable rights upon the new owner; and that any *mui tsai* was entitled to be restored to her natural parent without any payment on the application of the parent or the *mui tsai* herself, unless the Secretary for Chinese Affairs saw grave objections. This latter clause did no more than give formal legal sanction to the existing practice. The ordinance also repeated and in some respects strengthened the existing laws against the ill-treatment of *mui tsai*. The only real innovations were the clauses prohibiting the engagement of any new *mui tsai*, the employment of any domestic female servant under the age of 10 years, and the transfer of existing *mui tsai* except on the death of her employer and with the permission of the Secretary for Chinese Affairs. However, as Stubbs had himself admitted in a private letter, without a system of registration of existing *mui tsai* there was no means by which these new legal prohibitions could be made effective.[30] The law could only be enforced with the co-operation of the Chinese community, whose disapproval might discourage the engagement of new *mui tsai*, and by the willingness of individuals to give information on such transfers to the police to enable successful prosecutions to be initiated. Unfortunately, far from stigmatizing the custom of employing *mui tsai* as being reprehensible and uncivilized, the effect of the law seems rather to have been to rally support among the Chinese for a venerable Chinese institution that was under attack by foreigners. The problem was that the system did not depend for its continued existence upon the support of the law, but on the needs of poverty-stricken parents for sustenance, the economic interests of the better-off in obtaining cheap and docile labour at minimum cost, the helpless ignorance of the *mui tsai* themselves, and the tolerance of Chinese public opinion for a long-established custom. None of these facts was altered by the passage of the Female Domestic Service Ordinance 1923.

A year later Stubbs forwarded to London a report on the working of the ordinance prepared by the Secretariat for Chinese Affairs.[31] This was based on information supplied to the government by the District Watchmen Committee and reported that the number of *mui tsai* had been 'considerably reduced' and that the ban on the engagement of new *mui tsai* had been 'scrupulously observed'. Officials expressed their satisfaction at the success achieved by the new ordinance; a copy of the report was sent to the Anti-Slavery and Aborigines Protection Society. Then for the next five years the Colonial Office showed no further interest in what was happening to the *mui tsai*.

In later years a considerable amount of evidence was published which revealed that this reassuring picture of conditions in Hong Kong was far from accurate. A large number of witnesses who appeared before the Woods Commission in 1936 testified that the number of *mui tsai* had not diminished and had probably increased after 1923, although in deference to the new legislation they were often referred to not as *mui tsai* but as '*yeung nui*' — adopted daughters. Similarly the Loseby Committee reported in 1935 that 'for practical purposes the 1923 Ordinance did not come into force until 1929' and that new *mui tsai* continued to be engaged after its enactment. In the five years from February 1923 not a single prosecution was initiated under the new ordinance.[32]

But whatever the effect in Hong Kong may have been, the 1923 legislation was completely successful in stilling the agitation in Britain. All the societies and individuals who had assailed the Colonial Office with demands for the elimination of child slavery were completely satisfied that their mission had been accomplished once the ordinance was passed. Parliamentary criticism ceased and not a single question on the subject of *mui tsai* was put down for the next six years.

Stubbs had every reason to feel satisfied with his achievement. Faced with an order from the Secretary of State to implement changes in Hong Kong which he considered administratively impracticable and politically undesirable, since they would outrage the Chinese population, he had succeeded in obtaining successive modifications of Churchill's edict until it was rendered practically innocuous. Yet all the time he had professed his willingness to carry out the minister's wishes and showed an understanding of the political necessity to satisfy the critics of Hong Kong in Britain with a parade of compliance and purposeful activity. The only people left dissatisfied were the *mui tsai* themselves, and probably few of them ever heard of the efforts being made on their behalf.

9 The Abolition of the *Mui Tsai* System, 1925 to 1941

FOR the five years following the passage of the 1923 ordinance nothing more was heard of the question of *mui tsai* either in Britain or in Hong Kong. The philanthropists who had campaigned against the slavery endured by little children assumed that once the law had been passed the *mui tsai* system had thereby been brought to an end and turned their attention to other causes. The Hong Kong Anti-*Mui Tsai* Society for all practical purposes ceased to function. The general strike and boycott of 1925–6 and its aftermath pushed all lesser concerns into the background. Then in March 1927 the government in Kwangtung issued a decree abolishing any form of slavery and ordering the cancellation of all presentation deeds for the transfer of *mui tsai*. The new regulations provided that all *mui tsai* should in future be called 'adopted daughters', should not be ill-treated, but should be provided with adequate clothing, board, and lodging, and should be given some elementary education. All new purchases of *mui tsai* were forbidden, but existing *mui tsai* were apparently expected to remain with their employers until marriage. This decree did not differ greatly from the Hong Kong legislation of 1923, and little or no attempt was made to enforce the rules.[1] However, this move in Canton galvanized the Hong Kong Anti-*Mui Tsai* Society into holding its first meeting for four years. A new committee was elected and in the following months a number of representations were made to the Secretary for Chinese Affairs by the Society's Chairman.[2]

In October 1928 the Society held its annual meeting and the Hong Kong newspapers carried a full report of the Chairman's address in which he denounced the continued existence of the *mui tsai* system and the government's failure to introduce the compulsory registration of *mui tsai* and the payment of wages. This attack made little impact locally and the Secretary for Chinese Affairs formally advised the Governor that the time was not yet ripe for bringing into force Part III of the 1923 ordinance. But the report in the *South China Morning Post* was noted in Britain by John Harris, the Secretary of the Anti-Slavery and Aborigines Protection Society. He wrote a letter to the *Manchester Guardian*, a respected organ of liberal opinion, drawing attention to the allegations made by the Chairman of the Anti-*Mui Tsai* Society, in particular that the number of *mui tsai* in Hong Kong had increased in the past six years and that more cases of cruel treatment were occurring. He contrasted this with Churchill's pledge given to the House of Commons in March 1922 that the *mui tsai* system would be abolished 'within one year'. Harris's letter was backed by an editorial in the same newspaper and caused considerable comment.[3] The letter and editorial were soon republished as a pamphlet which achieved a wide circulation. The Colonial Office which had happily ignored the question for the past five years promptly telegraphed to the Governor for his observations on Harris's letter and asked for a full report on the working of the 1923 ordinance, correctly anticipating that parliamentary questions on the subject would soon have to be faced.

The Governor, Sir Cecil Clementi, replied with a lengthy dispatch which was in effect a vigorous defence of the whole *mui tsai* system, using all the arguments that had been deployed by May and Stubbs in the period before the enactment of the 1923 ordinance.[4] He denied that there was any evidence that would support the allegation that the number of *mui tsai* had increased and insisted that it was impossible to move faster in reforming a deep-rooted family custom than the moral sense of the Chinese community would allow. He also reiterated the old objections to the enforcement of registration, laying particular stress on the strong opposition to any such move expressed by the members of the District Watch Committee. The only changes he was prepared to support were the imposition of more severe penalties for anyone found guilty of cruelty to children, and the setting up of a Society for the Prevention of Cruelty to Children on the lines of the existing Society in Britain. Clementi's eloquent defence seemed very convincing to the civil servants at the Colonial Office, but it was useless for the purpose of stilling the onslaught of the government's critics in Britain, who claimed that the Colonial Office had deliberately deceived the public and reneged on solemn promises given to Parliament that the *mui tsai* system was in process of being abolished. All those who had been active in the 1920–2 agitation, the Haselwoods, Colonel Ward, Viscountess Astor, and many other individuals and organizations had now resumed their harassment of the Secretary of State with private letters and questions in Parliament. Articles were being published with such titles as 'Little Yellow Slaves Under the Union Jack', which claimed that the Secretary of State, Amery, had only to give the necessary orders and the whole evil system would promptly be brought to an end.[5] In these circumstances what Amery needed was not arguments such as Clementi deployed that the 1923 legislation had been misguided and in advance of public opinion, but evidence that could be put before Parliament to show that the legal abolition of *mui tsai* was being made as effective as possible in practice. So a further telegram was sent to Hong Kong requesting more information on specific points. This was accompanied by a private and personal note from Amery to Clementi emphasizing that while he appreciated the strength of Clementi's arguments what was needed was a dispatch that could be published which might quell the agitation in Britain.[6]

Clementi's next dispatch made some concessions to the public relations needs of the Secretary of State, but not many. Its main theme was the impossibility of abolishing the *mui tsai* system in Hong Kong so long as it continued to exist in China: 'This practice colours all the Chinese population that flows into Hong Kong. It would be as hard to free Hong Kong from it as it is to keep a space clear of mud at the mouth of the Canton River.' He gave a mass of evidence obtained from correspondence with the British consuls in southern China to show that the laws against taking *mui tsai* were in practice dead letters and had never been enforced. He rejected all Amery's suggestions for strengthening the rigour of the law as likely to prove impractical or ineffective: 'I am entirely opposed to any schemes of legislative eyewash.' The only new step he was prepared to take was to reissue in strengthened form the proclamation advertising the rights of *mui tsai* which had been published by Stubbs in 1922 on orders from London, and to see that in future it was kept permanently on display at police stations and the wharves where passenger steamers docked.[7] By the time this dispatch was received in London the Conservatives had been defeated at a general election and a Labour government had taken office. The new Secretary of State for the Colonies was Sidney Webb, a prominent Socialist intellectual and a leading member of the Fabian Society. Since he was not a Member of Parliament he was immediately given a peerage, and took the title of Lord Passfield. It was over two months before Passfield was free to attend to the problems of Hong Kong. Officials were inclined to accept Clementi's view that the best and most practicable course was to await a change in Chinese public opinion, while in the meantime attempting to discourage the system in every possible way. But Passfield decided to overrule the Governor's advice and a dispatch was sent directing that the provisions contained in

Part III of the 1923 ordinance for the registration and remuneration of *mui tsai* should be brought into effect forthwith, that the law should be amended to forbid the bringing of any new *mui tsai* into the colony, that inspectors should be appointed to ensure that the law was properly enforced, and that full reports on the measures taken should be sent to London every six months.[8]

Clementi made no further expostulations. He had already explained the administrative and political objections to registration several times and had pointed out that a ban on the entry of *mui tsai* would be unenforceable since there was no way of identifying a *mui tsai* on arrival in the colony. Since these warnings had proved ineffective, he bowed to the inevitable. The necessary amendments to the Female Domestic Service Ordinance were put before the Legislative Council in October 1929 and were passed with the minimum of debate. Regulations for the registration of *mui tsai* and for the payment of wages were published in November. When introducing the amending legislation the Attorney General made it clear that this was being enacted on the direct instructions of the Secretary of State and warned that the government had no intention of allowing the regulations to remain a dead letter. Clementi had a special meeting with the members of the District Watch Committee to enlist their support and that of the Chinese community in complying with the new regulations. However, Clementi did not submit meekly to the Secretary of State's directive. Without asking for permission from London he published the whole of the *mui tsai* correspondence as a Sessional Paper of the Legislative Council, thereby deliberately making public his strong personal objections to the policy he was introducing. Clementi remained convinced that all attempts to reform or abolish the *mui tsai* system would do more harm than good. He later told the Colonial Office that its policy had resulted in the deaths of many *mui tsai*.[9] He was not alone in holding this view: the supervisor of a Salvation Army hostel told the next Governor in 1931 that in her view the system had almost certainly been the means of saving the lives of many young children whose parents would have been unable to support them.[10] Every year the Sanitary Department collected the corpses of more than a thousand babies and young children which had been left abandoned on the streets of Hong Kong. In 1929, 1,851 such bodies were found, compared with 1,516 in 1928 and 1,185 in 1927.[11]

Registration began on 1 December 1929 and the initial response was very slow: in the first 18 days, only 21 *mui tsai* were registered.

Clementi had predicted that the Chinese would be reluctant to register and though there were still more than five months of the registration period remaining he seized upon this insignificant number as the pretext he needed to write to London urging a modification of policy. He pointed out that registration was unpopular and widely resented by the Chinese community, not only because of the inconvenience involved in reporting any change of address or temporary absence from the colony to the police after the initial registration, but also because of the stigma now attached to owning a *mui tsai*; in consequence a number of masters had sent their *mui tsai* out of Hong Kong, but some of these girls had been unwilling to accept a lower standard of living in the country with their parents, and had returned to their former masters of their own free will. In other cases masters who wished to be rid of their *mui tsai* were unable to do so, because the girls' parents could not be traced. So Clementi suggested that in order to encourage registration, provision should be made for the possibility of converting the *mui tsai* either into paid servants (*chu nin mui*) or into adopted daughters (*yeung nui*) if too young for domestic work. This change of status would take place at the time of registration when the original 'deed of presentation' would be formally destroyed, and the employer would then be under no further obligation to report the movements of his former *mui tsai*. As Clementi admitted, the outcome of this proposal would be very similar to what had taken place in China where the *mui tsai* system had been abolished merely by effecting a change of name.[12] Clementi was suggesting that the registration of *mui tsai* which the Secretary of State had ordered would be carried out, but the whole object of registration, the close supervision of *mui tsai* thereafter, would be abandoned.

Clementi's proposal was endorsed by senior officials at the Colonial Office, including the Permanent Under-Secretary, but the junior minister, Dr Drummond Shiels, who saw the file before it reached the Secretary of State, strongly dissented: in his view the Governor had encouraged a boycott of the registration by entertaining the possibility of a modification of the scheme, and he should be told that every effort must be made to ensure compliance. Passfield supported Shiels against the advice of his officials and the Governor was informed that no changes would be permitted and that he should report again after the period for registration expired in June.[13] This dispatch reached Hong Kong in April after Clementi had already left the colony to become Governor of the Straits Settlements, and a more determined effort was then made by the administration to encourage registration. A circular was prepared by the District Watch Committee, drawing attention to the penalty for failing to register a *mui tsai* — a fine of up to HK$250 — and thousands of copies were distributed to households throughout the urban area. This publicity produced a final rush to register and when the registers were closed on 1 June 1930 the number of *mui tsai* registered came to 4,183. Some late registrations subsequently increased this total to 4,368. This was roughly half the number of *mui tsai* recorded in the Census of 1921 (8,653) and well below the estimate of 10,000 which had been given by the Anti-*Mui Tsai* Society, taking into account the increase of the colony's population after 1921 and the lack of any effective measures to suppress the custom since then. However, the new Governor, Sir William Peel, considered the result to be highly satisfactory. In his report to London he suggested that the estimate of 10,000 was far in excess of the actual number of *mui tsai* and that any shortfall was to be accounted for by the fact that many *mui tsai* had been returned to their parents (though he knew of only 52 actual cases) and others had been sent out of the colony. He concluded by observing that since registration had been successfully completed he considered that no further measures were required to promote the policy expressed in the existing law.[14]

The Colonial Office was delighted with this result and for the moment chose to ignore the possibility that there were still several thousand unregistered *mui tsai* in the colony. Clementi's dire warnings that any attempt to enforce registration without the use of an army of inspectors would be a costly failure had proved false and the Secretary of State's decision to overrule a Governor's considered and maintained advice had been justified. Peel's dispatch was printed and laid before Parliament as evidence of the government's success in imposing reforms upon Hong Kong and a letter was sent congratulating the administration on its achievements. The Colonial Office implicitly agreed with Peel that all that was necessary had been done and the only new requirement laid down was that reports should be sent to London every six months giving details of the number of girls on the register and of any prosecutions.[15]

Reformers in Hong Kong and Britain, however, were not so easily satisfied. The Anti-*Mui Tsai* Society claimed that at least 4,000 *mui tsai* had escaped registration and their true status had been disguised by calling them 'adopted daughters'. Criticism also centred on the fact that the Governor had not appointed any inspectors, as he had been instructed to do by Passfield's dispatch of 1929, but proposed to rely on reports made to the Secretariat for Chinese Affairs by officers of the Anti-*Mui Tsai* Society and of the newly formed Society for the Protection of Children. The Colonial Office was at first prepared to accept the Governor's assurances that this would be sufficient; but under pressure from the various philanthropic societies in Britain, and from questions and speeches in Parliament, the Secretary of State directed the Governor to set up an inspectorate. In July 1931, a year after the registers had been closed, a police inspector was seconded to the Secretariat for Chinese Affairs for this work, and three months later two Chinese female inspectors were appointed to assist him. It was only then that any attempt was made to follow up the registration by regular visitation of the *mui tsai* on the register.[16]

These three inspectors bore little resemblance to the 'army of officials' that Clementi had insisted would be necessary to make registration effective. They were not concerned with ferreting out unregistered *mui tsai* and had no powers to carry out random house-to-house enquiries, but only to enter premises when they had some evidence that a *mui tsai* was employed there. On average about 40 cases involving unregistered *mui tsai* were brought before the courts every year in the 1930s. In many cases these were *mui tsai* brought into the colony by employers who had voluntarily made a report of their presence to the authorities in ignorance of the fact that bringing new *mui tsai* into the colony had been made a punishable offence in 1929. A few others were detected as a result of anonymous denunciations or were accidentally exposed in the course of other police enquiries. No special efforts were made by the administration to publicize the ban on bringing new *mui tsai* into the colony; the notices put up in 1929 at the steamer wharves and police stations disappeared within a few years and were not replaced, and no new posters or leaflets were distributed to inform any *mui tsai* who were unknown to the inspectorate of their rights.[17]

The inspectors of *mui tsai* normally visited every household where a *mui tsai* was known to be living about twice a year. These routine visits served as a check that the *mui tsai* were being properly treated and that the statutory wages were paid. On average four employers a year were prosecuted for failure to pay wages. This does not mean that in all other cases wages were regularly paid. In about 20 cases where the *mui tsai* were sent to school the school fees paid by the employer were allowed to count as the equivalent of wages. Elsewhere the wages were nominally accumulated by the employer on behalf of the *mui tsai*, and the girls were well coached to tell the inspectorate that they were free to draw on the unspent balance at any time. Very few cases of ill-treatment of registered *mui tsai* were discovered. There were on average five prosecutions a year for cruelty, assault, or ill-treatment, but practically all the cases concerned an unregistered *mui tsai*. In a few cases investigations were begun as a result of complaints made to the inspectorate by the *mui tsai* themselves.[18]

The number of *mui tsai* under the supervision of the inspectorate steadily diminished over the next 10 years. *Mui tsai* were removed from the register when they died, ran away, returned to their parents, left the colony permanently with their employers, were married, or began to earn their own living. Many of the last group were removed from the register when they chose to become paid domestic servants, '*chu nin mui*', but remained with their former mistress. This was a change of name that may well have made little difference in practice, although it freed their employers from the stigma of owning a *mui tsai* and being subject to supervision by the government inspectorate. This method of removing *mui tsai* from the register had been specifically forbidden by the Secretary of State in 1930, but by 1934 such transfers were being frequently carried out by the Secretariat for Chinese Affairs. For all these reasons the original number of 4,368 *mui tsai* on the register was reduced to 1,723 by 1936 and to 324 by 1939, when all *mui tsai* over 18 years of age were removed from the register. A major problem for the inspectorate was keeping track of the registered *mui tsai*. Employers frequently moved house, taking their *mui tsai* with them, without notifying the authorities, in spite of the penalties against this. Within two years 770 registered *mui tsai* could no longer be traced; by 1936 nearly half of those remaining on the register (912 out of 1,723) could not be contacted; and the last report sent to the Colonial Office in 1941 listed 75 out of a total of 127 *mui tsai* as missing.[19] Clementi had warned the Colonial Office of this problem in 1929 and had predicted that it would be impossible to keep the registers up to date because of the ebb and flow of population over the colony's borders and the frequency with which the poorer class shifted from one tenement to another, and his prophecy was now shown to be accurate. Registration had been advocated by the Anti-*Mui Tsai* Society in Hong Kong and by philanthropists in Britain as a means by which all *mui tsai* could be made aware of their right to freedom and those who remained with their masters could be given full protection. However, the evidence suggests that the failure to register all existing *mui tsai* in 1930, and the subsequent erosion of the numbers on the register, meant that the only *mui tsai* to receive the benefit of government supervision were those belonging to the more respectable and law-abiding members of the Chinese community, while those most in need of help from the inspectors were not contacted. Registration was not quite the 'eyewash' which Clementi had predicted: the visits of the inspectors no doubt served to remind some masters of their duties and contributed to the gradual change in public attitudes towards the whole *mui tsai* system which the 1923 and 1929 legislation had brought about; but it was certainly not the panacea which had been hoped for.

The institution of an inspectorate did not put an end to the pressures on the Colonial Office for further measures to accelerate the extinction of the *mui tsai* system. Resolutions continued to be passed at meetings of political, religious, and charitable societies, questions were asked in Parliament, and letters continued to arrive at the Colonial Office with fresh proposals for action. One frequent suggestion was that all adopted daughters should be registered, to avoid the possibility that the *mui tsai* system was being perpetuated under a different name.[20] It was claimed that according to Chinese custom only boys and never girls were adopted and the fact that a sum of money was commonly given to the natural parents as part of the transaction was taken as evidence that such girls were in fact being transferred as *mui tsai*. The proposal for the registration of adopted daughters was put to the Governor by the Colonial Office several times in 1931 and again in 1932, but Peel resisted it very strongly on each occasion, asserting that such a move would be extremely vexatious to law-abiding Chinese, and was also unnecessary since in any case of doubt the law provided that the onus of proof that a girl was a '*yeung nui*' and not a *mui tsai* rested with the employer. In 1932 Peel backed up his opposition by sending a long memorandum composed by the District Watch Committee. This set down a mass of historical evidence to show that the adoption of daughters was a long-standing Chinese custom, and that the transfer of a small sum of money was an integral part of the ceremonial and should not be taken as evidence that the girl had been purchased for domestic service. This document was signed by all the Chinese members of the Executive and Legislative Councils.[21] The Colonial Office had rejected similar advice before under the pressure of public opinion in Britain, but the Conservative Secretary of State, Sir Philip Cunliffe-Lister, declined to follow Passfield's example and overrule the Governor. He agreed that Hong Kong need take no new action so long as there was no evidence that the Chinese system of adoption was being abused as a cover for the purchase of new *mui tsai*.

The next moves for reform were set on foot by the League of Nations. In January 1934 the League's Permanent Advisory Committee of Experts on Slavery met in Geneva and invited its British member, Sir George Maxwell, to write a memorandum on the *mui tsai* system. Maxwell, who had formerly been Chief Secretary of the Federated Malay States, wrote a full survery of the operation of the *mui tsai* system in Hong Kong and Malaya which concluded with a list of points where further clarification was needed or where existing legislation could be strengthened. Before submitting his memorandum to the committee of the League Maxwell sent a copy to the Colonial Office suggesting that the Governors of Hong Kong and the Straits Settlements should be given an opportunity to comment. The Colonial Office welcomed this opportunity to anticipate criticism from the League. Maxwell's report was sent to the Governors and they were invited to set up local committees to report on his suggestions.[22] The Governor of Hong Kong accordingly set up a committee under the chairmanship of a local lawyer, Mr F.H. Loseby, consisting of a lady missionary from the Salvation Army and two Chinese actively involved in social work. All four members of the committee were on the executive committee of the Hong Kong Society for the Protection of Children. One of the Chinese members, Mr J.M. Wong, had previously served on the committee set up by Stubbs in 1922 as a representative of the Anti-*Mui Tsai* Society; the other was Mr Tang Shiu-kin, then at the beginning of a long career of public service. The committee was also asked to consider a resolution recently passed by the conference of the British Commonwealth League which called for the compulsory registration of all girls purchased in Hong Kong including those nominally adopted, and the institution of a far more comprehensive inspectorate.

The appointment of the Loseby Committee gave the Colonial Office a useful excuse for deferring any further actions in Hong Kong until the committee had completed its work. Its report was published in Hong Kong in September 1935.[23] The committee rejected most of Maxwell's suggestions as being unnecessary, inadvisable, or based on a misunderstanding of Chinese custom. It did not recommend an increase in the number of inspectors, largely on the grounds of cost, but instead proposed other administrative changes in the guardianship of girls who had been transferred, including the compulsory registration of adoptions. The main thrust of the report, however, was to emphasize the difficulty of defining who was and who was not a *mui tsai*. The committee specifically rejected the definitions used by the League of Nations and in the Hong Kong legislation. It pointed out that until very recent times the absolute right of the head of a Chinese family to sell his children was unquestioned, the sale of children was openly practised, and all transfers of children from one family to another by marriage or otherwise took the form of a sale. The main conclusion of the report was that there was an urgent need for a full enquiry into the sale and adoption of Chinese girls, the legal, moral, and social consequences, and the best method of avoiding the dangers likely to follow if official action hastened the changes of thought and custom then taking place in Chinese society. There was nothing very novel in the views expressed by the committee. The term '*mui tsai*' — 'little younger sister' — was a euphemism used in South China for the Mandarin term '*pei nu*' — 'slave girl', and the Hong Kong government itself had admitted in a report made to the League of Nations that the term '*mui tsai*' was commonly used in the sense of 'bought girl' and could sometimes refer to a girl who had been purchased as a prostitute.[24] Regrettably the committee did nothing to clarify the issue or to recommend clear directions for future administrative action.

The report of the Loseby Committee satisfied nobody. The District Watch Committee gave their comments on it, disagreeing with a number of its recommendations and reiterating their strong opposition to the compulsory registration of adopted daughters. The Governor then forwarded these divergent views to London, accusing the Committee of muddled thinking. He roundly asserted that every Chinese in the colony knew perfectly well the distinction between an adopted daughter and a *mui tsai* (even if the two Chinese members of the Loseby Committee did not), and that he was strongly opposed to any proposal which would treat them alike.[25] In London the Loseby Report was made available to Parliament and subsequently published as a White Paper. Critics seized upon various impolitic remarks in the report, such as the statements that the number of registered *mui tsai* was unknown, and that any attempts to stop the sale of girls were doomed to failure. The Secretary of State naturally rejected these views, insisting that all possible administrative measures were being taken to suppress the *mui tsai* system. But under pressure from Members of Parliament, the Anti-Slavery and Aborigines Protection Society, and other interested groups he conceded that a further enquiry was needed. Officials at the Colonial Office also favoured this course, in the hope that such an investigation would put a stop to the calumnies cast at the Colonial Office and the Hong Kong administration. As one official complained, 'People in this country find it incomprehensible that it is impossible to prevent isolated breaches of a law which runs contrary to ingrained Chinese tradition and which they can practise freely in their own country.'[26] A Commission of Enquiry was therefore set up. In order to satisfy one of the government's most persistent and influential critics, the Anti-Slavery and Aborigines Protection Society, the Colonial Office invited the Society to nominate one member of the Commission; the Society proposed Mr C.A. Willis, who had been a member of the Sudan civil service for 30 years. Another member was Miss Picton-Turberville, a militant feminist and former Labour Member of Parliament. The Chairman selected was Sir Wilfrid Woods, formerly Financial Secretary in Ceylon. The terms of reference of the Woods Commission were very wide: it was to investigate the whole question of *mui tsai* in Hong Kong and Malaya and the practices of transferring children for valuable consideration whether on marriage or adoption or in other circumstances, and to make recommendations. The Commission set out for the Far East in April 1936 in order to take evidence in Hong Kong, Singapore, and Malaya.

The Governor of Hong Kong at this time was Sir Andrew Caldecott. Unlike his predecessors he was convinced that the *mui tsai* system was a thoroughly nasty practice. He told the Colonial Office that as a result of legal prohibition and a change in public attitudes the system was already being crushed by popular contempt; the epithet '*mui tsai*' had become a term of abuse, and he was determined to bring about its final abolition both in word and deed. Accordingly he made no objection when the Secretary of State suggested that the Hong Kong courts should be able to impose a term of imprisonment as a deterrent instead of only a fine for offences under the Female Domestic Service Ordinance.[27] A bill to make this change was introduced into the Legislative Council in May 1936 at a time when the Woods Commission was taking evidence in the colony. The Chinese unofficial members objected strongly to the new penalty as being unnecessarily severe for such quasi-criminal offences as bringing an unregistered *mui tsai* into the colony or failing to report a change of address, and wanted the measure deferred until the Woods Commission had reported. The government argued that such a deterrent was needed in order to ensure that the *mui tsai* register was kept up to date and to prevent the disappearance of *mui tsai* from the supervision of the inspectorate. The amendment was carried by the votes of the officials and the European unofficials with the three Chinese members and one Portuguese member in opposition.[28]

The Woods Commission completed its report in January 1937. It contained a detailed account of the Chinese customs and ceremonial relating to marriage and adoption showing that bona fide adoptions of girls did take place in Chinese society. Such adoptions were less common than the adoption of sons and a different terminology was used, but an adopted daughter, like an adopted son, changed her surname upon transfer, while a *mui tsai* did not. A careful distinction was made between the mutual exchange of gifts (sometimes colloquially referred to as a 'sale' or 'purchase') which formed part of any ceremony of marriage or adoption, and the monetary arrangements involved in the sale or transfer of a girl to be a domestic servant or to be reared for a life of prostitution. It was admitted that sometimes the true purpose of the transaction might be disguised as an adoption, and that in extreme cases a poor family might dispose of a daughter without any payment merely to reduce the number of mouths to feed, and there might be no means of proving the nature or purpose of the transaction. The Commission then went on to consider the advisability of requiring the registration of all adoptions, as suggested by the Loseby Committee and the Hong Kong Anti-*Mui Tsai* Society. Such a procedure was rejected on the ground that no prescribed legal process of adoption existed, and so there was no way of proving whether any particular girl had or had not been adopted. If registration were made compulsory those who had adopted a child with the intention of bringing her up as a member of the family might register the adoption, but anyone who had acquired or purchased a girl to be a servant or to be reared to become a prostitute would be most unlikely to register and would merely cease to describe the child as an adopted daughter, describing her instead as a poor relative living in the household, or would give some similar explanation. Thus the compulsory registration of adoptions would not be an effective means for discovering any unregistered *mui tsai*.

At this point the members of the Commission failed to agree. The two former civil servants (Woods and Willis) went on to recommend various minor changes to strengthen the existing law, greater publicity for its provisions, and the appointment of more inspectors to detect unregistered *mui tsai*. Miss Picton-Turberville, in a minority report, recommended that all children transferred from their parents' custody to live with strangers before the age of 12 years should be notified to the authorities, whatever the reason might be. All such transfers would be investigated and where there was any doubt as to the safety or well-being of the child, the child would be registered and the household would be liable to continuing supervision by the inspectorate. The separate *mui tsai* register would then be amalgamated with the new register of wards and transferred children, and the stigma of being a *mui tsai* would thereafter be abolished. This proposal had the merit of providing a comprehensive system of child welfare, but only on the assumption that all transferred children would in fact be notified to the authorities. The other two commissioners considered this proposal but rejected it on the grounds that it would be administratively impracticable; that an army of inspectors would be needed to check the conditions of every transferred child and provide continuing surveillance; that there would be grave danger of misconduct and corruption on the part of the inspectorate; that the Chinese would not be ready to co-operate in such an invasion of the privacy of their homes; and that the abolition of the separate *mui tsai* register might open the door to the revival of domestic slavery under a new name.

The Colonial Office was quite satisfied with the Commission's report, since it generally supported the measures already adopted by the governments of Hong Kong and Malaya and rebutted many of the criticisms levelled against these policies by reformers in Britain. The proposals of Miss Picton-Turberville's minority report were thought to be altogether too drastic to be contemplated. The governments of Hong Kong and Malaya were asked for their comments on both reports and it was suggested that the measures for the effective abolition of the *mui tsai* system recommended in the majority report should be put into effect. Hong Kong was the first to reply: it was willing to adopt all the recommendations of the majority report and set about drafting the necessary legislation, but firmly rejected the minority report which had been condemned by unanimous votes in the District Watch Committee and the Executive Council.[29]

Meanwhile the reformers' lobby in Britain launched a new campaign to secure the adoption of the minority report. Sir George Maxwell (who had been the principal source of inspiration for Miss Picton-Turberville) wrote long memoranda to the Colonial Office; so did the Haslewoods, the National Council of Women, the Society of Friends, and many others. Questions were asked in Parliament, resolutions were passed by committees, and delegations waited upon the Secretary of State. A petition organized by the Anglican Bishop of Hong Kong and other Christian groups was sent to London and the Archbishops of Canterbury and York wrote to express their support.[30] The letter which made the most impression on the officials came from none of these bodies, but from a Mrs G.H. Forster who had been in contact with prostitutes in Hong Kong for 20 years and had helped to run a school for them in Yaumati. In the course of her social work she had interviewed a number of young prostitutes and she sent accounts of some of their lives to the Secretary of State. They had all been disposed of by their parents in infancy to women who had brought them up and had then sold them into brothels when they were sufficiently mature. These detailed case histories seem to have convinced officials that some wider scheme of child welfare was desirable which went further than merely strengthening the existing *mui tsai* legislation as the majority report recommended. The procuration of girls for prostitution was already subject to severe penalties in Hong Kong and Malaya, but the original adoption of these girls at an early age would not have been illegal, nor would the practice, which Mrs Forster reported to be common, of prostitutes buying and adopting small children as an insurance against their own weariness or old age. Copies of Mrs Forster's letter and the evidence she had collected were sent by the Colonial Office to Hong Kong and Malaya, but apart from this no clear lead was given to the governments as to what policy they should adopt.[31]

The reply from Malaya arrived several months after that from Hong Kong, since the various Chinese Advisory Boards in the Malay states and the Straits Settlements had to be separately consulted. The Governor of the Straits Settlements was Sir Shenton Thomas, who had succeeded Sir Cecil Clementi in 1934. His previous colonial career had been entirely spent in Africa, where he had been Governor of Nyasaland and the Gold Coast and he did not have Clementi's intimate knowledge of and respect for Chinese customs and institutions. The first reaction of the Chinese in Malaya had been strongly adverse to the minority report, but Shenton Thomas came to his own decision and took the view that a civilized government had a duty to protect children from exploitation, and that since their welfare was inadequately safeguarded under the existing legislation then the law must be changed along the lines proposed in the minority report. Further meetings were held with the Straits Chinese Consultative Committee and the Governor's determination was sufficient to overawe or persuade the Committee to accept the minority report, subject to certain minor changes. The Straits Settlements Executive Council then endorsed this recommendation.[32] Officials at the Colonial Office welcomed the Governor's decisive action. One commented, 'He has taken the right line and has recognized that the government has a duty in matters of reform and cannot necessarily bow to administrative difficulties and the conservative feelings of the local population.' It was also noted how the administrative difficulties on which Clementi had laid so much emphasis when opposing the introduction of registration in 1929 had proved to be easily surmountable in 1930 after Lord Passfield had given definite instructions that registration must be carried out.[33]

Once Malaya had taken the decision to adopt the recommendations of the minority report, Hong Kong was put under pressure to follow the same course, since it would be difficult for the Secretary of State to defend the adoption of divergent policies by two colonies in dealing with the same problem. The acting Governor of Hong Kong was informed that the Secretary of State proposed to defer any decision on the draft legislation to implement the majority report which had already been sent to London, although he welcomed the immediate adoption of any new administrative measures that were possible under existing law. This was a broad hint to Hong Kong that it should think again before legislating, and a copy of Shenton Thomas's dispatch was sent to indicate what was expected.[34] Meanwhile the new Governor of Hong Kong, Sir Geoffry Northcote, was briefed on the situation in the Colonial Office while on his way from British Guiana to Hong Kong.

Northcote arrived in Hong Kong in October 1937. The District Watch Committee and the Executive Council had already voted unanimously against the proposals contained in the minority report and the Secretariat for Chinese Affairs was not in favour of reopening the question, so the Governor had to proceed carefully if he wished to secure a reversal of these verdicts. He first canvassed a number of persons individually with a proposal that it should be made compulsory to notify all transfers of children by persons other than their parents. This would, it was hoped, deal with the problem of women who reared adopted children in order to pass them on to brothelkeepers in a second adoption, as had happened in the case of the four girls whose life histories had been sent to the Secretary of State by Mrs Forster. Sir Shou-son Chow, the Chinese member of the Executive Council, was prepared to accept this proposal, as were a number of other leading Chinese. Officials in London welcomed this as a step forward but pointed out the difficulties of enforcing such a partial measure, since there was no way of proving that the transferor of a girl was not her natural parent. The Governor continued his efforts at persuasion and three months later he was able to inform London that the leaders of public opinion had now agreed that all adoptions should be notified.[35]

Legislation was introduced into the Legislative Council in April 1938 and was passed in May without any opposition. This made it compulsory to register all adopted girls with the Secretary for Chinese Affairs, who was given the power to make any order he might think fit for their custody and control and to make regulations for their inspection. This new register of wards was to remain open indefinitely for the registration of all future adoptions including any such girls who were brought into the colony, who had to register within one week of entry. This register was to be kept separate from the existing register of *mui tsai*, which had been closed to new additions since 1930. The minority report had proposed that the two registers should be amalgamated, to free the girls from the stigma of being called a *mui tsai*, but Hong Kong decided (following the example of Malaya) to retain the separate *mui tsai* register to avoid the danger that domestic slavery might revive and appear to receive legal sanction under the new system of wards. In order to enforce the new system three additional Chinese female inspectors were appointed, together with a European woman as Assistant Secretary for Chinese Affairs to co-ordinate and supervise their work.[36]

Colonial Office officials congratulated Northcote on his achievement in persuading the Chinese, and at first assumed on the basis of the draft bills which he had sent to London in April that Hong Kong intended to follow Malaya in adopting the recommendations of the minority report that all transferred girls should be registered. In fact Northcote had not been so successful as Shenton

Thomas and the bill was subsequently amended during its passage through the Legislative Council on the suggestion of the unofficial members so as to confine the obligation to register to adopted girls only and not all girls living with strangers.[37] The existing powers of the Secretary for Chinese Affairs to declare himself to be the legal guardian of any girl who had been transferred and to make such arrangements for her welfare as he saw fit were extended, as the majority report had recommended, and the names of such girls would be added to the list of wards to be kept by the Secretariat; but there was no requirement that all girls living apart from their natural parents should be notified to the Secretariat, as the minority report had recommended and as had been done in Malaya. The Colonial Office criticized this change when notifying Hong Kong that the ordinance would not be disallowed, and asked for clarification.[38] The officials also suggested that the ordinance should be amended to require all wards to be regularly inspected if the Secretary for Chinese Affairs considered them to be in need of supervision. In his reply Northcote demurred to any statutory requirement for regular inspections, maintaining that this could be left to the discretion of the Secretary, and he avoided any direct answer to the Colonial Office's query about notification. The Office continued to press Northcote for an answer on this point and he eventually sent an explanation and justification of Hong Kong's action: those who had taken custody of children for improper or immoral purposes would not register them whatever the requirements of the law might be, and if the obligation to register were to be widened to include all transferred children the Secretariat would be swamped with a mass of notifications of amahs, servants, and children staying with relatives which would serve no useful purpose.[39] These were precisely the administrative objections which had persuaded the majority of the Woods Commission to reject the scheme proposed by Miss Picton-Turberville, but the government of the Straits Settlements had nevertheless decided that it was desirable and administratively practicable to register all transferred children. Colonial Office officials considered Northcote's arguments and acquiesced in them, in spite of the incongruity with what was being done in Malaya.[40] The matter was not brought to the attention of the Secretary of State, and the views of the Governor as 'the man on the spot' were on this occasion allowed to decide policy, whereas in 1929 the Colonial Office had insisted on registration over the protests of the local authorities.

Registration of adopted daughters began in June 1938. As had happened when the *mui tsai* register was opened in 1929, the public response was very slow at first and the government had to resort to widespread publicity and house-to-house distribution of handbills. As a result about 1,400 names had been registered by the end of the initial three-month period. By May 1939 the total had reached 2,720, and 3,070 a year later. It is impossible to say how successful the registration was since no other estimate of the number of adopted girls is available. Apart from adopted daughters the new register also included the names of some former *mui tsai* who had been removed from the *mui tsai* register when they left to earn their own living or attained the age of 19 years, but who remained under the protection of the Secretary for Chinese Affairs until they reached the age of 21 years.[41] All of these new wards had to be inspected, and as a result the number of inspectors was increased from 5 in 1938 to 10 in 1940. On average all wards were inspected twice a year. The *mui tsai* regulations had been amended in 1938 to require all *mui tsai* on the register to be inspected at least twice in each half year, in accordance with the recommendation of the majority report, but this was only to be done 'if practicable', and it was not in fact achieved.

The main reason that reformers in Britain and Hong Kong had, for the previous eight years, demanded the registration of all adoptions had been to discover the large number of *mui tsai* who allegedly had not been registered in 1930 and who were still being concealed and ill-treated. So far as this object was concerned the new register was failure. Investigations into the newly registered wards revealed only one case of a concealed *mui tsai*.[42] As in the past a few *mui tsai* continued to be discovered every year as a result of routine police enquiries into cases of cruelty to children and other crimes, but most prosecutions for keeping an unregistered *mui tsai* (175 in 1938) were the result of reports made to the police by refugees who had brought *mui tsai* into the colony with them and innocently attempted to register them, in ignorance of the fact that bringing them in was a statutory offence. Nor did the register of wards lead to the discovery of any young girls who were being procured for the purposes of prostitution. The inspectorate was able to carry out a number of successful raids on baby farms and houses where young girls were being detained before being shipped to the brothels of Siam (Thailand) and Malaya, but these investigations were all the result of information privately passed to the police or the inspectors, as had happened in the past, and were unconnected with the compulsory registration of wards.[43] The penalty for failing to register an adopted daughter, a fine of HK$50 or imprisonment for one month, was hardly sufficient to deter or trouble a hardened procuress.

The work of the inspectorate continued up to the time of the Japanese occupation in December 1941. By this time only 52 of the 4,368 *mui tsai* originally registered in 1930 still remained under the active supervision of the inspectorate. During the Second World War all records and registers of the Secretariat for Chinese Affairs were lost or destroyed, but three *mui tsai* were traced after the war and arrangements were made for their inspection.[44] In September 1946 a new register of wards was opened and all those having the custody of adopted daughters were required to re-register.[45] The Female Domestic Service Ordinance of 1923 which forbade the employment of *mui tsai* or the introduction of a *mui tsai* into the colony remained on the statute book, but its provisions were very rarely invoked. An isolated case occurred in 1956 when it was discovered that a farmer in the Sai Kung area of the New Territories had purchased a *mui tsai* in 1955 for HK$200. He was prosecuted and cautioned by the magistrate and the girl was placed under the care of the Secretariat for Chinese Affairs.[46] In 1969 the Female Domestic Service Ordinance was repealed by the Legislative Council. The Attorney General described it as obsolete and unnecessary. No member of the Council saw fit to comment on its demise. The only section of the ordinance still considered to be useful was that forbidding the employment of a domestic servant under the age of 12 years, and this was tacked on to another ordinance.[47]

The campaign to put an end to the *mui tsai* system was the longest and most successful effort made between the First and Second World Wars to force the Colonial Office to change its policy. The demand for the abolition of 'child slavery' had great emotional appeal and two Secretaries of State, Churchill in 1922 and Passfield in 1929, were persuaded by this powerful lobbying to overrule the advice of their officials and the objections of the Governors and insist that the necessary legislation must be passed and enforced. The first impetus for reform originated in Hong Kong in agitation by a few expatriates and some Chinese connected with the Christian churches. But the Anti-*Mui Tsai* Society was a feeble organization and by itself would never have made any headway against the entrenched opposition of the Chinese élite on whom the Hong Kong government relied.[48] It was the massive and sustained efforts of the philanthropic societies in Britain and the support that they were able to muster in Parliament that constrained the Colonial Office to insist on the enactment of reforms.

How far the legislation of 1923, 1929, and 1938 achieved its purposes is rather more doubtful. The 1923 ordinance was generally admitted to have had no more than a symbolic effect until compulsory registration was introduced in 1929. Registration achieved at best only a partial success in identifying all the *mui tsai* in Hong Kong, but this move, together with the appointment of inspectors in 1931, does seem to have helped to shift Chinese opinion from tolerance of the *mui tsai* system to distaste for it, and so prepared the ground for the acceptance of the wider registration of all adopted daughters instituted in 1938. The visits of the inspectorate may have helped to ameliorate the conditions of the decreasing number of *mui tsai* with whom they remained in contact, but did little or nothing to discover those *mui tsai* who had not been registered in 1930 and the additional *mui tsai* who continued to be brought into the colony by immigrants from China. These *mui tsai* could only have been found by rigorous house-to-house searches which would have alienated Chinese opinion and so were never contemplated by either the Hong Kong or the British government. The disappearance of the *mui tsai* by the 1950s can probably be ascribed to a number of causes: the ending of large-scale immigration from China, the change in Chinese attitudes to abhorrence of the *mui tsai* system as an outdated feudal custom, the rising standard of living which made it unnecessary for fathers to sell their daughters to escape starvation, and the wider availability and use of methods of birth control. Changing social and economic conditions and the altered climate of opinion were mainly responsible for the disappearance of the *mui tsai*, but the legislation which was so bitterly fought over in the 1920s and 1930s probably had some educative effect in accelerating the system's demise.

10 The State Regulation of Prostitution, 1857 to 1941

FROM its earliest days the male population of the colony greatly outnumbered the females. Chinese men came to find work, leaving their families in Kwangtung, and the European community was also predominantly male because of the presence of the army garrison, the ships of the Royal Navy, and the crews of merchant ships unloading their goods in the harbour. In 1872, when the first proper census was carried out, there were 3,264 European men compared to 669 European women, a ratio of practically 5 to 1, and Chinese men outnumbered women by 78,484 to 22,837, a ratio of 7 to 2.[1] This imbalance continued to exist, though to a diminishing extent, for the next 70 years: in 1931 Chinese men outnumbered women by 4 to 3, but the European ratio was 7 to 2.[2] In order to satisfy the needs of this predominantly male community, prostitutes quickly moved in to ply their trade, numerous brothels were established, and by the 1850s Hong Kong was already notorious for the prevalence of venereal disease.

In 1857 at the urgent request of the naval officer in command of the China station the Hong Kong government instituted a system for the registration and inspection of brothels, the compulsory medical examination of their inmates, the punishment of prostitutes who communicated venereal disease to their clients, and their detention in the Lock Hospital until cured.[3] This measure was approved by the Secretary of State primarily because it appeared that a system of licensed brothels and government inspection might provide a means of protecting the inmates from ill-treatment by and virtual enslavement to their brothelkeepers.[4] Ten years later the Hong Kong government was instructed by the Secretary of State to replace the ordinance of 1857 with a new one modelled on the Contagious Diseases Act which had just been passed by the British Parliament. This had set up a system of controlled brothels and compulsory medical examination of prostitutes in 12 garrison towns in England. The new 1867 ordinance, although more comprehensive, made few changes in the system already in force, except that the police were given much wider powers to investigate and break into any house suspected of being a brothel without a warrant and to arrest any inmate or any suspected prostitute on the streets.[5]

The legal system of control in operation from 1857 to 1889 placed the licensing of brothels under the control of the Registrar General. Brothels were confined to certain designated localities with separate districts for those catering for European and Chinese clients, and penalties were imposed for keeping a brothel outside these areas or an unlicensed brothel within them. Brothelkeepers were required to supply the Registrar General with an up-to-date list of their prostitutes and to display such a list in their brothels. Brothels were subject to inspection by the police and medical authorities at any time. All new prostitutes were brought by their brothelkeepers before the Registrar General who questioned them to ensure that they were entering the profession of their own free will and had not been kidnapped or otherwise forced into servitude. All prostitutes were required to attend for a weekly inspection at the Lock Hospital and were then issued with a certificate of good health which could be shown to their clients, and those found to be diseased were detained at the hospital until cured. This was the system as imposed by law; the practice was rather different.[6] Chinese prostitutes catering for Chinese clients had always objected vigorously to being examined internally by a European doctor and would prefer to suffer any punishment rather than submit to such an indignity.[7] So compulsory medical inspections were imposed only on the inmates of brothels frequented by the European population, principally servicemen and seamen. The Registrar General had the legal power to compel other prostitutes to be medically examined, but if they became diseased they normally made their own arrangements with Chinese doctors or herbalists or were sent back to Canton by the brothelkeepers. Regulations made by the Governor segregated the licensed brothels, those catering for Europeans being at the eastern end of the city and those for Chinese being at the western end, and brothelkeepers were required to ensure that their houses were not visited by clients from the other community. This regulation, together with the police campaigns to close down unlicensed houses (the so-called 'sly brothels'), made it less likely that servicemen would come into contact with prostitutes who had not been medically examined and certified to be free of disease. Thus the control system achieved its main objective, which was not the protection of women from exploitation but, as it was commonly expressed in Hong Kong, 'the provision of clean Chinese women for the use of the British soldiers and the sailors of the Royal Navy'.[8]

In Britain during the 1870s and 1880s the system set up by the Contagious Diseases Act came under attack by various moral reformers who considered that the licensing of brothels by the state implied official condonation of immoral behaviour. They also objected to the discrimination by which the women were compelled to submit to a demeaning medical examination. As a result of a long campaign the system was brought to an end and the Contagious Diseases Act was repealed by Parliament in 1886. This had no effect on the colonial ordinances, but colonial governments were then instructed by the Secretary of State to follow the British example. The Governor of Hong Kong protested vigorously to London, claiming that the repeal of the local Contagious Diseases Ordinance would be unanimously opposed by the Executive and Legislative Councils, by the naval and military authorities, and by all classes in the community, since it was the only means of controlling the spread of venereal disease, of preventing the proliferation of brothels in respectable areas of the city, and of protecting young girls from being forced into brothel slavery.[9] But the Secretary of State was adamant that the law imposing the compulsory inspection of women must be repealed, although he was prepared to allow the registration of brothels to continue solely for the purpose of providing a means for checking the possible enslavement of their inmates.[10] The Hong Kong government continued to prevaricate, forwarding petitions to London from the keepers of 42 brothels reserved for Europeans and from 23 European prostitutes begging that weekly examinations and the issuing of health certificates might be allowed to continue.[11] These pleas had no effect, and the Secretary of State sent Hong Kong a copy of an ordinance which had already been passed in the Straits Settlements with instructions to introduce a similar bill as soon as possible. He also ordered that the issuing of certificates should cease forthwith.[12] Finally in 1889, two years after the original directive from London, a bill entitled the Women and Girls' Protection Ordinance was introduced into the Legislative Council. Instead of following the model ordinance sent from London this bill repealed the Contagious Diseases Ordinance of 1867, but then immediately re-enacted most of its provisions for the licensing and inspection of brothels, omitting only the clauses providing for the compulsory inspections to which the Secretary of State had specifically taken exception. Other features of the existing Hong Kong system were retained in the regulations issued by the Governor in Council after the bill had been passed, and these regulations were not forwarded with the ordinance when it was sent to the Colonial Office for confirmation.[13] This deliberate flouting of a directive from London could not be permitted, and in 1890 the 1889 ordinance was itself repealed and a new ordinance enacted on the lines laid down by the Secretary of State. Both the 1889 and 1890 ordinances were only carried through the Legislative Council by the votes of the official members acting on the instructions of the Governor against the unanimous opposition of the unofficial members.

In spite of the dissension which it aroused it seems that the repeal of the Contagious Diseases Ordinance made little practical difference to the operation of the Hong Kong system of control. The inmates of the houses reserved for European clients continued to report at the Lock Hospital for their weekly examination as regularly as before, even though certificates of good health were no longer issued, and they had all been individually informed by the Colonial Surgeon and the Registrar General that attendance was no longer legally obligatory.[14] The prostitutes in the brothels catering for Chinese had never submitted to these examinations, so the repeal of the ordinance made no difference to them. The distinction between the two types of brothels was still maintained in the regulations issued under the 1890 ordinance and penalties could still be imposed on any brothelkeeper who allowed his or her house to be patronized by members of the wrong community, since the Hong Kong government had been successful in persuading the Secretary of State that this continued segregation was necessary if breaches of the peace were to be avoided.[15] So servicemen continued to enjoy some measure of protection against the danger that they might come into contact with a prostitute who had not been medically examined.

The continued existence of a system of licensed prostitution in Hong Kong soon came to the notice of the moral reform societies in Britain which had succeeded in abolishing such houses at home and were determined to end the system overseas as well. Pressure was brought to bear upon the Colonial Office by written appeals from the societies and by questions and speeches in Parliament.[16] So in 1893 a new Secretary of State, Lord Ripon, sent instructions to Hong Kong that the registration of brothels and the periodic examination of their inmates, whether nominally voluntary or not, must cease forthwith.[17] Once again the Governor expostulated, forwarding a petition from the leading Chinese who objected that with the abolition of registration, prostitutes would have no opportunity to complain about ill-treatment and that brothels would proliferate in respectable residential areas. The Colonial Surgeon also added his views, claiming that it would be cruel to forbid the women to attend for regular examinations; they were well aware of the need for early diagnosis of venereal disease and came of their own free will.[18] But the Secretary of State, under pressure from moral reformers in Britain, was obdurate, and a bill to repeal the 1890 ordinance and abolish the whole system of control was introduced into the Legislative Council in 1894 and passed by the official majority against the unanimous opposition of the unofficials. Hong Kong's long delaying action to avoid reform was apparently at an end.

The results of this measure were soon evident: prostitutes ceased to attend for their weekly examinations; a large number of new brothels were opened in areas of the city which had formerly been free of them; and the incidence of venereal disease in the garrison soared. In 1897 half of the soldiers in Hong Kong were under treatment for venereal diseases, compared to 15 per cent 10 years earlier. In Singapore, which had been given the same directive to abolish registered brothels as Hong Kong, the incidence of venereal disease among troops reached 60 per cent.[19] Faced with this situation the Governors of the Straits Settlements and Hong Kong submitted a succession of reports to London and proposed draft legislation which would broadly have had the effect of reintroducing the legal system of control that had existed before 1889. The China Association in London and its branches in Hong Kong and Singapore strongly supported the Governors' views and senior officials at the Colonial Office, including the Permanent Under-Secretary, favoured a return to the old system of control.[20] But because of the pressure of public opinion in Britain and the attitude of the House of Commons, the Secretary of State, Joseph Chamberlain, decided that it was politically impossible to sanction the re-enactment of the contagious diseases legislation in any form. He was, however, prepared to allow the introduction of amending legislation which would make it an offence for the keeper of a brothel to permit any woman suffering from venereal disease to remain on the premises; and also an amendment empowering a magistrate to close down any brothel if an application was made by the Captain-Superintendent of Police or the Registrar General.[21] This change was designed to meet the complaints voiced by the Chinese unofficials about the number of 'sly brothels' being opened in hitherto respectable areas of the city. The minutes written on the Colonial Office file make it clear that it was foreseen in London that this discretionary power to close down any brothel would in effect allow the Hong Kong government to reintroduce the zoning of certain parts of the city as areas where brothels were tolerated, but this implication was not spelled out in the dispatch that was sent since it was later to be published in a paper laid before the House of Commons.[22]

The Governor accepted these proposals with alacrity and informed the Colonial Office that they ought to give the government complete power to deal with the question. This was a remarkable statement in view of the Governor's previous contention that a full return to regulation and compulsory inspection was necessary. Even more surprisingly the subject of brothels and venereal disease then disappeared completely from the correspondence between Hong Kong and London for the next 20 years. The Colonial Office made no attempt to enquire exactly what the Hong Kong government was doing; ministers and officials were evidently only too glad that this politically embarrassing issue had disappeared from view and had also ceased to be raised in the House of Commons. But someone in the Hong Kong administration had realized that the discretionary power at the disposal of the government to order the closure of a brothel or to tolerate its continued existence could be used to reintroduce extra-legally the whole system of statutory control which had been dismantled by the repeal ordinance of 1894.[23] The fear of being forced to close down their businesses could be used to compel brothelkeepers to register their inmates and submit them for medical examination, just as had been done in the past, without the need to rely on any other legal enactment or penalty. Since there is no documentation available it is impossible to trace the development of the new system of tolerated houses, but by 1923 a highly complex system of regulation had been elaborated. The system was so well established that when the Colonial Office asked for information in that year in order to reply to a parliamentary question a full account was sent to London.[24] The Hong Kong government was quite open in describing its system of regulating prostitution and was obviously unconcerned or ignorant of the fact that the Secretary of State had ordered an almost identical system of control to be abolished 30 years earlier.

The administration described the arrangements as being based on the recognition of the impossibility of stopping prostitution but of the need for broad supervision to prevent abuse.[25] The Secretary for Chinese Affairs (the official who had formerly been entitled the Registrar General) kept a full list of tolerated houses, their mistresses, and their inmates. Brothels were classified into those catering for Europeans (with subclasses of those with European, Japanese, or Chinese prostitutes), brothels for Indians, and brothels for Chinese (subdivided into first-class, second-class, and third-class houses). The Secretariat fixed the charges which the mistresses might levy on their girls for board and lodging. All those wishing to practise the profession had to attend before the Secretary for Chinese Affairs, bringing three photographs with them, and they were closely questioned to ensure that they were entering the profession of their own free will. When the authority was satisfied on this point, and that the girl was over 19 years of age, she was given a card showing her number, name, and address, to which one photograph was attached. One photograph was retained by the Secretariat and the third by the brothel mistress, who pasted it in a record book kept in the brothel. The girl was also given a card informing her that she was free to leave the profession at any time and could appeal to the authorities for protection in the case of any ill-treatment. If any client complained to the Secretariat that he had been infected with venereal disease by a licensed prostitute the girl would be instructed to attend for a hospital examination; if she was found to be diseased her card was taken from her and her record was removed from the house book until she had received hospital treatment and was considered to be cured. There was never any difficulty in compelling the girl to receive treatment since the mistress of the brothel knew that her house would be liable to closure if she was found to be employing a girl without a card and she was also herself liable to be fined if she allowed a diseased prostitute to work in the premises under her control.

Stricter controls were enforced by the police on prostitutes catering for Europeans. Their brothels were confined to a particular area in the eastern end of the city and the girls were expected to attend for a weekly examination by a firm of private medical practitioners in the area. In addition to the sanctions imposed by the Secretariat for Chinese Affairs, brothels could be put out of bounds to servicemen by the naval and military authorities if a soldier or sailor suffering from venereal disease identified the girl he had patronized; each girl was required to keep a book in which every client was supposed to enter his name and address and the time of his visit, and these books were open to inspection by the police and military authorities whenever a complaint was made.

This system was generally approved by the Chinese and European unofficial members, and also by the military authorities. The government claimed that as a result the streets of Hong Kong were kept free of streetwalkers who might pester passers-by, and the navy and army garrison was kept free of disease. In 1922, only 7 per cent of the soldiers were under treatment for venereal disease, a proportion which was only slightly higher than the proportion infected in Britain. The system was much less effective in controlling the spread of venereal disease in the Chinese population. On the basis of examinations of patients admitted to the government hospital for other complaints it was estimated that at least 27 per cent of the Chinese male population were infected with syphilis, and it was possible that, if doubtful cases were included, the rate of infection could be as high as 40 per cent.[26] It was believed that the registered brothels used by Chinese in the West Point area were often the source of infection since their inmates were not subjected to periodic examination as were those catering for the European population. The Hong Kong authorities saw no need to take active steps to improve the situation.

Parliamentary pressure over social hygiene in Hong Kong largely lapsed after 1894, once the legal framework for the licensing of prostitutes and the registration of brothels had been repealed by the Legislative Council; thereafter Hong Kong was left free to set up its new extra-legal system of control without further interference from London. But after the end of the First World War agitation on the subject revived. The League of Nations appointed an Advisory Committee on the Traffic in Women and Children which published reports highlighting the connections between state regulation of prostitution and the procuration of women. The first warning to Hong Kong of the revival of concern in Britain was the arrival in the colony in 1921 of a commission from the National Council for Combating Venereal Disease which had been sent to report on conditions in the Far Eastern colonies. The Governor, Sir Edward Stubbs, had objected to any such visit and forbade government officials to give the commissioners any assistance; he also informed them when they arrived that they were not to hold any public meetings or advertise their presence in the press. In spite of this studied discourtesy the commissioners, Mrs Neville-Rolfe and Dr Hallam, set out upon a thorough exploration of the seedier areas of the city and various medical institutions, and were able to make contact with some business and religious groups and with some of the leading Chinese. On their return to London they submitted a scathing report to the Colonial Office on medical and social conditions.[27] According to the commissioners no serious attempt had been made by the government to improve the standard of health of the native population in 85 years of British rule; the infant mortality figures were disgraceful; the Tung Wah hospital was very dirty and badly equipped; the Po Leung Kuk, a place of refuge for Chinese girls, was largely used as a recruiting ground for cheap supplementary wives by members of the committee of the Po Leung Kuk. The Colonial Office was given its first description of the working of the system of tolerated brothels, which Mrs Neville-Rolfe dismissed as ineffective in preventing the kidnapping of girls into brothel slavery; on the contrary, she alleged that 'the artificial value put on the Chinese girl by the system of recognised brothels is the main inducement to the kidnappers'. This report was sent to Hong Kong for comment; a committee was appointed by the Governor which naturally refuted the more extreme of Mrs Neville-Rolfe's strictures, and disagreed with her recommendations. Correspondence between the Governor and the Colonial Office on the matter continued for several years.[28] Stubbs strongly supported the established system of regulation and the only suggestion that he was prepared to implement was the provision of free out-patient treatment for venereal diseases at the government hospital. Meanwhile in London the National Council for Combating Venereal Disease and various women's organizations continued to badger the Colonial Office to put pressure on Hong Kong, and the report by Mrs Neville-Rolfe and Dr Hallam provided a fine source of material for questions in the House of Commons, particularly from a small group of newly elected women Members of Parliament, led by Viscountess Astor.[29]

The main focus of parliamentary attention, however, was not on Hong Kong but Singapore. The government of the Straits Settlements had repealed its contagious diseases legislation in 1894 at the same time as Hong Kong and had set up a similar extra-legal system of tolerated houses. As in Hong Kong newly arrived prostitutes were interviewed by the staff of the Chinese Protectorate, lists of known brothels and their inmates were maintained, and brothel mistresses arranged for their girls to be inspected by private doctors under the implicit threat of the closure of their premises. But this system of control had become less effective and comprehensive by the 1920s.

All European prostitutes had been deported in 1916 as a wartime measure and the Japanese brothels had been closed and their inmates repatriated to Japan at the instance of the Japanese Consul-General in 1919. Their clientele then turned to the growing number of 'sly brothels' staffed by Chinese and Malay women who were not subject to any form of control and who were, it was alleged, normally infected with disease. This led to a rapid increase in venereal disease among both the European and Chinese population. Exact figures were not available, but various doctors estimated the incidence at between 50 and 75 per cent among the local Chinese and possibly as high a ratio among the Europeans. In 1923 the Governor appointed a small expert committee of medical men to investigate the problem. After painting a grim picture of the situation the committee unanimously recommended the re-enactment of the contagious diseases legislation in its entirety, including the registration of all brothels, the licensing of their inmates, and the compulsory medical examination of all prostitutes whether working in brothels or independently. The Governor quickly accepted the conclusions of the report; a bill was drafted to implement them without delay; and both were sent home for the approval of the Secretary of State.[30]

The draft bill immediately evoked a storm of protest. To calm the critics both inside and outside the House of Commons the Secretary of State appointed a new Advisory Committee on Social Hygiene and asked it to consider the bill and the report on which it was based. The committee included the redoubtable Mrs Neville-Rolfe and Viscountess Astor. It spent little time in considering the arguments put forward in the Straits Settlements for the state control of prostitution, which it considered to be completely discredited. Its final report asserted that, quite apart from the moral arguments, periodical examinations of prostitutes were medically ineffective in checking the spread of venereal disease; no examination could guarantee that a woman was free of disease, and even if she was she could become infected immediately afterwards or be the carrier of the contagion from one client to the next; such examinations merely gave men a false sense of security and encouraged promiscuity. The committee recommended various measures to improve social conditions, such as better housing, education, and more recreational facilities, as well as more doctors and free diagnosis and treatment. Its main conclusion was that all known brothels should progressively be closed down, commencing with those frequented by Europeans, and that all 'sly brothels' should be closed as soon as they were detected.[31] The committee's conclusions were unanimous and the Secretary of State, Leo Amery, had no alternative but to overrule the Governor and direct that the recommendations of the committee should be carried out. This was done and the closure of brothels in the Straits Settlements commenced in 1927.

The Advisory Committee on Social Hygiene had only been asked to consider what was to be done in Singapore, but its conclusions obviously applied equally to Hong Kong and other colonies. But no similar instructions were sent to Hong Kong so long as the Conservatives remained in power. However, as soon as the minority Labour government of 1929 came into office various pressure groups such as the Association for Moral and Social Hygiene and the National Council of Women of Great Britain set to work, writing to the Prime Minister and the new Secretary of State for the Colonies, Lord Passfield (formerly the Fabian Society reformer, Sidney Webb), demanding that Hong Kong should follow Singapore's example and suppress all of its brothels. There were also more parliamentary questions from Viscountess Astor and other sympathetic Members of Parliament.[32] In 1930 there was a change of Governor in Hong Kong: Sir Cecil Clementi left to govern the Straits Settlements, and Sir William Peel was promoted from the Federated Malay States to Hong Kong. Clementi had never shown himself very receptive to policy suggestions from London and his transfer gave the Colonial Office an opportunity to initiate a change of policy. Before taking up his appointment Peel saw Lord Passfield in London and was informed that it was the policy of the Labour government that all brothels should be suppressed, but that he should first look into the question and submit a report to London.[33]

Peel sent his views to the Colonial Office in August 1930, three months after his arrival.[34] He stressed that the abolition of licensed prostitution and tolerated houses was opposed by the military and naval authorities, senior government officials, and the leading members of the Chinese community who sat on the District Watch Committee. Abolition would probably lead to an increase in the number of 'sly brothels' and streetwalkers, and a greater incidence of venereal disease. It would also make it impossible to deal effectively with the international traffic in women: in Singapore some measure of control could be exercised at the point of entry where immigrants arrived in a few large vessels, but this was out of the question in Hong Kong where thousands arrived daily, on river steamers and junks and by land; so the licensing and interrogation of intending prostitutes at the Secretariat was the only way of checking that they were entering the profession of their own free will. The Governor finally suggested that if the Secretary of State was determined upon the suppression of brothels a start could be made by refusing to register any new prostitutes; but he would prefer to await full details of the results of the policy of suppression which had been adopted in Singapore. He strongly opposed the sending of an investigatory commission from London, which the Colonial Office had been pressing upon him. Peel's views were supported by the Permanent Under-Secretary and officials in London, who advised against any immediate action. A League of Nations commission to enquire into the international traffic in women and children was about to visit the Far East and this gave a good reason for delay, since any sudden change of policy would appear to be either designed to impress the commission or an admission of guilt. Lord Passfield accepted this advice.

For the next six months the question was allowed to rest. Then in June 1931 Peel again wrote to the Colonial Office, enclosing a long memorandum on the legal position of brothels in Hong Kong written by the Chief Justice, Sir Joseph Kemp.[35] This legal exposition concluded by warning that, although the suppression of all registered brothels might possibly lead to a lower incidence of illicit intercourse, it would probably arouse great resentment if the Chinese brothels patronized by the Chinese were to be suppressed. He continued:

I fear the danger of shaking the loyalty of the Chinese community as a whole and their confidence that the government will respect Chinese customs generally. The risk may have to be run, but I think it is a real one. It must be remembered that the Chinese do not view prostitution as we do. They look upon it with a more lenient eye, though excess is reprobated just as excess in other forms of self-indulgence is reprobated. Prostitutes are not social outcasts to the same extent as in 'Western' countries. A prostitute often becomes a highly respectable concubine ... I realise that this is a difficult defence to make, especially as the English public do not always realise the delicacy required in ruling an alien civilisation.

Peel offered up a small sacrifice to appease the Secretary of State: he suggested that the seven brothels containing European prostitutes should be closed down. This was not a sign that Peel had been converted to the moralists' point of view; European prostitutes were customarily deported from Hong Kong from time to time, since their presence was considered demeaning to European prestige in the East.[36] This decision to close the brothels employing European, Australian, and American women was endorsed by the Executive Council in July 1931.[37]

Meanwhile, at the Colonial Office, Dr Drummond Shiels, the Parliamentary Under-Secretary to Lord Passfield, had decided that action must be taken by the Hong Kong authorities before the League of Nations commission reported. Having consulted the Colonial Office Medical Adviser, and being assured that the balance of evidence was that the existence of tolerated houses did not keep down the incidence of venereal disease, and that this had been confirmed in the case of Malaya, he proposed that Hong Kong should follow the example of the Straits Settlements and close down all of its brothels, beginning with those served by European prostitutes, and the brothels with Chinese prostitutes which were used by British servicemen. Passfield approved this suggestion and a dispatch on these lines was in course of preparation when the Labour government fell from power in August 1931. The arrival of the Chief Justice's memorandum scarcely modified the draft: the possibility of strong local opposition to the closure of Chinese brothels catering for Chinese clients was noted by officials, but it was pointed out that similar warnings of Chinese resentment had not materialized when the *mui tsai* system had been abolished. The Governor was advised to proceed cautiously and to attempt 'to elicit the support of more enlightened Chinese opinion', but it was emphasized that it was the aim of the British government to bring about the suppression of all brothels in Hong Kong. This draft was presented by officials to the newly appointed minister of the National government, Sir Robert Hamilton, who authorized its dispatch.[38]

This directive reached Hong Kong in November 1931. The Governor had been hoping that his pleas for an indefinite delay would be successful and he had just told the Legislative Council that any action would be deferred until after the League of Nations commission had reported.[39] But this was not to be, and the Executive Council reluctantly agreed that further registration of new prostitutes should not be allowed and that six months' notice should be given to Chinese and Japanese brothels catering for Europeans. The completion of this stage was notified to London in July 1932. The closure of Chinese brothels catering for Chinese was undertaken much more slowly, and the last of the remaining houses was not closed down until June 1935.[40] Their inmates were individually interviewed and offered assistance in starting a new life, but all declined and stated their intention to continue their profession in Canton or Macau.[41]

The end of licensed prostitution was followed, as Peel had prophesied, by the opening of a large number of 'sly brothels' masquerading as dancing academies, bath houses, or massage parlours. The government had to decide what was to be done and the Executive Council directed that houses containing one or two prostitutes might be left undisturbed by the police so long as they did not constitute a nuisance to the neighbourhood, but that the keepers of larger establishments should be prosecuted, and deported if found guilty.[42] There was also a vast increase in the amount of soliciting on the streets, since prostitutes were obliged to advertise their services openly instead of being found in a recognized place of resort. The incidence of venereal disease soon increased among the soldiers and sailors of the garrison: during 1938, 24 per cent of servicemen were reported sick with venereal disease (29 per cent in the navy and 20 per cent in the army).[43] This compared with an infection rate of 7 per cent in 1922 when the tolerated houses were in business. There was also probably a similar increase among the general population: the number of new patients seeking treatment at government venereal disease clinics went up from 3,533 in 1932 to 8,573 in 1939, though part of the increase may have resulted from the increased availability of treatment and changing attitudes to European medicine.[44]

Alarm at the extent of venereal disease in the garrison led the Governor, Sir Geoffry Northcote, to appoint a local committee in 1938 to examine the situation. The Committee included representatives of the navy, army, police, and medical services. The committee clearly regretted the ending of the system of tolerated houses six years earlier; the report stated bluntly: 'The results of abolition, namely the increase in venereal disease with its appalling effect upon the defence forces of the colony, and the unpleasant conditions of the streets are much more of a disgrace than the tolerated houses ever were.'[45] It was noted that before 1932 any serviceman could identify the woman he had visited and she could be compelled to seek treatment at the expense of the keeper of the brothel; but in the new era there was no means of compelling a prostitute to seek treatment and it was estimated that three-quarters of the prostitutes in Hong Kong suffered from disease. The committee considered that an 'admirable arrangement' would be the restoration the old system of tolerated brothels confined to servicemen and subject to medical inspection, but they recognized that this was out of the question. So a variety of palliative measures were proposed, such as a wide definition of the offence of soliciting in the street, more police, the greater use by government of the power of deportation to rid the colony of known prostitutes, an increase in the provision of treatment facilities, and free hostel accommodation to encourage infected women to persevere to the end of their treatment. There is no information on how far these measures were implemented in wartime Hong Kong, or how successful they were.

After the occupation in 1941 the Japanese authorities reinstituted a system of controlled and medically inspected houses in Wanchai for the use of their own troops. These were closed down as soon as British rule was restored in 1945.

The system of licensed prostitution in Hong Kong originally had two purposes: the control of the spread of venereal disease, particularly among the soldiers and sailors of the garrison, and the prevention of the exploitation of Chinese prostitutes in conditions which often amounted to virtual servitude. In practice the first aim always had priority, and while the system of licensed prostitution was in operation, legally from 1857 to 1894 and extra-legally from 1900 to 1932, it seems to have been largely achieved. But control over Chinese prostitutes catering for Chinese clients was always less comprehensive and less strictly enforced. It served to curb the environmental pollution of brothels operating in respectable residential neighbourhoods (apparently the main concern of the Chinese élite), and it may have reduced somewhat the incidence of venereal disease, but it probably failed in its ostensible purpose of preventing brothel slavery. Practically all prostitutes appearing before the Secretary for Chinese Affairs in order to be registered were brought by their brothel mistresses and had been coached in the replies they should make to the stereotyped questions asked: 99 per cent claimed to be between 21 and 24 years of age and to have entered the colony only a few days previously.[46] Few if any attempted to avail themselves of the help of the Secretariat to escape from their profession.[47]

The action of the Secretary of State in overruling the Governors' advice in 1889, 1890, 1893, and 1931 was most unusual. It was, doubtless, a highly moral stand, and spared the Secretary from the obloquy of appearing as an advocate of vice in an unsympathetic

House of Commons. But the results were disastrous, so disastrous in fact that the official instructions were circumvented in Hong Kong for 30 years with the connivance of the Colonial Office. When they were enforced under a compliant Governor the results turned out to be as bad as had been predicted.

11 The Control of Opium, 1906 to 1919

THE knowledge and use of opium as a pain-killing drug in China can be traced back to the T'ang dynasty in the eighth century AD. The smoking of opium seems to have spread to China before the eighteenth century as a result of contact with Spanish traders from the Philippines and the Dutch in Taiwan who were accustomed to mix opium with their tobacco. The first imperial edict against opium was issued in 1729 by the Emperor Yung Cheng prohibiting the sale of opium for smoking and the opening of smoking divans. This decree seems to have been directed against locally produced opium, since imports at that time were minimal, about 200 chests a year. Similar anti-opium edicts were repeated at intervals throughout the eighteenth century with increased penalties, but the first prohibition on opium imports from abroad was not issued until 1796, and was repeated in 1800. This ban did not put a stop to the lucrative trade in imported opium from India which had been developed by British merchants who had found that opium-smokers preferred Indian opium to the native Chinese product and were prepared to pay a higher price for the imported article. After 1800 the traders turned to smuggling the drug with the connivance of corrupt Chinese officials, and imports grew from 2,000 chests in 1800 to 40,000 chests by 1839. In that year Commissioner Lin arrived in Canton determined to enforce the imperial edicts and stamp out the opium trade. But his energetic measures led to the outbreak of the First Opium War, China's defeat, and the cession of Hong Kong island to Britain.[1]

The treaty of peace made no specific mention of the opium trade (apart from the payment of HK$6 million compensation to the merchants whose opium had been confiscated and burnt by Commissioner Lin); but in practice the import of opium through the treaty ports that were then opened was not interfered with, and a lively smuggling trade in opium shipped in junks through Hong Kong developed. Following the Second Opium War (1856–60) the import of opium into China was officially recognized, the Chinese authorities being permitted to levy a duty of 30 taels per picul (slightly over 7 per cent), with the stipulation that foreign opium should be sold only at the treaty ports, and that the trade to the interior was reserved to the Chinese.[2] (A picul is 133 pounds or 60.5 kilograms, the normal weight of a chest of opium.) By the Chefoo Convention between Britain and China (which was negotiated in 1876, but only ratified by Britain in 1885), inland taxation (*li-kin*) on opium was to be collected simultaneously with the import duty and the total levy was set at 110 taels per picul. As a result of the treaties which ended the Second Opium War the opium trade inside China was effectively legalized, and the various edicts against opium-smoking and distribution were not renewed for the next 50 years. Chinese cultivation of the opium poppy increased rapidly alongside the growth in foreign imports and by 1906 it was estimated that native production provided about six-sevenths of the total consumption: 325,270 piculs of Chinese opium compared to 54,225 piculs of imported opium, almost all of which came from India. But hostility towards the opium habit had been growing in China, especially among students and the educated classes, who viewed opium as an unwanted import which had been forced upon China by foreigners and which resulted in the ruin of individual addicts and was a cause of national degeneracy and weakness. Societies were formed both in China and among overseas Chinese to agitate against the vice of opium-smoking and to help in the rehabilitation of addicts. These feelings were powerfully reinforced by China's humiliating defeat by Japan in 1896 and by the suppression of the Boxer rebellion by foreign intervention in 1900.[3] The example of Japan was a strong stimulus to action since Japan, as part of its drive towards modernization, had banned the growing, manufacture, and smoking of opium since 1880, and had imposed heavy penalties on offenders. By 1905 these efforts had been so successful that the Japanese were able to defeat a European power, Russia.

In the last decade of the Ch'ing dynasty, 1901 to 1911, a final effort was made by the imperial ministers to modernize China and stave off the threat of revolution. The education system was reformed and the old classical examinations for the civil service were abolished, the central administration was reorganized, and new military institutions were set up. Among other reforms an imperial edict was issued in September 1905 commanding that within 10 years the evils arising from foreign and native opium should be completely eradicated. Regulations were then promulgated in November which provided for the progressive extinction of Chinese cultivation of the poppy, the licensing of smokers, and restrictions upon opium divans.[4] These regulations were in general rigorously enforced throughout the provinces with measures which in some cases went much further than the original decree, and this was done with considerable popular support, as is testified by the reports filed by foreign consuls. Opium dens were closed down, farmers were ordered to dig up their poppy, and in a few cases farmers who refused were summarily tried and then beheaded among their poppy plants.[5] Meanwhile the Chinese government commenced negotiations with the British government to secure a reduction in the imports of Indian opium in line with the progressive diminution of the local crop. Before 1906 successive British governments, in response to pressure from missonary and philanthropic societies in Britain had professed themselves in principle in favour of some restriction of opium imports from India to China. In practice, however, they had taken no action on the matter, largely because of the loss to the finances of the Indian government that any such reduction would entail. But in February 1906 a new Liberal government had come to power with a large majority in a general election, and the new House of Commons had voted unanimously in May in support of a motion that the opium trade was 'morally indefensible'.[6] So, in accordance with the new national mood, an agreement was concluded between Britain and China in 1907 by which Indian exports of opium to China, then calculated to be running at an average rate of 51,000 chests a year, would be progressively reduced over a 10-year period by 5,100 chests a year until the trade was entirely extinguished by the end of 1917. Initially the agreement was to be in force for an experimental period of three years and further reductions from 1911 onwards were to be dependent on China's success in controlling the production of native opium. Restrictions were also placed on the small amounts of Turkish and Persian (Iranian) opium imported into China.[7]

Hong Kong's role in the opium trade was as an entrepôt for official imports and also as a base for the smuggling of illegal supplies. From 1842 to 1860 smugglers made use of the port to avoid the prohibition on opium imports which was still enforced against the Chinese junk trade. After 1860 they sought to evade the customs duty and *li-kin* levied by the Chinese authorities. The British administration made little or no effort to suppress this trade, maintaining that it was the responsibility of the Chinese government to enforce its own laws. But following the attempted Chinese 'blockade' of Hong Kong which was intermittently effective from 1867 to 1886 and the conclusion of the Chefoo Convention between Britain and China, an arrangement was reached with China by which all movement of opium in and out of Hong Kong was to be controlled by the Harbour-master, and a branch office of the Chinese Imperial Maritime Customs was established just beyond British territory to sell opium duty certificates. Information on all shipments was supplied by the Harbour-master to the Maritime Customs.[8] This arrangement reduced opium-smuggling but certainly did not eliminate it. Meanwhile the official trade in opium through Hong Kong contributed substantially to the port's prosperity. In 1906, 47,575 chests of opium were officially exported after being stored in warehouses in Hong Kong, quite apart from the 9,712 chests reported in ships' manifests but not unloaded. Exports of opium were valued at £5,312,645 in that year, or roughly 10 per cent of the value of all goods shipped through the port.[9]

Quite apart from the profit accruing to the colony from harbour fees and the charges for storage, freight, banking, and insurance on opium shipped to China, the Hong Kong administration also did very well out of internal consumption. Ever since the colony had been founded opium-smoking had been regulated in order to provide a source of revenue. From 1847 to 1857 fees had been charged for licences to sell raw or prepared opium and for opening smoking divans. From 1858, an opium monopoly was created and the right to boil and sell prepared opium was farmed out to the highest bidder. This system was continued until 1914, apart from a brief and unsuccessful experiment with direct government licensing in the years 1883–5. The farm was let for three-year periods by public tender and the farmer was entitled to withdraw up to 1,800 chests from bond to boil for consumption in Hong Kong or for export. This limit had been set in 1891; previously the farmer had been entitled to draw 3,600 chests. There had been strong grounds for believing that the opium-farmer was actively involved in the smuggling of prepared and raw opium into China, but the reduction in his permissible quota from 1892, and the concentration of his boiling operations in one establishment after 1900 (which made it impossible for him to explain any illicit opium found on junks in the harbour by the excuse that it was being transferred from one boiling establishment to the other) seems to have made smuggling more difficult.[10] The number of chests withdrawn by the farmer was considerably reduced, as Table 6 shows.

The opium farm was let to the highest tenderer for a period of three years. If the successful bidder miscalculated his likely profit (as the farmer for the years 1904–6 did) then the loss fell on his

Table 6   Chests of Opium Boiled by the Opium-farmer, 1888–1913

Year	Chests	Year	Chests
1888	3,771	1901	1,036
1889	1,746	1902	929
1890	2,511	1903	990
1891	1,878	1904	725
1892	1,620	1905	858
1893	1,760	1906	497
1894	n/a	1907	725
1895	1,607	1908	864
1896	1,515	1909	1,044
1897	1,589	1910	782
1898	1,704	1911	761
1899	1,749	1912	1,113
1900	1,098	1913	667

Sources: CO 882/5, p. 81; *Hong Kong Legislative Council Sessional Papers 1909*, p. 31; CO 129/411, p. 424

own shoulders and did not decrease the government's prospective revenue. The farmer could set his own price for sales in Hong Kong or abroad and he protected his internal monopoly against imported prepared opium (known as *chandu*) by employing a staff of detectives to search all persons arriving in Hong Kong. This searching, from which only government officials were exempt, was much resented by the Chinese public. The farmer also employed spies and rewarded informers who discovered any illicit opium-boiling.[11] Naturally the staff employed by the farmer had no incentive to prevent the smuggling of opium he had boiled out of the colony either to China or to other countries such as the Philippines which had come under American rule in 1900 and where the import, distribution, consumption, and smoking of opium had been prohibited since 1908. The percentage of the government revenue provided by the opium monopoly over the 20 years from 1886 to 1906 varied between 9 and 29 per cent. In 1906, as China renewed its campaign against opium, the revenue from opium reached its highest point to date, as can be seen from Table 7.

The colonial administration confessed to no disquiet at the large portion of its revenue that was derived from the opium farm. The

Table 7   The Proportion of Government Revenue Derived from the
Opium Monopoly, 1886–1913

Year	Total Revenue (HK$)	Opium Monopoly (HK$)	Percentage
1886	1,367,977	178,500	13.0
1887	1,427,485	182,400	12.8
1888	1,557,300	182,074	11.7
1889	1,823,549	428,400	23.5
1890	1,995,220	477,600	23.9
1891	2,025,302	389,900	19.3
1892	2,236,933	407,900	18.2
1893	2,078,135	340,800	16.4
1894	2,278,528	340,800	15.0
1895	2,486,228	295,133	11.9
1896	2,609,878	286,000	11.0
1897	2,686,914	286,000	10.6
1898	2,918,159	357,666	12.3
1899	3,610,143	372,000	10.3
1900	4,202,587	372,000	8.8
1901	4,213,893	687,000	16.3
1902	4,901,073	750,000	15.3
1903	5,238,857	750.000	14.3
1904	6,809,047	1,945,000	28.6
1905	6,918,403	2,040,000	29.5
1906	7,035,011	2,040,000	29.0
1907	6,602,280	1,550,000	23.5
1908	6,104,207	1,452,000	23.8
1909	6,822,966	1,452,000	21.3
1910	6,960,869	1,228,000	17.6
1911	7,497,231	1,183,200	15.8
1912	8,180,694	1,183,200	14.5
1913	8,512,308	1,183,200	13.9

Notes: 1. The opium farm was let every three years in March; variations in the
farmer's payments are caused by the discrepancy between the farmer's year
and the official financial year, which ran from January to December, and
by occasional payments by the farmer in advance or in arrears.
2. In addition to the main payment made by the opium-farmer, the
government also received a small sum in divan licences: in 1906, 194
divans each paid a fee of $10 a year, which was collected through the
opium-farmer.

Source: Hong Kong Blue Books (annual).

official view, as given in evidence to the Royal Commission on
Opium (1891–3) and by Governor Lugard in a memorandum laid

before the Legislative Council in 1909 was that the farm was a means to restrict and control the consumption of opium by keeping the price relatively high and by curbing competing imports. This method of financing government expenditure was no different from the licence fees charged on public houses and the taxes on alcohol levied in Britain. In any case, in Lugard's view, opium-smoking was 'a comparatively harmless habit' which was preferable to the consumption of alcohol since it acted as a sedative rather than a stimulant to the nervous system. Excessive consumption was, no doubt, harmful to some addicts but this was no more reason for banning the sale of opium than the existence of habitual drunkards in Britain was a reason for the prohibition of alcohol. Any such ban was likely to lead to smuggling and clandestine smoking or a resort to alcohol or morphia injections, which would have far worse results.

This benign view of the effects of opium had the support of the Royal Commission of 1893 and of the Straits Settlements Opium Commission which reported in 1908. But there were dissentients from this view even within the Hong Kong administration; four officials emphasized the baneful effects of the drug in the replies they sent to the questionnaire circulated by the Royal Commission; and all of the nine Hong Kong Chinese who responded condemned opium with varying degrees of severity including, with surprising candour, the then opium-farmer himself.[12] There was, however, no active anti-opium society in the colony such as existed in the Straits Settlements.[13]

The agreement negotiated between Britain and China in 1907 for the restriction and final extinction of opium exports from India was bound to have repercussions on Hong Kong. Imports of opium into China through the colony were in future to be confined to those chests 'certificated' for China at the Indian auctions; but it would still be possible for the opium-farmer to export prepared opium (*chandu*) to China out of any surplus he had after satisfying his Hong Kong customers. So in the course of the negotiations China proposed that the Hong Kong government should strictly prohibit the boiling of opium in Hong Kong for export to China; otherwise such exports from Hong Kong would be used to circumvent the limitation upon direct exports from India to China. This suggestion was passed to Hong Kong for comment and it fell to May, who was then Officer Administering the Government in the interval before Lugard's arrival, to make a reply.[14] He pointed out that any such prohibition would be a curtailment of the rights of the farmer under his three-year contract and could expose the administration to a claim for compensation. However, since the retail price of *chandu* made from Indian opium in Hong Kong was HK$3.30 to HK$3.50 a tael, while the same product was on sale in Canton for about HK$1.50 a tael (and Chinese opium at around HK$1.15), the farmer was more concerned with the smuggling of *chandu* from China into Hong Kong than with any trade in the reverse direction. May accordingly proposed that the farmer might consent to a prohibition on exports to China without making any claim for compensation if China would in turn prohibit exports of *chandu* to Hong Kong and take effective measures to curb the traffic.

May then added some further gratuitous comments. He pointed out the danger that the revenues of the colony might suffer if the farmer's supply of opium from India were to be restricted, and he went on to give grounds for doubting whether China's new-found enthusiasm for opium control would produce any more lasting effect on opium consumption than the innumerable edicts containing similar prohibitions promulgated in the past. May was in fact proved wrong on both points. His cynicism as to the effectiveness and dedication of the Chinese bureaucracy was unjustified, as consular reports showed and as Hong Kong was soon to discover to its cost. His fears for Hong Kong's opium supply were premature: Indian opium continued to be exported for the use of the Hong Kong monopoly for the next 28 years. But his compromise proposal for the mutual prohibition of exports was accepted and an ordinance to ban the export of *chandu* to China was passed by the Legislative Council in 1908. In practice China's promise to check smuggling had little effect; as Lugard later pointed out, seizures of *chandu* coming into the colony from China in the six months after this agreement was made averaged more than one a day.[15]

The next blow to the opium monopoly was completely unexpected. In May 1908 a zealous back-bencher in the House of Commons was lucky in the ballot for private members' motions and secured time to introduce a resolution welcoming the arrangements for diminishing India's opium exports and urging the government to take steps to bring to a speedy close the system of licensing opium dens prevailing in Hong Kong, the Straits Settlements, and Ceylon. A new Secretary of State for the Colonies, the Earl of Crewe, had just been appointed after a cabinet reshuffle, and he dispatched a telegram to Hong Kong instructing that all opium dens must be closed. As the debate was imminent there was no time for consultation with the Governor. The telegram was read out the next day by the minister speaking for the Colonial Office during the debate, enabling the government to secure the plaudits of the House of Commons, and the motion was accepted by the government and passed unanimously.[16]

This unheralded ministerial directive raised a number of questions, practical, financial, and constitutional. The practical point was whether closing the opium divans was the best way to reduce the number of addicts. Although many divans were being shut down in China, there were good reasons for doubting whether this was an effective way of curbing consumption. According to Lugard and his advisers in Hong Kong, opium divans were no more than rooms which sold opium and provided the pipes and other paraphernalia for smoking it on the premises. Women and children were excluded, and, being licensed, the divans were known to the police and subject to inspection. Unlike the operators of public houses in Britain, the divankeepers did not use any meretricious advertising devices to push sales. In Lugard's words, 'Divans are a concomitant or accessory of the habit and not an exciting cause. They serve a useful purpose in enabling government to exercise an effective control and by concentrating smokers they prevent the spread of the habit by example.' If divans were suppressed habitual smokers would indulge their craving at home in the domestic circle or in less salubrious surroundings which might even extend the habit instead of curtailing it; or if deprived of easy access to opium they might take to cheap alcohol, eating opium pills, or morphia injections, all of which would have far worse effects. Only about 3.5 per cent of the Chinese population frequented divans. Lugard wrote: 'The view that divans are in themselves agents for the demoralization of however microscopic a proportion of the population is not held by the bulk of the community here who by long residence in the East are better qualified to judge than those at home who with the best of motives advocate this particular method of restriction.' Accordingly Lugard suggested to London that the proposal for closing the divans should be withdrawn and that the restriction of opium should instead be carried out by a progressive reduction of the amount of opium boiled by the farmer, which would inevitably lead to a reduction in the number of divans as their trade decreased.[17]

Lugard's view that the opium divans should not be suppressed was not without support. The Straits Opium Commission of 1908, whose members included an American Methodist Bishop of 20 years residence in Singapore, had unanimously concluded that there was 'no necessity or justification for the abolition of smoking shops'. Sir John Jordan, the British minister in Peking who had 30 years experience of China and was no friend of the opium merchants, confessed himself 'entirely in accord' with Lugard's memorandum.[18] As late as 1931 the Far Eastern Opium Commission of the League of Nations favoured supervised smoking shops as the best means of controlling addiction. Lugard's arguments convinced the permanent officials of the Colonial Office who strongly supported his views in the minutes they wrote on his dispatches. Fiddes — a future Permanent Under-Secretary — wrote a scathing exposure of the evasions and illogicality of the ministers' position, and another civil servant pointed out that Lugard's opinion 'carried great weight with the public, irrespective of party, in this country'.[19] But the ministers were not prepared to humiliate themselves by retracting the pledge already given to the House of Commons. Lord Crewe went so far as to admit in a private and personal dispatch to Lugard that he was impressed by his arguments, 'but the situation presents great parliamentary difficulties'. So he insisted that the divans must be closed.

The financial consequences of the ministerial directive were also alarming. The immediate cancellation of all divan licences before they expired (as ministerial statements in the House of Commons Debate of 8 May apparently envisaged) would need new legislation. The licence-holders could justifiably demand compensation for the loss of their vested interests, while the opium-farmer could claim that the closure of the 192 divans which sold his product represented a substantial change in the terms on which he had tendered for the opium farm. Such compensation payments would be very costly to the colony: the capital value of the assets of the divankeepers could amount to HK$20,656; the profits of the farm could be diminished by as much as HK$66,000 a month, and the farmer intimated that his claim would be for not less than HK$45,000 a month, or well over HK$500,000 in a full year. Since it was already estimated that the colony's budget in 1908 would be HK$630,000 in deficit, such an additional burden on the colony's finances would be quite insupportable, particularly when the colony was affected by a trade depression. Lugard rather melodramatically pointed out to London that, if money had to be found for compensation payments to the opium-farmer and the divankeepers, he might be forced to curtail expenditure on sanitation to combat the current outbreak of plague which was causing from 16 to 20 deaths a day.[20]

This potential financial crisis also had constitutional implications. The unofficial members of the Legislative Council were incensed at this ministerial fiat imposed without consultation with the representatives of the taxpayers. Such high-handed treatment from London was unprecedented and the unofficial member who represented the Chamber of Commerce, Murray Stewart, moved a resolution which was in effect a vote of censure on the Secretary of State. He hinted in his speech that unless proper respect was paid to the constitutional position of the Legislative Council as the arbiter of the budget he and other unofficials might consider resigning from the Council. All but one of the unofficials voted for the motion, which was, of course, defeated by the use of the official majority, as was a similar motion debated on 24 September.[21] Lugard immediately sent a full account of the debate to London and, building on the hint given in the debate, emphasized the grave danger that the whole body of the unofficials would resign together if an ordinance were to be introduced closing down the divans while their current licences were valid or if proposals for new taxation were to be brought forward in order to find money for compensation. The possibility that they might resign their seats in a body and so precipitate a constitutional crisis if an attempt was made to force through the immediate abolition of the divans was taken seriously by Colonial Office officials. They minuted to ministers that concessions were advisable since the unofficials were on strong ground in maintaining their right to have a consultative voice in a matter affecting Hong Kong's prosperity and revenue.[22]

Lugard's arguments and his weighty support, the financial consequences and the possibility of a political crisis (which Lugard may have exaggerated) had their effect on ministerial resolve. One civil servant — Stubbs, a future Governor of Hong Kong — did point out Lugard's lack of logic in claiming that the closing of divans would lead to no reduction in smoking, and at the same time postulating that it would so decrease the opium-farmer's sales that half a million dollars in compensation would be needed;[23] but the weight of official advice persuaded Lord Crewe and his more fiery Parliamentary Under-Secretary, Colonel Seely, to face the implications of their policy. In the absence of further directives from London, Lugard became increasingly bold in proposing possible compromises. In June he suggested that half of the divans, 96 out of 192, should be closed on the expiry of their licences in February 1909, and the rest a year later. In October he modified his proposal, reducing the number to be closed to 52 to be chosen by the opium-farmer. In December the number to be closed was cut down again to 26. This final figure was accepted by the Secretary of State, subject to the proviso that all the rest must be closed in March 1910 when the farmer's current contract expired.[24] Lugard also proposed, as an earnest of Hong Kong's willingness to restrain consumption, that the farmer should be prohibited from boiling more than 1,200 chests (1,000 for home consumption and 200 for export) in the final year of his contract. This was a reduction by one-third in the maximum permitted by the terms of his lease, and Lugard assured Lord Crewe that he had been successful in persuading the farmer to accept this diminution without making any claim for compensation. This was in fact no great sacrifice on the part of the farmer; he had never drawn as many as a thousand chests in any year since 1901. But this token gesture was gratefully accepted by the Secretary of State who promised, with Cabinet approval, that a substantial contribution would be provided out of imperial funds to assist the colony in the loss of revenue expected when the farm was next put out to tender in 1910.

Looked at in one way, Lugard lost his battle with London: less than two years after the May 1908 debate in the House of Commons and Lord Crewe's directive, all the opium divans in Hong Kong were closed down. But from another angle Lugard had won a substantial number of points: the rate and terms of the closures were as he had suggested; the new restrictions on the opium-farmer were entirely cosmetic; and he had secured the promise of imperial aid for the colony's budget, which would certainly not have been forthcoming if he had meekly accepted Lord Crewe's directive. But how far the closing of the divans might help in the long term to diminish opium addiction was rather obscure.

The lease of the opium farm was put out to tender again in 1909. Lugard anticipated objections from ministers by proposing to London that various new restrictions should be placed on the farmer which took account of the pledges given to Parliament and the recommendations made by the International Opium Conference which met in Shanghai in February 1909. The new terms prohibited sales of *chandu* to women and children, limited the number of chests which might be drawn by the farmer for boiling to 900 a year, and forbade exports except with the written permission of the Superintendent of Imports and Exports. All divans were to be closed from March 1910. In view of these restrictions Lugard gloomily forecast that the letting value of the farm would be reduced by HK$600,000 a year.[25] The new conditions were approved by ministers, but Lugard's fears proved unjustified. The farm was let at an annual rental of HK$1,183,000, a drop of only HK$268,800 on that paid by the previous farmer. The British government kept to its pledge to ease the transition by paying half the loss incurred by the colony for three years, and grants were made of £9,000 (equivalent to HK$102,857) in 1910–11 and £12,000 in 1911–12 and 1912–13 (that is, less than half the decrease in the first year and more than half in the following two years).[26]

But even without the reduction in the opium revenue the Hong Kong budget for 1910 would still have been in deficit, so new sources of revenue were required. In 1909 a bill was introduced to impose excise duties on alcoholic liquors for the first time, at rates approximately half of those prevailing in Britain. These duties were further increased in the following year. As a consequence Hong Kong was forced to set up a Preventive Service for the first time in its history. This was felt to be a great blow to its traditional status as a free port. So, until the end of the opium farm in 1914, Hong Kong had two kinds of excise officers: those directly employed by the government and the agents of the opium-farmer, who were authorized by the Governor to exercise identical powers.

Meanwhile in China the drive to suppress cultivation of the opium poppy was going ahead with unexpected momentum alongside the rigorous enforcement of the 1906 anti-opium legislation. British officials had at first been sceptical of the ability of the Chinese bureaucracy to extirpate every trace of opium within 10 years, as China had bound itself to do by the terms of the Ten-Year Agreement with India, under which exports of Indian opium would cease only if local production were similarly extinguished. But by 1911 Sir John Jordan, the British minister in Peking, was writing in his dispatches to London of 'China's unexpected but unmistakable determination to stamp out the opium habit in a shorter period than was ever contemplated or thought possible' and of the 'marvellous reduction' that had been effected. In March 1911 he reported that in the province of Szechuan (Sichuan), which formerly produced two-thirds of China's opium crop, cultivation of the poppy had been practically suppressed: 'the Chinese government have amply demonstrated their ability to impose their will on the provinces'.[27]

The immediate result of this successful campaign was a shortage of opium for smokers in China, and a consequent rise in the price of the drug. In some parts native opium had quadrupled in price by 1910 and there were enormous rises everywhere. Another factor affecting the price was the fear that soon no opium at all would be available and those smokers who could afford it tried to lay in stocks to last the rest of their lifetimes. Naturally the rise in the price of native opium also affected the imported product. The opium merchants of Shanghai and Hong Kong hoped to take full advantage of the situation. Indian opium imports appeared to be guaranteed until 1917 (though on a declining basis) by the Ten-Year Agreement, and the suppression of native opium cultivation seemed to leave the way clear for the Indian product. Feverish speculation drove up the price at the Indian opium auctions from a normal average price over the previous five years of 1,380 rupees per chest to 3,900 rupees a chest in April 1910.[28]

It is obvious that it had not been the intention of the Chinese authorities that native opium should be suppressed in order to leave the market open for imported opium from India, and so various hindrances and restrictions were imposed on the transit and sale of Indian opium which technically contravened the Chefoo Convention of 1885 and the Ten-Year Agreement of 1907. In May 1910 the provincial authorities in Kwangtung imposed a new tax, nominally on prepared opium, but in fact levied on the raw imported article. Collection of the tax was farmed out to a Chinese firm and severe penalties were imposed for evasion. These new restrictions thoroughly demoralized the opium trade and Chinese merchants refused to take delivery of foreign opium. The legality of the new regulations was dubious; the British Consul at Canton at first refused to protest in spite of the fact that the opium merchants, strongly supported by the Hong Kong government, took the contrary view. Eventually the British government accepted the merchants' contention, and the British minister made a protest in Peking, which he repeated on a number of occasions. The *Wai-chiao Pu* (Chinese Foreign Office) replied with sophisticated and evasive arguments which covered either an inability or an unwillingness to call the Kwangtung provincial authorities to order.[29]

Meanwhile the opium trade between Hong Kong and Canton was at a standstill. Prices at the Indian auctions dropped again by half to 2,000 rupees a chest in July and the opium merchants felt obliged to support the market to protect their investments. There was talk of bankruptcies among the commercial houses, and the banks who had advanced money for the purchase of opium at the Indian auctions were anxious for the security of their loans. By September stocks of opium had accumulated to the value of HK$4,000,000, an enormous sum at that time, and there were fears of a financial panic. The great opium firm of David Sassoon and Co. sent repeated cables and letters to the Foreign Office in London urging the necessity for action to compel China to adhere to the treaties or at least that the Indian government should suspend further opium sales. These representations were supported by the Hong Kong Chamber of Commerce, the China Association in Britain, and various other interested parties. Between June and November, Sir Henry May, who was administering the colony in Lugard's absence, sent to the Secretary of State 17 dispatches totalling (with enclosures) 322 pages on this subject. But although Sir John Jordan reiterated his protests in Peking there was little more that Britain could do. The use of force to compel China to take opium she did not want was out of the question; gunboats had been used for this purpose in 1840 and 1856, but such action was not politically acceptable in 1910. The Foreign Office laid part of the blame for the difficulties in clearing the stocks of opium on the action of the merchants in artificially forcing up the price at the Indian auctions; but hints were dropped in Peking that negotiations on the renewal of the Ten-Year Agreement might be broken off if the existing treaties regarding the import of opium were not adhered to. In consequence there was some modification of the Canton regulations and sales of Indian opium were resumed by the end of the year.[30]

Meanwhile negotiations were slowly proceeding in Peking between Sir John Jordan and the *Wai-chiao Pu* for the renewal of the 1907 Ten-Year Agreement, which had originally been concluded for an experimental period of three years only. A new convention was finally concluded in May 1911. This confirmed the arrangement for the progressive ending of Indian imports by 1917, in line with a similar diminution of local production, but specified that the period could be reduced if clear proof could be given of the extinction of Chinese cultivation of the opium poppy before them. During the period to 1917 any Chinese province declared by a joint Chinese-British commission to be clear of the cultivation and import of native opium could be completely closed to Indian opium. Britain agreed that a consolidated import duty could be charged on Indian opium at an increased rate of 350 taels per chest (replacing the 1885 figure of 110 taels), provided that an equivalent tax was levied on native opium. In return China conceded that all extraordinary provincial

taxes and restrictions on foreign opium would be lifted. The sign-
ing of this agreement was one of the last significant acts of the
government of the Chinese emperor before the revolution of
November 1911. In the intervening few months the provinces of
Szechuan and Shansi (Shanxi) and the three Manchurian provinces,
Hei-lung-chiang (Heilongjiang), Fengtien (Liaoning), and Kirin
(Jilin), were declared free of native opium and closed to foreign
imports in accordance with the terms of this convention.[31]

The restrictions and taxes on foreign opium at Canton were lifted
on the conclusion of the convention and the opium traffic between
Hong Kong and Canton was resumed. All talk of a financial crisis
in Hong Kong vanished and was replaced by renewed optimism. At
the July 1911 auctions in India, opium certificated for China was
sold at 3,370 rupees a chest; by October the price had touched 6,000
rupees and it remained at around 5,500 rupees until May 1912.[32]
The only apparent impediment to the prospect of an immensely
profitable end to the hundred-year-old opium trade lay in activities
in Macau, where enormous quantities of uncertificated opium were
being imported at half the price of certificated opium, nominally
for internal consumption or for re-export to South America, but in
fact intended for smuggling into China. The Portuguese government
proved recalcitrant to diplomatic pressure from Britain to curb this
extremely profitable trade.

The euphoria of the opium merchants was very short-lived. The
revolution of November 1911 created a completely new situation.
The central government lost effective control of many of the
provinces and there was a widespread recrudescence of opium-
planting as some of the new provincial governments were unwilling
to risk unpopularity by enforcing the former decrees or even officially
permitted the planting of the opium poppy, as in Kansu (Gansu).[33]
But elsewhere the reformers who had come to power vigorously
revived and reinforced restrictions against both native and foreign
opium, claiming that the new republican regime could not be bound
by the Ten-Year Agreement concluded by the deposed monarchy.
In Hunan (Henan) province where the authorities acted with unusual
but not unparalleled severity at least 42 men and 5 women were
executed by shooting for sowing the poppy or smoking opium. In
Peking, President Yüan Shih-k'ai, who was seeking recognition from
the British government, assured Sir John Jordan of his determination
to honour international agreements and to suppress native opium
as soon as his government had obtained effective control. But the

opium merchants soon became convinced that the real policy of the new republican government was to exclude Indian opium completely in order to replace it by the native drug. However, by the end of 1912 there was sufficient evidence to convince Sir John of the determination of the new government to stamp out every vestige of the drug in the shortest possible time.[34]

These new anti-opium measures brought a renewed panic to the opium market, far worse than the crisis of 1910, since now both Hong Kong and Shanghai were affected. Chests of opium which could not be disposed of to the interior began to pile up at the treaty ports as more and more certificated opium was shipped from India. Prices at the Indian auctions dropped by 1,700 rupees in June 1912 and by the end of that year stocks in the treaty ports, in Hong Kong, and in transit from India had reached over 29,000 chests, valued at £10–£12 million. These could only be disposed of into the interior with the greatest difficulty because of the rigour of the new anti-opium restrictions. Frantic cables and letters from the opium merchants and the British banks in the East who had advanced money for opium purchases and now saw their collateral halved in value demanded forcible action by the British government to ensure observance of the 1911 treaty. All to no avail. The only possible action open to Britain was to ask the government of India to suspend further auctions of certificated opium. But, as the Permanent Under-Secretary at the Colonial Office pointed out in minuting on one of May's voluminous dispatches on the subject, 'The Indian Government is by no means ready to stop sales which would injure the native cultivators and benefit only Sassoons.'[35] Finally, faced with mounting evidence of the imminence of a financial panic in the East, the government of India announced in January 1913 that auctions of certificated opium would cease in three months' time, and that in the meantime a minimum price would be set at the auctions. Although this was meant to be only a temporary suspension it was in fact the end of official Indian opium exports to China. In May 1913 the Secretary of State for India announced in Parliament that sales had finally been ended four years before the date set in the Ten-Year Agreement.[36] The Liberal government publicly took credit for a highly moral action, but it was primarily motivated by the desire to save the investments of the opium merchants. The government of India did not suffer unduly: as a result of the rise in prices at the auctions it had already received twice as much revenue in the first five years of the Ten-Year Agreement as it had hoped to obtain over its full term.[37] Although exports to China were now prohibited, the India opium auctions were allowed to continue for sales to other destinations, and the Macau opium-farmer and the Macau smugglers took full advantage of this. Their example was quickly followed by the French leased territory of Kwongchow Wan (Guangzhou Wan). Opium was also smuggled into China on ships sailing from Britain, since the British government did not impose any controls on opium exports until 1915.

Meanwhile international moves had been under way to assist the Chinese government's anti-opium campaign. On the initiative of the American government (which was also anxious to curb smuggling into the Philippines) a conference of experts from all the major powers connected with the opium traffic in Asia convened at Shanghai in February 1909 and made various recommendations dealing with the gradual suppression of opium-smoking, the prohibition or the careful regulation of the use of opium, the supervision of opium exports to prevent the shipment of opium to any country prohibiting its entry, and the strict control of the manufacture, sale, and distribution of morphine and other harmful derivatives of opium. In September 1909 the United States issued invitations to the governments represented at Shanghai to attend a further International Opium Conference in order to turn the resolutions passed at Shanghai into a full international treaty. Britain agreed to attend provided that the conference also agreed to place restrictions on the manufacture and distribution of morphia and cocaine. This stipulation was accepted and the conference met at The Hague from December 1911 to January 1912, where agreement was reached on an International Opium Convention (hereafter cited as the Hague Convention). The contracting powers agreed to control the production and distribution of raw and prepared opium and to take measures for the gradual and effective suppression of the internal trade in and use of prepared opium and to prohibit its import and export. Those powers not yet ready to prohibit exports completely were to institute rigorous controls and in particular to forbid export to any country which prohibited imports. The manufacture of morphia, cocaine, heroin, and so on was to be confined to that needed for legitimate medical uses. The contracting powers having treaties with China (termed the 'Treaty Powers') agreed to co-operate with China in the prevention of smuggling, to restrain and control the retail trade in opium in their concessions and leased territories, and *pari passu* with the Chinese government to suppress opium dens and reduce the number of shops where raw and prepared opium was sold.[38]

The British colonies in the Far East (Ceylon, the Straits Settlements, Hong Kong, and Weihaiwei) were consulted before the final draft was completed and all agreed to the British delegation signing the Convention at the end of the conference on their behalf. In the case of Hong Kong the Governor consulted with his Executive Council who agreed with this decision.[39] The convention was not to come into force until ratifications were received from all the signatory powers. These were not all received before the outbreak of the First World War in 1914. The convention did not finally come into force until 1920, as a result of a provision inserted in the peace treaties (Article 295 of the Treaty of Versailles). So neither Britain nor Hong Kong was technically bound to observe the convention until eight years after it was drawn up. But, by then, the British government and the Hong Kong government had accepted by Article 6 the legal and moral obligation to take 'gradual and effective measures' to suppress the use of prepared opium, and this clause was to be quoted against the colony and its opium monopoly for the next 29 years.

The first occasion was in May 1912 when the Hong Kong government wrote to London asking for permission to let the opium farm for a further three-year period from March 1913. In view of the possibility of swift ratification of the convention, and the uncertainties of the situation in China and India, Hong Kong was told that a new three-year contract for the opium farm would commit the government too far ahead, and it was suggested that it would be best to negotiate with the present farmer for a year's extension, coupled with a reduction in the number of chests permitted for boiling. May replied that the farmer would agree to an extension with a reduction in the permissible boilings from 900 to 720 chests a year (540 for domestic consumption and 180 for export). However May preferred, with the unanimous concurrence of the Executive Council, to put the farm out to tender for three years, since this was a particularly favourable time to get a high bid for the contract. May's proposed terms for a new farm would have allowed 540 chests a year to be boiled for internal consumption and 180, 150, and 120 chests in successive years to be boiled for export. He argued (rather implausibly, as the Colonial Office noted) that 540 chests a year for three years would in fact mean a reduction in opium consumption per head since the population was increasing.[40]

May did not elaborate as to why the time was peculiarly favourable for letting the farm, but the reasons are not difficult to infer. By July 1912 the determination of the new Republican government in China to extinguish all opium consumption both domestic and foreign had been clearly revealed, and the farmer was thus assured of no competition for his monopoly from the mainland, so long as there was no backsliding on the part of China. Since he boiled uncertificated Indian opium which was selling in India at half the price of opium certificated for export to China, there was now every incentive for his customers to smuggle the *chandu* he retailed into China, in addition to using the well-established smuggling routes to America and the Philippines. In the face of this new demand for his product the farmer had increased his selling price from HK$3.50 per tael in 1909 to HK$5.50 in 1912, and in the farm year 1911–12 he had drawn his full entitlement of 900 chests for boiling.[41] It is small wonder that he was willing to accept the lease of the farm for a further year at the same rental, even though the number of chests was to be reduced, or that other syndicates were eager to bid for the contract against him.

The Colonial Office was unconvinced. May was told to extend the farm for one year only. An official minuted, 'Our hands will be tied for the shortest time possible, our revenue will for the time be maintained, and our window is nicely dressed by a reduction in the number of chests to be imported'.[42] May was also asked to consider the possibility of abolishing the farm system and adopting that in force in the Straits Settlements where a direct government monopoly had been established in 1910 for the import, preparation, and sale of opium.[43] Previous Governors of Hong Kong had argued against such a system on the ground that it would involve the institution of a costly preventive service which might be less efficient than that organized by the opium-farmer. His agents were largely his own relatives and clansmen who had a strong personal incentive to safeguard the farmer's profits, and it was feared that government employees would be less zealous and more corruptible. But since Hong Kong had already been forced to employ its own excise men after the decision had been taken to levy duties on alcoholic liquors in 1909, Colonial Office officials argued that if the farmer could afford to pay his staff and still make a handsome profit the Hong Kong government could do the same. So the farm was extended until 1914 while May considered the possibility of a government monopoly.

Later in 1912 May submitted a draft bill to amend the Opium Ordinance. The Colonial Office noticed that an individual was allowed to have 30 taels of *chandu* in his possession without committing an offence, and suggested to May that this amount should be reduced to three taels to discourage purchases for smuggling. The Colonial Office had consulted the head of the government opium monopoly in the Straits Settlements who confirmed that five-tael tins (equivalent to about 6⅔ oz. or 190 grams) were very convenient and much used for smuggling, and that this size had consequently been discontinued in Singapore since 1910. May demurred to this suggested reduction, pointing out that the farmer strongly objected to any reduction below 10 taels, and suggested that a five-tael limit would be sufficient. May's plea was supported by a visit of Severn, the Hong Kong Colonial Secretary, then on leave in London, to the Colonial Office. He argued in conversation with the officials that the farmer had been so reasonable and had already made so many concessions that it was undesirable to try to wring further concessions from him. But the Colonial Office was adamant; the Permanent Under-Secretary minuted, 'The Hong Kong government is far too much in the hands of the opium farmer in this matter', and the Secretary of State, Harcourt, agreed. May immediately telegraphed to ask for the decision to be reconsidered: the farmer had a large stock of five-tael tins and labels; subdivision of opium already packaged would be expensive; if a limit of three taels were insisted on the farmer might refuse to extend the lease and it would be too late to call for new tenders before March, causing a hiatus in supplies and a loss of revenue.

Under this assault the Colonial Office gave way; 'Since all the men on the spot are against us', ran the minute, '5 taels may be allowed for this year only'. May was informed by telegraph and promptly expressed his thanks.[44] It is difficult to believe that there was any real danger of the farmer withdrawing from his lucrative contract if this concession had not been made. The Colonial Office then forgot about the matter and never checked that its instructions were carried out. The five-tael tins were apparently phased out in 1914, but the limit of five taels permitted to an individual remained in the opium legislation for the next 30 years.

In June 1913 May reported to London that he and the Executive Council had concurred in accepting the Colonial Office proposal that from the expiry of the term of the present opium-farmer the government should set up a monopoly for the preparation and sale of opium. The reasons in favour were that 'under a monopoly the Government can maintain a closer and stricter control over the use of opium, that its policy with regard to opium can more quickly and easily be adapted to meet changing circumstances, and that abuses can be checked as they arise without the danger of being involved in the payment of large sums in compensation for a breach of agreement'. May proposed to buy out the opium-farmer's appliances, to rent his premises, and to take over his staff of boilers. The number of preventive officers was to be increased from 38 to 96 and there were various other charges to meet for fuel, packaging, and retailing. A very conservative estimate of the profits to be expected from the monopoly was enclosed with the dispatch which assumed that only 40 chests a month would be boiled (as compared with 45 a month permitted to the farmer in his last year), that raw opium would cost HK$2,114 a chest, and that the farmer's retail price of HK$5.50 a tael would be retained. Even so May calculated that the annual revenue from opium sales of HK$2,851,200 would exceed the additional recurrent expenditure by HK$1,727,500. This was HK$544,300 (46 per cent) more than the rent of HK$1,183,200 paid by the farmer in the year 1913–14. Each tael of *chandu* sold by the monopoly at HK$5.50 would thus bring in a profit of HK$3.33 for the government revenue. This high rate of profit was, as May pointed out, entirely consistent with the purposes of the Hague Convention, since the high price served to discourage smoking.[45]

These proposals were approved by the Colonial Office officials and the Secretary of State and announced to the Legislative Council in the Budget Debate of 1913. This was noticed by the anti-opium campaigners in Britain, and Mr Theodore Taylor (the Member of Parliament who had moved the 1906 motion in the House of Commons) wrote to the Secretary of State asking why there had been a change from the farming system to a government monopoly, and why the Hong Kong government had told the Legislative Council that it was considering the erection of permanent offices for the monopoly. Officials at the Colonial Office who composed the reply for the Secretary of State's signature expressed impatience over the tactlessness of the Hong Kong administration, but side-stepped the point in their draft reply, which assured Mr Taylor that the British government fully intended to proceed with the suppression and complete abolition of opium-smoking as soon as effective regulation of the traffic in morphia and cocaine under the Hague Convention made this possible; but in the interim period the establishment of a government monopoly would provide a more effective means of control than the farming system.[46]

The estimates of the likely profitability of the monopoly were soon out of date. Before the farmer's contract expired he had put up the price to HK$6.50 a tael and one of the first actions of the government monopoly in March 1914 was to announce a further increase to HK$8 a tael for standard-quality Bengal *chandu*, with corresponding increases for lower grades and for dross opium. (Dross opium was produced by reboiling the residues left in a pipe after smoking.) May explained to the Colonial Office that these advances had been made possible by the high prices then ruling in China, which ensured that there was no likelihood of the smuggling of *chandu* into the colony. He said nothing about the probability of *chandu* being smuggled out of the colony into China. Three months later May informed London that he had reduced the price of third-quality opium by 20 per cent (from 15c. to 12c. per 0.02 tael) since it had been found that the price had been set at too high a level, as compared with the price of dross opium.[47] The Colonial Office made no comment on May's sharp marketing tactics, even though this action hardly squared with his professed aim of discouraging sales by raising prices. In September 1914 the price was again increased to HK$10 a tael, but May neglected to notify this change to London, and in the press of business following the outbreak of the First World War in August 1914 this omission passed unnoticed.

The gross revenue from opium in the first 10 months of the new monopoly from March to December 1914 was HK$3,594,284, compared to the estimate of HK$2,376,000. Sales would have been even higher, May reported, but for the successive price increases and the outbreak of war, which caused an immediate exodus of population to Canton, and further departures later in the year as a consequence of the trade depression which the war induced.[48] Opium thus provided 34 per cent of the gross revenue of the colony in 1914 compared to 13.9 per cent in 1913. This calculation does not take account of the monopoly's production costs; if these are subtracted the net opium revenue was 26.1 per cent of the total.

Accordingly, when the Budget Estimates were drawn up for 1915, opium sales were expected to bring in HK$4,000,000, or 35.7 per cent out of a gross revenue of HK$11,200,000 (30.1 per cent of net revenue). This excessive reliance on opium revenue was criticized during the Budget Debate in the Legislative Council by an unofficial member, Mr Hewett, who asked how this sum would be replaced if the colony were forced to abolish the monopoly in future, in view of the known attitudes of the Secretary of State and the House of Commons. In his reply the Governor declined to speculate on such hypothetical questions as the future of the monopoly and rebuked the unofficials for raising the question: 'I would have been glad if the unofficial members had said nothing about the subject. I am strongly of the opinion that it is a subject about which the less one says the better.'[49] The unofficials took the hint, and the subject of the opium revenue was not raised again in the Legislative Council. Similar reticence was shown in the annual report on the colony which was presented each year to Parliament. Sales of opium were not separately specified in listing the sources of the colony's revenue but were concealed under the heading 'Licences and Internal Revenue not otherwise specified'.

In the years that followed May took every opportunity to increase the price of *chandu,* taking advantage of the changing opium situation in China and the price set by the opium-farmer in Macau. When reporting these rises to the Colonial Office May always began by referring to the need to raise prices in order to restrict consumption, but the rest of the dispatch made it clear that the chief motive was his assessment of the supply and demand position in the local market. A high point of HK$14.50 a tael for the monopoly's standard grade of Bengal opium was reached in June 1918, and this price remained unchanged for the next 12 years. The prices for this grade which were set by the farmer and the government monopoly are shown in Table 8.

The year 1918 also marked the highest point for sales of opium by the monopoly and of its contribution to the revenue of the colony, as can be seen from Table 9.[50]

The costs of the monopoly were kept down by the use of smuggled opium seized by the Preventive Service. Until 1920, when numerous discoveries of raw Chinese opium began to be made, almost all of the opium seized was Indian opium which could be blended into the boiling of the monopoly's *chandu*, which used only Patna and Benares opium from Bengal. These purchases were made under a contract with the government of India which enabled the Hong Kong monopoly to buy a maximum of 540 chests a year at 2,000 rupees a chest (approximately HK$1,350). There was no obligation to take a minimum number in any year and in fact Hong Kong's purchases over the period of the contract from 1915 to 1920 averaged 390 chests a year because of the supply conveniently provided by the smugglers.

Table 8   The Retail Price of Standard-grade Monopoly Opium,
           1900–1940

Year	Price per Tael (HK$)
1900	1.50
1901	2.00
1904	3.30
1905	3.50
1912	5.50
1913	6.50
March 1914	8.00
September 1914	10.00
December 1915	11.00
February 1916	11.50
April 1916	12.00
June 1918	14.50
October 1927	8.33
January 1928	14.50
February 1931	17.00
April 1936	12.00
July 1940	15.00
November 1940	18.00

Note: The price was set by the opium-farmer in the period 1900–13 and
by the government monopoly thereafter.

Sources: *Hong Kong Legislative Council Sessional Papers 1909*, p.30; CO
129/410, pp.265 and 418; *Hong Kong Government Gazettes*, 1914
onwards.

Informers who led the Preventive Service to caches of illicit opium
were rewarded at the rate of HK$1 per tael of opium discovered,
which was below the cost of buying and shipping opium from India.
In July 1915 the Hong Kong monopoly introduced a special cut-price
line in *chandu* made from confiscated Persian opium at HK$8 a tael,
which was HK$2 below the price of its standard Bengal *chandu*. This
followed the seizure of the equivalent of 50 chests of Persian opium
shipped from London for smuggling into China in the first five
months of that year.

It is possible to calculate how much confiscated opium was boiled

Table 9   Sales, Revenue, and Costs of the Hong Kong Government
Opium Monopoly, 1914–1941

| Year | Sales of Opium (taels) | | Gross Revenue of Monopoly | Direct Costs of Monopoly | Opium Revenue as Percentage of Total Government Revenue |
	Bengal and Pensian	Dross Opium	(HK$)		
1914	397,439	28,242	3,594,284	913,667	34.0
1915	425,954	14,768	4,701,877	703,300	42.7
1916	459,690	10,832	5,811,110	668,110	42.0
1917	481,826	9,524	5,887,475	613,571	39.0
1918	651,696	4,516	8,686,622	691,793	46.5
1919	457,969	3,415	6,803,034	687,830	41.2
1920	293,272	1,104	4,317,970	363,560	29.4
1921	262,133	672	3,938,197	427,690	22.2
1922	370,332	—	5,551,305	484,254	24.9
1923	384,124	—	5,712,056	726,180	23.0
1924	351,559	—	5,147,043	694,834	21.3
1925	233,489	—	3,392,381	696,985	14.6
1926	195,224	—	2,831,305	619,209	13.4
1927	292,830	—	3,344,370	736,061	15.7
1928	247,352	—	3,318,225	716,157	13.3
1929	179,983	—	2,651,491	665,247	11.3
1930	191,774	—	2,835,286	753,337	10.2
1931	173,244	—	3,019,724	752,729	9.1
1932	128,765	—	2,314,226	732,200	6.9
1933	59,209	—	1,152,851	518,075	3.6
1934	31,876	—	655,067	195,175	2.2
1935	17,293	—	352,713	199,905	1.2
1936	15,496	—	264,300	194,265	0.9
1937	22,168	—	314,769	242,767	0.9
1938	25,029	—	345,090	254,950	0.9
1939	83,178	—	1,025,269	232,665	2.5
April 1940–March 1941	?200,000	—	3,032,851	280,342	5.1

Sources: See note 50.

by the monopoly by converting the amount retailed into its equivalent
in chests of opium and comparing this figure with the number
of chests boiled which had been officially purchased from India.

Each chest of opium was expected to produce 1,040 taels of *chandu* after it had been boiled and processed.[51] During the four years 1915 to 1918, the monopoly sold 2,019,165 taels of *chandu,* equivalent to 1,941 chests. But in this period it drew only 1,596 chests from its stock. So the equivalent of 345 chests, approximately 18 per cent of the total sold, consisted of opium confiscated from the smugglers.

In 1918 each tael of Bengal opium retailed by the monopoly at HK$14.50 had cost only HK$1.06 to produce, including the cost of the raw opium.

The opium farm at Macau was making similar high profits. It had been let for five years in 1913 at an annual rent of HK$1,056,666 on the condition that the farmer was limited each year to boiling 260 chests for home consumption and 240 for export to countries that permitted such trade. In 1918 the farm was put out to tender again on the same terms and even though the last outlet for legitimate export, Mexico, had been closed the previous year the farm was relet at an annual rent of HK$6,676,000, the highest of 18 tenders. The superintendent of the Hong Kong monopoly estimated the costs of the Macau farm at approximately HK$2 a tael: the cost of raw opium in 1918 was 50 per cent more than Hong Kong paid on its fixed contract with India, but the new syndicate hoped to produce 1,400 taels of *chandu* from each chest boiled (presumably by adulterating the product), compared with the average of 1,040 taels obtained from each chest by the Hong Kong monopoly, and to sell at a higher price than the HK$12 a tael charged by the previous farmer. 'The quality of Macau opium in already a byword', May reported scathingly of the rival firm; 'the success of a price increase is very problematical in view of the evil repute of the opium now supplied by the present Macau farm'. The farmer could not hope to make enough to pay the annual rent out of sales to Macau's tiny population. He was entitled to boil 240 chests for export out of the 500 chests officially imported from India, but it was believed that at least as many chests of Indian opium were unofficially imported through Kwongchow Wan and Indo-China, together with other illicit supplies from Yunnan and elsewhere. This production found a ready market when smuggled into China or to more distant customers in the Philippines, Australia, and the United States.[52]

The profits of the Hong Kong monopoly, unlike those of Macau, were almost entirely derived from retail sales inside the colony. If any of the monopoly's customers tried to smuggle the drug into China or elsewhere this did not concern the administration, unless large quantities were involved. It was not a criminal offence for a man to have up to five taels of opium in his possession and travellers were allowed to carry half a tael (five mace) of opium for every day of their voyage. Official exports of *chandu* were confined to 360 taels dispatched annually to Weihaiwei for the use of the 36 registered addicts there and 1,200 taels to the New Zealand authorities in Western Samoa.[53] The entrepôt trade in raw opium that had once provided a substantial part of the business of the port of Hong Kong was also practically finished. By 1919 it had dwindled to less than 1,000 chests a year, consisting of several hundred chests shipped to the Macau farm and the Japanese monopoly on Taiwan, which were transhipped at Hong Kong. The Foreign Office was pressing the Colonial Office to make the passage of Persian opium through Hong Kong to Taiwan illegal, but the Governor successfully resisted this proposal, on the ground that the opium would only reach Taiwan through another port, thereby depriving the colony of the harbour dues on the transaction to no purpose.[54]

The steady rise in the sales of the Hong Kong monopoly from 1914 to 1918 and the frequent advances in the price charged were only made possible by the success of the Chinese government's anti-opium drive and the manoeuvres of the British opium merchants. During 1913 provincial inspections by joint teams of Chinese officials and British consular staff were resumed in conformity with the terms of the Ten-Year Agreement, and five further provinces — in addition to the five closed in 1911 — were declared free of native opium and closed to foreign imports. Four more provinces were closed in 1914, leaving only three provinces which habitually consumed Indian opium open for sales: Kiangsi (Jiangxi), Kiangsu (Jiangsu), and Kwangtung. All such inspections were preceded by vigorous efforts on the part of the local administrations to ensure that all signs of the cultivation of the poppy were eradicated. The extinction of the native product naturally increased the demand for the remaining stocks of Indian opium and the opium merchants took full advantage of this situation. In February 1913 they concluded an agreement among themselves to corner the market. The minimum price set by this merchants' combine for Bengal opium was 2,400 Chinese taels of silver (HK$3,037) and for Malwa opium 2,300 taels (HK$2,910). These values were based on the upset prices set at the last Indian auctions. But this was only the starting-point. By December 1913 both brands were selling at around 4,000 taels (HK$5,063). In February 1914 the combine succeeded in forcing up the price of

Bengal opium by 70 per cent to 6,800 taels (HK$8,607) and Malwa by 40 per cent to 5,600 taels (HK$7,088).[55] Sales were actually concluded at these prices and the chests were somehow moved out of the International Settlement at Shanghai and the concessions at the other treaty ports in spite of the heavy penalties imposed almost everywhere in China for smoking or trafficking in opium. It was at this time, March 1914, that the Hong Kong government opium monopoly commenced operations and immediately raised its price to HK$8 a tael and subsequently to HK$10 in September.

The effect of these high prices was to delay the disposal of the huge stockpile of opium that had accumulated in Hong Kong and the treaty ports or was on its way there before the Indian auctions were suspended. In January 1913 this amounted to over 29,000 chests. By the end of the year this stock had dwindled to 11,739 chests and to 8,131 by the end of February 1914. If sales had continued at this rate the balance of the chests would have been disposed of by the end of 1914, but the manoeuvres of the opium combine to force up the price frustrated this hope and in November 1914, 6,340 chests still remained unsold. The Foreign Office and Sir John Jordan strongly disapproved of the merchants' greed which was preventing the final settlement of the opium question but they were powerless to take action. However in November 1914 the combine was warned by Sir John Jordan that if the three remaining provinces still nominally open to Indian opium were inspected in the spring of 1915 when the poppy was in flower and declared free of opium the merchants would be required to remove all their stocks from China.[56] Shanghai was in the middle of Kiangsu province and the International Settlement there could not be allowed to be an exception when the province was closed.

The opium combine was now faced with the prospect of losing the massive profits on which they had been counting and being forced to dispose of their surplus stocks on the world market at around HK$1,088 a chest (the upset price at the Indian auctions of uncertificated opium at the end of 1914). Accordingly they entered into private negotiations with the Chinese government, which was very short of money, and at the end of May 1915 an agreement was signed with the Opium Prohibition Commissioner for the provinces of Kwangtung, Kiangsu, and Kiangsi by which the opium combine would be allowed to dispose of their stocks freely in these three provinces and the Chinese government would not apply for their closure before April 1917. Meanwhile controls over the distribution of native Chinese opium and the smuggling of opium from Macau and Kwongchow Wan were to be vigorously enforced in order to give a free market for the combine's Indian opium. In return for this the combine agreed to make a contribution to the Chinese government of HK$3,500 on every chest sold, in addition to the existing official duty of 350 taels (HK$443) per chest payable to the Maritime Customs. In effect the opium merchants were being forced to disgorge a portion of their profits to the Chinese government in payment for the right to dispose of their stock in the provinces not yet closed. This was a right which they should have been entitled to exercise freely in accordance with the Sino-British Ten-Year Agreement, but which the British government was impotent to enforce. The opium combine, now given a new lease of life, promptly advanced prices in Shanghai by 2,000 taels (HK$2,500) a chest as soon as the contract was signed.[57] This marked the first step backward by the Chinese government from a policy of the total suppression of opium. But there were no protests against this move since public attention was preoccupied with the 'Twenty-one Demands' which had been presented by the Japanese in January 1915 and the ultimatum which followed in May.

Further backsliding occurred in October 1915 when a supplementary contract was signed in Canton between the Hong Kong merchants in the opium combine and the Opium Prohibition Commissioner, by which the combine agreed to sell 1,200 chests to him at an average price of HK$9,000. The first signatory on the contract for the Hong Kong combine was Mr Shellim, who was the general manager of David Sassoon and Co. and an unofficial member of the Hong Kong Legislative Council. The opium was to be used by a syndicate to establish a new opium monopoly in Kwangtung province. A company was set up for this purpose (whose shares promptly doubled in price) and an elaborate network of retail outlets was organized throughout the province. The opium suppression police had been conveniently disbanded the month before the contract was signed. The official explanation put forward by the Kwangtung administration was that the *chandu* retailed by the new monopoly would be sold only to licensed addicts and would include an ingredient designed to cure them of their craving. This rationale deceived nobody. Since the syndicate had to pay HK$12,500 for each chest (HK$9,000 plus the HK$3,500 contribution to the government) for its raw opium, the retail price was set at HK$15 a tael. This promised a rather low rate of return to the syndicate since each chest should produce only around 1,100 taels of *chandu* and there were the production expenses and the profit margin for the retail outlets to be met; the British Consul at Canton confidently predicted that the temptation to adulterate the product with lard, pigs' blood, and cheap illicit Chinese opium from Yunnan would prove irresistible. The syndicate also made plans to import additional uncertificated Indian opium by devious routes and to make purchases in Persia.[58]

In Hong Kong the Governor's first reaction was anxiety that the syndicate would be so successful in these endeavours that it might dump cheap *chandu* in the colony to compete with the government product. But the effective abolition of the restrictions on opium in Canton encouraged many Chinese to resume the habit of opium-smoking and this in turn led to an increase in the sales of Hong Kong opium as the transitory population which moved in large numbers between Kwangtung and Hong Kong each day continued to indulge in the habit while in the colony.[59] May promptly took advantage of this to put up the Hong Kong retail price to HK$11 a tael, both to restrict consumption (his usual excuse) and to make it less attractive to smuggle *chandu* to the mainland. He explained to the Colonial Office that he would have advanced the price further but for the fact that the price in Macau remained at HK$10; however he hoped to persuade the Macau farmer to raise his prices in step with Hong Kong, and if he could do so he would increase the price still more. The officials at the Colonial Office made no adverse comments and only noted the likely effects on the Hong Kong revenue.[60] The sales of Hong Kong *chandu* did not diminish and the Hong Kong price was raised by a further 50c. in February 1916 and again by 50c. in April. These price rises were not reported to the Colonial Office until a year later, in a routine dispatch of May 1917, enclosing the opium return for 1916.[61]

Although the arrangements between the opium combine and the Chinese government were made without the knowledge or consent of British officials in China, it was thought that the agreements would at least lead to the final disposal of the remaining stocks of Indian opium. But political changes and the greed of the opium merchants frustrated this hope. By March 1916 the combine had pushed up their prices in Shanghai to 11,500 taels (HK$14,556) for a chest of Bengal opium and 12,500 taels (HK$15,822) for Malwa, and clearances of opium in stock naturally diminished. The Opium Prohibition Commissioner who had made the agreement with the Hong Kong combine was assassinated in Canton in March 1916 when only 300 chests out of the 1,200 contracted for had been delivered. His brother who succeeded him as Commissioner refused to continue to carry out the agreement, and Sir John Jordan refused to intervene on behalf of the combine.[62] The upshot was that in March 1917 when both agreements were due to expire some 3,000 chests of Indian opium were still left in the hands of the combine. The opium merchants then entered into further negotiations with the Chinese government represented by General Feng Kuo-chang, the military governor of Nanking (Nanjing) and titular Vice-President of the Republic, to take over the stocks. Agreement was delayed by disagreements over the price to be paid, popular protests, and political upheavals, such as the attempted restoration of the monarchy under P'u-i. But finally in September 1918 after General Feng had become President the remaining stock, which had now shrunk to 1,577 chests, was purchased by the Chinese government at 6,200 taels per chest, payable in Chinese government 6 per cent bonds which were not due to mature for 10 years. The government promptly resold 300 chests at 16,000 taels (HK$20,253) each. President Feng was succeeded by Hsu Shih-chang, an honest and dedicated reformer, who gave orders that the remaining 1,200 or so chests should be publicly destroyed. Special kilns were constructed on the banks of the Yangtze river (Chang Jiang) and in January 1919 the opium was conveyed there, checked by foreign experts to prove that it was genuine, publicly burnt, and the ashes were dissolved in the river. This was the largest pyre of opium since the burning of the stocks at Canton by Commissioner Lin in 1839. The opium destroyed had a market value of over 19,000,000 taels (HK$24,000,000), a sum which China could ill afford to spare.[63]

Meanwhile in Hong Kong the opium monopoly had just completed its most successful year. A total of 651,696 taels of *chandu* had been sold at HK$14.50 a tael, which, together with sales of 4,516 taels of dross opium, brought in revenue of HK$8,686,622. The monthly quantity sold was 37 per cent greater than in 1914, the first year of the monopoly, when the price was only HK$8 a tael. Such an increase in sales despite successive price rises could only have been achieved by supplying the demand of addicts in Kwangtung and elsewhere who were prevented from obtaining their supplies locally by the vigorous measures being taken to eradicate the drug. These measures were being enforced, with minor backslidings, all over China. The Preventive Service put little effort into preventing the smuggling of the monopoly's *chandu* into China: in 1917, only 81 taels of Hong

Kong opium were discovered out of 47,589 taels seized and in 1918, only 518 taels out of a total of 72,513 taels seized.[64] The Hong Kong monopoly's profits increased in proportion to the success of China's efforts at eradication and the large revenues derived by the colonial government from opium provided a standing temptation to China to relax its efforts and do the same.

12 The Control of Opium, 1919 to 1941

THE end of the First World War in November 1918 brought a resumption of international efforts to control the use and distribution of addictive drugs. Even before fighting ceased the United States government had tried to initiate moves to bring the 1912 Hague Convention into force at least among those countries that had ratified it. Britain preferred to wait until Germany, Austria-Hungary, and Turkey had adhered to the Convention and suggested that the matter should be raised at the Peace Conference.[1] The result was the inclusion of clauses in the peace treaties compelling the belligerent states to accept the 1912 Hague Convention, which was then brought into force in 1920. Article 23 of the Covenant of the League of Nations entrusted the League with the 'general supervision of the traffic in opium and other dangerous drugs'. At the first Assembly of the League of Nations in Geneva in December 1920 the League formally took over the duties of collecting data and dealing with disputes which the Hague Convention had laid upon the Netherlands government. A resolution was passed entrusting the Secretariat of the League with the task of collecting this information and authorizing the appointment of an Advisory Committee which would make reports to the annual Assembly of the League on all matters regarding the arrangements to control the traffic in dangerous drugs.[2]

These moves were viewed with considerable misgivings inside the Colonial Office. In December 1918 a dispatch to the Governor of Hong Kong permitting him to set up a Salaries Commission to adjust the pay of the public service after the period of wartime inflation warned him that it should be borne in mind that the colony might have to face the total loss of its opium revenue in the near future. In February 1919 an official noted on a dispatch which described the appalling housing conditions and proposed measures to alleviate overcrowding: 'We have before us the awful spectre of the loss of our opium revenue which amounts to quite half the total.'[3] Indeed, the finances of the Hong Kong government had become as dependent on opium as any addict on his drug. The opium revenue in 1918 was more than the total revenue of the colony in 1913. Between 1913 and 1918 the annual revenue had more than doubled from

HK$8,512,000 to HK$18,600,000; three-quarters of this increase was due to the opium revenue, which had increased from HK$1,183,200 in 1913 to HK$8,686,622 in 1918. The only significant new tax imposed during the First World War was an excise duty on tobacco, which yielded HK$619,000 in 1918.

Moves against opium did not come only from the United States and the international community. Sir John Jordan, the British minister in Peking, who was convinced, following the pyre of opium in Shanghai in January 1919, that the Chinese government was sincere in its determination to eradicate opium, pressed upon the Foreign Office the desirability of a complete ban on opium shipments from India to the Far East and the need for the abolition of the opium monopolies in Hong Kong, the Straits Settlements, North Borneo, and Macau, arguing that the large revenues obtained from opium sales by the colonial administrations provided a bad example and a standing temptation to China to do the same. By ending the Indian opium trade with China, Britain had finally broken her connection with the trade and had thereby removed the cause of the stigma attached to her by public opinion; should there be a relapse on China's part it was important, he argued, that Britain should have no share in such a calamity.[4] The Foreign Secretary, Lord Curzon, agreed with this point of view. The Foreign Office had recently been embarrassed by the action of the Straits Settlements in renewing its five-year agreement with India for supplies of opium. Even though the quantities to be purchased were to be less than those purchased under the previous agreement, the Foreign Office was able to defend the new agreement only on the weak argument that no minimum annual quantity was specified. Therefore, it argued, the agreement was not incompatible with the aim of the Hague Convention, which was to confine the use of opium to medicinal purposes only. The views of Sir John Jordan were passed on to the Colonial Office in April and July 1919, and officials subsequently asked Hong Kong and the Straits Settlements to comment. Both objected strongly to any proposal to abolish their opium monopolies within a fixed period. After giving a highly selective review of events in Hong Kong over the past six years, Severn, the Officer Administering the Government, warned that if the government manufacture of opium were to cease smokers would experience 'wholly unnecessary inconvenience and a good deal of mental and bodily suffering which they would take immediate means to alleviate'. Since the Chinese would have opium if it could be procured, the closure of the government monopoly would lead to increased smuggling (which could only be kept in check by a greatly enlarged Preventive Service at prohibitive cost), or indulgence in alcohol, or the use of injections of morphine or cocaine. The existence of the monopoly, he averred, enabled the government to keep the opium habit within bounds which made it 'practically innocuous'. The only effective way to control addiction was to cut off the supply of raw opium at its sources.[5]

Severn's arguments against the abolition of the monopoly closely followed those advanced by Lugard 10 years before, and they were subsequently endorsed by the new Governor, Sir Edward Stubbs, when he arrived. But Stubbs, who had been an official at the Colonial Office for many years before moving to Ceylon in 1913 as Colonial Secretary, appreciated the need to make some gesture in the direction of the 'gradual and effective suppression of the use of opium' agreed to in 1912. So in October 1919 he reported that it had been decided to cease production of dross opium, which was prepared by the government factory from the dross purchased from opium-smokers and which was generally regarded as more deleterious than prepared opium. In future the government would purchase dross and then destroy it. The colony would lose an expected revenue from sales of around HK$14,000 a year while continuing to incur the cost of purchasing dross at about HK$44,000 a year. Stubbs paraded this as 'a clear indication of the Hong Kong government's *bona fide* desire to restrict opium smoking without regard to financial considerations'. The Colonial Office officials were little impressed: an official minuted that the loss amounted to less than 1 per cent of the colony's opium revenue. In any event Stubbs did not move with undue haste to discontinue sales of dross opium. A supply of dross opium sufficient to enable sales to continue for two more years was laid down before the factory for manufacturing it was closed. Within a few years the monopoly ceased to purchase opium dross.[6]

This dispatch was written while the Budget for 1920 was under consideration by the Legislative Council and for the first time since the government monopoly was established the estimated revenue from opium sales showed a decline on the previous year, amounting to HK$1,500,000. This fall was a consequence of reduced sales in 1919, but Stubbs took the opportunity to warn the Council that as a result of the setting up of the League of Nations there was likely to be a determined effort to suppress the opium trade: 'We must therefore reconcile ourselves to doing without the revenue from opium in the near future.'[7] However in a private dispatch to the

Colonial Office he was more sanguine, explaining that he did not regard this as an immediate danger: 'Until China ceases to grow and consume enormous quantities of opium it would be useless for the colony to abandon its present system, as the only result would be that the consumer would be supplied with opium smuggled from China and the money now received by the government would go into the pockets of private persons.'[8]

A year later, in December 1920, the Foreign Office returned to the attack with a letter to the Colonial Office stating that Lord Curzon was emphatically of the opinion that the time had now come for a serious effort to be made to limit the duration of the opium monopolies of the Straits Settlements and Hong Kong. The first meeting of the League of Nations was about to take place and the Foreign Office referred to the increased international scrutiny of British actions which was now to be expected. It also pointed to the danger of the smuggling of opium from Hong Kong to China and the embarrassment which the continued existence of the colonial monopolies caused in the British government's efforts to persuade Portugal to accept a reduction in the excessive quantity of opium legally imported into Macau. (A Colonial Office official annotated on this: 'It is difficult to see why a British colony should be crippled in order that the Foreign Office may more effectively protest against the misbehaviour of a Portuguese one.') Another reason for action was the decision of the Japanese government to close down its monopolies in the leased territories of Kwantung (now part of Liaoning province) and Tsingtao (Qingdao) and to supply opium only on production of a medical certificate.[9]

The Colonial Office was quick to reply. It pointed out that there was no danger of government-prepared opium being smuggled from Hong Kong to China because it was sold in Hong Kong at a price maintained at an artificially higher level than that in the neighbouring countries. The colonies were fully and conscientiously complying with the Hague Convention. 'Any premature attempt to replace the present system of effective and increasingly stringent regulation and control by one of total prohibition must under present conditions inevitably result in a vast increase in the illicit traffic in opium (which is already increasingly difficult to circumvent), an upheaval of popular indignation and resentment among the races long accustomed to its use and the substitution of that wide-spread indulgence in morphine and far more dangerous and insidious drugs which, as Lord Curzon is well aware, has been an immediate consequence of the efforts made to suppress the consumption of opium in China.'[10]

Similar arguments were used in a Colonial Office memorandum to the Cabinet in February 1921. It is not at all clear whence the Colonial Office derived its fears of 'an upheaval of popular indignation and resentment' if the opium monopolies were abolished. Severn's dispatch from Hong Kong had referred merely to the inconvenience and bodily suffering of the addicts deprived of their drug. But no doubt it proved an effective argument. Colonial Office officials were determined to protect the colonies' revenue and the Secretary of State, Lord Milner, fully supported these efforts. The Cabinet meeting of 18 February 1921 accepted the arguments of the Colonial Office and rebuffed Curzon's attempt to have the monopolies closed down.[11]

The whole international effort to control opium had been inspired by the desire to support China's campaign, begun in 1906, to eradicate opium. By the end of 1918 China's efforts seemed at last to have been extraordinarily successful. All the provinces had been declared free of native cultivation to the satisfaction of the British government, and the last chests of imported Indian opium were incinerated in Shanghai in January 1919. But before the year was over there were reports that the opium poppy was again being cultivated in several provinces that had once been declared clear of it. This evidence was eagerly seized upon by the Hong Kong authorities. Severn had remarked tartly on Sir John Jordan's optimism, 'I can see little gain in exulting over the burning of foreign opium in Shanghai while Chinese opium is being freely produced in Shensi' (Shaanxi). By 1920 consular reports showed that opium was being grown again in more than half the provinces of China with the connivance and sometimes the open encouragement of the military governors (*tuchan* or war-lords) who had effectively taken over the administration. The government in Peking might be sincere in its wish to suppress opium but the provinces paid little attention to its commands. So abundant was the supply that, for example, in Fukien (Fujian) province the price of raw opium had dropped from HK$16 to 90c. a tael in the space of two years.[12] The Maritime Customs authorities were incapable of controlling the illegal traffic in opium throughout the country and its officers were increasingly subject to bribery or demoralized when their efforts were frustrated by local officials acting under the orders of the war-lords. By November 1920 the Inspector-General of the Customs was advocating the legalization of opium again and the imposition of a tax on opium as the only means of bringing the scandal under any sort of control.[13] In effect China had now attained what many believed to have been her long-standing aim, dating back to 1796, which was to exclude Indian opium and force all Chinese addicts to consume only the native product.[14] Since opium continued to be officially banned, although in fact it was freely available in increasing quantities, India was barred by Article 3 of the 1912 International Opium Convention from resuming exports to China.

The ready availability of cheap opium in China naturally affected the sales of the Hong Kong monopoly. In 1919 raw and prepared opium from China reappeared in seizures of smuggled opium for the first time since the government monopoly was established, though the amounts were small: only 1,558 taels of raw opium and 6,088 of *chandu*, a mere 15 per cent of the total seizures. But in 1920, 8,828 taels of raw opium and 100,911 taels of *chandu* (approximately 4 tons of opium) originating from China were discovered, amounting to 85 per cent of the total seizures. Chinese *chandu* was inferior to the Indian *chandu* produced by the government monopoly. Stubbs considered that it was comparable only to the monopoly's dross opium which was about to be discontinued. Since the confiscated Chinese opium could not be blended with the monopoly's product, as had been done in the past with seized Bengal and Persian opium, it had to be destroyed. This meant that the money paid out as a reward to informers was unproductive expenditure for the government, because most convicted smugglers preferred to go to prison rather than pay any fine imposed, thereby creating a further charge on the colony's revenue. Stubbs accordingly cut by half the rate of rewards paid to informers when opium of the inferior grade was discovered.[15] None the less, in spite of its poor quality, the Chinese *chandu* found a ready market among the colony's addicts because it was so much cheaper (retailing at HK$2 a tael) than the monopoly's standard blend of Indian opium, which retailed at HK$14.50 (and which Stubbs privately described as 'admittedly the best product in existence'). As a result sales of the monopoly's *chandu* were cut by more than half between 1918 and 1920, falling from 651,696 taels in 1918 to 293,272 taels in 1920. There was a similar decline in the monopoly's contribution to the government's revenue, from a net profit of HK$7,994,829 on sales in 1918 to HK$3,954,410 in 1920.

The Hong Kong monopoly was not alone in being affected by the surge of cheap supplies from China. Its rival, the opium-farmer in

Macau, suffered similarly. The Macau opium farm had been let in February 1918 for a period of five years at an annual rent of HK$6,676,000, when the ban on opium-growing in China was still being rigorously enforced. But the upsurge of Chinese opium production from 1919 onwards, which was permitted or encouraged by the war-lords, proved ruinous; in 1920 the Macau farmer abandoned his contract after only two years. The farm was relet in July 1920 for three years at an annual rent of HK$3,950,000 (roughly equal to the profit on the Hong Kong monopoly for 1920) and the new farmer promptly reduced his retail price to HK$9 a tael in order to maintain his sales.[16] This was a marketing tactic which was not open to the Hong Kong monopoly since for many years Hong Kong had claimed that its sole motive for increasing the price of its product was to curb consumption. The question of reducing the price of the monopoly's opium in order to make it more competitive was discussed in the Executive Council in June 1921, but Stubbs resisted the suggestion on the ground that any decrease in the price might stir up agitation in Britain for the complete suppression of the monopoly.[17]

However, the colonial government was not prepared to see its opium sales, and consequently its revenue, decline because of competition from smuggled supplies from China. In the second half of 1921 a vigorous campaign was mounted by government revenue officers to raid illegal opium divans. Divankeepers were prosecuted and smugglers and those convicted of opium offences were banished from the colony if they could not prove that they were born in Hong Kong. Since 90 per cent of those convicted refused to pay fines the number of persons imprisoned for opium offences increased from 242 in 1920 to 4,036 in 1921.[18] The difficulty and risks of buying smuggled opium were accordingly increased, and the sales of monopoly opium rose substantially in 1922 and 1923. But the profits of opium-selling were so large (both for illicit divankeepers and for the government) that police action had only a limited deterrent effect so long as opium could easily be smuggled into the colony in small junks landing at quiet beaches or on the persons of the thousands of transients who thronged the ferries between Hong Kong and the mainland every day. In the Eastern District of Hong Kong, Hakka divankeeepers were so well organized that they set up a mutual protection society which charged a fixed monthly subscription and in turn paid watchers to give warning of police raids, engaged lawyers whenever a member was arrested, paid compensation while he was in prison, and then set him up in business again with a new divan outfit as soon as he was released. It was frequently found that a cubicle used as a divan reopened under a new keeper as soon as the former proprietor was arrested. In some cases children acted as managers of divans, since it was impossible to imprison or punish children for doing what their parents or employers would punish them for refusing to do. Other reasons for the increased sales in 1922 were the unsettled conditions existing in the neighbouring province of Kwangtung and the temporary interruption of communications caused by the seamen's strike of that year.[19]

These increased sales of government *chandu* found the monopoly temporarily short of supplies of raw opium. In 1920, faced with a declining demand and large stocks of Indian opium accumulated in the past, Hong Kong had reduced its imports from India from 45 to 10 chests a month. At that time there were fears that the monopoly might be closed down as the result of international pressure and every effort was made to use up its accumulated stocks. By mid-1922 these were nearly exhausted and an urgent request was sent to India for the supply to be increased to 20 chests a month. This request was fully in accordance with the agreement on opium purchases which had been renewed with India in 1921; this set no maximum limit on supplies provided that six months' notice of any increase or decrease was given. But the request was extremely embarrassing for the British government, which had already taken credit for the reduction in the amount of Indian opium purchased by Hong Kong in 1920. The request was received just before the meeting of the League of Nations Assembly in September 1922, and the matter was raised at a meeting of the Advisory Committee on the Traffic in Opium by Sir John Jordan (one of the assessors attached to the Committee), who strongly attacked the increase as excessive and as setting a bad example to China. The matter was also raised in the Assembly where the British delegation, led by Lord Balfour, was attacking the failures of the Chinese and Japanese to abide by the 1912 Hague Convention. When the request by Hong Kong for increased supplies became known other delegations took malicious pleasure in this fine example of British hypocrisy. At Balfour's request the Colonial Office telegraphed to Hong Kong asking if the increase in supply could be delayed until March 1923 when the Advisory Committee was next due to meet. But Hong Kong replied that this was impossible as by then its stocks would be completely exhausted and consumers would be forced into total dependence on smuggled opium. So, since the

Colonial Office was unwilling to intervene to deny Hong Kong's request, the British delegate at Geneva felt obliged to give a public undertaking that, subject to the Advisory Committee's future recommendation, the amount of opium placed on sale by the monopoly in future would not exceed the average consumption for the past few years.[20]

The terms of this pledge were somewhat vague, and the Colonial Office attempted to argue that the calculation of the 'average consumption', which determined the amount that the government might put on sale, should include the amount of smuggled opium which had been consumed in previous years, before vigorous preventive measures had diverted this demand to the purchase of government *chandu*. But Sir Malcolm Delevingne, the British member and first Chairman of the League of Nations Advisory Committee on the Traffic in Opium, insisted that only the consumption of government opium was to be used in the calculation.[21] Delevingne had been chosen as the British delegate in 1921, and he remained on the Committee until 1934, to the great discomfort of the Colonial Office. When the appointment was under discussion, the Colonial Office had wished, if possible, to secure special representation on the League of Nations Committee for the interests of Hong Kong and Malaya, or alternatively to ensure that the British representative should be specifically instructed to safeguard the interests of the colonies and maintain a close association with the Colonial Office, just as the Indian government had a separate representative on the Committee who proved to be a forceful defender of India's opium policy. Instead the British government chose Delevingne, a civil servant from the Home Office who, as a Colonial Office official minuted at the time, was 'strongly anti-opium'.[22] One of his first actions as Chairman of the Advisory Committee was to insert into the Committee's questionnaire to governments a request that they should set a date for ending the manufacture of, trade in, and use of prepared opium (that is, when they proposed to enforce their obligations under Article 6 of the 1912 Convention). None of the British colonies and dependencies in the Far East was prepared to set such a date, and their replies variously emphasized the dangers that the premature ending of government supplies of *chandu* would lead to an increase in opium-smuggling, or to an indulgence in morphia injections or alcohol as an alternative, or that Chinese emigration, which was necessary to the continued progress of the colonies, would be diverted to territories where opium was still available, unless similar restrictions were imposed everywhere. The Colonial Office summarized these arguments and passed them on to Delevingne, adding the observation that the abolition of opium manufacture would lead to a 'huge and paralysing financial loss for the colonies', although this loss would not be allowed to interfere with further restrictions or the ultimate goal of the complete suppression of opium-smoking.[23]

The question of the terminal date for the government monopolies was not pursued at the 1922 meetings of the League of Nations and its Advisory Committee, which were largely concerned with proposals to censure China for its backsliding over opium production, and with Chinese rebuttals of these charges. The question was deferred pending the receipt of information from all states on their legitimate requirements of opium and other drugs. But in April 1923 Delevingne sent to the Colonial Office a set of proposals which he intended to put before the Advisory Committee to secure effective application of Article 6 of the 1912 Convention. Delevingne stigmatized the present position as one of drift: the colonial monopolies continued to put unlimited quantities of *chandu* on sale and any reduction in demand (for which the governments took credit) was in practice due either to customers' shortage of cash to pay the high prices demanded (owing to trade depressions or similar causes) or to the availability of cheaper illicit supplies. He proposed that the farming system where it still remained should be replaced by government monopolies (this was principally directed against Macau); that *chandu* should be sold only at government shops (thus taking the trade out of the hands of private retailers who had an incentive to push sales); that all smokers should be registered and issued with a ration card allowing them to purchase only a fixed amount; and that this ration of *chandu* should be periodically revised and reduced. Delevingne had already discussed these proposals with officials from Hong Kong and Singapore who had been with him in Geneva, and they considered them practicable. He pointed out that the registration of smokers was already in operation in the Dutch East Indies and the Japanese colony of Formosa (Taiwan) — to which list he could also have added Weihaiwei and Ceylon; and he hoped that, if he could announce that the British colonies were prepared to adopt the scheme, it might be possible to secure an agreement among all the colonial powers to take similar action.[24]

Colonial Office officials were prepared to agree to all of these suggestions except for the registration of smokers, which was the crucial point of the whole scheme. They emphasized the practical difficulties of enforcing such a scheme in Hong Kong and this point was emphatically affirmed by Stubbs in a telegram and subsequent dispatch as soon as the proposition was put to him.[25] Nevertheless Delevingne's proposals, with slight modifications, were put to the Advisory Committee, which decided to recommend to the Council of the League that a fresh conference of all the powers with Eastern possessions should be called to negotiate on these lines about measures for more effective control of the sales of prepared opium. An American delegation was present at the meeting of the Advisory Committee, mandated by a joint resolution of both houses of Congress to press for the limitation of the production of narcotic drugs strictly to the quantity required for scientific and medical purposes.[26] According to the Congressional Resolution more than a million Americans were addicted to morphia, heroin, or opium and there were strong demands upon the United States president to put pressure on the states involved in the production of or trade in these drugs. The subsequent decision of the League to call two conferences to meet in 1924, one to consider the trade in prepared opium, and the other to consider limits on the production and manufacture of narcotic drugs, was thus largely taken at the instigation of the United States, just as the conferences of 1909 in Shanghai and of 1911–12 in The Hague had been.[27] The United States had just adopted by the constitutional amendment of 1919 the policy of the complete prohibition of alcohol within its borders and its reforming zeal was now directed to the world-wide prohibition of opium and its derivatives.

In September 1923 dispatches were sent to the Governors of the Far Eastern colonies inviting them to set up local committees of officials and unofficials, including, it was stressed, prominent Chinese, to consider what effective action could be taken on the lines of Delevingne's proposals, so as to enable the British delegation to the forthcoming conferences to resist international criticism, particularly from the United States, of Britain's failure to carry out the provisions of the 1912 Hague Convention by closing down the colonial opium monopolies. Accordingly a Hong Kong committee of three officials and four unofficials was set up to examine the position. It included the two Chinese members of the Legislative Council, Chow Shou-son and R.H. Kotewall and also a missionary, Revd T.W. Pearce. The report which they produced in March 1924 was unanimous. It began by resolving to ignore the financial aspect completely and admitted that the measures then in force would never lead to the complete suppression of opium-smoking but were only effective in keeping the opium habit within bounds by setting a high price for the monopoly's *chandu* and imposing penalties on the use of illicit supplies. But, the Committee went on to argue, no further measures were possible: the registration of smokers would lead to impersonation and the sale of ration cards; a reduction of the amount put on sale would not wean smokers from the habit but merely increase the demand for smuggled supplies; total prohibition would lead to a massive increase in smuggling and to the corruption of the Preventive Service; and more drastic searching of those entering the colony would be bitterly resented by the Chinese population who already objected to the existing checks. Since public opinion was generally tolerant of opium-smokers and smuggling nothing more could be done for the present. The only cure was for China (and Persia and Turkey) to cease growing opium. Until this occurred attempts to stop the Hong Kong Chinese from smoking opium were merely 'beating the air'. The committee concluded by reiterating its entire accord with the principle of opium suppression both in Hong Kong and throughout the world.[28]

The Governor of Hong Kong naturally concurred in the views of the Committee. He had already told the Colonial Office when the proposals were first put to him that if a registration and rationing system for supplies of *chandu* were to be enforced effectively, Hong Kong might lose the greater part of its immigrant labour; such a loss would mean 'ruin to a flourishing colony and disaster to British trade in South China'. The existing measures to search all entrants had been the cause of constant protests by the representatives of the Chinese community, he wrote. 'An extension of them which would make them thoroughly efficient would result in setting the whole Chinese population against us and would lead in no long time to the loss of Hong Kong as a British Colony.' Meanwhile Severn, the Hong Kong Colonial Secretary who was on leave in London, had visited the Colonial Office to reinforce Stubbs's views. His chief argument against the licensing of smokers was the intense dislike felt by the Chinese against any form of registration, although he did not deny that registration might be possible.[29]

The views of the Hong Kong Committee received a chilly reception from the Home Office and the Foreign Office. Delevingne stigmatized the Hong Kong Committee's report as 'frankly negative', contrasting it unfavourably with the report of the Singapore and

Malaya Committee which was at least prepared to countenance some preliminary moves towards registration and rationing. With the support of the Foreign Office he argued that Britain was committed by adherence to an international convention to the effective suppression of opium-smoking; that Britain's efforts to persuade other countries to enforce the Convention were compromised by the continued existence of the colonial opium monopolies; and that there was strong pressure to remedy this state of affairs from public opinion in the United States which had the support of the American government. Delevingne accordingly argued that prohibition of the use of *chandu* for smoking should be imposed within a definite period, even if in the case of Hong Kong such a law could not be effectively enforced. The situation in Hong Kong would be little worse than it was already, he argued since the colonial government admitted that there was at least as much illicit opium smoked as opium provided by the monopoly. It was unfortunate, he continued, that Chinese public opinion in Hong Kong would not support a strong anti-opium policy. But if one Chinese war-lord, Yen Hsi-shan in the province of Shansi (Shanxi), had been able to enforce the prohibition of opium, then the Hong Kong government could do the same. Hong Kong was a British colony, where British standards must prevail. Delevingne was of the opinion that if smoking was declared illegal decent people would turn against it. The Colonial Office naturally opposed Delevingne's proposal, and the Secretary of State submitted a counter-memorandum to the Cabinet, in which be rehearsed the arguments provided by the Governor and the Hong Kong Committee that prohibition would be unenforceable and would lead to worse evils.[30]

A government formed by the Labour Party was then briefly in office, but with only a minority of the seats in the House of Commons. The government was defeated on a division in the House of Commons and Parliament was dissolved in October 1924 before a Cabinet decision had been taken which could have resolved the conflicting views on opium policy held by the Colonial Office and the Home and Foreign Offices. The first opium conference was due to open in November and could not be postponed to suit Britain's convenience, so a meeting of civil servants agreed that the British delegation should adopt a temporizing line, express its good intentions and, if pressed, should propose an impartial League of Nations Commission to investigate the problem. This was not the strong initiative which Delevingne had wanted to take, but it was out of the question to impose the registration of addicts or a closure of the opium monopolies on the colonies in the absence of a Cabinet decision. The Labour government had been committed to a 'one hundred per cent League of Nations policy', and the fall of that government may have postponed the closure of the colonial opium monopolies for a further 20 years.[31]

The two opium conferences were scheduled to be held consecutively in Geneva, beginning in November 1924, but in fact the first conference did not complete its business before the second one opened, and both continued until February 1925. The first conference comprised the governments of the Far Eastern territories where the use of prepared opium was still temporarily permitted under the provisions of Chapter Two of the 1912 Hague Convention (Britain, France, India, Japan, the Netherlands, Portugal, and Siam), together with China. Delevingne had hoped that agreement would be reached to strengthen control of opium-smoking on the lines of his original proposals of 1923 but it soon became clear that the other colonial powers had no such intention. The conference only agreed on minor amendments to the Convention, such as the prohibition of the re-export or transhipment of prepared opium, and a decision that the importation, manufacture, sale, and distribution of prepared opium should be made a government monopoly 'as soon as conditions permit'. (The qualifying phrase was inserted to accommodate Macau, the only territory where the farming system was still in operation.) But there was no agreement on the registration and rationing of addicts or on a progressive limitation on the amount of prepared opium to be put on sale. Delevingne had expected to be embarrassed by the attenuated proposals he was authorized to make on behalf of Britain, but found that the other states were not prepared even to go so far.[32]

The United States did not take part in the first conference; indeed, one reason for splitting the conferences had been to keep the Americans out of the discussion of Far Eastern matters. The Americans quickly denounced the meagre results achieved by the first conference, claiming that the emphasis laid on the problem of opium-smuggling from China was a mere subterfuge by the colonial powers to enable their profitable opium monopolies to continue. Britain in particular was criticized on the ground that in Britain opium-smoking was considered so reprehensible that it was a criminal offence, but in the colonies Britain supplied the material for this crime and drew revenue from it. The second conference, which comprised 40 nations, was nominally concerned with the control of the manufacture and trade in prepared drugs such as morphia, heroin, and cocaine, but the American delegation insisted on raising their proposal, which had been ignored by the first conference, that the production of prepared opium should be progressively reduced by 10 per cent a year until it was totally abolished over a 10-year period. The colonial powers considered that this proposal was out of order, and the conference was deadlocked over the issue when it adjourned for Christmas. In the interval the new Conservative government, which was anxious to avoid antagonizing the United States, decided, with the reluctant agreement of the Colonial Office, to give a pledge that the colonial opium monopolies would be phased out within 10 to 15 years, as soon as China had taken effective measures to suppress the growth of the opium poppy; the date when this could be said to have occurred was to be determined by an impartial League of Nations Commission.[33] Unfortunately this undertaking, which in effect postponed any action to the indefinite future, did not satisfy the United States delegation which walked out of the conference, followed by that of China. The remaining delegations then cobbled together the few new measures on which they were able to agree into two new agreements and protocols which were signed in February 1925. The powers represented at the first conference also agreed to meet again in 1929 to review the position.

Thus the immediate threat to the Hong Kong government opium monopoly from international action backed by the British government appeared to have passed away. The changes embodied in the conference agreements were notified to the colonies, but no new action was required by Hong Kong. By 1924, in anticipation of the results of the conference, the system of selling *chandu* through private distributors who were paid a commission on sales had been abolished, and retail sales were put in the hands of licensed agents who were paid a fixed salary.[34] But in 1926 new dangers arose from an unexpected quarter. The government of India had always firmly opposed any reduction in its opium exports on the ground that such self-denial on India's part would only lead to increased sales by Turkey and Persia. However, in February 1926 the Viceroy announced that the opium auctions would be discontinued and that all future sales would be made direct to governments; these would be on a diminishing basis over 10 years so that India's opium exports would be entirely brought to an end in 1936.[35] In effect India was acceding to the American demands against which she had voted a year earlier at the Geneva conference. When this policy was under discussion at the end of 1925 the Secretary of State for the Colonies, Leo Amery, made vigorous protests, claiming that a restriction of the amount of *chandu* put on sale by the colonial monopolies as a consequence of reduced supplies from India would lead to the hoarding of stocks and profiteering by speculators, increased smuggling, and the possibility of rioting by the poorer classes. He officially informed the colonies, with the agreement of the Foreign Office and the India Office, that diminishing supplies from India could be supplemented by purchases from other sources such as Persia, so far as this was consistent with the international obligations which the colonies had accepted.[36] The government of the Straits Settlements promptly took advantage of this permission to make considerable purchases of Persian opium. Malaya was enjoying an economic boom at the time and sales of *chandu* to the local Chinese community had increased rapidly from 1923 onwards although there had been no change in retail prices. This caused considerable diplomatic embarrassment for the British government.

There was no similar necessity to supplement Indian supplies in Hong Kong. Sales by the government monopoly had remained roughly stable at about 1,000 taels a day from 1922 to 1924, after Stubbs had instituted severe measures against illegal divans purveying smuggled Chinese opium in 1921. This campaign was continued at full intensity in the years that followed, with the result that on average over one-third of those serving sentences in the colony's gaols had been convicted of opium offences, quite apart from several hundred a year who were deported for the same reasons. Most of those in prison were convicted for keeping an illicit divan, opium-smuggling, or boiling opium. Smoking illicit (that is, non-monopoly) opium was also a crime, but offenders were usually fined only one or two dollars, or were sentenced to a day's imprisonment.[37] In June 1925 the great strike and boycott of the colony began. Large numbers of strikers left the colony, some voluntarily, others as the result of intimidation, and sales of monopoly *chandu* decreased to a daily average of less than 600 taels by the end of the year. Some of the population drifted back during 1926, but the boycott was not officially ended until December; sales throughout 1926 averaged only 535 taels a day.

In 1927 the political situation was once more back to normal and those who had left the colony had returned, but government hopes that this would lead to a revival of opium sales were disappointed. In the first nine months of the year sales averaged less than 500 taels a day. The main reason was the competition from smuggled Persian and Chinese opium with which the colony was said to be 'inundated'. The cheapest Chinese *chandu* retailed at as little as HK$2 a tael; the new Macau government opium monopoly which was set up in July 1927 had promptly reduced its price from HK$6 to HK$2.80 a tael;[38] but the Hong Kong monopoly was selling its special 'Kamshan' brand of pure Indian opium at HK$15 a tael and its 'Bengal' brand (a blend mainly of Indian opium mixed with Persian and other confiscated opium) at HK$14.50. This price had been set in 1918 at a time when the cultivation of opium in China had practically ceased. But in 1927 opium was more widely grown throughout China than it had ever been before. In many places the peasants were forced to grow the poppy by the military governors in order to pay their taxes, in spite of the fact that the laws against opium-growing and smoking formally remained in force. In Kwangtung the sale of opium was controlled through a fully organized government monopoly operating under the title of the 'Opium Suppression Bureau' and opium was freely sold, labelled as 'anti-opium medicine'. In 1927, 150 different brands of opium were seized by the Hong Kong revenue service, all originating in South China.[39]

Faced with this situation the Governor, Sir Cecil Clementi, decided that the monopoly must enter into competition with the smugglers to regain control of the local market. The recent sharp reduction in the price of Macau opium may have influenced his decision. Large stocks of confiscated Persian and Chinese opium, both raw and boiled, had been accumulated, and these provided Clementi with the stocks he needed for his experiment. At the beginning of October 1927 the monopoly's standard 'Bengal' brand was withdrawn and two new blends were put on sale: 'Blue Label', made up of one-third Indian opium mixed with Persian and Chinese, selling at HK$8.33 a tael, and 'Red Label', a blend of Persian and Chinese opium only, selling at HK$6.66 a tael. These prices were fixed to compete with known illicit brands. The experiment was an immediate success. In the first week sales of monopoly *chandu* soared from 500 to 2,000 taels a day and then settled down to a daily level of around 1,600 taels, and there were fears that the stocks of confiscated opium would soon become exhausted. The Governor promptly telegraphed to London asking for permission to make purchases of Persian opium forthwith at the rate of 40 chests a month. In the interim, before

Persian supplies could arrive, be asked to be allowed to borrow 80 chests from Singapore.[40]

This telegram, dispatched on 7 October, four days after the experiment had begun, was the first information that the Colonial Office had of Clementi's plans. The official dispatch explaining the rationale of the scheme had been sent by sea and did not reach London until November. Officials were extremely annoyed at Clementi's failure to ascertain their views beforehand. Clementi had obviously doubted whether he would have been permitted to proceed with the experiment if he had notified London in advance. His telegram and subsequent dispatch explained that his aim was to secure stricter control of opium-smoking by capturing the Hong Kong market from smugglers, to reduce the pressure on the colony's gaols caused by the number of opium offenders, and to decrease the opportunities for corruption of the revenue staff. He also mentioned that the government's revenue from opium had steadily declined over the past few years, in spite of a continuing increase in Hong Kong's population, and he hoped that this experiment would reverse this trend. The Colonial Office suspected that this was in fact Clementi's main motive and subsequent correspondence made it all too clear that this was indeed the case.

A mild rebuke was administered to Clementi for his initiative, which was likely to cause diplomatic embarrassment to the British government: 'It would have been well that I should have been consulted before you authorized such a radical change from existing practice. It is of the greatest importance that you should realize that the opium problem cannot be treated as a domestic concern of the Hong Kong Government only but that it has much wider repercussions.' Nevertheless officials decided to support Clementi's request to buy Persian opium. The leading considerations were the need to maintain the prestige of the colonial government by not forcing it to abandon its new policy, and the importance of preserving Hong Kong's right of access to Persian opium when it should become necessary in future.[41] Although the acting Secretary of State, Ormsby-Gore, agreed with the views of his officials (Amery was on a world tour) a decision could not be taken by the Colonial Office alone. The matter was referred first to the Interdepartmental Opium Committee and then to the Cabinet, where the Colonial Office was opposed by the Foreign Office and the Home Office, briefed by Delevingne. The arguments put forward against the experiment by

Delevingne were that even if the Hong Kong government succeeded in driving the smugglers out of business (which was considered to be very doubtful) the monopoly would be committed to supplying unlimited quantities of the new brands to addicts for the indefinite future. Any attempt to restrict supplies or raise prices would merely lead to the return of the smugglers. Clementi was asking for 480 chests from Persia in 1928 which, with the 196 chests due to be received from India in that year, would make 676 chests, far more than the monopoly had imported in any year since its inauguration in 1914. Such an increase in sales and the consequential increase in the government's opium revenue, would give a handle to anti-British propagandists in the United States, China, and Japan and weaken Britain's efforts at Geneva to bring the world-wide drug traffic under control. In particular it would impede the efforts being made by the League of Nations to persuade Persia to restrict opium production. The Colonial Office memorandum to the Cabinet used the arguments provided by Clementi, that the experiment would lead to a decline in the wholesale violation of the law, lower the prison population, and prevent the corruption of junior officials. It was denied that the experiment would lead to increased consumption; it would only end the hypocrisy of a situation where the monopoly supplied the rich and the poor were supplied by smugglers. Government control over sales was an essential preliminary to eventual restriction and similar experiments in price reductions were being considered in the Netherlands East Indies and Siam with the same object of confining opium-smuggling within reasonable bounds. The weakness of Hong Kong's case was that it could not be shown that the experiment would lead to any decrease in consumption, and the most obvious benefit was to the government's revenue, a point which the Colonial Office could hardly advertise. So it was not surprising that the Cabinet, faced with these conflicting views, refused to sanction purchases of Persian opium to continue the experiment, though it did agree that a memorandum should be drafted to be sent to the League of Nations asking for the appointment of an impartial commission to examine the position in the Far East.[42]

Clementi was informed of the Cabinet decision and immediately sent a long and frantic telegram reiterating his arguments and begging that the question might be reconsidered. But these expostulations were in vain. The Secretary of State declined to reopen the question at Cabinet level, and so the experiment was abandoned on 26 January 1928 when the confiscated supplies of Persian and Chinese opium

Table 10   Offences against the Opium Ordinance, 1919–1929

	Number of Prosecutions	Offenders Convicted	Offenders Banished
1919	314	686	2
1920	452	875	—
1921	2,147	3,040	58
1922	1,879	2,396	167
1923	2,775	3,510	285
1924	5,019	6,167	469
1925	4,407	5,835	592
1926	4,644	6,428	566
1927	5,114	6,726	681
1928	568	544	234
1929	760	732	197

Source: *League of Nations, Commission of Enquiry into the Control of Opium Smoking in the Far East* (Geneva, League of Nations, 1930), Vol. II, p. 374.

were exhausted. Over the three-month period of the experiment smugglers did indeed suffer some set-back in the Hong Kong market, as shown by the threefold increase in the sale of the new brands and a decline in the average daily number of opium offenders in gaol from 540 to 361 over the period.[43] Unfortunately this also had the result that less illicit opium was discovered and seized to augment the stocks held by the monopoly, and this hastened the end of the experiment. In February 1928 the 'Bengal' brand of the monopoly was again placed on sale at the former price of HK$14.50, although the proportion of Indian opium in the blend was increased. In March the price of the superior 'Kamshan' opium, which had remained on sale throughout the experiment, was raised to HK$16.66 a tael. Sales of monopoly opium quickly dropped back to around 500 taels a day, the same level as before the experiment.

At the same time, following a suggestion made by Delevingne to the Interdepartmental Opium Committee, the revenue officers who had been detailed to suppress divans were withdrawn in order to concentrate efforts on the bigger smugglers, and the rewards offered for the detection of divans and petty trafficking in illicit opium were cancelled, while the rewards for large seizures were increased. The natural result was a reduction in the number of convictions and relief from the overcrowding of the gaols, as can be seen from the figures in Table 10 for offences against the Opium Ordinance.

In April 1929 Clementi attempted to revive his proposal in a different form. Arguing that it would soon be essential to purchase Persian opium as imports from India continued to diminish in accordance with the 10-year programme, he suggested that the price of the monopoly's Kamshan and Bengal brands should be raised and a new blend of Indian and Persian opium should be put on sale at HK$10 a tael. He made little attempt to conceal that his primary motive was to augment the opium revenue:

This government is very willing to prohibit the consumption of opium in the colony and to forego its revenue from this source as soon as production and consumption of opium in China is suppressed. But when we know that for each dollar of opium revenue we receive the less, a dollar or more has gone to swell the funds of smugglers, to facilitate increased opium consumption and to postpone the date of final suppression then we regard the subject in a different light; and we definitely consider that it is preferable that the Hong Kong Government rather than smugglers should make money out of such opium as comes to this colony. There are most necessary public works which have remained for years on our waiting list owing to lack of funds.

Clementi supplemented his official dispatch by a personal letter to the Secretary of State, Leo Amery, but to no avail. Amery, acting on the advice of his officials, decided that no change could be made until the investigatory commission which was being sent to the Far East by the League of Nations had made its report. Clementi thereafter made his own views public in a memorandum laid before the Legislative Council.[44]

Shortly after this, in May 1929, the Conservative government was defeated in a general election and the second minority Labour government came to power. The new Parliamentary Under-Secretary, Mr W. Lunn, was associated with the British Anti-Opium League, and he proposed to his officials that the Hong Kong authorities should be asked to take more drastic and determined action against illicit opium and especially against illegal divans, and that the keepers should be heavily fined. Officials were quick to point out that the policy of concentrating on the large smugglers had been agreed by an Interdepartmental Committee in July 1928 and that experience had shown that those convicted for keeping a divan were usually men of straw put up by the real owner who were quite content to serve a term of imprisonment in lieu of a fine while the divan soon reopened elsewhere, or even in the same building. Any change of policy, it was suggested, should be left until the League of Nations Commission had reported. Lunn, with Passfield's agreement, reluctantly accepted this advice.[45]

In December 1930 Hong Kong, with the agreement of the Colonial Office, again raised the price of its de luxe 'Kamshan' brand from HK$50 to HK$60 for a three-tael tin. This was to offset the rise in the cost of Indian opium caused by the depreciation in the value of the silver-based Hong Kong dollar against the gold-based Indian rupee. The Colonial Office considered whether to insist that all opium prices should be raised by an equivalent amount, in order to make the change easier to defend at Geneva, but finally decided merely to endorse Hong Kong's decision.[46]

Britain's proposal that, before another international conference on opium was held, a small impartial commission should conduct a thorough investigation into the opium situation in the Far East, was accepted by the League of Nations Assembly in September 1928. Mr Eric Ekstrand, a Swedish diplomat, was chosen as chairman, the other members being a Belgian economist and a Czechoslovakian diplomat. The Commission set out in September 1929 on an extensive tour of South and East Asia lasting seven months. No investigations were conducted in China since the Chinese delegation to the League had objected to the appointment of the Commission unless the enquiry were extended to all countries producing drugs and China was represented on it. When this proposal was not accepted China gave no facilities to the Commission, presumably because she was unwilling to allow it to probe the hypocrisy of her proclaimed system of opium control. However, the Commission found and published ample evidence of the extent to which opium was cultivated and smuggled out of China, in spite of the stringent new anti-opium laws promulgated in 1928 by the Nanking government.[47]

The Commission's report, published at the end of 1930, proved to be largely a vindication of the opium policies of the colonial powers, particularly in its frank acknowledgement that effective suppression of opium-smoking was unattainable so long as vast illicit imports from China continued. Its most surprising recommendations concerned the price to be charged for government *chandu* and the opening of opium divans, in both of which areas the commissioners advocated the reversal of policies that had been followed by governments for the past 20 years. During their stay in Hong Kong Clementi had taken the opportunity to give the commissioners a full account of his experimental reduction of the price of monopoly *chandu* from October 1927 to January 1928 and the justification he had put forward for the move. His arguments so convinced the commissioners that in their report they recommended that the government monopolies, instead of charging a high price to discourage demand, should reduce prices to make smuggling unprofitable and drive the illicit trade out of business.[48] With regard to opium divans the Commission was so impressed by Siam's system of restricting smoking to public smoking establishments as a means of control that they recommended the setting up of a sufficient number of publicly managed smoking establishments to accommodate all authorized addicts. The commissioners' arguments unconsciously echoed those used by Lugard in 1908 when he expostulated against the British government's order to close down Hong Kong's licensed divans. The course advocated by the Commission was directly contrary to Article 4 of the 1925 Geneva Agreement, which obliged the signatories to limit the number of divans as far as possible.

Most of the Commission's other recommendations were less controversial: better international co-operation against smugglers, strict control over the purchase of opium dross, the disinfection of opium pipes, sales of opium to be for cash only, the prohibition of sales to those under the age of 21 years, more propaganda and health education, more scientific research, and increased provision in hospitals for the cure of addicts. The only proposals likely to cause difficulty were those that all addicts should be registered, licensed, and rationed; that the revenue from the government opium monopolies should be separated from the general government budget and expended solely on anti-opium measures and for social and sanitary purposes; and that licensed retail shops should be abolished and replaced by government shops staffed by government employees.

The three volumes of the report contained a mass of detail obtained by the Commission about the actual workings of the opium monopolies. Some of this information caused surprise in London. Officials had been under the impression that in Hong Kong monopoly *chandu* was sold only through government shops, as was the case in Malaya and the Straits Settlements. The report revealed that it was in fact sold as a sideline in retail shops whose owners were licensed and paid a fee ranging from HK$20 to HK$105 a month. Delevingne was particularly annoyed at this revelation, and not without reason. In May 1923 Stubbs had agreed to accept

Delevingne's original proposal, as communicated to him by the Colonial Office, that private retailers should be abolished and sales made from government shops only. The Colonial Office had welcomed Stubbs's agreement and asked him to implement the new arrangements at once. But in fact all that the Hong Kong administration did was to issue licences to the existing retailers and change their title to 'Government agents', paying them a fixed fee rather than a commission on sales. Presumably this was done to save the colony the expense of setting up government shops. This change of policy had not been concealed from the Colonial Office; it had been reported in the routine annual *Administrative Report*; but no effort had been made to draw the attention of officials in London to the change, and the matter had passed unnoticed there until the report of the Opium Commission was received.[49] The Hong Kong government was promptly asked for an explanation, and in reply it was claimed that what had been done was permissible according to Article 1(3) of the Geneva Agreement (which was formally correct) and that the licensed retailers did not receive any increase in salary if they increased their sales, and so had no incentive to push them. Hong Kong did not add the fact, which the commissioners had discovered, that a licensee might find his licence cancelled if his sales decreased considerably, and that more than 30 licences had been cancelled for this reason in the past 10 years.[50]

In accordance with normal practice the colonial governments were asked for their comments on the report of the Opium Commission before the British government decided on its attitude. Surprisingly the Hong Kong administration gave only a tepid welcome to the Commission's recommendation that opium prices should be reduced, largely because of the consequences for the government's finances. Clementi had by this time left Hong Kong to be Governor of the Straits Settlements and his successor, Sir William Peel, pointed out that, in order to compete with smuggled Chinese opium, government *chandu* would have to be reduced in price to around HK$3.50 a tael from the current price of HK$14.50; but the monopoly's *chandu* could not be sold at less than HK$7.50 a tael for Indian opium or for less than HK$4.50 for Persian opium without incurring a loss. (This was because the Hong Kong dollar, being based on silver, had depreciated in value against the gold-based Indian and Persian currencies.) Effective competition with the smugglers was thus impossible unless the price paid for Indian opium could be substantially reduced or unless Hong Kong was allowed to purchase

Chinese opium. The latter expedient was not possible since China had officially abolished opium-growing and so could not openly export it. It was also out of the question to subsidize the cost of monopoly *chandu* at a time when the government's finances were already feeling the effects of the world depression.[51] It appears that Peel was quite content to accept the existing profits of the monopoly, which still provided 10 per cent of the government's revenue, without indulging in risky experiments; in fact in February 1931 he had increased the price of the monopoly's standard blend to HK$17, and Kamshan opium to HK$23.66 a tael (partly to offset the fall in exchange), with the result that there was a small increase in the opium revenue from HK$2,835,256 in 1930 to HK$3,019,724 in 1931.

With regard to the Commission's other recommendations Peel was amiably prepared to fall in with most of them, although he emphasized the practical difficulties. He would consider the establishment of government shops in the urban districts, while warning that the expense would be incomparably greater than under the existing system. He would even consider the registration of smokers, in spite of the problems posed by Hong Kong's transient population. He mildly pointed out the drawbacks and cost of establishing public smoking establishments and enforcing their use in the face of strong public opposition. The allocation of hospital beds for the cure of opium addicts was all very well, he wrote, but the likely effect would be that unemployed coolies would volunteer to be 'cured' for the sake of a few weeks free bed and board in hospital, but would quickly relapse as soon as they left. Similar comments came from other colonial Governors.

A conference of the Far Eastern powers to consider the Commission's report was held in Bangkok in November 1931. The British delegation was again led by Delevingne. China did not attend and her absence enabled all the other delegations to join in denouncing her connivance in the smuggling of opium, which gave such a convenient excuse for their own slow progress in opium suppression. The outcome of the conference was a short international convention supplementing and modifying the 1925 Geneva Agreement. The only important change was a tightening of the requirement that sales of government opium should take place only in government shops; licensed retailers were only to be permitted where local circumstances made it difficult to establish a government shop. There was general opposition at the conference to the proposal for price reductions, the main arguments against being the possible encouragement of new smokers and the difficulty of obtaining sufficient supplies of opium to ensure that a policy of price reduction could be continued over a long period. Only Siam supported the proposal for restricting smoking to public divans only, and this proposal was accordingly dropped. Other recommendatons of the Commisson, such as the registration and rationing of smokers, were generally endorsed by the conference in an hortatory final communiqué, but were not made mandatory by their inclusion in the new convention.[52]

As was expected the somewhat meagre results of the conference were denounced by China and the other powers at the next meeting of the League of Nations Assembly in Geneva, where it was claimed that the colonial powers were motivated solely by revenue considerations. To forestall these criticisms Hong Kong was instructed by the Colonial Office to begin the establishment of government shops immediately, and to implement the other resolutions of the conference as soon as possible. Six shops were opened in October 1932 and 34 salaried retailers were consequently abolished, leaving 28 retailers, of whom 17 were in the New Territories. Peel then sent a dispatch pointing out that the shops had cost HK$30,000 to set up and sales from the new outlets had greatly diminished; could he not be excused from further action? The Colonial Office reply was firm: all licensed retailers in the urban area must be done away with, although some flexibility might be permitted in the rural areas; the drop in sales could not be regarded as a reason for failing to implement the Bangkok agreement.[53]

The institution of the government shops was not the only reason for the decline in sales. One minor change agreed at Bangkok had been to permit a government factory in one colonial territory to supply prepared opium to the other territories of the same power. This had technically been illegal under the 1925 Geneva Agreement which prohibited any exports of prepared opium. This change enabled Hong Kong, North Borneo, and Sarawak to draw their future supplies from the new factory which had been set up in Singapore in 1930 to produce *chandu* in metal tubes. It was hoped that this method of packing would make it more difficult to adulterate the monopoly's product. Hong Kong *chandu* had hitherto been sold in earthenware pots which could easily be refilled with illicit opium and passed off as the government brand. Hong Kong had considered setting up its own factory to pack its *chandu* in tubes in 1927, but found that the volume of sales would not justify the investment, so it was happy to accept the proposed new arrangements to draw supplies from Singapore. The Hong Kong plant for boiling and packing opium was closed down in January 1933 and surplus chests of Indian opium were transferred to Singapore, except for the stock of Kamshan opium. A sufficient quantity of this was prepared and put in stock to serve those addicted to this de luxe blend for a further period of years.[54]

Unfortunately the Straits Settlements and Malaya had for some years been supplementing decreasing supplies of Indian opium by purchases from Persia, and in 1929 for the first time more Persian than Indian opium was imported. The Singapore factory produced a standard blend for all its customers, and no special arrangements were made for the new Hong Kong market. Tubes of Singapore opium first reached the Hong Kong shops in January 1933. Sales immediately dropped by almost half, from 7,106 taels in December 1932 to 3,690 taels in February 1933 and continued to decline throughout the year, although sales of the exclusive Kamshan brand were not affected. The former Hong Kong 'Bengal' brand had been largely blended from Indian opium and smokers considered that the Singapore mixture with its high proportion of Persian opium was of inferior quality and not worth the premium at which monopoly opium was sold.[55] Quite apart from the unpopularity of the new blend there was another reason for the fall in demand: in 1933 there was an abundant harvest of opium in China. In places the cultivator had to sell his crop at less than 10c. a tael and illicit opium was available in the colony at a new low price of HK$1.20 a tael for raw opium and HK$2.20 a tael for prepared opium, while the monopoly product was selling at HK$17 a tael. So abundant was the supply of smuggled opium in the colony that the Preventive Service seized an amount equivalent to 150 per cent of the total of all prepared opium sold officially by the monopoly. Another reason for the fall in sales was a trade depression and consequent unemployment, which reduced the number of addicts who could afford to buy the monopoly's *chandu*.[56]

Faced with this decline in sales Peel ordered a renewed campaign against divans purveying illicit opium which lasted from April to October 1933. This resulted in a threefold increase in convictions to an average of 232 a month. This campaign was not so intense as those conducted under Stubbs and Clementi, when the monthly average of convictions was as high as 500. Only those discovered keeping an illicit divan, boiling opium, or smuggling it were brought before the courts; those found smoking in divans or in possession of non-government opium, numbering some 9,000, were not prosecuted. Nevertheless, the gaols were soon overcrowed with opium prisoners, most of whom had refused to pay the fines imposed, and many had to be released before they had served the full sentence imposed by the courts, in order to relieve the pressure on the prisons. But these measures did not stem the fall in the sales of Singapore opium, which dropped steadily to no more than 2,363 taels in December. As a result the government's income from opium sales fell to the lowest level to date, less than 4 per cent of total revenue. The only bright spot was the steady demand for Kamshan opium. By the end of the year the remaining 166 connoisseurs of this luxury brand were providing just under half (47 per cent) of the monopoly's gross income. Accordingly the Hong Kong government took advantage of this steady demand to raise the price from HK$70 to HK$80 for a three-tael tin.[57]

In April 1934 Peel sent a long dispatch to the Colonial Office making a fervent plea that the colony's entire opium policy should be reviewed. He set out the facts in detail — the massive inflow of illicit opium, the corruption of the staff of the Police and Revenue Departments, the overcrowded prisons, and the widespread undermining of respect for the law — and emphasized the evident failure to achieve any real limitation or diminution of the habit of opium-smoking, which was supposed to be the whole object of the control system. He then drew a parallel with the experience of the United States in attempting to enforce Prohibition, the noble experiment which had been finally abandoned at the end of 1933 after 13 years:

In both cases the basic facts are the same. A legislative ban has been placed on the use of something which the greater part of the community of the territory in question regards as a legitimate amenity if not a necessity of life. In both cases a plentiful supply of the forbidden article has been available in adjacent territories. Violent measures of enforcement become necessary and bring in their train corruption and moral deterioration menacing the social body far more than the forbidden indulgence would ever have done.

Accordingly he suggested the repeal of the laws prohibiting the use of opium and the import and export of opium to and from China. Exportation elsewhere would be prohibited, and divans would still be banned to encourage smoking in private. The government opium monopoly would be abolished, though the Kamshan brand would still be sold as long as stocks lasted. The effect on government revenue would be a net loss of about HK$500,000 immediately (approximately 1.6 per cent of total revenue) and a further similar loss in three years' time when stocks of Kamshan were expected to be exhausted. Peel admitted that the loss of revenue would be painful: 'But I must repeat that the control of opium smoking, which is the object of all the conventions, is today in Hong Kong further from attainment than ever and that the effects of the cure are demonstrably far worse than the disease.' As an alternative, he suggested that the government monopoly be allowed to reduce its prices, even though this would only be a palliative: 'I do not claim that a competitive price for government opium would in any way promote the abolition of opium smoking. The sole object of reduction would be to remove the intolerable evils of repression until such time as abolition of supply imposes a natural repression.'[58]

The Governor's dispatch led to extended consultations both within the Colonial Office and with the other departments of the British government that were concerned. There was general agreement that Peel's first alternative must be rejected since it would be contrary to Britain's treaty commitments under the 1925 Geneva and 1931 Bangkok Agreements and would give colour to the allegations frequently made in America and elsewhere that Britain was not acting in good faith in carrying out her obligation to achieve the ultimate suppression of the traffic in opium. But some officials also argued against Peel's alternative proposal of price reductions. The parallel with Clementi's experiment in 1927 was drawn, and it was argued that a price reduction would lay the government open to the charge that it was motivated solely by revenue considerations. Other officials took a more strong-minded attitude, pointing out that a policy of price reduction was in accordance with a recommendation of the 1929 League of Nations Commission and that Britain's actions in Malaya where the registration and rationing of addicts had been introduced were sufficient proof of her bona fides; so long as money was being spent on opium, the government was entitled to tax it by the device of a government monopoly and to take measures to protect this revenue, particularly when the abandonment of the monopoly would not lead to any decrease in opium-smoking. One senior official commented bluntly:

It is unfortunate that consideration of the opium question is veiled in an atmosphere of calculated hypocrisy. We have entered into undertakings based on the entirely erroneous assumption that in the near future the Chinese government would be able and willing to prohibit the cultivation of the poppy, while the reports that reach us show that such an assumption is quite fantastic. Nevertheless we have got to play the game according to the rules. We cannot abandon the policy to which however hopelessly we are bound. But possibly 'we need not strive officiously to keep alive'.[59]

In February 1935, 10 months after the original dispatch, a compromise reply which had been agreed by all departments was finally sent to Hong Kong. The Secretary of State sympathized with Hong Kong's problems but could not agree to a radical reversal of its existing opium policies, which would be contrary to international agreements. However, the Governor was to be permitted to reduce the prices of monopoly opium, provided he would be able to obtain sufficient supplies to meet any greatly increased demand. It was also suggested that Hong Kong might ask Singapore to produce a blend more to the taste of the Hong Kong smoker. By the same post the Governor was instructed to carry out the complete substitution of government shops for licensed retailers in the urban area.[60]

Hong Kong did not immediately take advantage of this permission to reduce prices, probably because of the six-month gap between the end of Peel's governorship in May and the arrival of Sir Andrew Caldecott in December. Meanwhile the sales of monopoly opium continued to fall. In 1935 the consumption of Singapore opium dropped by half and the gross receipts from opium sales were reduced to a mere 1.2 per cent of the total government revenue, the lowest proportion ever. This drop in demand was attributed to the continuing unpopularity of the Singapore blend, the plentiful supply of smuggled Chinese opium, the effect on incomes of the economic depression, and, for the first time, to an alarming increase in the use of heroin pills.[61]

In January 1936 Hong Kong reported to London that agreement had been reached with the Singapore factory for the production of a special blend of *chandu* for the Hong Kong market, which would make use of the chests of Indian opium that had been transferred to Singapore in 1933 when the Hong Kong factory closed down; at the same time the Governor requested approval for a reduction of the price per tael from HK$17 to HK$12. Caldecott did not expect to have any difficulty in maintaining supplies if demand increased, presumably because illicit prepared opium continued to be retailed at HK$3.50 or less. The Colonial Office approved the price reduction. But any hopes that these changes would increase demand for monopoly opium were quickly disappointed. The new blend went on sale in April, but sales for the whole of 1936 were practically the same as in 1935, while demand for the luxury Kamshan blend continued its steady decline as the holders of ration books died or left the colony. The gross receipts from opium sales in 1936 amounted to less than 1 per cent of the colony's revenue, the lowest point ever. This compared with the situation in the Straits Settlements, where opium continued to provide a quarter of the revenue, in spite of the fact that all addicts were registered and rationed, and the registers had been closed.[62]

Sales continued to decline in the first half of 1937, but the outbreak of the Sino-Japanese War in July caused an unanticipated reversal of the trend. Hong Kong experienced an influx of refugees, many of whom were opium-smokers, as the fighting reached Shanghai and Nanking. At the same time the conflict led to the disruption of the normal patterns of legitimate and illicit trade, with the result that the supplies of smuggled opium became scarcer, and its price in Hong Kong accordingly increased considerably. This made the monopoly's product more competitive, and so sales of the Singapore blend increased by 75 per cent in 1937 and by a further 12 per cent in 1938, proving that the main objection of the Hong Kong addicts had been to the price rather than to the flavour of the monopoly's product. However, the receipts from opium sales continued to provide less than 1 per cent of the colony's revenues, since the Sino-Japanese War provided a welcome stimulus to the Hong Kong economy and consequently to the government's receipts from taxation.[63]

Meanwhile international pressure for the imposition of stricter controls on opium-smoking continued. In 1935 the International Labour Organization (ILO) published the results of an enquiry which it had carried out into the effects of opium on workers in the East. In its replies to the ILO questionnaire the Hong Kong government had argued that the total suppression of opium-smoking would cause unrest and resistance among the working class and would tend to discourage the immigration of labour on which the manufacturing and trade of the colony depended.[64] These and similar viewpoints expressed by other colonial governments were not accepted by the ILO, and its conference in 1936 passed a resolution advocating the registration of all smokers and the progressive reduction of the quantity of opium put on sale by the monopolies, leading to the complete abolition of the monopolies within five years. This proposal was endorsed by the League of Nations Advisory Committee on the

Traffic in Opium in 1937. The Foreign Office strongly favoured compliance, particularly because of the need to conciliate American opinion, but the Colonial Office as usual first forwarded the proposal to Governors for comment. In its reply the government of Hong Kong repeated its usual stand that the ready availability of illicit opium and the constant flow of population across its border made any attempt to register addicts or to suppress opium-smoking completely impracticable. The other Far Eastern territories also rejected the ILO proposal, and the Colonial Office endorsed their views when forwarding them to the Foreign Secretary. The Colonial Office suggested that Britain should reiterate the undertaking set out in the protocol of the 1925 Geneva Conference: to suppress completely the consumption of opium in its territories within 15 years of the date when the poppy-growing countries had ceased to export opium and had thereby removed this serious obstacle to control. In the mean time no action should be taken pending the outcome of an international conference which was due to meet in Geneva in 1940 to draw up a convention to restrict the production of raw opium.[65] This was the last general pronouncement by the Colonial Office on the opium question before the outbreak of the Second World War. The Foreign Secretary, Halifax, apparently accepted the Colonial Office view, since he did not attempt to raise the matter at Cabinet level.

In October 1938 the Japanese advance reached Canton and the steady inflow of refugees into Hong Kong which had persisted throughout the year became a flood. The disruption of communications with the main opium-growing areas of China, such as Yunnan, caused an acute shortage of raw opium which deepened throughout the following year. The same factor affected the neighbouring Chinese province of Kwangtung, and in November and December 1938, for the first time for many years, smugglers were caught in the New Territories attempting to carry opium into China, rather than in the reverse direction. After September 1939 smuggling was also impeded by the controls introduced as a result of the outbreak of the Second World War in Europe. These included strict entry and clearance control of all ocean-going vessels and the censorship of letters and cables. In addition the movements and ports of call of ships became uncertain, so that the co-ordination of smuggling operations became more difficult. Illicit opium from China or Persia was now so scarce that government opium was even found being purveyed in illegal divans.[66] Sales of the monopoly product consequently soared, reaching 1,000 taels a day in October 1939. In 1936, by comparison, sales had been less than a 1,000 taels a month. The Hong Kong government feared that its stocks might quickly be exhausted, and so supplies to government shops were promptly rationed to 500 taels a day. Hong Kong had not found it necessary to purchase any raw opium since 1933 and the Singapore factory had supplied the colony's needs by using the 250 chests transferred to Singapore when the Hong Kong factory closed down. These were supplemented by periodic transfers of usable illicit opium seized by the Preventive Service, but in 1939 such seizures had dropped by half. (These transfers were strictly contrary to Article 6 of the 1925 Geneva Convention, but Delevingne had agreed to such transfers provided no attention was called to them.)[67] To satisfy the level of demand experienced in October 1939 Hong Kong would have needed to use up practically the equivalent of a chest of opium a day, and there were fears that its reserve of chests in Singapore would quickly be exhausted. So in addition to limiting deliveries to 500 taels a day the Governor, Sir Geoffry Northcote, telegraphed to London for permission to buy 100 chests of Persian opium.[68]

The Colonial Office drew a different conclusion. For the past 20 years Hong Kong had argued that it was impossible to impose effective controls on opium-smoking and enforce the registration and rationing of smokers because of the ready availability of illicit opium, the vast daily influx and egress of population across its borders, and the lack of sufficient room in the colony's prisons to accommodate all those who broke the opium laws. Now it seemed that most of these objections had disappeared: the great influx of refugees had forced Hong Kong to institute immigration controls for the first time, detention camps had been set up to supplement the prisons, and the supply of smuggled opium from the mainland had almost dried up. Accordingly a semi-official letter was sent to the Governor in December 1939 by Gent, the Assistant Secretary in charge of the Eastern Department, mildly suggesting that the situation was now propitious for instituting a greater measure of control. Meanwhile any shortfall in opium supplies could be met by borrowing from Singapore stocks.[69]

Northcote replied in January 1940, declining to take any action. He pointed out that the absence of smuggled opium was purely ephemeral and the situation would change as soon as wartime conditions eased. The rules to control immigration were largely ineffectual and the detention centres were not sufficiently secure to ensure the isolation of addicts. Instead Northcote put his faith in the greater commitment to physical fitness and athleticism of the younger generation of Chinese. With a candour rare in the whole of the opium correspondence he pointed to the main obstacle to effective opium control: 'So long as the government sells monopoly opium, the offence of the smuggler or the illicit boiler has little more criminality than defrauding the revenue by distilling alcoholic liquor on the sly and this puts curative action somewhat on the lines of treating alcoholic excess.'[70] He was however prepared to consider a reorganization of preventive work, and the setting up of a special anti-narcotics branch of the police. In the press of wartime business at the Colonial Office Northcote's letter was lost for six months and was then put away unanswered.

What Northcote did not mention in his letter was that the Hong Kong opium account was now showing a very healthy surplus: in 1939 gross opium revenue tripled to over a million dollars, providing 2.5 per cent of government revenue, the best result since 1933. Demand remained strong throughout 1940, and the Hong Kong government fretted that it could not supply a demand estimated at 25,000 taels a month. In May 1940 Hong Kong asked the Colonial Office for permission to buy 300 chests of Persian opium direct from Nemazee, a firm notorious for its involvement in the illicit trade; permission was refused. At the same time Northcote wrote to Singapore grumbling about hold-ups in deliveries from the Singapore factory, but requesting that the existing policy of borrowing from Singapore stocks should continue until the Colonial Office authorized further purchases. He explained that the Hong Kong government was anxious to increase sales up to 25,000 taels a month: 'This limit is small compared to the population of the colony and the direct rationing in force at present is unsatisfactory both from the point of view of the government and the consumer.' This argument must have seemed very odd in the Straits Settlements where the opium registers had been closed in 1934 and supplies to addicts were strictly limited. The Controller of Customs for the Straits Settlements and the Federated Malay States wrote a memorandum suggesting that the attention of the Hong Kong government should be drawn to the 1925 and 1931 Opium Conventions and the obligation contained therein, which Hong Kong had so far avoided, to set up a system of licensing and rationing and to issue identity cards for all purchasers. But this suggestion was not followed up.[71]

The Singapore factory was itself finding difficulty in obtaining supplies from Persia where the government was taking full advantage of a world shortage of opium to raise prices and insist on payment in United States dollars rather than sterling. This demand was unacceptable to the British Treasury, faced with the wartime need to conserve foreign exchange, and officials asked the Colonial Office why the Far Eastern colonies could not use up their stocks first, or find other sources of supply. The Colonial Office, vigilant as always to defend colonial interests, replied that opium purchases were essential since, if the government monopolies did not supply opium, addicts would turn to illicit supplies and the measure of control already achieved would be lost. (This was an argument which applied to Malaya, but hardly to Hong Kong.) As to alternative sources of supply, Turkish opium would be unacceptable to local addicts. The possibility of buying from Afghanistan was investigated.[72]

Faced with this difficulty of obtaining supplies Hong Kong began to restrict demand, and incidentally to maximize its revenue, by raising the price, a policy which it had been unable to follow since the First World War. In July 1940 the price per tael was raised from HK$12 to HK$15, and then to HK$18 in November.[73] Consequently the opium revenue for the last 12 months for which figures are available, April 1940 to March 1941, reached over HK$3,000,000, tripling the 1939 figures, and supplied over 5 per cent of the colony's gross revenue. In early 1941 orders were placed with Persia for 500 chests, half of which were allocated to the Hong Kong account, and negotiations were in progress for the purchase of a further 750 chests in November 1941, just before the Japanese invasion.[74] In its last year of operation the Hong Kong opium monopoly sold more opium than in any year since 1928 and made a greater profit than in any year since 1924.

With the Far Eastern colonies under Japanese rule the Colonial Office was at last free to determine policy without the restraining influence of objections by the colonial governments. A post-war opium policy was not discussed in the dark days of 1942, but the question was revived in March 1943 by the American government. The British embassy in Washington had learned from a meeting addressed by the United States Commissioner for Narcotics, Mr Anslinger, that it was the intention that United States forces in the Pacific would close down the opium monopolies in all Japanese-occupied territories which they reconquered. The ambassador noted the continual friction caused to Anglo-American relations by disagreements over opium and asked for an updated statement on

British policy. This request was passed on to the Colonial Office by the Foreign Office which reiterated its long-standing view that the monopolies should be closed down, and further asked that an announcement to this effect should be made as soon as possible to forestall criticism, because the question was likely to become salient as the prospect of the liberation of Japanese-occupied territories came closer. The matter was exhaustively discussed in the Colonial Office. Pressure to reach a decision increased after information was received from the Netherlands government in exile in London that the decision had been taken to close down the opium monopoly in the Dutch East Indies after Japan's defeat. The Dutch were prepared to delay publication of this decision to allow Britain to make a simultaneous announcement.[75]

Faced with this *fait accompli* by the Dutch, Britain's policy could hardly be in doubt. The crucial decision was taken at a meeting of three Colonial Office officials, Gent, Paskin, and Thorogood, on 27 August 1943. The leading considerations were that in Malaya, North Borneo, and Sarawak, control of opium by the system of registration and rationing of addicts had gone as far as was possible, and the next logical step was total prohibition. It would, in any case, be very difficult to revive the registration system after the chaos of the Japanese occupation, and the initial problems of enforcing total prohibition would be easier under the martial law regime that would be imposed by the returning Allied forces. Prohibition would be much more difficult to enforce in Hong Kong but there was some hope that China would take more effective action in the post-war years to stamp out cultivation of the opium poppy. If Malaya prohibited opium-smoking, Hong Kong would have to follow suit, since there could not be diametrically opposed policies in separate parts of the colonial empire. Moreover, if the Singapore factory was closed down Hong Kong would have to reinstate its own factory which had been closed down in 1933, and any such move would be extremely embarrassing politically. So the decision was taken for total prohibition. Some colonial officials then in London were asked for their views beforehand, but the question could not be referred to the colonial governments, as would have been normal pre-war practice. The recommendation for complete prohibition was quickly approved by the Interdepartmental Opium Committee and the ministers concerned and was announced on 10 November 1943 in concert with similar announcements by the French and Dutch governments. In the interim there had been renewed pressure for a decision from the United States government, in an *aide-mémoire* delivered to the British ambassador on 6 October, but the Foreign Office was happy to be able to tell the Americans that the decision had already been taken. In Hong Kong the decision was implemented by Proclamation 13 of the British Military Administration issued on 20 September 1945.

So ended the colonial opium monopolies, 33 years after Britain had undertaken by the Hague Convention of 1912 to take measures for the gradual and effective suppression of the internal trade in and use of prepared opium. Like so many other changes in the colonies, the closure of the monopolies would clearly have been delayed further but for the events of the Second World War. Throughout the period every Governor of Hong Kong did his best to maximize the government's revenue from the sale of monopoly opium, while at the same time proclaiming the desirability of the complete suppression of opium consumption. All of them seem to have shared the view, which was common among Europeans in the East, that there was little that was reprehensible about opium-smoking, though most did not express this view as openly as Lugard and Clementi. The availability of plentiful supplies of opium from China provided a very convenient excuse for the government's failure to put its professed principles into effect; but when supplies from China were temporarily interrupted, as happened in both world wars, the government made use of this occurrence as an opportunity to raise the price and increase the sales of government opium rather than as an occasion for a campaign to eradicate drug addiction.

Officials at the Colonial Office found no fault with the colony's opium policy since their overriding concern was to safeguard the colony's revenue. Apart from Gent's private initiative in 1939, they made no attempt of their own volition to encourage the Governor to implement measures for the control of drug addiction. All the Secretaries of State after the Earl of Crewe in 1906 were quite content to follow the advice of their officials and supported the Governors' views to the limit of their ability.

Moves to compel Hong Kong to change its policy and to conform to the international conventions on the control of drugs came primarily from the Foreign Office and the Home Office and successive Secretaries of State for the Colonies found themselves obliged to send directives to Hong Kong to tighten controls over opium in order to prevent the British government from being embarrassed internationally. The Foreign Office in turn was primarily motivated by the need to conciliate opinion in the United States, which played the leading role in the international campaign against drug addiction. After 1914 pressure from Parliament and from philanthropic groups in Britain had hardly any effect on the determination of colonial policy, compared with the sustained campaigns mounted to free the *mui tsai* or to close the tolerated brothels. The most effective proponent of opium control in Britain seems to have been a civil servant, Delevingne of the Home Office, who made full use of his strategic position as Chairman of the League of Nations Advisory Committee to push the Colonial Office into instituting reforms.

13 Conclusion

FROM 1912 to 1939 there were about 120 occasions when the Colonial Office refused to agree to a proposal put forward by the Governor of Hong Kong or instructed him to change his policy, an average of just over four rejections a year out of some 600 dispatches, telegrams, and reports that were sent to London annually. The largest number of refusals, a total of 10, occurred during the 12-month period 1918–19 when Severn was acting as Governor. In many of these cases the Governor may well have expected a negative response, especially when his proposals affected the interests of the Foreign Office, the Treasury, or the War Office, or were in breach of some international agreement, or were contrary to settled Colonial Office policy; for example, when he recommended the promotion of a local officer to a vacant senior post, knowing full well that it was established policy that such vacancies should be open to officers throughout the colonial empire. On issues that concerned the Colonial Office alone, particularly on financial matters such as the approval of a particular item of expenditure or a change in salary or allowances, the decision to overrule the Governor was normally taken by an official. This was often the end of the matter. But when the Governor was unwilling to accept the decision and pressed for it to be reconsidered, and if the officials came to the conclusion that 'the man on the spot' could not be allowed to have his way, the file was always seen and approved by a minister.[1] On such occasions, the Secretary of State always supported his officials except where the decision complained of had originally been taken by him.

There were only five instances between 1912 and 1941 where the Secretary of State insisted on imposing his own views against the advice of his officials and the reiterated protests of the Governor. Three of these involved the *mui tsai* system: Churchill's demand in 1922 that the system be abolished within one year, Passfield's decision in 1929 that registration should be brought into force, and his further decision in 1930 that the transformation of *mui tsai* into domestic servants to escape registration could not be permitted. The other cases were the decision of Dr Shiels in 1931 that the licensed brothels should be closed down, and Cunliffe-Lister's rejection of the Hong Kong government's comprehensive plans for the reclamation and redevelopment of the foreshore of the harbour in 1935. On all five occasions the Secretary of State was under extreme pressure from Members of Parliament and from groups in Britain, philanthropic societies, women's organizations, and churches in the first four cases and business associations in the last one. In at least three of these cases ministerial disregard for the Governor's advice had little or no permanent effect in Hong Kong. Stubbs succeeded in having the terms of Churchill's edict modified and reinterpreted so that the bill that was eventually passed by the Legislative Council was practically innocuous, and even then its provisions were not enforced. Passfield's directive forbidding the deregistration of *mui tsai* was obeyed at first, but four years later the practice that he had refused to sanction was being routinely performed by the Secretariat for Chinese Affairs. When forbidden to bring in a single comprehensive measure for the redevelopment of the harbour the Hong Kong government drafted a series of bills to accomplish the same object over a longer period and these were all approved by later Secretaries of State. Apart from these five cases ministers invariably accepted the advice of their officials on the comparatively few occasions when a file relating to Hong Kong was put before them.

   Was there any change in the attitudes of the Colonial Office and in its relationship with the colonial governments over this period? Two different points of view have been expressed. Sir Cosmo Parkinson, who served in the Colonial Office from 1909 to 1945, ending as Permanent Under-Secretary, has recorded his impression that in his early days the Secretary of State had been accustomed to make *ex cathedra* pronouncements and to issue directions to colonial governments, but that in more recent times governors were more often consulted before important policy papers were published.[2] On the other hand Walter Ellis, the head of the Eastern Department, minuted as follows in 1930: 'There was for a long time a policy, now abandoned, of assuming that governors were always right and the permanent staff of the Colonial Office always wrong.'[3] It is difficult to decide which view is closer to reality. Certainly personal relations between the minister and governors became less formal and hidebound. In the years before the First World War governors were expected to approach the Secretary of State with a proper show of deference. In 1913 May received a sharp reprimand for impertinence on the direct instructions of the Secretary of State, Lewis Harcourt, who had taken offence at the wording of a dispatch from the Governor recommending the appointment of an officer as Deputy Superintendent of Police.[4] In contrast to this, 15 years later Clementi was corresponding personally with Amery explaining his policies and seeking to enlist his support. A possible indicator of changing attitudes is the number of times that the Colonial Office turned down a governor's requests: these averaged six a year from 1912 to 1919; four a year in the 1920s; and just under three a year in the 1930s. However this decline may merely reflect the fact that a higher proportion of the Hong Kong files for the earlier period survived the weeding-out process before being sent to the Public Record Office. Another possible explanation for the larger number of refusals in the first decade is the system of economic controls imposed from London on Hong Kong's trade during the First World War, which gave rise to more requests for special exemptions.

One area in which there was certainly a move towards stronger leadership from the Colonial Office and greater pressure on colonial governments to conform to standards set by the centre was in the matter of labour legislation and the regulation of conditions of employment. In the 1920s circular dispatches were sent out giving the texts of newly drafted conventions of the International Labour Organization, but governors were expressly informed that there was no obligation on the British government to extend these conventions to the colonies and that it was a matter for colonial administrations to decide whether to adhere to the conventions or not. After the Labour government came to power in 1929, a new circular dispatch was sent out stating that the British government was under a moral obligation to apply the conventions to the greatest extent possible and with the minimum of modification. A later dispatch warned that the Secretary of State would scrutinize very carefully any reasons that governors might put forward for the inapplicability of the conventions to their territory. This stress on the need for colonial administrations to take effective action on labour matters was continued throughout the 1930s even after the fall of the Labour government, and was further reinforced when Malcolm MacDonald became Secretary of State in 1938.[5]

Perhaps the most important question to ask about imperial control is whether the colonies were better or worse governed as a result. Did the peoples of the Empire live better lives because the colonial governments were checked, admonished, and occasionally directed by London, or did the elaborate machinery of supervision and control achieve very little beyond the production of a vast amount of paperwork? If we look at various specific instances where the Secretary of State or civil servants overruled the Governor it is difficult to claim that the Colonial Office was wiser or the results achieved were more beneficent than if the Governor's advice had been followed. After the tolerated brothels were closed down in 1932 unlicensed houses quickly took their place, spreading more venereal disease than before. The complex system of the registration and inspection of *mui tsai* and wards instituted in the 1930s probably did very little to improve the miserable conditions of the daughters of poverty-stricken families, whether they were forced into ill-paid domestic service or were transferred surreptitiously as *mui tsai*. The measures to control opium introduced in order to conform to international agreements were completely ineffective in decreasing the number of opium addicts so long as China continued to produce and put on sale vast quantities of the drug; all they achieved was to diminish the government's revenues and increase the profits made by smugglers. In all these cases the measures imposed by directives from London may have had some long-term educative effect on the climate of opinion in Hong Kong, but they achieved very little more.

However, the policies recommended in circular dispatches were generally enlightened and exerted useful and necessary pressure on the colonial administrations to implement social reforms. Take for example the question of colonial penal codes. A circular dispatch of 1915 strongly urged the repeal of any legislation which allowed the infliction of a double flogging upon a prisoner; a dispatch of 1928 required that the cat-o'-nine-tails used in colonial prisons should not be knotted; and in 1939 a dispatch asked governors to consider the possible abolition of all forms of corporal punishment, or at least its limitation to juvenile offenders only.[6] Similarly the Colonial Office Medical Adviser and his advisory committee inspired a number of dispatches emphasizing the need for preventive medicine and public health measures to reduce disease. The course of action proposed in such dispatches was rarely mandatory and governors could and did decline to follow the exhortations addressed to them from London, citing what they considered to be good local reasons against. But this stream of advice had some effect and served to counteract the danger that a governor might become too self-satisfied with local conditions or be too impressed by the possibly reactionary views of his local councillors and advisers. Hong Kong's first labour law enacted in 1922 prohibiting the industrial employment of children under the age of 10 years was passed at least partly as a result of the interest shown and the pressure exerted by the Colonial Office. The Hong Kong Executive Council had twice refused to sanction any action being taken to deal with this problem when the matter was put on its agenda in July 1919 and March 1920. The Secretary of State, whose attention had been drawn to this issue by a question in the House of Commons, then sent a dispatch to the Governor asking for information as to what measures were being contemplated to deal with child labour. This led the Governor to set up a local commission of enquiry which reported in 1921, revealing the deplorable conditions existing in many of the colony's workshops. This report paved the way for the 1922 ordinance.[7]

As well as encouraging colonial administrations to adopt more progressive policies the Colonial Office also provided some check against the danger that they might be tempted to abuse their powers. The concentration of power in the hands of the Governor under the colonial system of government was mitigated by the requirement that he must seek the advice and consent of the Executive and Legislative Councils and by the political need to pay heed to the views of important groups within the community and to take account of public opinion. But most ordinances received only a very perfunctory examination during their passage through the Legislative Council, and it was left to the legal advisers in the Colonial Office to scrutinize their provisions in detail and call attention to cases where the colonial government had granted itself excessive or unusual powers or diminished the rights and liberties of its subjects. Appointed unofficial members of the Legislative Council rarely challenged the government in debates or sought to expose the faults of government officials by detailed investigation of the complaints of individuals; and there were no other local channels through which those who were aggrieved at any administrative decision could ask that their complaint should be examined with some prospect that they might obtain redress. The only available resort was to approach the Secretary of State and this right was exercised by groups, organizations, and individuals who either wrote a letter of complaint direct to the Colonial Office or submitted a formal petition through the Governor.

Most often the Colonial Office saw no reason to interfere with the decisions taken by the administration; but there were occasions when officials decided that the Governor had acted unreasonably or high-handedly, and he might then be pressed to reconsider the decision or offer appropriate compensation. A good example of this occurred in 1919. The Hong Kong government had decided to regulate the cross-harbour ferry services. An ordinance was passed authorizing the Governor in Council to license ferry services and to grant the exclusive right to maintain a service on any route. This power was then used to put up for auction the right to operate services between Victoria and the Kowloon peninsula. The lowest tender came from a new company, which was granted the monopoly franchise, putting the existing operators out of business. These companies petitioned the Colonial Office for compensation for the loss of their vested interests in a ferry service which they had carried on since 1902. The petition was referred to the Colonial Office Legal Adviser for comment and he was outraged: 'The action of the Hong Kong government appears to me to be most extraordinary. What they have done is to create by legislation a monopoly which they have sold to the highest bidder without the slightest regard to the long-established interests of the petitioner. This is a highly interesting method of raising money which I thought had died with the Stuarts.'[8] He considered that the ferry companies were entitled to full compensation for the loss of their business, and not merely the value of the piers which they had built, which was all that the government was willing to pay. This view was put to Hong Kong, but the Governor, Stubbs, vigorously defended the action taken by his predecessor and refused to increase the compensation offered. The Colonial Office continued to press for fairer treatment of the companies and suggested that the amount should be settled by arbitration. Eventually Stubbs conceded a sum which the Colonial Office considered to be adequate.[9]

Most petitions came from members of the public service. The Colonial Office was particularly concerned to ensure that public servants in the colonies were fairly treated and sought to protect their terms of service against unilateral action by the Governor, since they had no legal redress if their salaries or allowances were cut or the rate of exchange was altered when the government budget could not otherwise be balanced. In the financial crises of the 1930s the Colonial Office agreed to cuts in pay only with the greatest reluctance and successfully pressed the Governor to restore full payment at the earliest opportunity. All disciplinary cases sent to London for confirmation, and petitions from quite junior staff who had been dismissed, were carefully examined to see that justice had been done. Although the Governor's decision was upheld in the vast majority of cases, there were a few instances where the penalty imposed was reduced, and the knowledge that the Colonial Office might intervene no doubt provided a safeguard against arbitrary action by the Governor.

In general a British Governor was allowed a very wide measure of discretion to rule his colony as he saw fit. Enquiries, suggestions, and occasional rebuffs from London were no more than a tiresome irritant, and the authorities at home could normally be pacified by a soothing report composed of carefully selected facts which showed that all was well. The staff of the Colonial Office shared a common set of values and beliefs about the aims of imperial policy with the officers of the colonial administrative service and were normally content to trust the Governor's judgement as to what was necessary or practicable in existing circumstances. Officials were more often a Governor's allies in his attempts to persuade the Foreign Office of the need to modify British policy to suit the territory's interests than captious critics seeking to dictate to him how his colony should be run. Ministers were an unpredictable element: normally they were kept too busy to concern themselves with Hong Kong's affairs, but on rare occasions they could intervene with potentially devastating effects. However, such crises could normally be handled by a resourceful Governor, ministers passed on to other offices of state, and the even tenour of colonial administration could once more be resumed.

Notes

Note to the Preface

1. Sir S.Y. Chung once complained in the Legislative Council, 'When it comes to internal affairs we are remotely controlled by London and cannot decide for ourselves' (*Hong Kong Hansard*, 1969–70, p. 343). On another occasion he stated, 'Since Hong Kong is a colony officials in the Hong Kong Government are basically members of the U.K. civil service and are, strictly speaking, under the directives of Whitehall' (*Hong Kong Hansard*, 1973–4, p. 63).

Note to the Introduction

1. See F.J. Moreno, *Legitimacy and Stability in Latin America* (New York, New York University Press, 1969), pp. 27–43; J.H. Parry, *The Spanish Seaborne Empire* (London, Hutchinson, 1966), pp. 181–2, 193–211, and 276–8.

Notes to Chapter 1

1. CO 129/381, pp. 343–8 and CO 129/388, pp. 219–23; *Hong Kong Hansard*, 30 November 1911, pp. 243–5.

2. CO 129/388, pp. 51–9 and CO 129/389, pp. 110–15 and 146.

3. *South China Morning Post*, 3,5,8,9, and 19 July 1912; CO 129/391, pp. 150–3; a full account of this incident is given in N.J. Miners, 'The Attempt to Assassinate the Governor in 1912', *Journal of the Hong Kong Branch of the Royal Asiatic Society*, Vol.22, 1982, pp. 279–85.

4. CO 129/402, pp. 281–5; CO 129/392, p. 7; CO 129/391, pp. 459–63; *Administrative Reports*, 1912, pp. 29–30.

5. CO 129/393, pp. 252–5; CO 129/394, pp. 5–6, 85–91, and 175–96; CO 129/399, pp. 40–50, 387–8, and 413–14; CO 129/402, pp. 272–93.

6. For details of these events see *Administrative Reports*, 1913–18, section entitled 'General Observations', and CO 129/494, pp. 393–410, Memorandum, 'Outline of Cantonese History 1911–1926'.

7. *Hong Kong Legislative Council Sessional Papers 1911*, 'Report of 1911 Census', Table III, p. 12, gives the resident European civil population as British: 3,761, Portuguese: 2,558, and German: 342; *The Times History of the War*, p. 137, states: 'In 1914 the whole business and administration of the colony was permeated by German influence', quoted in CO 129/448, p. 284.

8. CO 129/429, pp. 196–201; CO 129/430, pp. 112–24; CO 129/431, pp. 414–19 and 521–30; CO 129/442, pp. 225–39.

9. Lists of Hong Kong's contributions to the war effort are given in *Hong Kong Hansard*, 29 March 1917, pp. 18ff. and 3 October 1918, pp. 72ff.

10. For example, Sir Robert Ho Tung donated the cost of two aeroplanes. The HK$2,000,000 raised from the rates is included in the grand total of HK$10,000,000.

11. Dr Olitsky's report is at CO 129/449, pp. 87–134. Severn, OAG, sent his comments on it to the Colonial Office on 16 December 1918, CO 129/450, pp. 368–78.

12. *Hong Kong Legislative Council Sessional Papers 1920*, 'Preliminary Report on the Purchase and Sale of Rice by the Government of Hong Kong During the Year

1919'. No final report was ever published, in spite of pressure from the Colonial Office; see Stubbs to Colonial Office, 12 October 1921, CO 129/469, pp. 174–5.

13. There is a detailed account of this strike in A. Coates, *A Mountain of Light*, pp. 79–85. See also *Administrative Reports*, 1920 and 1921, Appendix C, 'Report of the Secretary for Chinese Affairs', p. C14; and Stubbs to Fiddes, 14 April 1920, CO 129/460, p. 177.

14. *Sessional Papers 1921*, Report on the Census, p. 156.

15. *Sessional Papers 1920*, pp. 47–9, gives details of housebuilding in the years 1910–19; *Minutes of the Executive Council*, 14 August 1919; *Hong Kong Hansard*, 18 July 1921, pp. 84–96; Stubbs to Colonial Office, 5 August 1921, CO 129/468, pp. 437–44.

16. Stubbs to Colonial Office, 17 March 1924, CO 129/484, pp. 152–6: 'It is not pleasant to hear the methods of the Army Council compared with those of Chinese militarists, with a slight leaning in favour of the latter.' *Hong Kong Hansard*, 7 February 1924, pp. 2–16 and 13 March 1924, pp. 25–9; Stubbs to Colonial Office, 17 June 1925, CO 129/488, p. 295.

17. Jamieson to Alston, 13 May 1921, with enclosures, CO 129/471, pp. 305–8.

18. See, for example, reports on the development of Whampoa discussed in Stubbs to Colonial Office, 4 August 1922, CO 129/478, pp. 735–40. Later proposals are discussed in Clementi to Colonial Office, 7 September 1929, CO 129/519/6, and Caldecott to Colonial Office, 19 February 1937, CO 129/562/20.

19. The fullest account of the strike, with full documentation, is in Stubbs to Colonial Office, 18 March 1922, CO 129/474, pp. 224–66.

20. Stubbs to Colonial Office, 31 March 1922 and 12 April 1922, CO 129/474, pp. 329–37 and 386–90.

21. Stubbs to Colonial Office, 18 March 1922, CO 129/474, pp. 224–66.

22. Stubbs to Colonial Office, 11 March 1922, CO 129/474, p. 288. *Minutes of the Executive Council*, 18 May 1922.

23. *Administrative Reports*, 1922, pp. C12–C15. Memorandum by Kotewall on the 1925 Strike, CO 882/11, p. 14.

24. Foreign Office memorandum of August 1923, CO 129/483, pp. 212–16.

25. Stubbs to Masterton-Smith, 21 July 1923, CO 129/482, pp. 252–8.

26. Stubbs to Colonial Office, 26 June, 10 July, and 24 July 1925, CO 129/488, pp. 468–72, 580–4, and 646–9.

27. Memorandum by R.H. Kotewall on the strike, CO 129/489, pp. 428–64. Stubbs wished to impose the penalty of flogging with a cat-o'-nine-tails for crimes involving violence, intimidation, and breaches of the peace, as Lugard had done in 1911. The Colonial Office warned him of the danger that similar punishment might be meted out to Europeans living in China in retaliation; the emergency regulations to impose flogging were therefore promulgated but not enforced; see CO 129/491, pp. 348–55.

28. Jamieson to Macleay, 2 November 1925, CO 129/495, pp. 517–18.

29. The number of ships calling at Hong Kong dropped from 764,492 in 1924 to 310,361 in 1926. See *Administrative Reports*, 1924 and 1926, Appendix D2, 'Report of the Harbour Office', p. D2.

30. Stubbs to Colonial Office, 2 October 1925, CO 129/489, pp. 269–72.

31. All possible courses of action, and the objections to them, were reviewed in a Foreign Office memorandum by Ashton-Gwatkin, CO 129/495, pp. 405–501.

32. All Clementi's dispatches about these abortive negotiations are printed in *Colonial Office Confidential Print, Eastern No. 144*, CO 882/11. There is a full account of the strike in an unpublished MA thesis: Rosemarie Chung Lu-cee, 'A Study of the 1925–6 Canton-Hong Kong Strike and Boycott', University of Hong Kong, 1969. This makes use of Chinese as well as British sources.

33. CO 882/11, pp. 138–71.

34. The estimate of HK$500,000,000 is in Ward to Amery, 16 December 1925, CO 129/491, pp. 536–7. Another calculation by D.J. Orchard, in 'China's Use of the Boycott as a Political Weapon', *Annals of the American Academy of Political and Social Science*, Vol. 152, 1930, pp. 252–61, estimates the depreciation in property values and Hong Kong industrial companies at HK$500,000,000.

35. In 1935 the commission appointed to enquire into the causes of the trade depression cited lack of confidence in the future of the colony as one reason for the depressed property market. This was omitted from the published version of the report: see Peel to Colonial Office, 14 May 1935, CO 129/554/5.

36. Clementi's dispatches on the situation in Canton during 1927 are collected in *Colonial Office Confidential Print, Eastern No. 145*, CO 882/11.

37. *Administrative Reports*, 1928, p. 3. In 1929 Clementi was referring in his dispatches to 'my little friend Li Chai-sum' (CO 129/515/5), and when Li was arrested by Chiang Kai-shek, Clementi tried to induce the British minister to intervene on his behalf (CO 129/512/1).

38. For loan proposals, see *Minutes of the Executive Council*, 16 February 1928 and CO 129/510/10. After the crushing of the Canton uprising in December 1927 the Hong Kong government handed over a number of Communists who had taken refuge in Hong Kong, who were then executed by the Kwangtung authorities; see CO 129/508/1, and FO 371/13199, Clementi to Amery, 22 December 1927. Extradition procedures were simplified and those who were accessories or abetters of crimes committed in China were made liable to prosecution in Hong Kong; see CO 129/505/10 and CO 129/511/20.

39. The Emergency Regulations were consolidated and reissued in 1931 and 1938, but without significant changes.

40. H.R. Butters, 'Report on Labour and Labour Conditions in Hong Kong', pp. 117–18, in *Hong Kong Legislative Council Sessional Papers 1939*; Memorandum on Trade Unions by the Secretary for Chinese Affairs, 30 August 1938, in CO 129/572/6.

41. The measures taken to deal with the shortage are set out in *Hong Kong Hansard*, 20 June 1929, pp. 65–73.

42. A long account of Hong Kong's water supply problems was given by Clementi in *Hong Kong Hansard*, 5 September 1929, pp. 134–50. When the reservoir at Tai Tam Tuk was completed in 1917, it was expected to satisfy the colony's needs for 15 years, but in fact it sufficed for only five, *Hong Kong Hansard*, 4 November 1926, p. 90.

43. *Hong Kong Legislative Council Sessional Papers 1931*, Report of the Census, Table 39; *Sessional Papers 1935*, 'Report of the Commission to Enquire into the Causes and Effects of the Present Trade Depression', pp. 80 and 87–90.

44. See the annual *Administrative Reports* from 1924 onwards, specifically Appendix C, Report of the Secretariat for Chinese Affairs, the section on factories.

45. The detailed account of the negotiations and the reasons for their failure is in CO 129/517, files 1, 12, 13, and 14, and CO 129/531/15. See also W. Peel, *Notes Concerning His Colonial Service*, pp. 143ff (referred to hereafter as Peel, *Notes*).

46. Peel to Colonial Office, 28 September 1931, with reports by the Inspector-General of Police and the General Officer Commanding British Troops, CO 129/536/6.

47. The revenue from land sales in 1930 was HK$2,864,897, in 1931, HK$3,177,807, and in 1932, HK$1,370,658. The possibility of reviving the Rent Restriction Ordinance was discussed by the Executive Council on 12 December 1929, but was rejected.

48. The Statistics Branch was abolished by Stubbs in 1925 as part of the general retrenchment of staff to save money during the strike and boycott. It was re-established in April 1930. For the trade figures see the section headed 'Commerce' in the annual *Administrative Reports*.

49. For a full discussion, see *Hong Kong Legislative Council Sessional Papers 1935*,

Report of the Commission to Enquire into the Causes and Effects of the Present Trade Depression, pp. 63–134.

50. *Sessional Papers 1935*, Report of Commission, pp. 81–7. Peel to Colonial Office, 14 May 1935, CO 129/554/5, contains passages from the Report critical of Canada's discrimination against Hong Kong which were omitted from the published version.

On the threat of quotas against Hong Kong's exports of rubber footwear, see *Minutes of the Executive Council*, 28 June 1935, and Palmer (Board of Trade) to Colonial Office, 18 September 1935, CO 852/16/10 and subsequent letters. The British manufacturers of rubber shoes were attempting to persuade Canada to limit its exports of rubber footwear to Britain, but the Canadian manufacturers would only agree to this if a quota was placed on Hong Kong's exports to the British market. The Colonial Office was prepared to ask Hong Kong to limit its exports, but disagreed about the size of the proposed quota. Negotiations reached deadlock on this point, so no quotas were imposed.

51. *Administration Reports*, 1937, p. 17 and Table 1.

52. CO 129/558/3.

53. See Northcote to Colonial Office, 13 October 1938, CO 129/576/1; and Report of the Housing Commission in *Legislative Council Sessional Papers 1938*, pp. 257–88. The Treasury in London suggested that this surplus might be used to purchase the leasehold of the New Territories from China, see minute by Gent, 28 March 1939, in CO 129/576/1.

54. Caldecott to Colonial Office, 24 September 1936, CO 129/559/13. The British financial expert, Sir F. Leith-Ross, who had advised China on its currency devaluation, suggested that Hong Kong should enter into a customs union with China, since he had reason to believe that some ministers in Nanking were in favour of such a union. Colonial Office officials were doubtful if the benefits to Hong Kong's trade and manufacturing industry would outweigh the disadvantages of an increase in the cost of living in Hong Kong as a result of applying the high Chinese tariffs, and the political cost of allowing increased Chinese influence in Hong Kong; see the discussions recorded in CO 129/558/11. Caldecott emphatically rejected the proposal when it was put to him; see his dispatch to the Colonial Office, 23 February 1937, CO 852/124/6.

55. *Administration Reports*, 1938, pp. 62–4; Northcote to Colonial Office, 22 June 1939 and 13 September 1939, CO 129/578/11 and CO 129/577/7.

56. *Administration Reports*, 1938, p. 62; CO 129/564/11.

57. *Administration Reports*, 1939, Appendix C, p. C7. The gas-mask factories were reported by Northcote to Colonial Office, 24 November 1939, CO 129/580/9.

58. CO 129/571/15 and CO 129/580/4. The possibility of allowing military aircraft to be assembled in Hong Kong and then flown to China was discussed by the British Cabinet on 17 November 1937 and it was decided to refuse permission, primarily from fear of Japanese reactions.

59. See CO 129/569/11. During this visit high officials in Canton assured the Governor that there was no possibility of labour and similar internal troubles in Hong Kong when relations between Canton and Hong Kong were good.

60. *Hong Kong Hansard*, 30 May 1940, p. 68, speech by the General Officer Commanding British Forces.

Notes to Chapter 2

1. The exact number of colonies depends upon how a separate administrative unit is defined. Some governors ruled over a territory consisting of a colony and one or more protectorates. The figure of 50 is given by C. Jeffries in *Whitehall and the Colonial Service: An Administrative Memoir 1939–1956*, p. 1.

2. The only issues of Hong Kong domestic policy discussed by the British Cabinet, or reported to the Cabinet for approval by a Cabinet committee between 1916 and 1939 were: various defence decisions on the strengthening or reduction of the size of the garrison; measures to deal with the 1925–6 strike and boycott; naval action against the pirates' lair at Bias Bay (in 1926, 1927, and 1929); Hong Kong's request to purchase supplies of opium from Persia (1927); the disposal of the Boxer Indemnity Fund (1928 and 1930); the Hong Kong currency reform (1935); exports of war material from Hong Kong to China (1937); and the introduction of compulsory service for Europeans in Hong Kong (1939). See CAB 23 Cabinet Minutes.

3. See S. Constantine, *The Making of British Colonial Development Policy 1914–1940*, pp. 269–72.

4. As occurred, for example, in 1959 when the Secretary of State for the Colonies, A. Lennox-Boyd, was severely criticized for the deaths of 11 Mau Mau detainees at Hola Camp in Kenya.

5. MacDonald, quoted in D.J. Morgan, *The Origins of British Aid Policy, 1924–1945*, p. xv.

6. Letter of Lord Passfield to his wife, 15 September 1930, quoted in B.C. Roberts, *Labour in the Tropical Territories of the Commonwealth*, p. 179.

Two ministers in this period have written autobiographies which describe their activities as Secretary of State: L.S. Amery, *My Political Life, Vol. Two*, see pp. 176–213 and 300–70; and Viscount Swinton (formerly Sir Philip Cunliffe-Lister), *I Remember*, see pp. 64–103.

7. Circular dispatches of 6 August 1930, 11 September 1930, and 17 September 1930 in CO 854/78. See Shiels's speech to the conference of colonial governors, 10 July 1930, as recorded in CO 854/173. Shiels's activity during his brief ministerial career has already been noted in B.C. Roberts, *Labour in the Tropical Territories of the Commonwealth*, pp. 175–80.

8. These figures ignore the brief four-month tenure of Sir George Gater from February to May 1940.

9. Maffey had been a member of the Indian Civil Service before moving to govern the Sudan. Wilson's practical experience in the army and as a governor did not compensate for his lack of intellectual achievements in the eyes of certain officials at the Colonial Office. One remarked, 'How would you like to serve under a Permanent Secretary who can neither read nor spell?' — quoted in R. Furse, *Aucuparius, Recollections of a Recruiting Officer*, p. 146.

10. Minute by Anderson, 15 September 1913, CO 129/402, pp. 270–1.

11. C. Parkinson, *The Colonial Office from Within, 1909–1945*, pp. 95–6.

12. For example, Stubbs's minute on a dispatch from May to the Colonial Office, 19 June 1904, CO 129/323, p. 134: 'As the ordinance has been approved it is useless to pick the obvious holes in Mr. May's arguments.' See also, on this point, M. Perham, *Lugard: the Years of Authority*, p. 368.

13. L.S. Amery, *My Political Life, Vol. Two*, p. 337.

14. R. Furse, *Aucuparius*, p. 147; C. Parkinson, *The Colonial Office from Within*, p. 100.

15. Memorandum by McEldery, 20 October 1927, commenting on Clementi's scheme for the reduction of opium prices, CO 129/506/3, pp. 130–6; see also his memorandum of 7 December 1926 in CO 825/1/30811.

16. D.J. Morgan, *The Origins of British Aid Policy*, pp. xviii–xx; C. Parkinson, *The Colonial Office from Within*, pp. 24–5 and 52–5; and S. Constantine, *The Making of British Colonial Development Policy*, pp. 278–86.

17. Circular dispatches of 17 September 1930 and 24 August 1937 in CO 854/78 and CO 854/78. The Governors' replies are printed in the *Colonial Office Confidential Print, Miscellaneous No. 427*.

18. Parkinson, *The Colonial Office from Within*, p. 25; Constantine, *The Making*

of British Colonial Development Policy, pp. 281⁻4; K. Robinson, *The Dilemmas of Trusteeship*, pp. 34⁻6.

19. Minutes on Caldecott to Colonial Office, 26 October 1936, CO 323/1375/3704/3.

20. For example, in 1938 Northcote wrote to the Colonial Office asking if it was in order for the local Eugenics League (which advocated birth control) to advertise its services in a government health clinic. This file was passed up to the Secretary of State, Malcolm MacDonald, who agreed that the Governor might exercise his own judgement on the issue; minutes on Northcote to Colonial Office, 14 April 1938, CO 129/571/17.

21. C. Jeffries, *Whitehall and the Colonial Service: An Administrative Memoir*, pp. 5⁻6. Jeffries states that it was an established custom that all petitions were seen by one of the ministers. This was generally true in the 1930s, but not before then.

22. May, OAG, to Colonial Office, 4 May 1904, CO 129/322, pp. 631⁻40. The ordinance was approved by Sir C. Lucas. This omission to consult ministers was noted by Lord Emmott and by Harcourt in CO 129/400, pp. 373⁻4, when a similar European reservation was set up at Taipo in 1913. The Cheung Chau reservation was approved by Sir G. Fiddes, minute dated 9 January 1919, on Severn, OAG, to Colonial Office, 20 October 1918, CO 129/450, p. 147.

23. Minutes on Northcote to Colonial Office, 2 October 1939, CO 129/582/17. A similar case where a possibly fruitful ministerial initiative was effectively smothered by officials occurred in 1928. The question at issue was whether the Governor could be permitted to sell the leasehold of Crown land in the New Territories for a period extending beyond the expiry date of the New Territories Lease in 1997. Clementi wished to do so, claiming that otherwise long-term investments in the area would be discouraged; but the Legal Adviser to the Colonial Office and the Foreign Office objected on the ground that any such extended leases would be in breach of the 1898 Convention and would justify China in making a strong diplomatic protest. When perusing one of the Foreign Office replies Amery unexpectedly put forward the idea that the Hong Kong government should sell the freehold of land in the New Territories, since this was not forbidden by the Convention and a freehold sale remained valid for all time. This novel suggestion was not followed up by the officials, who decided that Amery could only have put it forward as a possible argument to deploy in discussions with the Foreign Office, and not as a serious proposal for implementation in Hong Kong. See CO 129/513/4.

24. See, for example, minutes on CO 129/569/1, a petition from the New Territories Unemployed Chinese Seamen's Association, 21 November 1938.

25. C. Jeffries, *The Colonial Office*, p. 40; C. Parkinson, *The Colonial Office from Within*, pp. 63 and 137.

26. K. Robinson, *The Dilemmas of Trusteeship*, p. 21, quoting Sir D. Cameron, *My Tanganyika Service and some Nigeria* (London, Allen and Unwin, 1939), p. 20.

27. *The Colonial Empire 1947⁻48*, Cmd. 7433 of 1948, quoted in C. Jeffries, *The Colonial Office*, p. 38.

28. The normal term of a governor was reduced from six years to five in 1938.

29. Circular dispatches of 2 April 1931 and 3 August 1938 in CO 854/80 and CO 854/110.

30. This statement is taken directly from C. Jeffries, *Whitehall and the Colonial Service*, p. 6. A minute summarizing the conclusions of an interdepartmental committee on measures to be taken against piracy in the South China Seas noted that 'the normal procedure would be to transmit the conclusions to Hong Kong and invite the Governor to implement them'. Minute by Paskin dated 1 January 1925, CO 129/487, p. 450.

31. In 1927 Clementi sent a dispatch strongly advocating that the British embargo on the supply of arms to China should be modified in favour of General Li Chai-sum. The Permanent Under-Secretary, Wilson, minuted, 'I agree that the governor

of Hong Kong is bound to urge on the Secretary of State the adoption of whatever line of policy in South China he thinks would be in the interests of Hong Kong, and that we should press the Foreign Office accordingly' (30 May 1927). The Foreign Secretary opposed this proposal, and the disagreement went to the Cabinet, which decided in favour of the Foreign Office view that the embargo should be maintained, CO 129/504/13.

32. L.S. Amery takes the credit for this decision in *My Political Life, Vol. Two*, p. 365. See CAB 23/58(28)3 and CAB 23/8(30)1 for the discussions in Cabinet, and CO 129/512/4 and 5.

Notes to Chapter 3

1. A. Grantham, *Via Ports*, p. 107.

2. *Colonial Regulations 1928*, No. 5.

3. Colonial governorships were divided into four classes for the purpose of pensions. A full list with classifications as at 1938 is given in C. Jeffries, *The Colonial Empire and its Civil Service*, p. 254.

4. *Report of the Salaries Commission*, pp. 76–7, in *Sessional Papers of the Hong Kong Legislative Council 1928*.

5. Stubbs to Wilson, 31 January 1926, CO 129/492, pp. 88–9; Peel, *Notes*, p. 162; Des Voeux, *My Colonial Service*, Vol. II. pp. 230–2; Grantham, *Via Ports*, pp. 122–6; M. Perham, *Lugard: the Years of Authority*, p. 357.

6. Peel, *Notes*, pp. 125 and 138–50. The vacancy in Hong Kong was unexpected. It was caused by the sudden mental breakdown of the Governor of the Straits Settlements, Sir Hugh Clifford, who was replaced by Clementi, who was transferred from Hong Kong.

7. These reasons for May's selection may be deduced from the minutes on the unofficials' petition, CO 129/381, pp. 550–63, and from Fiddes's minute dated 10 September 1913 on CO 129/402, p. 270.

8. Des Voeux, *My Colonial Service*, Vol. II, p. 244.

9. See Peel, *Notes*, p. 151, and Clementi's list of his visits in *Hong Kong Hansard*, 23 June 1930, p. 17.

10. Peel, *Notes*, p. 152. May was also a very active sportsman, see G.R. Sayer, *Hong Kong 1862–1919*, p. 116.

11. May to Colonial Office, 14 March 1913, CO 129/400, pp. 93–6. This action is described by G.R. Sayer, *Hong Kong 1862–1919*, p. 115, as 'an immense leap forward' in education.

12. See Chapter 6, p. 105. The correspondence on this subject was collected in the *Colonial Office Confidential Print Eastern No. 150*, CO 882/11.

13. See, for example, Clementi's dispatches in CO 129/500/4 and CO 129/517/7, such as Clementi to Colonial Office, 20 September 1927: 'I take this opportunity of urging once again that the policy of regional recognition is the only practicable method of solving the Chinese problem.'
In a semi-official letter to Hankey of the Cabinet Office, the Permanent Under-Secretary, Wilson, commented on Clementi: 'The trouble appears to be that he thinks that in his capacity as Governor of Hong Kong he is also responsible for the control of all the naval, military and air forces in South China, as well as shaping our policy there'; Wilson to Hankey, 20 December 1926, CO 129/494, p. 497.

14. See FO 371/11622, a dispatch from Clementi which has been lost from the Colonial Office files; also CO 129/503/2, CO 129/507/6, and CO 129/513/4.

15. Stubbs to Colonial Office, 10 February 1920, CO 129/460, pp. 120–2. May's plans for a salt tax had already been rejected by Severn, who was Officer Administering

the Government for a year before Stubbs arrived; see Severn, OAG, to Colonial Office, 22 July 1919, CO 129/455, p. 65.

16. Clementi to Colonial Office, 26 April 1926, CO 129/498, p. 491.

17. Peel to Colonial Office, 17 December 1931, CO 129/538/3. Peel, *Notes*, p. 143. Northcote to Colonial Office, 11 July 1938, CO 129/573/15.

18. When the Colonial Office criticized one of his dispatches, Northcote apologized that he had signed it in a fit of absence of mind: 'I am afraid that my previous dispatch lay under my "blind spot" when I signed it, for I do not now find myself in agreement with its proposals and I regret that I put them forward; indeed I had to enquire whence they came. I am sorry that the Secretary of State was put into the position of having to turn down such an obviously wrong-headed suggestion'; Northcote to Gent (semi-official), 5 August 1939, CO 129/577/2.

In 1937 the Governors of Hong Kong and the Straits Settlements were asked to send in their comments on the Report of the *Mui Tsai* Commission in two separate dispatches: one an official dispatch which could be published in a Command Paper to be laid before Parliament and one containing 'anything really confidential or private which in your opinion it would be definitely undesirable to publish'; Ormsby-Gore to Caldecott and Shenton Thomas, private, 24 March 1937, CO 882/169, p. 62.

19. See Stubbs's dispatches of 25 October, 21 and 27 November 1919, and 31 March 1920, CO 129/456, pp. 137, 250, and 268 and CO 129/460, p. 332. Stubbs argued that the need to submit lease modifications to London for approval delayed urgently needed rebuilding schemes. He was also allowed to dispense with public auctions when he reported that certain rich Chinese were bidding up the premiums on new sites on Cheung Chau and elsewhere to a prohibitive figure in order to frustrate the intention to create European reserves.

20. Stubbs was not allowed to fix revised increments for the salaries of junior cadets, nor to engage his own auditors in place of the staff of the Director of Colonial Audit as an economy measure. The Colonial Office also insisted that full reports must be forwarded in all cases where he exercised the prerogative of mercy. See Stubbs to Colonial Office, 3 May 1920, CO 129/461, p. 10; 14 June 1920, CO 129/461, p. 233; and 13 September 1924, CO 129/485, p. 60.

21. Clementi's use of this tactic caused a number of complaints at the Colonial Office; see, for example, the minute by Sir G. Grindle of 5 December 1927, 'The present government of Hong Kong is much inclined to rush important decisions and tell us afterwards. This seems a good occasion for a hint on the subject', CO 129/506/3, p. 30.

22. Circular dispatches of 30 March 1932 and 15 December 1940, CO 854/83 and CO 854/115.

23. See F. Gilbert Chan, 'An alternative to Kuomintang–Communist Collaboration: Sun Yat-sen and Hong Kong January–June 1923', *Modern Asian Studies*, Vol. 13, 1979, pp. 127–39.

24. CO 129/482, p. 212.

25. Stubbs to Masterton-Smith, 21 July 1923, CO 129/482, pp. 252–8; Stubbs to Duke of Devonshire, 23 December 1923, CO 129/481, pp. 554–62; Foreign Office memorandum, 29 August 1923, CO 129/483, pp. 212–16.

26. Stubbs to Colonial Office, 25 August 1923, CO 129/481, pp. 203–7.

27. Stubbs to Colonial Office, 11 December 1923, CO 129/481, p. 447; Macleay to Foreign Office, 14 December 1923, CO 129/483, pp. 206–8.

28. Curzon to Devonshire, 19 December 1923, CO 129/483, pp. 204–5.

29. Colonial Office to Stubbs, 22 December 1923, CO 129/483, pp. 197–8; Memoranda by G. Grindle, CO 129/483, pp. 209–11 and 217–21.

30. Stubbs to Devonshire, 23 December 1923, CO 129/483, pp. 554–62.

31. Stubbs to Colonial Office, 24 December 1923, CO 129/481, p. 526; Colonial Office to Stubbs, 28 December 1923, CO 129/483, p. 200.

32. Tyrrell to Lambert, 30 June 1925, CO 129/491, pp. 335-40.

33. Peel, *Notes*, pp. 140 and 151.

34. *Royal Instructions* X.

35. See further discussion of this committee on p. 62. It was commonly referred to in the earlier period as the District Watchmen Committee, but after 1929 as the District Watch Committee.

36. *Minutes of the Executive Council*, CO 131/43, meetings of 4 November 1909, 7 February 1910, 28 April and 8 December 1910, and 1 August 1911. Later joint meetings were on 14 February 1922, 24 December 1925, and 4 February, 26 April, 25 May, and 17 June 1926.

37. A system of pipes to supply salt water for flushing purposes was not laid until after the Second World War. So the erection of water closets which would draw on the colony's limited reserves of fresh water had to be strictly controlled.

From 1926 such decisions were considered in the first instance by the Sanitary Board, and the Executive Council only dealt with appeals from that body.

38. The ordinance of 1904 had forbidden the leasing of property on the Peak to Asians, but did not prevent Chinese from buying houses and living there themselves. Another reason for the 1918 ordinance was the fact that Hong Kong had adhered to the Anglo-Japanese Treaty of 1906 which protected Japanese from any discriminatory treatment. Mme Chiang Kai-shek was permitted to reside on the Peak by an Executive Council decision of 14 April 1936.

39. CO 131/49, p. 521. *Minutes of the Executive Council*, 16 December 1915. See also CO 129/422, pp. 241-2 and 276-80, and CO 129/428, pp. 518-20.

The Volunteer Corps was a territorial force who did military training in their spare time. At this time it consisted of Europeans, together with a company of Hong Kong-born Portuguese who originally came from Macau.

40. *Royal Instructions* XII. May to Colonial Office, 27 September 1912, CO 129/392, p. 109, and May to Colonial Office, 28 December 1916, CO 129/436, p. 449. May also upheld a decision of the Military Service Tribunal against the majority view of the Executive Council that an appeal should be allowed, May to Colonial Office, 30 July 1918, CO 129/449, p. 222.

41. On one occasion Stubbs informed the Council that he proposed to act against the advice of the majority and would so inform the Secretary of State. The other members of the Council then changed their votes to conform with the Governor's opinion, since the issue was a minor one, and they had not been aware of his view when they voted. The question was whether to order the carrying out of a death sentence on receipt of a Colonial Office telegram, or to await the arrival of a dispatch confirming that the prisoner's appeal to the Privy Council had been dismissed. *Minutes of the Executive Council*, 13 and 20 July 1922, CO 131/60, pp. 378 and 382.

42. *Minutes of the Executive Council*, 23 August and 13 September 1917, CO 131/54, pp. 143-4 and 155. Similarly on 13 January 1916 May was outvoted by four to two on the question of whether to allow four water closets to be erected in a new development in Kowloon. May deferred a final decision until he had reconsidered the report of the Sanitary Board. On 27 January the matter was brought up again and at this meeting the Council was equally divided, three to three, enabling the Governor to give his decision against the application. CO 131/49, pp. 550 and 556.

43. *Royal Instructions* XXXIV.

44. *Minutes of the Executive Council*, 19 January 1933 and 11 October 1934, CO 131/89, p. 23, and CO 131/92, p. 210.

45. A full statement of the policy customarily followed by the Secretary of State in cases where a prisoner was condemned to death was given to Parliament by A. Creech Jones (Secretary of State for the Colonies, 1946-50), in *House of Commons Debates*, 11 August 1947, Written Answer, cols. 232-3. For an earlier statement of the settled policy of the Colonial Office see G.V. Fiddes, *The Dominions and Colonial*

Offices, p. 48. Fiddes expressed his views much more forcibly in the minutes he wrote on such requests: 'As I have said twenty times, I don't agree. I do not recollect that my view has ever been upset, viz. that the prerogative must be exercised solely on the Governor's responsibility and that there would be a risk, amounting to certainty, of miscarriage of justice if the Secretary of State attempted to interfere.' Minute of 21 May 1915, quoted in CO 129/550/6.

46. Colonial Office to Peel, 18 December 1934, CO 129/550/6. The Secretary of State, Cunliffe-Lister, minuted: 'I have repeatedly told the House of Commons that the prerogative is vested in the Governor personally. It would be most improper to intervene. The Bishop should have made his representations to the Governor'. Minute dated 14 December 1934.

The official who suggested intervention was H.E. Bader, an administrative officer from Kenya who was on secondment to the Colonial Office, acting as a Principal. One month previously he had criticized Peel's decision to commute a death sentence against the majority view of the Executive Council in what the Chief Justice considered to be a carefully planned and premeditated murder. Bader's minute was firmly rejected by all five senior officials who added their comments. Minutes on Peel to Colonial Office, 18 October 1934, CO 129/550/2.

47. *South China Morning Post*, 19, 22, and 23 November, and 10 and 17 December 1912; CO 129/416, pp. 507–10 and 641–3; CO 129/411, pp. 343–8 and 396–7; CO 129/412, pp. 81–2.

The expenses of sepoy Ibrahim's appeal to the Privy Council *in forma pauperis* were paid by the Hong Kong government.

48. Papers on the appeal of Chung Chi Cheung to the Privy Council, 7 January to 23 December 1938, CO 129/568/9. This was also an appeal *in forma pauperis* at the government's expense.

For a fuller discussion of the exercise of the prerogative of mercy see N.J. Miners, 'The Governor, the Secretary of State and the Prerogative of Mercy', *Hong Kong Law Journal*, Vol.17, 1987, pp. 77–89.

Notes to Chapter 4

1. CO 129/511/5.

2. The Governor voted in support of the motion to increase public service salaries in 1930; see *Hong Kong Hansard*, 19 June 1930, p. 100.

3. There is a full list of the unofficial members of the Legislative Council from 1850 to 1941 in G.B. Endacott, *Government and People in Hong Kong 1841–1962*, pp. 251–3. Endacott states that A.G. Stephen (Legislative Council, 1921–3) was from Jardine, Matheson and Co. He was in fact the chief manager of the Hongkong and Shanghai Banking Corporation. In 1916 D. Lansdale, the Hong Kong head of Jardine, Matheson declined to sign the petition in favour of the reform of the Legislative Council on the ground that the Hong Kong head of Jardines had always been nominated by the Governor to a seat on the Legislative Council without the necessity of any election, and that it would therefore be an ungracious act for him to sign such a petition, CO 129/433, p. 222.

4. *Hong Kong Hansard*, 23 January 1930, p. 14.

5. *Hong Kong Hansard*, 19 June 1930, p. 51.

6. *Hong Kong Hansard*, 22 October 1931, p. 177.

7. *Hong Kong Hansard*, 14 November 1921, p. 177.

8. *Hong Kong Hansard*, 28 August 1919, pp. 63–5.

9. See H.J. Lethbridge, 'The District Watch Committee: The Chinese Executive

Council of Hong Kong?', *Journal of the Hong Kong Branch of the Royal Asiatic Society*, Vol. 11, 1971, pp. 116–41.

10. CO 129/394, p. 5; CO 129/443, p. 18; CO 129/476, p. 244; CO 129/499/1; CO 129/522/3; CO 129/555/6.

11. See Clementi's frank remarks about the Committee in his dispatch to Amery, 6 March 1928, CO 129/510/11.

12. CO 129/443, p. 8, enclosure by Secretary for Chinese Affairs in Stubbs to Colonial Office, 27 July 1921; CO 129/468, p. 426.

13. *Hong Kong Hansard*, 19 March 1936, p. 52, and 26 August 1936, p. 179.

14. The official report of the debate in the Legislative Council was normally sent to London when the ordinance was forwarded for notification of non-disallowance. The Colonial Secretary assured Holyoak that the Colonial Office was normally informed of all dissenting votes in the Legislative Council, see *Hong Kong Hansard*, 19 April 1917, pp. 81–2.

15. *Hong Kong Hansard*, 28 May 1908, p. 47.

16. CO 129/411, pp. 35ff; CO 129/443, pp. 340–4.

17. See Stubbs's comments on CO 129/453, p. 164, written before he arrived in Hong Kong. Details of the reorganization were given in *Hong Kong Hansard*, 29 January 1920, p. 3.

18. *Hong Kong Hansard*, 10 December 1931, p. 214.

19. CO 129/463, p. 119.

20. CO 129/405, p. 52, and *Hong Kong Hansard*, 29 January 1920, p. 3.

21. *Minutes of the Executive Council*, 16 October 1919; *Hong Kong Hansard*, 31 October 1919, pp. 114–15.

22. *Hong Kong Hansard*, 6 September 1923, pp. 86–92.

23. *Hong Kong Hansard*, 14 June 1923, pp. 55–7.

24. Stubbs to Milner, 16 June 1920, CO 129/461, p. 243.

25. *Minutes of the Executive Council*, 18 May and 27 July 1922; *Hong Kong Hansard*, 17 August 1922, pp. 76–7.

26. CO 129/509/4; OAG to Colonial Office, 6 October 1928; *Hong Kong Hansard*, 24 January 1929, p. 8, and 2 May 1929, p. 44.

27. CO 129/510/8, 'Report of the Conference of the Interdepartmental Opium Committee', 9 July 1928.

28. CO 129/524/1.

29. CO 129/524/1, Minutes on OAG to Colonial Office, 24 March 1930. The question had previously been raised by May to Colonial Office, 15 May 1917, CO 129/442, p. 248.

30. CO 129/525/3 and CO 129/533/13. Until 1971 the pound sterling was divided into 20 shillings (s.), and each shilling was divided into 12 pence (d.). Prices were denominated as £.s.d. So in 1930 the value of the Hong Kong dollar declined from 1s.6d. in January to 1s.3d. in June, and to 11¾d. in December.

31. CO 854/47, circular dispatch of 1 November 1911; CO 854/176, secret circular dispatch of 16 October 1937.

32. See circular dispatch, CO 854/115 of 8 December 1939, which gives a summary of the objectionable provisions often found in legislation examined at the Colonial Office. The only unofficial member of the Hong Kong Legislative Council who ever raised a protest about excessive powers being given to the executive was Lo Man-kam; see *Hong Kong Hansard*, 29 June 1939, p. 71, debate on the Telecommunications Bill which gave the Postmaster-General very wide powers to authorize searches and arrests.

33. CO 129/387, p. 246, petition dated 8 April 1911.

34. CO 129/537/11.

35. CO 129/515/3.

36. See files CO 129/537/6, CO 129/542/3, CO 129/554/12, and CO 129/557/3.
37. CO 129/404, p. 40, and CO 323/633.
38. Minute by Anderson dated 29 January 1912 in CO 129/394, p. 83; CO 129/402, pp. 268–97; CO 129/439, p. 585.
39. CO 129/454, p. 63.
40. CO 129/506/6.
41. *Hong Kong Hansard*, 28 August 1924, pp. 71–3.
42. *Hong Kong Hansard*, 27 October 1932, p. 226.
43. CO 129/465, p. 435.
44. CO 129/530/9.
45. CO 129/559/2.
46. Other cases are CO 129/390, p. 277; CO 129/444, p. 285; CO 129/479, p. 454; CO 129/511/7; CO 129/548/15; and CO 129/584/16.
47. CO 129/505/7; CO 129/551/5.
48. CO 129/504/7.
49. CO 129/551/10.

Notes to Chapter 5

1. All data in this chapter about the size, composition, and payment of the public service have been calculated from the figures given in the annual *Blue Books*, the annual *Estimates of the Hong Kong Government*, and the annual *Staff List*.
2. Reports of the Censuses of 1911, 1921, and 1931 were published in the annual volume of the *Hong Kong Legislative Council Sessional Papers*. The 1939 estimate is from the *Administration Report*, 1939, p. 2.
3. For example, May in *Hong Kong Hansard*, 7 May 1914, p. 46; Stubbs to Colonial Office, 11 December 1919, CO 129/456, p. 370; Peel to Colonial Office, 4 November 1931, CO 129/534/3, p. 37.
4. *Hong Kong Hansard*, 7 May 1914, p. 44; *Hong Kong Hansard*, 18 November 1920, pp. 64 and 73–4.
5. CO 129/534/3, p. 195; *Hong Kong Hansard*, 19 March 1936, p. 71.
6. Severn, OAG, to Colonial Office, 22 August 1922, CO 129/476, pp. 96–8.
7. Stubbs to Colonial Office, 29 October 1924, CO 129/485, p. 195; Clementi, CO 129/493, p. 175, and CO 129/511/16.
8. CO 129/460, p. 7, and Crown Agents to Colonial Office, 26 April 1920, CO 129/464, pp. 97–9. On recruitment from the British army see CO 129/526/6 and CO 129/539/1.
9. *Hong Kong Hansard*, 21 February 1918, pp. 3–4, and CO 129/434, p. 394.
10. May explained the system in a dispatch dated 14 September 1912, CO 129/392, pp. 57–60. The Secretary of State, Harcourt, expressed his agreement.
11. Peel to Colonial Office, 20 May 1930, CO 129/523/11. In the minutes on this dispatch, the Parliamentary Under-Secretary, Dr Drummond Shiels, expressed strong reservations about the rules and practice of the Hong Kong government, but he did not issue instructions that any changes should be made.
12. CO 129/449, p. 13.
13. *Hong Kong Legislative Council Sessional Papers 1931*, p. 62.
14. *Hong Kong Hansard*, 19 March 1936, p. 72. Peel to Colonial Office, 1 November 1934, CO 129/546/7.
15. Stubbs to Colonial Office, 12 April 1923, CO 129/480, p. 26.
16. CO 129/534/3; CO 129/561/4; *Hong Kong Hansard*, 12 September 1932, pp. 149 and 152, 12 October 1933, p. 125, 19 March 1936, p. 70, 22 April 1936, p. 82, and 16 September 1936, pp. 217 and 222.

17. Caldecott to Colonial Office, 6 March 1936, CO 129/558/3; Northcote to Colonial Office, 15 March 1939, CO 129/578/7.

18. *Hong Kong Hansard*, 22 April 1936, pp. 81-2.

19. Northcote to Colonial Office, 7 July 1938, CO 129/574/4.

20. K. Robinson, *The Dilemmas of Trusteeship*, pp. 43-4. R.O. Tilman, *Bureaucratic Transition in Malaysia*, pp. 46-8 and 112. J. de Vere Allen, 'Malayan Civil Service, 1874-1941: Colonial Bureaucracy/Malayan Elite', *Comparative Studies in Society and History*, Vol.12, 1970, pp. 174-7.

21. For a detailed study of cadets' family and educational background, see H. Lethbridge, 'The Hong Kong Cadets 1862-1941', *Journal of the Hong Kong Branch of the Royal Asiatic Society*, Vol. 10, 1970, pp. 36-56.

22. For example, CO 129/420, p. 324; CO 129/518/6; CO 129/548/1; and CO 129/562/5.

23. CO 129/489, pp. 644-6 and CO 129/492, pp. 27 and 88. In 1912 Claud Severn was brought in from Malaya to be Colonial Secretary. In 1941 F.C. Gimson was similarly transferred to be Colonial Secretary just before the Japanese invasion.

24. CO 129/518/6.

25. CO 129/552/4.

26. CO 129/503/6; CO 129/548/2; CO 129/549/19; CO 129/553/12; and CO 825/12/83053.

27. Criticism of cadets and their attitudes was voiced by the British Consul-General at Canton, Jamieson, to Alston, 11 March 1922, CO 129/477, p. 286. See the long critical memorandum from Swire and Sons Ltd. to Colonial Office, 20 February 1930, CO 129/523/6. Also CO 129/491, pp. 39-43, and CO 129/548/2.

28. For a detailed account of conditions of service in the colonial service and the changes brought about by unification in the 1930s, see Charles Jeffries, *The Colonial Empire and its Civil Service*.

29. Clementi to Colonial Office, 29 June 1926, and reply, CO 129/498/22.

30. CO 129/423, p. 412; CO 129/434, p. 575; CO 129/441, p. 263.

31. Cunliffe-Lister to Peel, 31 January 1935, CO 129/546/7, *Hong Kong Hansard*, 3 October 1935, p. 100.

32. CO 129/558/8; *Hong Kong Hansard*, 22 September 1937, p. 74.

33. CO 129/448, p. 532; CO 129/450, pp. 393-5; CO 129/453, pp. 244ff.

34. CO 129/456, pp. 356-81. Stubbs to Milner, 11 December 1919, and reply, 20 March 1920. A Colonial Office official later commented that Stubbs had been rather stingy, minute by A.E. Collins, 17 March 1925, CO 129/488, p. 447.

35. Clementi to Colonial Office, 27 April 1928, and minute by Clutterbuck, 30 June 1928, CO 129/511/6.

36. Salaries Commission Report in *Hong Kong Legislative Council Sessional Papers 1929*, pp. 71-112, and *Sessional Papers 1930*, pp. 51-64. Representations to the Colonial Office and its decision are in CO 129/524/1.

37. *Hong Kong Hansard*, 22 October 1930, pp. 218 and 229. The suggestion was made by Mr P. Lauder who had been a member of the Salaries Commission. The sterling values of the Hong Kong dollar during 1930 are given in Chapter 4, note 30, on p. 295 above.

38. Decision by Lord Passfield, acting in accordance with the advice of the Permanent Under-Secretary, 5 January 1931, in CO 129/525/3.

39. Telegram from Peel, 12 January 1931, CO 129/525/3.

40. CO 129/533/13.

41. Smith, OAG, to Colonial Office, 4 October 1935, and Caldecott to Colonial Office, 3 January 1936, in CO 129/555/2. Successive revisions of the salary levy are in CO 129/558/3. A table giving the monthly value of the Hong Kong dollar in shillings and pence from January 1931 to December 1934 can be found in *Hong Kong Legislative Council Sessional Papers 1935*, p. 133.

42. *Colonial Regulations 1928*, Nos. 16–26. Before this revision, the limits were £100 and £300 a year.

43. Stubbs to Colonial Office, 12 April 1923, and reply, CO 129/480, pp. 26–30.

44. One of the rare cases where the Governor's provisional appointment was rejected occurred in 1939 when Northcote proposed to appoint a Lieutenant-Commander in the Royal Navy directly to the post of Assistant Superintendent of Prisons, CO 129/578/9.

45. CO 129/523/3.

46. *Colonial Regulations 1928*, Nos. 39–51.

47. CO 129/392, pp. 109ff, gives the evidence and report; the decision is given on pp. 274–8. *Minutes of the Executive Council*, 14 December 1916; May to Colonial Office, 28 December 1916, CO 129/436, pp. 449–94. In an attempt to exculpate himself Mr Bowen-Rowlands made accusations of drunkenness against other senior officers. These unsubstantiated allegations were noted on the officers' confidential files in the Colonial Office.

48. CO 129/433, pp. 347–59, and CO 129/435, pp. 209–11. Further details of this incident and its consequences can be found in N.J. Miners, 'Why Civil Servants Retire at 55: The Curious Origins of a Government Rule', *Hong Kong Law Journal*, Vol.13, 1983, pp. 209–17.

49. CO 129/535/4; CO 129/554/15.

Notes to Chapter 6

1. According to D.J. Morgan, *The Origins of British Aid Policy 1924–1945*, p. 9, the proportion of general revenue received from customs duties in 1933 was: Kenya, 33 per cent, Nigeria, 58 per cent, Ceylon, 52 per cent, and Jamaica, 60 per cent.

2. *Hong Kong Hansard*, 25 May 1917, pp. 41–2. *Hong Kong Legislative Council Sessional Papers 1939*, Taxation Committee Report, pp. 83–102.

3. All details of revenue and expenditure are calculated from the annual *Blue Book* and the annual *Estimates of Revenue and Expenditure*.

4. *Hong Kong Hansard*, 7 April 1921, p. 21, and 7 May 1931, p. 54.

5. *Hong Kong Hansard*, 1 June 1911, pp. 102–10, 23 October 1913, pp. 79–81, 29 October 1930, pp. 205–8, 27 September 1934, pp. 147–8, and 7 October 1936, p. 251.

6. Stubbs to Colonial Office, 23 March 1920 and 2 February 1923, CO 129/460, p. 299, and CO 129/479, pp. 337–41.

7. The voluminous correspondence on this subject between 1926 and 1933 is printed in *Confidential Print Eastern No. 50*, CO 882/11.

8. Northcote to Colonial Office, 22 June 1938, CO 129/566/21. The Hong Kong government paid lower salaries and deducted only 6 per cent for the rent of government quarters, because if it paid higher salaries and charged an economic rent, this would have attracted a higher defence contribution; see *Hong Kong Hansard*, 14 November 1921, p. 176. See also note 17 below.

9. Another argument against increased expenditure on health and education was that the provision of such social services would stimulate a flood of indigents from Kwangtung province; see, for example, CO 129/553/12, private letter from Forster, 4 October 1935.

10. CO 129/566/21 contains the official dispatch of 22 June 1938 signed by Northcote and also a semi-official private letter commending the proposals.

11. *Colonial Regulations 1928*, Nos. 261, 283, 210, and 281.

12. Peel to Colonial Office, 1 August 1930, CO 129/527/15; Secretary of State to Peel, 10 April 1935, CO 129/552/1.

13. Southorn, OAG, to Colonial Office, 20 February 1930, CO 129/525/3. For another example see Peel to Colonial Office, 31 May 1933, CO 129/544/7. The Governor proposed to build a dispensary launch to provide medical services for boat dwellers. A junior official, Gent, was in favour of rejecting the proposal as being too expensive. The file went up to the Permanent Under-Secretary, Wilson, who supported the Governor.

14. CO 129/401, p. 305; CO 129/574/10; CO 129/389, pp. 30–6; CO 129/577/2.

15. Clementi to Colonial Office, 26 September 1929, CO 129/519/1, p. 32, and CO 129/519/2, pp. 2 and 174.

16. Peel to Colonial Office, 20 March 1933, CO 129/543/11.

17. Minute by Campbell, 24 January 1932, CO 129/536/1; CO 129/541/2; CO 129/545/1. Secretary of State to Peel, 20 January 1934. One reason why the Hong Kong government preferred to finance the building of the gaol by a loan was that otherwise it would be obliged to raise additional revenue, equivalent to 25 per cent of the cost of the gaol, in order to pay the increased military contribution; see Peel to Colonial Office, 7 August 1931, CO 129/534/6.

18. Secretary of State to Northcote, 12 January 1938, CO 129/561/10.

19. Stubbs to Colonial Office, 5 March 1925, CO 129/488, pp. 166–72; Stubbs to Grindle (personal), CO 129/488, pp. 180–2.

20. Stubbs was wrong about the expected yield from death duties on Sir Paul Chater's estate. Ten years later the amount to be paid was still the subject of litigation and the case was finally settled by an appeal to the Privy Council in 1936; see CO 129/557/12.

21. For example, Colonial Office to Peel, 16 January 1935, CO 129/550/1.

22. See *Hong Kong Legislative Council Sessional Papers 1907*, pp. 617–27; May to Colonial Office, 21 November 1912, CO 129/393, pp. 251–4; *Hong Kong Hansard*, 6 November 1914, pp. 137 and 139.

23. Telegram, Colonial Office to May, 16 December 1915, CO 129/424, p. 521; CO 129/425, pp. 702–7.

24. May to Colonial Office, 9 February 1916 and 28 March 1916, CO 129/431, pp. 371–4, and CO 129/432, pp. 364–7.

25. Stubbs to Colonial Office, 19 and 21 August 1920, CO 129/462, pp. 206 and 225–8. Colonial Office officials agreed that there was no alternative to making a grant to the university in order to save it from insolvency. They similarly approved retrospectively the expenditure and losses on the rice purchases, although they delayed for two years before signifying non-disallowance of the Rice Ordinance 1919, waiting for a further report which was never sent; see CO 129/469, pp. 174–5.

26. There were minor alterations during 1926 in the charges for water, fees for hospital treatment, and liquor duties, but these were routine adjustments.

27. *Hong Kong Hansard*, 2 October 1930, p. 177, 4 December 1930, p. 248, 29 January 1931, pp. 9 and 13, 26 February 1931, pp. 30 and 35, 7 May 1931, p. 54, 22 October 1931, pp. 198–200, and 10 December 1931, p. 212.

28. Minute by Cowell, dated 19 November 1932, and dispatch of 10 January 1933 in CO 129/541/2.

29. CO 129/541/5.

30. CO 129/558/11, especially the memorandum on pp. 58–61.

31. *Hong Kong Hansard*, 12 September 1935, pp. 155–7, and 3 October 1935, p. 189.

32. Colonial Office to Caldecott, 24 January 1936, CO 129/558/3.

33. *Minutes of the Executive Council*, 10 February 1937.

34. Circular dispatch of 10 June 1932, CO 854/84. Circular dispatch of January 1937, CO 854/104. The latter dispatch is reproduced in C. Jeffries, *The Colonial Empire and its Civil Service*, pp. 243–7.

35. Colonial Office to Clementi, 1 April 1929, CO 129/515/6. Colonial Office to Clementi, 2 October 1929, CO 129/518/6.
36. Described in Caldecott to Colonial Office, 19 August 1936, CO 129/558/3.
37. Interview with Sir Sydney Caine.
38. *Hong Kong Legislative Council Sessional Papers 1939*, Taxation Committee Report, pp. 83–102.
39. Northcote to Colonial Office, 8 October 1939, CO 129/582/7 and subsequent papers in this file. The Secretary of State, MacDonald, accepted the advice of his officials that the official majority in the Legislative Council should not be used to impose a full income tax, but that the compromise should be accepted; see minute of 2 November 1939. *Hong Kong Hansard*, 14 March 1940, pp. 22–31, and 25 April 1940, p. 66.

Notes to Chapter 7

1. The petition and the replies to it by Lord Ripon and Chamberlain were printed in *Hong Kong Legislative Council Sessional Papers 1896*, pp. 423–48.
2. May to Colonial Office, 15 March 1914, CO 129/410, p. 5; Stubbs to Colonial Office, 29 July 1920, CO 129/462, pp. 122–31.
3. Caldecott to Colonial Office, 19 February 1936, CO 129/556/17, recommending the appointment of Kotewall to the Executive Council. From 1896 to 1916 Kotewall was a clerk in the Colonial Secretariat. This experience later enabled him to criticize the presentation of the Budget accounts with an insider's knowledge.
For an account of the Eurasian community in Hong Kong see Irene Cheng, *Clara Ho Tung: A Hong Kong Lady, Her Family and Her Times*, especially pp. xv–xvii, 24, and 27.
4. May to Colonial Office, 18 May 1913, CO 129/403, pp. 122–31.
5. *Hong Kong Hansard*, 26 February 1914, pp. 28–9, 30 July 1914, p. 79, 3 December 1914, p. 150. Colonial Office officials commented on May's account of Sir Kai's final appearance in the Legislative Council: 'The Hong Kong government have rather overdone it; they must be considerably afraid of him.' Minute on May to Colonial Office, 5 March 1914, CO 129/409, p. 410.
6. May to Colonial Office, 1 April 1912, CO 129/400, p. 259; 16 June 1913, CO 129/401, p. 360; 15 March 1914, CO 129/410, pp. 3–7.
7. Stubbs to Alston, 17 May 1921, CO 129/471, p. 601; Northcote to Colonial Office, 15 December 1937, CO 129/565/17.
8. Colonial Office to May, 27 March 1914, CO 129/409, p. 85.
9. Northcote to Colonial Office, 1 September 1939, CO 129/576/2.
10. Peel to Colonial Office, 30 December 1930, on the reappointment of Kotewall for a third term, CO 129/530/1.
11. *Hong Kong Hansard*, 23 December 1915, p. 98; 5 October 1916, p. 52.
12. May to Colonial Office, 18 December 1915, CO 129/425, pp. 616–35.
13. Stubbs to Colonial Office, 22 March 1920, CO 129/460, pp. 303–10. At the outbreak of the Second World War in September 1939 the commodore in command of the Royal Navy in Hong Kong was added to the Executive Council.
14. The petition, together with the Governor's dispatch on it and the Colonial Office reply, was published in *Hong Kong Legislative Council Sessional Papers 1916*, pp. 57–91.
15. Minutes on May to Colonial Office, 26 May 1916, CO 129/433, pp. 205–9.
16. May to Colonial Office, 19 September 1917, CO 129/443, p. 479.
17. The petition of 1894 had asked for an electorate composed of British subjects. But at that time the colony consisted of only Hong Kong island and the Kowloon peninsula and almost all the Chinese living there were migrants from Kwangtung.

The acquisition of the New Territories in 1898 brought in a large settled Chinese population, all of whom were compulsorily naturalized as British subjects.

18. Severn, OAG, to Colonial Office, 30 January 1919, CO 129/453, pp. 138–64.

19. Stubbs to Colonial Office, 29 July 1920, CO 129/462, pp. 122–32.

20. Chater to Colonial Office, 15 November 1920, CO 129/466, pp. 74–9.

21. *Hong Kong Hansard*, 3 March 1921, p. 17. *House of Commons Debates*, 7 June 1921, p. 1705.

22. Petition dated 16 March 1922, CO 129/478, pp. 346–58.

23. Minute by Beckett dated 8 May 1923 on Stubbs to Colonial Office, 14 March 1923, CO 129/479, pp. 469–76.

24. This was the view of the Colonial Secretary, as stated in *Hong Kong Hansard*, 18 October 1923, p. 152.

25. Enclosure in Clementi to Colonial Office, 6 March 1926, in *Confidential Print Eastern No. 144*, CO 882/11, pp. 68–70.

26. Clementi to Colonial Office, 29 May 1926, CO 129/492, pp. 585–93. The second Chinese to be knighted was Sir Boshan Wei Yuk in 1919. Sir Robert Ho Tung, knighted in 1915, was a Eurasian.

27. Clementi to Colonial Office, 24 June 1926, CO 129/493, pp. 83–8.

28. Colonial Office to Clementi, 8 November 1926, CO 129/495, pp. 408–9.

29. Guillemard to Colonial Office, 18 December 1920, CO 273/503; 6 July 1921, CO 273/510/39839, pp. 171–204.

30. Minute by Beckett, dated 14 September 1921, in CO 273/510/39839.

31. *Hong Kong Hansard*, 19 April 1928, p. 28. *Minutes of the Executive Council*, 12 April 1928, CO 131/75, p. 67. Clementi to Amery, 25 April 1928, CO 129/511/5.

32. Minute dated 8 October 1928 in CO 129/509/14, p. 18.

33. *Hong Kong Legislative Council Sessional Papers 1939*, p. 97.

34. *Hong Kong Hansard*, 24 January 1929, pp. 2–3; 13 October 1937, p. 127. The papers relating to the appointment of D'Almada and Dr Li are missing from the files of CO 129. Dr Li had previously been elected to the Sanitary Board in 1932; see G.B. Endacott, *Government and People in Hong Kong*, p. 160.

35. Clementi to Colonial Office, 6 March 1928, CO 129/510/11.

36. See G.B. Endacott, *Government and People in Hong Kong*, pp. 170–5.

37. Minute by Colonial Office Legal Adviser, 6 July 1920, CO 129/460, pp. 375–6.

38. Stubbs to Colonial Office, 14 April 1920, CO 129/460, pp. 377–9.

39. Commodore, China Station to Admiralty, 24 June 1940, CO 129/583/19.

40. G.B. Endacott, *Government and People in Hong Kong*, pp. 148–59. *Hong Kong Legislative Council Sessional Papers 1902*, pp. 637–8.

41. *Hong Kong Legislative Council Sessional Papers 1907*, pp. 185(3)–185(45).

42. May, OAG, to Colonial Office, 29 May 1907, CO 129/340, pp. 412–45.

43. 'Report on Public Health in Hong Kong' by A.R. Wellington, November 1930, CO 129/531/13, p. 26.

44. Memorandum enclosed with Peel to Colonial Office, 15 May 1935, CO 129/553/10. *Administrative Reports 1924*, M(1)16.

45. *Hong Kong Hansard*, 28 August 1924, pp. 60–70.

46. Memorandum of 15 May 1935, CO 129/553/10, p. 16.

47. CO 129/511/15, especially the minutes by Dr Stanton, the Colonial Office Medical Adviser. *Hong Kong Hansard*, 20 September 1928, p.70.

48. *Minutes of the Executive Council*, 31 October 1929, CO 131/78, p. 221.

49. Report in Peel to Colonial Office, 18 November 1930, CO 129/531/13.

50. Accounts of these complex changes are given in Peel's memorandum of 15 May 1935, CO 129/553/10, and *Hong Kong Legislative Council Sessional Papers 1937*, 'Memorandum on Changes in the Public Health Organization 1929 to 1937'

by A.R. Wellington. *Minutes of the Executive Council*, 18 August 1932, CO 131/87, p. 162.

51. Minutes by J.A. Calder, dated 6 August 1931 and 20 August 1932, in CO 129/531/13. 'Dr Wellington explained that he had received considerable help and sympathy from Sir C. Clementi, but that under Sir W. Peel the old regime of persistent obstruction and suspicion of the medical authorities had revived.'

52. See Section 11(2) of the Urban Council Ordinance 1935. Northcote to Dr O'Brien, Colonial Office, 13 August 1938, CO 129/566/2; 'There have been a number of instances in which the Director of Medical Services and the Medical Officers of Health have been over-ruled by the Chairman of the Urban Council on technical points.'

53. *Hong Kong Legislative Council Sessional Papers 1937*, 'Memorandum on Public Health Organization', p. 107.

54. See Wellington's Report, CO 129/531/13, pp. 9–12, and comments made by the Colonial Office on the annual *Administrative Reports*, 'Sanitation and Health Report', for example, that of 1926, CO 129/506/7.

55. Southorn, OAG, to Colonial Office, 31 July 1935, CO 129/553/10.

56. Confidential Appendix to the Report of the Retrenchment Commission, para. 35, in Peel to Colonial Office, 22 May 1931, CO 129/534/3. This proposal had earlier been raised by an unofficial member in the Legislative Council, but Stubbs quickly squashed the idea, *Hong Kong Hansard*, 3 November 1924, pp. 107 and 117.

57. On the post-war developments, see N.J. Miners, 'Plans for Constitutional Reform in Hong Kong, 1946–52', *China Quarterly*, No. 107, September 1986.

Notes to Chapter 8

1. W.W. Woods, *Mui Tsai in Hong Kong and Malaya, Report of Commission*, 5 January 1937, p. 124 (hereafter cited as *Woods Commission*).

2. Descriptions of the *mui tsai* system by its defenders and critics can be found in: Lau Chu-pak, 'Girl Slavery in Hong Kong', CO 129/467, pp. 250–2; E.R. Hallifax, 'The Hong Kong *Mui Tsai* System', *Colonial Office Confidential Print Eastern No. 137*, CO 882/10; speech by Chow Shou-son in *Hong Kong Hansard*, 8 February 1923, pp. 5–9; F.H. Loseby, 'Mui Tsai in Hong Kong', *Hong Kong Legislative Council Sessional Papers 1935*, pp. 195–282 (hereafter cited as *Loseby Committee*), also printed in Britain by HMSO, *Cmd. 5121* of 1936; the *Woods Commission*. See also M.H.A. Jaschok, 'A Social History of the *Mooi Jai* Institution in Hong Kong', unpublished Ph.D. thesis, 1981, School of Oriental and African Studies, University of London.

3. A '*sung tip*' with detailed explanations by the Secretary for Chinese Affairs is enclosed in Stubbs to Colonial Office, 19 May 1921, CO 129/467, pp. 515–26.

4. See, for example, the speech by Dr Yeung, reported in *Hong Kong Daily Press*, 2 August 1921, CO 129/468, pp. 592–4; Manifesto of the Anti-*Mui Tsai* Society, CO 129/478, pp. 318–20; H.L. Haslewood, 'Child Slavery under British Rule' in CO 129/473, p. 181.

5. Trafficking in children and young women for the purpose of prostitution was a criminal offence, but this did not apply to transfers of *mui tsai* for domestic service. The Hong Kong government admitted in one dispatch that some girls ostensibly purchased as *mui tsai* were in reality intended for prostitution, reply to League of Nations Questionnaire, 28 October 1921, CO 129/469, p. 237. However, the Hong Kong government always insisted that *mui tsai* were in a completely different category from prostitutes; see, for example, Clementi to Colonial Office, 16 May 1929, paragraph 9, CO 129/514/2.

6. See *Woods Commission*, pp. 133-6, and May to Colonial Office, 9 August 1918, CO 129/449, pp. 254-8.

7. Protection of Women and Girls Ordinance 1897, sec. 32, as amended in 1910. *Loseby Committee*, pp. 146-8.

8. May to Colonial Office, 9 August 1918, CO 129/449, p. 254. Statement by Hallifax at Colonial Office, 10 March 1921, CO 129/470, p. 343.

9. See, for example, the case of a *mui tsai* found serving a poor family living in a sampan, reported to the Colonial Office in a dispatch dated 7 January 1932, CO 129/539/4, p. 148.

10. The report by Russell is reproduced in *Loseby Committee*, pp. 235-46. For a full account of these discussions see *Woods Commission*, pp. 122-47.

11. Ward wrote to Appleton, Secretary of the General Federation of Trade Unions, who sent the letter on to the Secretary of State, 27 October 1917, CO 129/446, pp. 342-64.

12. May to Colonial Office, 9 August 1918, CO 129/449, pp. 251-9.

13. Minutes by Collins, 15 October 1918, and Fiddes, 18 October 1918, CO 129/449, p. 253.

14. Severn, OAG, to Colonial Office, 20 March 1919, CO 129/453, pp. 469-71.

15. Stubbs to Colonial Office, 10 July 1920, CO 129/461, pp. 418-20.

16. Colonial Office to Stubbs, 16 April 1920, enclosing three letters from Haslewood, CO 129/466 pp. 196-211. Stubbs to Colonial Office, 10 July 1920, CO 129/461, pp. 415-20.

17. Colonial Office to Stubbs, 28 September 1920, CO 129/461, p. 438; Stubbs to Colonial Office, 21 December 1920, CO 129/463, pp. 375-80.

18. Stubbs to Colonial Office, 27 July 1921, CO 129/468, pp. 422-6; 17 October 1921, CO 129/469, p. 198; Colonial Office to Stubbs, 13 October 1921, CO 129/473, p. 392.

19. Wedgwood to Churchill, 19 December 1921, CO 129/478, p. 315. Churchill's minute is at CO 129/478, p. 297. Churchill's statement to Parliament is in *House of Commons Debates*, 21 March 1922, pp. 214-15.

Colonial Office officials were unhappy at Churchill's abrupt reversal of previous policy. Two years later in a briefing for a new Secretary of State, J.H. Thomas, an official rationalized the decision as follows: 'We have taken in Hong Kong a big step which would never have been taken unless there had been an Anti-*Mui Tsai* Society in Hong Kong. It is no use pretending that the Chinese generally like the ordinance we have imposed; they generally acquiesce, but that is all. We have to be extremely careful not to go too fast and give an impression that we want to interfere recklessly in the private affairs of the Chinese. Any pressure to go faster should be resisted.' Minute by Beckett, 20 March 1924, CO 129/487, p. 148.

20. CO 129/478, pp. 312-13.

21. Telegram from Stubbs to Colonial Office, 16 March 1922, CO 129/474, p. 216.

22. Stubbs to Colonial Office, 28 March 1922, CO 129/474, pp. 299-301.

23. Stubbs to Colonial Office, 21 December 1920, CO 129/483, p. 376.

24. Stubbs to Colonial Office, 10 June 1922, with enclosures, CO 129/475, pp. 332-9. This dispatch was published in *Hong Kong Legislative Council Sessional Papers 1929*, pp. 202-10.

25. Telegrams from Severn, OAG, to Colonial Office, 5 and 9 September, CO 129/426, pp. 124 and 135.

26. Stubbs to Grindle (semi-official), 16 September 1922, CO 129/478, pp. 764-6.

27. Stubbs to Colonial Office, 24 January and 6 March 1923, CO 129/479, pp. 287-9 and 435-6. A detailed account of these manoeuvres can be found in C.T. Smith, 'The Chinese Church, Labour and Elites and the *Mui Tsai* Question in the

1920s', *Journal of the Hong Kong Branch of the Royal Asiatic Society*, Vol. 21, 1981, pp. 91-113.

28. *Hong Kong Hansard*, 28 December 1922, pp. 152-4, 8 February 1923, pp. 3-16, 15 February 1923, pp. 20-2.

29. Stubbs to Colonial Office, 6 March 1923, CO 129/479, pp. 435-9.

30. Stubbs to Grindle, 1 October 1922, CO 129/478, pp. 794-7.

31. Enclosure in Stubbs to Colonial Office, 30 May 1924, CO 129/484, pp. 400-1.

32. *Woods Commission*, pp. 39-54. *Loseby Committee*, p. 209. Report by Secretary for Chinese Affairs enclosed with Clementi to Colonial Office, 22 February 1929, CO 129/514/2.

D. MacDougall told me in an interview that one of the cadets who arrived in Hong Kong with him in 1928 acquired a *mui tsai* by purchase, but had to dispose of her very quickly in 1929 when registration was introduced.

Notes to Chapter 9

1. A copy of the Canton regulations was enclosed in Clementi to Colonial Office, 16 May 1929, CO 129/514/2.

2. *South China Morning Post*, 9 April 1927, in CO 129/514/2.

3. *South China Morning Post*, 22 October 1928; *Manchester Guardian*, 16 January 1929.

4. Clementi to Colonial Office, 22 February 1929, CO 129/514/2. This and other official dispatches of 1929 were published in *Hong Kong Legislative Council Sessional Papers 1929*, pp. 233-54.

5. *John Bull* magazine, 30 March 1930, copy in CO 129/514/2.

6. Amery to Clementi, 20 April 1929, CO 129/514/2, p. 137. Clementi had already sent a personal letter to Amery in amplification of his dispatch on 23 February 1929, in which he warned Amery that a storm of protest would arise throughout the colony if any drastic steps were taken, CO 129/514/2, p. 148A.

7. Clementi to Colonial Office, 16 May 1929, CO 129/514/2.

8. Minutes by Caine, 18 July 1929, Grindle, 24 July 1929, and Wilson, 25 July 1929; Colonial Office to Clementi, 22 August 1929, CO 129/514/2.

9. Minute by Ellis, dated 24 January 1931, in CO 129/532/3.

10. Peel to Colonial Office, 19 August 1931, CO 129/532/3.

11. *Administrative Reports 1929*, Appendix K, Report of Inspector-General of Police, p. K5.

12. Clementi to Colonial Office, 18 December 1929, CO 129/522/6.

13. Minute by Shiels dated 13 February 1930; Colonial Office to Clementi, 5 March 1930, CO 129/522/6.

14. *Hong Kong Weekly Press*, 2 May 1930; Peel to Colonial Office, 25 June 1930, CO 129/522/6, pp. 44-8.

15. Colonial Office to Peel, 19 August 1930, CO 129/522/6.

16. Meeting of the Anti-*Mui Tsai* Society reported in *Hong Kong Weekly Press*, 31 October 1930 and *South China Morning Post*, 27 October 1930; *House of Commons Debates*, 1930-31, Vol. 252, pp. 943-4, Speech by Dr Shiels; Colonial Office to Peel, 24 June 1931, CO 129/523/4; Peel to Colonial Office, 19 August 1931, CO 129/532/5.

17. See the account of the inspectors' work in *Woods Commission*, pp. 50, 54-7, and 64-5.

18. *Woods Commission*, pp. 57-60. In May 1934, 141 *mui tsai* were attending school, *Woods Commission*, p. 169. The Governor's report for the six-month period, June to November 1932, stated that 10 out of 40 prosecutions were instituted as a

result of complaints by *mui tsai*, Peel to Colonial Office, 4 January 1933, CO 129/543/2.

19. A summary of the number of *mui tsai* removed from the register up to May 1936 is given in *Woods Commission*, p. 60. Note by Secretary for Chinese Affairs, enclosed in Peel to Colonial Office, 15 October 1934, in *Confidential Print Eastern No. 169*, 'The Mui Tsai System in Hong Kong and Malaya', CO 882/16, pp. 28–9. Report of 31 May 1939 in CO 852/27/55019/5. Report of 31 May 1941 in CO 825/30/55019/5.

20. See CO 129/532/4, CO 129/532/5, CO 129/539/3, and CO 129/542/10.

21. Peel to Colonial Office, 5 May 1932, CO 129/539/4.

22. *Confidential Print Eastern No. 169*, CO 882/16, pp. 1–28.

23. *Loseby Committee*, pp. 195–282.

24. Hong Kong government replies to League of Nations Questionnaire, 16 January 1931, CO 129/533/10, p. 57.

25. Caldecott to Colonial Office, 18 March 1936, with enclosures, *Confidential Print Eastern No. 169*, CO 882/16, pp. 50–7.

26. Minute by Cowell, dated 13 March 1936, in CO 825/20/55019/2.

27. Caldecott to Colonial Office, 18 March 1936, especially paragraphs 3, 5, and 31; Caldecott to Maxwell, 13 April 1937, CO 825/22/55019/1/37; Colonial Office to Caldecott, 13 February 1936, CO 825/20/55019/1.

28. CO 825/21/55019/7; *Hong Kong Hansard*, 27 May 1936, pp. 118–31.

29. Minutes in CO 825/22/55019/1/37; Smith, OAG, to Colonial Office, 27 May 1937, CO 882/16, pp. 81–2.

30. See CO 825/22/55019/9/37, *passim*, and CO 882/16, pp. 63–78 and 87–90.

31. Mrs G.H. Forster to Ormsby-Gore, 2 June 1937, CO 882/16, pp. 78–81. Minutes on this letter in CO 825/23/55019/37, No. 36.

32. Shenton Thomas to Colonial Office, 26 September 1937, and Shenton Thomas to Ormsby-Gore, 27 September 1937, CO 882/16, pp. 83–6.

33. Minute by Gent, 14 October 1937, in CO 825/23/55019/2/37.

34. Colonial Office to Northcote, 6 December 1937, CO 882/16, p. 91.

35. Northcote to Gent, 26 November 1937, CO 825/22/55019/37. Northcote to Gent, 10 February 1938, CO 825/24/55019/1/38.

36. Northcote to Cowell, 20 October 1938, CO 825/25/55019/2/38.

37. The original text of the bill made the Secretary for Chinese Affairs the legal guardian of all girls whose parents had voluntarily parted with them for the purpose of adoption, or had received money for parting with them, and all such girls had to be registered with the Secretariat for Chinese Affairs (*Supplement to Hong Kong Government Gazette 1938*, p. 213). The bill as amended by the Legislative Council stated that: 'Whenever any person adopts as his own and obtains the custody of the child of another person, such child being a girl under the age of 21 years' the legal guardianship of the child was vested in the Secretary for Chinese Affairs and the adopter was required to register the child (sections 31 and 32 of the Protection of Women and Girls Ordinance, 1938, reproduced in CO 882/16, pp. 108–9).

38. Colonial Office to Northcote, 20 July 1938, CO 882/16, p. 125. The Secretary for Chinese Affairs sent a memorandum to the Colonial Office explaining the bill which was deliberately misleading, since he misquoted section 31 of the bill as: 'Whenever any person adopts as his own *or* obtains the custody...' (emphasis added); see Northcote to Colonial Office, 21 June 1938, with enclosure, CO 882/16, pp. 121–2.

39. Northcote to Colonial Office, 18 October 1938, CO 882/16, pp. 131–2; Northcote to Colonial Office, 28 February 1939, CO 882/16, pp. 134–5; Northcote to Cowell with enclosure, 23 March 1939, CO 882/16, pp. 135–6.

40. Minute by Goldsworthy on Governor's dispatch of 28 February 1939, CO 825/28/55019/1/39.

41. Northcote to Colonial Office, 18 October 1938, CO 882/16, pp. 131–2. Report on *mui tsai*, June to November 1938, in Northcote to Colonial Office, 25 February 1939, CO 825/27/55019/5/39.

42. Northcote to Colonial Office, 23 August 1939, containing *mui tsai* report, December 1938 to May 1939, CO 825/27/55019/5/39.

43. See the book written by the English woman appointed as Assistant Secretary for Chinese Affairs, Phyllis Harrop, *Hong Kong Incident*, pp. 42–53. Northcote to Colonial Office, 8 December 1938, CO 129/573/12.

44. Hawkins to Ruston, Colonial Office, 2 July 1946, CO 825/39/55019/46.

45. Protection of Women and Girls Amendment Ordinance, No. 17 of 1946, 20 September 1946.

46. *South China Sunday Post-Herald*, 15 July 1956.

47. Law Revision (Miscellaneous Repeals) Bill 1969, *Hong Kong Hansard*, 22 December 1969, p. 177.

48. Willis, a member of the Woods Commission, gave a scathing account of the Anti-*Mui Tsai* Society in a private letter to the Colonial Office, describing it as an insignificant group which was mainly concerned to annoy the established Chinese élite: 'I have never met so wet a lot of liars.' Willis to Gent, 6 March 1937, CO 825/22/55019/1/37.

Notes to Chapter 10

1. *Hong Kong Government Gazette*, 15 February 1873, p. 55.

2. *Hong Kong Legislative Council, Sessional Papers 1931*, pp. 102 and 111.

3. *Correspondence Relating to the Working of the Contagious Diseases Ordinances of the Colony of Hong Kong, C. 3093*, p. 21 (hereafter cited as *Correspondence, C. 3093*); also in *British Sessional Papers, House of Commons 1881*, Vol. LXV, p. 699.

4. Mr Labouchere to Governor Bowring, 27 August 1858, reproduced in *Report of the Commissioners Appointed to Inquire into the Working of the Contagious Diseases Ordinance 1867* (Hong Kong, Noronha, 1879), p. 207 (hereafter cited as *Report of the Commissioners*, 1879).

5. *Correspondence, C. 3093*, p. 22; also in *British Sessional Papers, House of Commons 1881*, Vol. LXV, p. 700.

6. For a full description of the system in operation in 1878 see *Report of the Commissioners*, 1879, Appendix, especially the evidence of C. Clementi Smith and A. Lister, pp. 1–8.

7. *Report of the Commissioners*, 1879, Appendix, p. 6. 'The examinations were the greatest punishment [the women] could have and the mere threat of sending them to examination was generally sufficient to keep them in order.' See also CO 129/259, pp. 132ff. for the situation in 1893.

8. Quoted by Governor Sir J. Pope Hennessy in a dispatch to the Earl of Kimberley, dated 13 November 1880, in *Correspondence, C. 3093*, p. 46; also in *British Sessional Papers, House of Commons 1881*, Vol. LXV, p. 724.

9. W.H. Marsh, OAG, to Secretary of State, 10 January 1887, in *Contagious Diseases Ordinances (Colonies), Copies of Correspondence, September 1887, H.C. 347*, pp. 7–12 (hereafter cited as *Contagious Diseases 1887, H.C. 347*); also in *British Sessional Papers, House of Commons 1887*, Vol. LVII, pp. 697–702.

10. Sir H.T. Holland to Governor of Hong Kong, 2 July 1887, in *Contagious Diseases 1887, H.C. 347*, pp. 53–4; also in *British Sessional Papers, House of Commons 1887*, Vol. LVII, pp. 743–4.

11. Sir W. Des Voeux to Lord Knutsford, 8 October 1888, with enclosures, in *Contagious Diseases Ordinances (Colonies), Copies of Correspondence, March 1889*,

H.C. 59, pp. 23–32 (hereafter cited as *Contagious Diseases 1889, H.C. 59*); also in *British Sessional Papers, House of Commons 1889*, Vol. LV, pp. 163–72.

12. Knutsford to Des Voeux, 30 November 1888 and 15 February 1889, in *Contagious Diseases 1889, H.C. 59*, pp. 33–4 and 39, and *British Sessional Papers, House of Commons 1889*, Vol. LV, pp. 173–4 and 204.

13. Knutsford to Des Voeux, 3 and 13 January 1890, in *Contagious Diseases Ordinances (Colonies), Copies of Correspondence, June 1890, H.C. 242*, pp. 30–7 and 43 (hereafter cited as *Contagious Diseases 1890, H.C. 242*); also in *British Sessional Papers, House of Commons 1890*, Vol. XLIX, pp. 50–7 and 63.

14. Des Voeux to Knutsford, 29 July 1889, in *Contagious Diseases 1890, H.C. 242*, pp. 19–20 and *British Sessional Papers, House of Commons 1890*, Vol. XLIX, pp. 39–40. Lord Ripon to Sir William Robinson, 17 March 1893, in *Contagious Diseases Ordinances (Colonies), Copy of Correspondence, 1894, H.C. 147*, pp.39–40 (hereafter cited as *Contagious Diseases 1894, H.C. 147*); also in *British Sessional Papers, House of Commons 1894*, Vol. LVII, pp. 39–40.

15. Knutsford to Des Voeux, 12 December 1890, and Des Voeux to Knutsford, 13 April 1891, in *Contagious Diseases 1894, H.C. 147*, pp. 26–31, and *British Sessional Papers, House of Commons 1894*, Vol. LVII, pp. 26–31.

16. See, for example, CO 129/218, pp. 487–8, letter to the Secretary of State from the National Association for the Repeal of the Contagious Diseases Act, 28 March 1884.

17. Ripon to Robinson, 17 March 1893, in *Contagious Diseases 1894, H.C. 147*, pp. 39–40, and *British Sessional Papers, House of Commons 1894*, Vol. LVII, pp. 39–40.

18. Robinson to Ripon, 17 June 1893, with enclosures, and Ripon to Robinson, 17 April 1894, in *Contagious Diseases 1894, H.C. 147*, pp. 46–52 and 56–7, and *British Sessional Papers, House of Commons 1894*, Vol. LVII, pp. 46–52 and 56–7.

19. See the tabulated returns for the Straits Settlements and Hong Kong in CO 129/286, pp. 86–7.

20. See *Correspondence Regarding the Measures to be Adopted for Checking the Spread of Venereal Disease, C. 9523*. Minute by Sir Edward Wingfield at CO 129/276, p. 132.

21. J. Chamberlain to Governor, Sir H.A. Blake, 11 May 1899, CO 882/6, p. 117.

22. Minute by J. Chamberlain, 25 January 1898, CO 129/276, p. 132.

23. This possibility had been mentioned earlier in an unpublished letter from the Attorney General; see minute in CO 129/286, p. 75, dated 18 March 1899.

24. Memorandum by the Secretary for Chinese Affairs, 4 June 1923, CO 129/480, pp. 254–9.

25. The following paragraphs are based on the memorandum by the Secretary for Chinese Affairs; a long description by Dr Wellington, Director of Medical and Sanitary Services, not dated, item 5 in CO 129/533/10 of 1931; and note by the Chief Justice, J.H. Kemp, dated 16 May 1931, item 3 in CO 129/533/10.

26. H. Macfarlane and G.E. Aubrey, 'Venereal Disease Among the Natives of Hong Kong', *The Caduceus, Journal of the Hong Kong University Medical Society*, Vol. 1, April 1922, pp. 22–7, quoted in CO 129/480, p. 260.

27. In CO 129/472, pp. 356–82, April 1921.

28. See CO 129/474, pp. 338–58, CO 129/484, pp. 257–8; CO 129/485, pp. 2–18 and 122–6.

29. See CO 129/472, pp. 603–5; CO 129/475, pp. 326–31; CO 129/483, pp. 66–75 and 156–70.

30. *Straits Settlements Legislative Council Sessional Papers 1923*, Report of the Venereal Diseases Committee, 17 December 1923, pp. C286–327; CO 882/11,

Confidential Print Eastern No. 147, Correspondence 1923–1925 Relating to Social Hygiene in Singapore.

31. *First Report of the Advisory Committee on Social Hygiene*, August 1925, *Cmd. 2501*. See also *Report of a Committee Appointed by the Secretary of State for the Colonies to Examine and Report on Straits Settlements Ordinance No. 15 of 1927*, March 1929, *Cmd. 3294*.

32. CO 129/522/3.

33. Peel, *Notes*, pp. 138 and 146. *House of Commons Debates*, 27 June 1930, p. 1500, speech by Dr D. Shiels.

34. Peel to Passfield, 22 August 1930, CO 129/522/3.

35. Peel to Passfield, 9 June 1931, with enclosure, CO 129/522/10. Kemp had originally been appointed to Hong Kong as a cadet officer. He was Attorney General for 15 years from 1915 to 1930.

36. For example in 1908; see CO 129/352, pp. 416–19 and *Minutes of the Executive Council*, 26 March 1909 and 1 March 1910.

37. *Minutes of the Executive Council*, 2 July 1931.

38. Secretary of State to Peel, 29 September 1931, CO 129/533/10.

39. *Hong Kong Hansard*, 22 October 1931, p. 193.

40. *Minutes of the Executive Council*, 6 December 1934.

41. Southorn, OAG, to Cunliffe-Lister, 18 July 1932, CO 129/532/3, p. 133.

42. *Minutes of the Executive Council*, 25 April 1935.

43. M.J. Abbott, *Report of the Committee Constituted in Accordance with the Directions of the Governor* (Hong Kong, Noronha, 1939), p. 19 (hereafter cited as *Abbott Report*). (Copy available in Hong Kong Secretariat Library, Ref. CSO 5661/32.)

44. *Administration Reports*, 1932 and 1939, Reports of the Medical Department.

45. *Abbott Report*, p. 5.

46. Replies by the Hong Kong Government to a Questionnaire sent by the League of Nations Commission of Enquiry into the Traffic in Women and Children in the Far East, in CO 129/533/10, p. 6. Interview with Mr R.R. Todd who first arrived in Hong Kong as a cadet in 1925 and served in the Secretariat for Chinese Affairs before 1930.

47. For the results of the system before 1894 see minute in CO 129/259, p. 129, dated 23 November 1893, quoting the views of the Registrar General.

Notes to Chapter 11

1. For further details see I.C.Y. Hsü, *The Rise of Modern China*, pp. 220–47.

2. Hsü, *The Rise of Modern China*, p. 267.

3. J.T. Pratt, *Memorandum Respecting the Opium Problem in the Far East*, pp. 3–4, in FO 415/26; also in CO 825/4/63038; (cited hereafter as Pratt, *Memorandum*).

4. See D.E. Owen, *British Opium Policy in China and India*, pp. 324–54.

5. Eric Lewis, *Black Opium*, pp. 101–2. *Foreign Office Confidential Print, Further Correspondence Respecting Opium*, FO 415, Part III, pp. 102 and 194. This will be cited hereafter as FO 415, *Opium*.

A facsimile reproduction of the whole of FO 415 has been published in six volumes, under the title *The Opium Trade 1910–1941*.

6. M. Perham, *Lugard: the Years of Authority*, p. 320.

7. Owen, *British Opium Policy*, pp. 335–7; Pratt, *Memorandum*, p. 4.

8. G.B. Endacott, *A History of Hong Kong*, pp. 188–94 and 213–14.

9. *Hong Kong Legislative Council Sessional Papers 1909*, 'Memorandum Regarding

the Restriction of Opium in Hong Kong and China' by F.D. Lugard, p. 26. Hereafter this will be cited as Lugard, *Memorandum*.

10. Endacott, *A History of Hong Kong*, p. 214; Lugard, *Memorandum*, pp. 30–2; *Confidential Print, Eastern No. 63, Correspondence on the Consumption of Opium in Hong Kong and the Straits Settlements 1883–1896*, CO 882/5.

11. Lugard, *Memorandum*, pp. 30–1; *Hong Kong Hansard*, 28 May 1908, p. 50.

12. J. Rowntree, *The Imperial Drug Trade*, pp. 165–76.

13. Lugard to Colonial Office, 11 December 1908, CO 129/349, pp. 395–8.

14. May, OAG, to Colonial Office, 15 May 1907, CO 129/340, pp. 355–72.

15. Lugard, *Memorandum*, p. 27.

16. *House of Commons Debates*, 6 May 1908, Vol. 188, pp. 341–5. Lugard to Colonial Office, 6 May 1908, CO 129/347, pp. 220–5.

17. Lugard to Colonial Office, 13 June 1908, CO 129/347, pp. 492–502, and 27 October 1908, CO 129/349, pp. 90–116.

18. CO 129/349, p. 88; Jordan to Grey, 12 October 1909, FO 371/616.

19. Minute dated 5 December 1908, CO 129/349, pp. 86–9. Perham, *Lugard: the Years of Authority*, p. 331.

20. Lugard to Colonial Office, 13 June 1908, CO 129/347, pp. 492–501, and 27 October 1908, CO 129/349, pp. 90–116.

21. *Hong Kong Hansard*, 28 May 1908, pp. 46–52, 24 September 1908, pp. 116–19.

22. Lugard to Colonial Office, 13 June 1908, and minutes on this dispatch, CO 129/347, pp. 492–501.

23. Minute dated 3 December 1908, CO 129/349, p. 860.

24. Lugard to Colonial Office, 13 June 1908, CO 129/347, p. 499, 27 October 1980, CO 129/349, p. 103, and 12 December 1908, CO 129/349, p. 228. Colonial Office to Lugard, 8 January 1909, CO 129/349, pp. 76–119.

25. Lugard to Colonial Office, 19 April 1909, CO 129/356, pp. 80–5.

26. Colonial Office Memorandum in CO 129/386, pp. 44–6.

27. Jordan to Grey, 28 January 1911, 19 April 1911, 3 March 1911, in FO 415, *Opium, Part III*, pp. 48, 64, 140, and 168.

28. *House of Commons Debates*, 26 July 1911, p. 2015. FO 415, *Opium, Part II*, p. 26.

29. David Sassoon and Co. to Foreign Office, 14 June 1910, FO 415, *Opium, Part I*, p. 73; FO 415, *Opium, Part II, passim*.

30. FO 415, *Opium, Part II*, pp. 15, 26, 91, and 110; FO 415, *Opium, Part III*, pp. 2, 3, and 15.

31. FO 415, *Opium, Part III*, pp. 168ff.; FO 415, *Opium, Part IV*, pp. 53–5.

32. FO 415, *Opium, Part IV*, pp. 4, 8, and 10; *House of Commons Debates*, 30 July 1912, p. 1939.

33. Pratt, *Memorandum*, pp. 9–10; FO 415, *Opium, Part V*, pp. 56, 61, and 132.

34. FO 415, *Opium, Part VI*, p. 142; FO 415, *Opium, Part VII*, pp. 9 and 88.

35. FO 415, *Opium, Part V*, p. 151; FO 415, *Opium, Part VI*, p. 76; CO 129/394, p. 32.

36. FO 415, *Opium, Part VI*, pp. 150–2; *House of Commons Debates*, 7 May 1913, pp. 2150–94.

37. *House of Commons Debates*, 30 July 1912, p. 1939.

38. Pratt, *Memorandum*, pp. 5–6; FO 415, *Opium, Part V*, pp. 2–53.

39. Lugard to Harcourt, 6 January 1912, FO 415, *Opium, Part V*, pp. 4–5.

40. May to Colonial Office, 2 May 1912, CO 129/390, pp. 26–9, and 12 July 1912, CO 129/391, pp. 75–81.

41. Lugard to Colonial Office, 21 November 1912, CO 129/393, p. 245, 21 January 1913, CO 129/399, p. 212, and 27 March 1913, CO 129/400, p. 196.

In fact the farmer boiled 1,113 chests in 1912, but when this discrepancy in the opium statistics for 1912 was noticed by the Colonial Office May 'corrected' the figures by allocating the surplus chests to the previous year. See May to Colonial Office, 24 June 1914, CO 129/411, pp. 422–6.

42. Minute by Collins, 16 July 1912; Colonial Office to May, 20 July 1912, CO 129/391, pp. 75–80.

43. The Straits Settlements had set up a government opium monopoly in 1910 following the report of the local 1908 Opium Commission. See Cheng U Wen, 'Opium in the Straits Settlements, 1867–1910', *Journal of South-East Asian History*, Vol. 2 (1961), pp. 83–8. The government monopoly system had previously been adopted in the Netherlands East Indies.

44. CO 129/391, pp. 366 and 388; CO 129/393, pp. 241 and 415; CO 129/394, p. 116; CO 129/399, pp. 212 and 309–11.

45. May to Colonial Office, 5 June 1913, CO 129/401, pp. 271–84.

46. Harcourt to Taylor, 17 October 1913, CO 129/408, p. 396.

47. May to Colonial Office, 7 April 1914, CO 129/410, pp. 265–70, and 23 June 1914, CO 129/411, pp. 417–19.

48. May to Colonial Office, 10 April 1915, CO 129/421, pp. 380–2; *Administrative Reports 1914*.

49. *Hong Kong Hansard*, 6 November 1914, pp. 130 and 138.

50. The sources for Table 9 are as follows: opium sales for the years 1914 to 1919 are from the Governor's dispatches to London in CO 129; thereafter figures are given in the annual Hong Kong *Administrative Reports*, 'Report of the Superintendent of Imports and Exports'; the gross revenue of the monopoly and the total government revenue are from the annual *Hong Kong Blue Book*; the direct costs of the monopoly are from the Governor's dispatches of 1914–17, 1922, 1933, and 1934; for other years, from *Revised Estimates of the Hong Kong Government*. These costs were calculated in accordance with a formula agreed between the Colonial Office and the War Office in 1914 for the purpose of assessing Hong Kong's military contribution to the cost of the garrison. They cover only the cost of raw opium (by far the largest item), boiling, packaging, and retailing. The costs of the monopoly as calculated for the annual reports to the League of Nations from 1933 onwards, *Report of the Government of Hong Kong on the Traffic in Prepared Opium*, include charges for the police, the prisons, the Preventive Service, hospitals, pensions, and so on, which enabled the Hong Kong government to claim that the monopoly was running at a heavy loss. Different figures are given in *Hong Kong Legislative Council Sessional Papers 1929*, p. 118. All Hong Kong government files for the period before 1941 were destroyed during the Japanese occupation. Consequently the history of the opium monopoly has to be written on the basis of the statistics published by the Hong Kong government at the time, and what was privately communicated in dispatches to London.

51. Opium Report for 1915, May to Colonial Office, 18 May 1916, CO 129/433, p. 65.

52. May to Colonial Office, with enclosures, 25 January 1918, CO 129/447, pp. 327–30.

53. May to Colonial Office, 18 April 1914, CO 129/440, p. 330; 9 November 1915, CO 129/425, p. 185.

54. Annual *Administrative Reports*, 1914–20; Stubbs to Colonial Office, 13 July 1921, CO 129/468, p. 296.

55. FO 415, *Opium, Parts VII and VIII, passim*, especially *Opium, Part VII*, p. 62, and *Opium, Part VIII*, pp. 12 and 48–9.

56. FO 415, *Opium, Part VIII*, pp. 7, 51, and 148.

57. Jordan to Grey with enclosures, 15 May 1915, FO 415, *Opium, Part IX*, pp. 20–5.

58. FO 415, *Opium, Part IX*, pp. 30–3; FO 415, *Opium, Part X*, pp. 1–6.

59. May to Colonial Office with enclosures, 30 November 1915, CO 129/425, pp. 363–75.

60. May to Colonial Office, 13 December 1915, CO 129/425, pp. 516–18.

61. May to Colonial Office, 2 May 1917, CO 129/442, pp. 153–6.

62. FO 415, *Opium, Part X*, p. 16; FO 415, *Opium, Part XI*, p. 13; CO 129/434, pp. 641–4; CO 129/435, p. 313.

63. FO 415, *Opium, Part XIII*, pp. 5–7 and 20–1, dispatches by Sir John Jordan to Foreign Office, 5 December 1918 and 29 January 1919.

64. FO 415, *Opium, Part XV*, p. 140, Stubbs to Colonial Office, 7 March 1921.

Notes to Chapter 12

1. FO 415, *Opium, Part XIII*, p. 13.

2. FO 415, *Opium, Part XV*, pp. 2, 44, and 66–7.

3. Minute by Collins, 20 February 1919, on CO 129/450, p. 368.

4. Jordan to Foreign Office, 30 December 1918, 29 January 1919, and 4 March 1919, in FO 415, *Opium, Part XIII*, pp. 9 and 21 and FO 415, *Opium, Part XIV*, pp. 3–4.

5. Severn, OAG, to Colonial Office, 25 September 1919, CO 129/455, pp. 416–21 and 435–6.

6. Stubbs to Colonial Office, 15 October 1919, CO 129/456, pp. 86–9. The repurchase of dross had ceased some years before the League of Nations Commission visited Hong Kong in 1930 (*League of Nations Commission of Enquiry into the Control of Opium Smoking*, Vol. II, p. 356). The Hong Kong government claimed that repurchasing dross was merely subsidizing smuggling, since it was impossible to distinguish the dross of monopoly opium from smuggled opium, CO 825/11/83003, minutes of meeting of 28 July 1931.

7. *Hong Kong Hansard*, 30 October 1919, p. 112.

8. Stubbs to Colonial Office, 6 November 1919, CO 129/456, pp. 178–9.

9. Foreign Office to Colonial Office, 2 December 1920, CO 129/465, pp. 123–43. FO 415, *Opium, Part XIV*, pp. 51–2.

10. Colonial Office to Foreign Office, 5 January 1921, FO 415, *Opium, Part XV*, pp. 4–5.

11. FO 415, *Opium, Part XV*, pp. 51–2 and CO 129/472, pp. 244–53. Cabinet Minutes 8(21) of 18 February 1921, Conclusion 2(b).

12. FO 415, *Opium, Part XV*, p. 29. For reports of renewed opium-growing in China, see FO 415, *Opium, Parts XIV, XV*, and *XVI*, *passim*.

13. FO 415, *Opium, Part XV*, pp. 30–1. Letter from Sir F. Aglen to Commissioner of Customs, 17 August 1921, FO 415, *Opium, Part XVI*, pp. 123–4.

14. See, for example, *Hong Kong Legislative Council Sessional Papers 1924*, 'Report of the Hong Kong Opium Committee', p. 59: 'Since the earliest days of the opium question in China the principal concern of the provincial governments has been to eradicate not the opium habit but the Indian opium habit and the failure to attain this end until India cooperated may be attributed to the fact that public taste vastly prefers the Indian to the home grown drug.'

15. Stubbs to Colonial Office, enclosing table of opium seizures for the period 1917–20, 7 March 1921, CO 129/467, pp. 227–30. Stubbs to Collins (personal), 13 September 1922, CO 129/478, p. 755.

16. May to Colonial Office, 25 February 1918, CO 129/447, pp. 328–30; FO 415, *Opium, Part XVI*, pp. 79–80.

17. *Minutes of the Executive Council*, 30 June 1921, CO 131/60.

18. Stubbs to Colonial Office, 17 February 1922, FO 415, *Opium, Part XVII*, pp. 63-5.

19. *Administrative Reports 1922*, Report of Superintendent of Imports and Exports 1922, p. E2 and *Administrative Reports 1923*, pp. E2-4. Memorandum by Paskin, April 1923, CO 129/483, p. 295.

20. FO 415, *Opium, Part XVIII*, pp. 15-16, 31, and 43-5. Memorandum by Paskin, CO 129/483, pp. 294-8. Stubbs to Collins, 13 September 1922, CO 129/478, pp. 752-8.

21. Severn, OAG, to Colonial Office, 14 September 1922, and correspondence between Delevingne and Grindle, CO 129/476, pp. 180-97.

22. Memorandum from Colonial Office, 10 February 1921, CO 129/472, p. 246. Minute by Collins, CO 129/472, p. 265. In a private letter to Leo Amery, Sir L.N. Guillemard, Governor of the Straits Settlements, referred to 'ignorant enthusiasts like Delevingne whom I regard as a crank', CO 825/1/30811 of 1927. See also the strong criticism of the Home Office and Delevingne in the Colonial Office memorandum to the Cabinet of 8 May 1927, CO 825/1/30811.

23. CO 129/478, pp. 14-24.

24. Delevingne to Grindle, 28 April 1923, CO 129/483, pp. 325-46. Also in *Confidential Print Eastern No. 155, Correspondence 1923-1931 Relating to Opium*, CO 882/11. This will be cited hereafter as *CP Eastern No. 155*.

25. *CP Eastern No. 155*, pp. 2-4 and 6-8.

26. FO 415, *Opium, Part XIX*, pp. 59-61; FO 415, *Opium, Part XX*, pp. 2-12.

27. *Report of Committee on the Traffic in Opium to the League of Nations Assembly*, 26 September 1923, in CO 129/483, pp. 225-7.

28. *Hong Kong Legislative Council Sessional Papers 1924*, Report of the Hong Kong Opium Committee, pp. 59-64; see also *CP Eastern No. 155*, pp. 22-7.

29. Stubbs to Colonial Office, 16 May 1923, *CP Eastern No. 155*, pp. 6-8; CO 129/480, p. 114.

30. *CP Eastern No. 155*, pp. 34-7, 41-4, and 48-56.

31. *CP Eastern No. 155*, pp. 54 and 60-1.

32. Delevingne's full report on the conferences, FO 415, *Opium, Part XXII*, pp. 16-55. See also an American denunciation of the 1925 conferences, J.P. Gavit, *Opium* (Routledge, London, 1925).

33. *CP Eastern No. 155*, pp. 89-91.

34. Stubbs to Colonial Office, 26 July 1923, *CP Eastern No. 155*, p. 6. *Administrative Reports 1923*, p. E2.

35. *CP Eastern No. 155*, pp. 154-61. FO 415, *Opium, Part XXIII*, pp. 1-8.

36. Colonial Office to Hong Kong and Straits Settlements, 25 January 1926; *CP Eastern No. 155*, p. 160.

37. Statement by McEldery at the Interdepartmental Opium Committee, 31 October 1927, *CP Eastern No. 155*, p. 131.

38. *CP Eastern No. 155*, p. 133.

39. *CP Eastern No. 155*, p. 100; *Administrative Reports 1927*, p. E6.

40. Clementi to Colonial Office, 6 and 7 October 1927 and 12 January 1928, *CP Eastern No. 155*, pp. 126, 133, and 137-45. The original correspondence about Clementi's experimental price reduction is in CO 129/506/30236 and CO 129/510/52836.

41. Telegram, Colonial Office to OAG, Hong Kong, 15 October 1927. Minutes on Hong Kong telegram of 7 October 1927, CO 129/506/30236.

42. *CP Eastern No. 155*, pp. 126-7 and 130-2. Memoranda of the Cabinet in CO 129/506/3. Cabinet meeting 57 of 1927, conclusion 11.

43. Clementi to Colonial Office, 12 December 1927, *CP Eastern No. 155*, pp. 155-6.

44. Clementi to Colonial Office, 3 April 1929, *CP Eastern No. 155*, pp. 152-3; minutes on this dispatch in CO 129/516/5; *Hong Kong Legislative Council Sessional Papers 1929*, 'Memorandum on the Use of Opium in Hong Kong', pp. 263-72.

45. See minutes by S. Caine, 16 July, W. Ellis, 16 August, S. Wilson, 19 August, and W. Lunn, 19 August 1929, in CO 129/516/5.

46. Peel to Colonial Office, 12 November 1930, CO 129/520/8.

47. *League of Nations Commission of Enquiry into the Control of Opium-Smoking* in the Far East (Geneva, League of Nations, 1930), 3 volumes. Hereafter cited as *League Commission*.

48. *League Commission*, Vol. I, pp. 90 and 140, and Vol. II, pp. 350-3.

49. *League Commission*, Vol. II, p. 348. *Administrative Reports 1924*, p. E2.

50. Peel to Colonial Office, 13 May 1931, paragraph 9 of enclosure, in *Colonial Office Confidential Print Eastern No. 160, Papers on Opium Conference Bangkok 1931*, CO 882/12, p. 17 (hereafter cited as *CP Eastern No. 160*).

51. *CP Eastern No. 160*, pp. 12-19. Original in CO 825/9/83014.

52. Report on the conference by Delevingne, *CP Eastern No. 160*, pp. 43-54; also in FO 415, *Opium, Part XXIX*, pp. 1-18.

53. *CP Eastern No. 160*, pp. 63-5, 74-5, and 77-8.

54. *League Commission*, Vol. II, p. 51. Memorandum by Lloyd dated 25 July 1932, CO 825/15/92881.

55. *League Commission*, Vol. II, p. 53; Peel to Colonial Office, 22 May 1933, *CP Eastern No. 160*, p. 75.

56. *Administration Reports 1933*, p. E5. *Report of the Government of Hong Kong for the Calendar Year 1933 on the Traffic in Opium*, pp. 1 and 4. Peel to Colonial Office, 5 April 1934, *Confidential Print Eastern No. 171, Opium Papers 1934-40*, CO 882/18, pp. 1-5 (hereafter cited as *CP Eastern No. 171*).

57. *Report of the Government of Hong Kong for 1933 on the Traffic in Opium*, pp. 5, 9, and 10.

58. *CP Eastern No. 171*, pp. 1-5.

59. Minutes on dispatch of 22 May 1933 in CO 825/18/34027/1. The quoted minute is by Cowell and is dated 9 August 1934.

60. Colonial Office to Peel, 20 February 1935, *CP Eastern No. 171*, pp. 18-19.

61. *Administration Reports 1935*, p. E2.

62. Caldecott to Colonial Office, 14 January 1936, CO 825/20/55002. *Report of the Government of Hong Kong on the Traffic in Prepared Opium*, 1935 and 1936.

63. *Report on the Traffic in Prepared Opium*, 1937, pp. 4 and 5. *Administration Reports 1937*, pp. E3 and E4.

64. International Labour Office of the International Labour Organization, *Opium and Labour, Report of a Documentary Enquiry*, p. 36. Colonial Office comments on the Report are in CO 825/19/1935.

65. *CP Eastern No. 171*, pp. 33-4 and 40-6.

66. *Administration Reports 1938*, pp. E3 and E5. *Administration Reports 1939*, p. E3. *Report on the Traffic in Prepared Opium*, 1939.

67. Memorandum by Lloyd, 25 July 1932, and letter by Delevingne, CO 825/15/92881.

68. Northcote to Colonial Office, 3 November 1939, CO 825/27/55001/39.

69. Gent to Northcote, 2 December 1939, CO 825/27/55001/39.

70. Northcote to Gent, 13 January 1940, CO 825/29/55001/40.

71. Northcote to Colonial Office, 11 May 1940; Northcote to OAG, Straits Settlements, 15 May 1940; memorandum of discussion by Controller of Customs, Straits Settlements, 6 June 1940. All in CO 825/29/55006/40.

72. Colonial Office to Governor, Straits Settlements, 5 May 1940; Colonial Office to Treasury, 15 August 1940; and correspondence and minutes in CO 825/29/55006/1/40.

73. Smith, OAG, to Colonial Office, 5 July 1940, CO 825/29/55006/2/40.

74. Details taken from Colonial Office Eastern Register (CO 872) of file 55006/41 'Destroyed Under Statute'.

75. See CO 825/30/55006/3 of 1943: 'Opium: Post War Policy' for this and the following paragraph.

Notes to Chapter 13

1. The only exception to this generalization occurred in December 1935. Caldecott had been allowed to impose a cut in all public service salaries from January 1936. He then requested permission to pay European officers whose salaries were denominated in sterling for the month of December at the rate of HK$12 = £1, instead of the actual Treasury rate of HK$14 = £1. In effect Caldecott was proposing to impose the salary levy one month earlier by using a fictitious rate of exchange. This request was refused, but Caldecott sent a further telegram asking for the decision to be reconsidered in view of the colony's impending financial deficit. This plea was rejected by the Permanent Under-Secretary, Maffey, on his own responsibility on 13 December, and the Governor was so informed. The decision had to reach Hong Kong by 15 December in order that the salary slips for December could be prepared, so presumably Maffey decided that the time was too short to consult the minister. CO 129/555/14.

2. C. Parkinson, *The Colonial Office From Within, 1909–1945*, p. 142.

3. Minute by Ellis, dated 7 March 1930, in CO 129/524/6, p. 3. A similar viewpoint is expressed in B.C. Roberts, *Labour in the Tropical Territories of the Commonwealth*, pp. 171–81.

4. CO 129/399, pp. 185–95. In his original dispatch May recommended the promotion of Wodehouse to the vacant position of Deputy Superintendent of Police, but doubted his ability to act as head of the police force; so he put forward his name 'on the understanding that recommendations which may be made by me involving his supersession in the acting appointment of Captain Superintendent of Police will not be overruled'. This was considered to be an attempt to bargain with the Secretary of State over his prerogative to make any appointment he chose. May was obliged to send a humble letter of apology to Harcourt.

5. Circular dispatches of 6 November 1923, CO 854/59; 6 August 1930, CO 854/77; 17 September 1930, CO 854/78; 2 April 1931, CO 854/80; 16 May 1931, CO 854/81; and 30 June 1938, CO 854/109.

6. Circular dispatches of 26 April 1915, CO 854/51; 14 December 1928, CO 854/70; and 18 January 1939, CO 854/112.

7. *Minutes of the Executive Council*, 12 June 1919, 24 July 1919, and 25 March 1920; *House of Commons Debates*, 20 December 1920, pp. 1328–9; CO 129/465, pp. 307–11; CO 129/468, p. 114; *Hong Kong Legislative Council Sessional Papers 1921*, pp. 119–41, 'The Industrial Employment of Children'; CO 129/469, pp. 315–29; CO 129/476, pp. 244–52.

8. Minute by H.G. Bushe, 28 May 1919, CO 129/454, pp. 50–132. The reference to the Stuarts is to the practice of James I (1603–25) in creating monopolies in certain items of trade by use of the royal prerogative and granting them to court favourites or selling them to augment royal revenues.

9. Stubbs to Colonial Office, 14 July 1920, CO 129/461, pp. 460–7. Further petition by the Tai Yau Steam Launch Company, 2 June 1922, CO 129/475, pp. 248–92. Minutes on Severn, OAG, to Colonial Office, 6 October 1922, CO 129/476, pp. 274–82.

Bibliography

Official Papers at the Public Record Office, London

Cabinet Papers
  CAB 23, Minutes of Cabinet Meetings (1916 onwards).
Colonial Office
  CO 129, Hong Kong, Original Correspondence.
  CO 131, Minutes of the Hong Kong Executive Council.
  CO 133, Hong Kong Blue Books (annual digest of statistics).
  CO 273, Straits Settlements, Original Correspondence.
  CO 323, General Correspondence.
  CO 349, Hong Kong, Register of Correspondence.
  CO 825, Eastern, Original Correspondence (1927 onwards).
  CO 852, Economic, Original Correspondence (1935 onwards).
  CO 854, Circular Dispatches.
  CO 872, Eastern, Register of Correspondence.
  CO 882, Confidential Print, Eastern.
Foreign Office
  FO 371, Political Correspondence (1906 onwards).
  FO 415, Confidential Print, Correspondence Respecting Opium
    (1910–1941).

Private Papers at Rhodes House Library, Oxford

Sir Alexander Grantham, Transcript of Recorded Interview.
Sir Frederick Lugard's Papers.
Sir Matthew Nathan's Papers.
Sir William Peel, Notes Concerning His Colonial Service 1897–1935.
Sir Claud Severn's Papers.

Hong Kong Government Serial Publications

Administrative Reports for the Year —— (called Administration Reports
    after 1931).
Colonial Reports—Annual, Hong Kong (London, His Majesty's Stationery
    Office).
Colony of Hong Kong: Estimates of Revenue and Expenditure for the Year
    ——.
Hong Kong Blue Book for the Year ——.
The Hong Kong Civil Service List for —— (annually).
Hong Kong Government Gazette.

Hong Kong Hansard, Reports of the Meetings of the Legislative Council.
Hong Kong Legislative Council Sessional Papers (annually).
Report of the Government of Hong Kong for the Calendar Year —— on the Traffic in Opium and Dangerous Drugs (1930–1939).
Report of the Government of Hong Kong for the Calendar Year —— on the Traffic in Prepared Opium (1934–1939).

Books, Articles, and Reports

Abbott, M.J., *Report of the Committee Constituted in Accordance with the Directions of H.E. the Governor Contained in his Letter dated 9 April 1938* (Hong Kong, Noronha, 1939).

Allen, J. de Vere, 'Malayan Civil Service, 1874–1941: Colonial Bureaucracy/Malayan Elite', *Comparative Studies in Society and History*, Vol. 12, 1970, pp. 149–87.

Amery, L.S., *My Political Life, Volume Two, War and Peace 1914–1929* (London, Hutchinson, 1953).

Bailey, S.H., *The Anti Drug Campaign, An Experiment in International Control* (London, King & Son, 1935).

British Parliamentary Papers, China (Shannon, Ireland, Irish Universities Press, 1971).

British Sessional Papers, House of Commons (E.L. Erickson, editor) (New York, Readex Microprint, 1967).

Butters, H.R., 'Report on Labour and Labour Conditions in Hong Kong', *Hong Kong Legislative Council Sessional Papers 1939*, pp. 103–68.

Carland, John M., *The Colonial Office and Nigeria, 1898–1914* (London, Macmillan, 1985).

Chan, F. Gilbert, 'An Alternative to Kuomintang–Communist Collaboration: Sun Yat-sen and Hong Kong January–June 1923', *Modern Asian Studies*, Vol. 13, 1979, pp. 127–39.

Cheng, Irene, *Clara Ho Tung: A Hong Kong Lady, Her Family and Her Times* (Hong Kong, Chinese University Press, 1976).

Cheng, T.C., 'Chinese Unofficial Members of the Legislative and Executive Councils in Hong Kong up to 1941', *Journal of the Hong Kong Branch of the Royal Asiatic Society*, Vol. 9, 1969, pp. 7–30.

Cheng U Wen, 'Opium in the Straits Settlements, 1867–1910', *Journal of South-East Asian History*, Vol. 2, 1961, pp. 63–88.

Chung Lu-cee, Rosemarie, 'A Study of the 1925–6 Canton-Hong Kong Strike and Boycott' (unpublished MA dissertation, University of Hong Kong, 1969).

Coates, Austin, *A Mountain of Light* (Hong Kong, Heinemann, 1977).

Colonial Office, *Colonial Regulations, being Regulations for His Majesty's Colonial Service* (London, His Majesty's Stationery Office, 1934).

——*Regulations for His Majesty's Colonial Services* (London, His Majesty's Stationery Office, 1928).

Constantine, Stephen, *The Making of British Colonial Development Policy 1914–1940* (London, Frank Cass, 1984).

Contagious Diseases Ordinances (Colonies). Copies of Correspondence or Extracts therefrom relating to the Repeal of Contagious Diseases Ordinances in the Crown Colonies. H.C. 347 (London, Colonial Office, 1887).

Contagious Diseases Ordinances (Colonies). Copies of Correspondence or Extracts therefrom relating to the Repeal of Contagious Diseases Ordinances in the Crown Colonies. H.C. 59 (London, Colonial Office, 1889).

Contagious Diseases Ordinances (Colonies). Copies of Correspondence or Extracts therefrom relating to the Repeal of Contagious Diseases Ordinances in the Crown Colonies. H.C. 242 (London, Colonial Office, 1890).

Contagious Diseases Ordinances (Colonies). Copy of Correspondence which has taken place since that comprised in the Paper presented to the House of Commons in 1890 (H.C. 242) relating to the Repeal or Enactment of Contagious Diseases Ordinances in the Colonies. H.C. 147 (London, Her Majesty's Stationery Office, 1894).

Correspondence Regarding the Measures to be Adopted for Checking the Spread of Venereal Disease: Ceylon, Hong Kong and Straits Settlements (London, Her Majesty's Stationery Office, C.9523, 1899).

Correspondence Relating to the Mui-Tsai Question, *Hong Kong Legislative Council Sessional Papers 1929*, pp. 199–261.

Correspondence Relating to the Petition for Greater Representation of the Public on the Executive and Legislative Councils, *Hong Kong Legislative Council Sessional Papers 1916*, pp. 55–91.

Correspondence Relating to the Working of the Contagious Diseases Ordinances of the Colony of Hong Kong (London, Her Majesty's Stationery Office, C.3093, 1881).

Correspondence Respecting the Alleged Existence of Chinese Slavery in Hong Kong (London, Her Majesty's Stationery Office, C.3185, 1882).

Cross, Colin, *The Fall of the British Empire* (London, Hodder and Stoughton, 1968).

Darwin, John, 'Imperialism in Decline? Tendencies in British Imperial Policy Between the Wars', *Historical Journal*, Vol. 23, 1980, pp. 657–79.

Des Voeux, Sir William, *My Colonial Service, Volume II* (London, John Murray, 1903).

Endacott, G.B., *Government and People in Hong Kong 1841–1962* (Hong Kong, Hong Kong University Press, 1964).

—— *A History of Hong Kong* (Hong Kong, Oxford University Press, 1964).

—— and Birch, Alan, *Hong Kong Eclipse* (Hong Kong, Oxford University Press, 1978).

Endicott, Stephen L., 'British Financial Diplomacy in China: The Leith-Ross Mission, 1935–1937', *Pacific Affairs*, Vol. 46, 1973, pp. 481–501.

Fiddes, Sir George V., *The Dominions and Colonial Offices* (London, Putnam, 1926).

First Report of the Advisory Committee on Social Hygiene, Cmd. 2501 (Chairman, W. Ormsby-Gore), (London, His Majesty's Stationery Office, 1925).

Fisher, Warren, *Report of a Committee on the System of Appointment to the Colonial Office and the Colonial Service, Cmd. 3554* (London, His Majesty's Stationery Office, 1930).

Fung, Edmund S.K., 'The Sino-British Rapprochement, 1927–1931', *Modern Asian Studies*, Vol. 17, 1983, pp. 79–105.

Furse, Sir Ralph, *Aucuparius, Recollections of a Recruiting Officer* (London, Oxford University Press, 1962).

Gavit, J.P., *Opium* (London, Routledge, 1925).

Grantham, Alexander, *Via Ports, From Hong Kong to Hong Kong* (Hong Kong, Hong Kong University Press, 1965).

Hall, Henry L., *The Colonial Office, A History* (London, Longmans, 1937).

Hallifax, E.R., 'The Hong Kong Mui Tsai System', *Colonial Office Confidential Print, Eastern No. 137*, CO 882/10.

Harrop, Phyllis, *Hong Kong Incident* (London, Eyre & Spottiswoode, 1943).

Hsü, Immanuel C.Y., *The Rise of Modern China* (New York, Oxford University Press, 1975).

International Labour Office of the International Labour Organization, *Opium and Labour, Report of a Documentary Enquiry* (Geneva, International Labour Organization, 1935).

Jaschok, Maria H.A., 'A Social History of the *Mooi Jai* Institution in Hong Kong, 1843–1938' (unpublished doctoral dissertation, University of London, 1981).

Jeffries, Charles, *The Colonial Empire and its Civil Service* (Cambridge, Cambridge University Press, 1938).

—— *The Colonial Office* (London, Allen & Unwin, 1956).

—— *Whitehall and the Colonial Service: An Administrative Memoir 1939–1956* (London, Athlone Press, 1972).

Kirk-Greene, Anthony H.M., 'On Governorship and Governors in British Africa', in L.H. Gann and Peter Duignan (eds.), *African Proconsuls: European Governors in Africa* (New York, Free Press, 1978).

Kotewall, R.H., 'Memorandum on the Strike and the Measures Taken to Meet It', in *Colonial Office Confidential Print, Eastern No. 144*, CO 882/11, pp. 5–39.

League of Nations, Commission of Enquiry into the Control of Opium-Smoking in the Far East (Geneva, League of Nations, 1930).

Lee, J.M., and Petter, Martin, *The Colonial Office, War, and Development Policy* (London, Maurice Temple Smith, 1982).

Leeming, Frank, 'The Earlier Industrialization of Hong Kong', *Modern Asian Studies*, Vol. 9, 1975, pp. 337–42.

Lethbridge, Henry, 'The District Watch Committee: The Chinese Executive Council of Hong Kong?', *Journal of the Hong Kong Branch of the Royal Asiatic Society*, Vol. 11, 1971, pp. 116–41.

—— 'The Hong Kong Cadets 1862–1941', *Journal of the Hong Kong Branch of the Royal Asiatic Society*, Vol. 10, 1970, pp. 36–56.

—— *Hong Kong: Stability and Change* (Hong Kong, Oxford University Press, 1978).

Lewis, Eric, *Black Opium* (London, Marshall Brothers, 1910).

Loseby, F.H., 'Mui Tsai in Hong Kong, Report of the Committee appointed by the Governor, Sir William Peel', *Hong Kong Legislative Council Sessional Papers 1935*, pp. 195–282.

Lugard, F.D., 'Memorandum Regarding the Restriction of Opium in Hong Kong and in China', *Hong Kong Legislative Council Sessional Papers 1909*, pp. 25–40.

Macfarlane, H., and Aubrey, G.E., 'Venereal Disease Among the Natives of Hong Kong', *The Caduceus, Journal of the Hong Kong University Medical Society*, Vol. 1, 1922, pp. 22–7.

Maxwell, Sir George, 'The Mui Tsai System in Hong Kong', *Colonial Office Confidential Print, Eastern No. 169*, pp. 2–18.

'Memorandum on the Use of Opium in Hong Kong', *Hong Kong Legislative Council Sessional Papers 1929*, pp. 262–72.

Miners, N.J., 'The Attempt to Assassinate the Governor in 1912', *Journal of the Hong Kong Branch of the Royal Asiatic Society*, Vol. 22, 1982, pp. 279–85.

—— *The Government and Politics of Hong Kong* (Hong Kong, Oxford University Press, fourth edition, 1986).

—— 'The Governor, The Secretary of State and the Prerogative of Mercy', *Hong Kong Law Journal*, Vol. 17, 1987, pp. 77–89.

—— 'Plans for Constitutional Reform in Hong Kong, 1946–52', *China Quarterly*, No. 107, September 1986, pp. 463–82.

—— 'Why Civil Servants Retire at 55: the Curious Origins of a Government Rule', *Hong Kong Law Journal*, Vol. 13, 1983, pp. 209–17.

Moreno, Francisco Jose, *Legitimacy and Stability in Latin America* (New York, New York University Press, 1969).

Morgan, D.J., *The Official History of Colonial Development, Volume 1: The Origins of British Aid Policy 1924–1945* (New Jersey, Humanities Press, 1979).

The Opium Trade 1910–1941, a facsimile reproduction of Foreign Office Confidential Print 'Correspondence Respecting Opium (1910–1941)', FO 415 (Wilmington, Delaware, Scholarly Resources Ltd., 1974).

Orchard, Dorothy J., 'China's Use of the Boycott as a Political Weapon', *Annals of the American Academy of Political and Social Science*, Vol. 152, 1930, pp. 252–61.

Owen, David Edward, *British Opium Policy in China and India* (New Haven, Yale University Press, 1934, reprinted Hamden, Conn., Archon Books, 1968).

Parkinson, Sir Cosmo, *The Colonial Office from Within, 1909–1945* (London, Faber and Faber, 1947).

Parliamentary Debates, House of Commons (London, His Majesty's Stationery Office).

Parry, J.H., *The Spanish Seaborne Empire* (London, Hutchinson, 1966).

Perham, Margery, *Lugard: the Years of Authority* (London, Collins, 1960).

Pratt, J.T., 'Memorandum Respecting the Opium Problem in the Far East', in FO 415/26, *Foreign Office Confidential Print, Opium*, August 1929.

Pugh, R.B., 'The Colonial Office 1801–1925', in *The Cambridge History of the British Empire, Volume III* (Cambridge, Cambridge University Press, 1959), pp. 731–68.

Report of the Commission Appointed to Enquire into the Administration of the Sanitary and Building Regulations (Chairman, E.A. Hewett), *Hong Kong Legislative Council Sessional Papers 1907*, pp. 185(3)–185(45).

Report of the Commission Appointed to Enquire into the Causes and Effects of the Present Trade Depression in Hong Kong (Chairman, W.J. Carrie), *Hong Kong Legislative Council Sessional Papers 1935*, pp. 63–137.

Report of the Commission Appointed to Enquire into the Conditions of the Industrial Employment of Children (Chairman, S.B.C. Ross), *Hong Kong Legislative Council Sessional Papers 1921*, pp. 119–41.

Report of the Commissioners Appointed to Inquire into the Working of the Contagious Diseases Ordinance 1867 (Hong Kong, Noronha, 1879).

Report of the Committee Appointed to Consider the Colony's Position with Regard to the Obligations Incurred Under the International Opium Convention 1912 (Chairman, Claud Severn), *Hong Kong Legislative Council Sessional Papers 1924*, pp. 59–64.

Report of a Committee Appointed by the Secretary of State for the Colonies to Examine and Report on Straits Settlements Ordinance No. 15 of 1927, Cmd. 3294 (Chairman, Lord Balfour of Burleigh), (London, His Majesty's Stationery Office, 1929).

Report of the Housing Commission 1935 (Chairman, R.A.C. North), *Hong Kong Legislative Council Sessional Papers 1938*, pp. 257–88.

Report of the Salaries Commission (Chairman, H.C. Gollan), *Hong Kong Legislative Council Sessional Papers 1929*, pp. 71–112.

Report of the Venereal Diseases Committee (Chairman, W.H. Lee Warner), *Straits Settlements Legislative Council Sessional Papers 1923*, pp. C286–327.

Roberts, B.C., *Labour in the Tropical Territories of the Commonwealth* (London, Bell and Sons, 1964).

Robinson, Kenneth, *The Dilemmas of Trusteeship* (London, Oxford University Press, 1965).

Rowntree, Joshua, *The Imperial Drug Trade* (London, Methuen, 1905).

Sayer, G.R., *Hong Kong 1862–1919, Years of Discretion* (Hong Kong, Hong Kong University Press, 1975).

Smith, Carl T., 'The Chinese Church, Labour and Élites and the Mui Tsai Question in the 1920's', *Journal of the Hong Kong Branch of the Royal Asiatic Society*, Vol. 21, 1981, pp. 91–113.

Swinton, Viscount, *I Remember* (London, Hutchinson, 1948).

Tilman, R.O., *Bureaucratic Transition in Malaysia* (Durham, North Carolina, Duke University, 1964).

Turnbull, C.M., 'Sir Cecil Clementi and Malaya: the Hong Kong Connection', *Journal of Oriental Studies*, Vol. 22, 1984, pp. 33–60.

Watson, James L., 'Transactions in People: The Chinese Market in Slaves, Servants and Heirs', in James L. Watson (ed.), *Asian and African Systems of Slavery* (Oxford, Basil Blackwell, 1980).

Wellington, A.R., 'Changes in the Public Health Organization of Hong Kong During the Period 1929 to 1937', *Hong Kong Legislative Council Sessional Papers 1937*, pp. 103–12.

——'Public Health in Hong Kong', in CO 129/531/13, pp. 20–70.

Woods, W.W., *Mui Tsai in Hong Kong and Malaya, Report of Commission* (London, His Majesty's Stationery Office, Colonial 125, 1937).

Index

ABERDEEN RESERVOIR, 67–8
Acts of Parliament, 29, 71, 78, 153, 191, 193
Administrative Officers, *see* Cadets
Admiralty, 64, 145–6, 159
Adopted children, 156, 160, 168, 170, 174–5, 178–82, 186–9
Advisory Committee on the Traffic in Opium, 240, 247–50, 270–1, 277
Advisory Committees in Colonial Office, 36, 87, 98, 151, 200–1, 203, 281
Afghanistan, 57, 274
Air raids, 25, 27, 71, 122
Alabaster, Sir C. G., 66, 76, 99
Alcohol duties, 23, 26, 102, 116–18, 121, 213, 219, 226, 299n.26
Amery, Leopold S., 30–4, 171, 201, 255, 257, 260, 280, 289n.6, 290n.23
Anderson, Sir John, 33, 75, 227
Anslinger, United States Narcotics Commissioner, 274
Anti-*Mui Tsai* Society, 161, 163–4, 170–1, 175–7, 179, 182, 189, 302n.19, 306n.48
Anti-Opium League, 260
Anti-Slavery and Aborigines Protection Society, 160, 161, 168, 170–1, 181
Apathy in Hong Kong, 126, 135, 138, 141
Army, 4, 5, 11–12, 14, 16, 22, 26–7, 42, 46, 55, 57–8, 70, 76, 77, 80, 103–6, 127, 145, 191–3, 195, 197–8, 201, 204–5
Assessed taxes, *see* Rates
Astor, Viscountess, 160, 171, 199–201
Asylums, 78
Attorney General, 58, 59, 60, 65, 70, 76, 86, 88, 130, 131, 149, 173, 189
Audit, 49, 86, 123, 292n.20
Australia, 28, 55, 233
Austria, 7, 55, 115, 240

BADELEY, F.J., 99–100
Balfour, Lord, 247
Bangkok Opium Conference of 1931, 264–5, 268, 273
Bank of England, 71, 120
Banknotes, 6, 120, 129
Banks, banking, 21, 62, 70, 71, 120, 129, 210, 220, 223

Barracks, 11–12
Bermuda, 88
Bias Bay, 20, 25, 75, 289n.2
Bishops, 57, 160, 184, 215
Blake, Sir Henry, 153
Blockade of Hong Kong of 1867–86, 209; threatened, 1930, 22
Board of Education, 98
Board of Trade, 41, 71, 74
Boxer Indemnity Fund, 41, 208
Boycott of tramway, 1912, 5–6, 75, 128
Boycott Prevention Ordinance, 6, 75
Braga, Jose Pedro, 60, 63, 142
British American Tobacco Co., 72
British Guiana, 44, 88, 185
Brussels Sugar Convention, 74
Budgets, 24, 26, 29, 38, 49, 59, 60, 69–70, 92, 94–6, 101–25, 283
Building Authority, 54, 146, 151
Burney, E., 87
Butterfield and Swire, 72–3, 297n.27

CABINET, BRITISH, 29, 244, 252–3, 257–8, 271, 289n.2, 290–1n.31
Cadets, 35, 85–9, 91–2, 99, 123, 147–51
Caine, Sydney, *vii*, 106, 124, 300n.37
Caldecott, Sir Andrew, 24–5, 44–5, 47, 92, 123, 181, 269, 314n.1
Calder, J.A., 34
Campbell, Sir John, 110
Canada, 28, 288n.50
Canton, 2, 5, 7, 9, 12–19, 22, 24–7, 42, 46, 51–3, 86, 89, 128–9, 137–9, 144, 167, 170–1, 192, 204, 214, 220–2, 229, 237–8, 271, 288n.59
Capital punishment, 56–8, 293–4n.45
Castro, L. D' Almada E., 142
Cement factory, 21
Censorship, 20, 63, 71
Censuses, 10, 21, 79, 156–7, 164, 175, 191
Ceylon, 8, 35, 44, 53, 64, 79–80, 85, 87–8, 90, 99, 126, 136, 140, 181, 214, 225, 249
Chadwick, Osbert, 145, 146
Chamberlain, Joseph, 126–7, 133, 152, 195
Chan Ming-shu, General, 20

DATE DUE